DYING IN THE LAW OF MOSES

The Modern Jewish Experience
Paula Hyman and Deborah Dash Moore, editors

DYING
IN THE LAW
OF MOSES

CRYPTO-JEWISH MARTYRDOM
IN THE IBERIAN WORLD

Miriam Bodian

INDIANA UNIVERSITY PRESS
Bloomington and Indianapolis

This book is a publication of

Indiana University Press
601 North Morton Street
Bloomington, IN 47404-3797 USA

http://iupress.indiana.edu

Telephone orders   800-842-6796
Fax orders   812-855-7931
Orders by e-mail   iuporder@indiana.edu

Library of Congress Cataloging-in-Publication Data

Bodian, Miriam, date
Dying in the law of Moses : crypto-Jewish martyrdom in the Iberian world / Miriam Bodian.
p. cm. — (The modern Jewish experience)
Includes bibliographical references and index.
ISBN 978-0-253-34861-6 (cloth : alk. paper)
1. Marranos—Latin America—Biography. 2. Marranos—Spain—Biography. 3. Marranos—Portugal—
Biography. 4. Jews—Persecutions—Latin America—History—16th century. 5. Jews—Persecutions—
Latin America—History—17th century. 6. Jews—Persecutions—Spain—History—16th century.
7. Jews—Persecutions—Spain—History—17th century. 8. Jews—Persecutions—Portugal—History—
16th century. 9. Jews—Persecutions—Portugal—History—17th century. I. Title.
F1419.J4B63 2007
296.8'2—dc22
2007000631

1 2 3 4 5   12 11 10 09 08 07

Here it is the roots that are seeking. They burst
from the ground, overturn gravestones,
and clasp the broken fragments in search
of names and dates, in search
of what was and will never be again.

—Yehuda Amichai, "And Who Will Remember the Rememberers?"

Contents

LIST OF ILLUSTRATIONS AND MAPS • ix

PREFACE • xi

ACKNOWLEDGMENTS • xv

LIST OF ABBREVIATIONS • xvii

1. The Historical Setting — 1

2. The Dogmatista Crypto-Jewish Martyrs — 23

3. A Conquistador's Nephew in New Spain — 47

4. A Monk of Castanheira — 79

5. A Converso Surgeon in the Viceroyalty of Peru — 117

6. A Hebrew Scholar at the University of Salamanca — 153

7. Echoes in the Portuguese-Jewish Diaspora — 178

APPENDIX A

Commemoration of Individual Martyrs in
the Literature of the Portuguese-Jewish Diaspora, to 1683 • 197

APPENDIX B

Summary of Luis Carvajal's Nine Reasons for Adhering to
the Law of Moses, Audience of February 15, 1595, *PLC,* 235–238 • 199

GLOSSARY • 201

NOTES • 203

BIBLIOGRAPHY • 253

INDEX • 269

ILLUSTRATIONS AND MAPS

Illustrations

1. *The Last Judgment.* Jan van Eyck and Workshop Assistant. • 19
2. An auto-da-fé in Madrid, 1680. • 28
3. Map of a village in the Pánuco region, New Spain, 1593. • 53
4. Bird's-eye view of Mexico City in the late sixteenth century. • 59
5. Image of condemned prisoner in a sambenito. • 77
6. Signature of Diogo d'Asumpção, "Christus Dominus." • 102
7. *Quemadero* scene in Lisbon in 1682. • 110
8. Francisco Maldonado de Silva's signature. • 136
9. Frontispiece of Fernando Montesinos, *Auto de la fe celebrado en Lima 23. de enero de 1639.* • 145
10. Frontispiece of Paulus de Santa Maria, *Scrutinium Scripturarum.* • 149
11. Title page of Inquisitor-general Gaspar Quiroga's *Index of Prohibited Books.* • 160
12. Courtyard of a building of the Spanish Inquisition, with cells. • 173
13. The *hashkavah* prayer for martyrs, in Spanish and Hebrew, from *Seder Berakhot* (Amsterdam 1687). • 187
14. Burning at the stake of the Protestant martyr William Hunter in 1554, from John Foxe, *Actes and Monuments.* • 190
15. Frontispiece of Daniel Levi de Barrios, *Contra la verdad no hay fuerça.* • 194

Maps

1. Late-sixteenth-century Mexico, with locations important to the career of Luis Carvajal. • 56
2. Early-seventeenth-century Portugal, with locations important to the career of Diogo d'Asumpção. • 105
3. The Viceroyalty of Peru in the seventeenth century, with locations important to the career of Francisco Maldonado de Silva. • 119
4. Seventeenth-century Spain, with locations important to the career of Lope de Vera. • 154

Preface

This book explores the careers of a handful of men who were tried by the Spanish and Portuguese inquisitions, who became celebrated martyrs among some of their Jewish contemporaries. It will examine what drove them to choose a path of martyrdom, and how they both improvised and drew on established patterns as they asserted and reaffirmed their convictions.

All of these men were "judaizers"[1]—that is, baptized Christians prosecuted by the Iberian inquisitions in the sixteenth and seventeenth centuries for secretly embracing "the Law of Moses." But unlike most accused judaizers, they decided at some point after their arrest to declare their beliefs openly and defiantly before the tribunal. They almost invariably announced that they intended "to live and die in the Law of Moses"—a formula borrowed from the pledge of pious Catholics to "live and die in the Law of Christ." This was not just a statement of belief. It was also an implicit assertion of their right to determine religious truth independently, relying on revealed Scripture (in tandem with reason or divine illumination).

In their challenge to ecclesiastical authority, these martyrs[2] drew in part from medieval Jewish anti-Christian polemical arguments that had been absorbed into crypto-Jewish lore. (They sometimes reinforced or refined their arguments by subversively reading Church authors.) But they also drew from Reformation currents that—contrary to popular belief—were significant in early modern Iberian society. Echoing voices that could be heard throughout Europe, they insisted that Scripture, understood in its literal sense, was the only source of religious truth. (Unlike Protestants and sectarians, of course, they rejected the New Testament.) They borrowed, too, from Protestant anticlerical rhetoric: indeed, one of them cited Martin Luther. Some of them tapped into an Iberian form of spirituality known as *alumbradismo*. The *alumbrados*, to simplify their characterization greatly, were religious seekers who stressed interiority, de-emphasized objects of worship, and aroused inquisitorial suspicions of Protestant heresy.

More generally, the celebrated martyrs' behavior reflected the aggressive and confrontational religious climate of the Reformation. One of the hallmarks of the great judaizing martyrs was their readiness (and ability) to engage the inquisitors in disputations for months or years on end. Death at the stake was inevitable. But if the martyrs rejected a compromise and chose to be burned *alive* (rather than being garroted first), they achieved the crowning distinction.

In this book I have not tried to define what does or doesn't constitute martyr-

dom. *Martyrdom* is a concept that eludes definition: like beauty, it is in the eye of
the beholder. Besides, no definition can satisfactorily embrace the different behaviors that have been gathered together under the rubric of *martyrdom* over
the centuries and across cultures. I have tried only to understand what martyrdom meant to the conversos (forcibly baptized Jews and their descendants) and
judaizers (most, but not all of them, drawn from the converso population) of
Iberian lands, as well as to members of the "rejudaized" converso diaspora in early
modern Europe.

This episode in the history of martyrdom would merit a book if only because
of the unusual nature of the evidence about it. Most historical episodes of martyrdom are preserved only in didactic, idealized, convention-bound literary forms:
evidence rarely extends far beyond a set of partisan accounts written as propaganda
or in commemoration. Scholars often find themselves analyzing such texts more
for what they say about the authors and audiences than for what they reveal about
the martyrs. The contrast is striking when we turn to evidence about the careers of
the subjects of this book. The key documents for their careers are not heart-stirring
martyrological accounts targeting a wide public, but inquisitorial dossiers: that is,
detailed legal records of individual trials, compiled by trained and disciplined
(albeit biased) officials for their own use alone.

These dossiers are actually much more than trial records. They include genealogical information, intercepted messages, wardens' accounts of conversations between prisoners in the so-called "secret cells," reports about the prisoners' eating
habits, and so on. It is true that the documents must be used with caution (though
the view that they are inherently unreliable is no longer tenable). In particular, we
must keep in mind that the interrogations, formulated as indirect speech in the
third person and often paraphrased, are not strictly verbatim transcripts. But they
are *close* to verbatim. However deeply, then, we might wish this evidence had never
been produced, its unparalleled wealth renders crypto-Jewish martyrdom a particularly fertile field for understanding the psychic, social, and cultural dimensions
of martyrdom in a specific historical context.

All of the cases I have examined in detail, with one exception, have been
explored previously by Jewish historians.[3] Moreover, in the broader literature dealing with Iberian judaizing, a number of scholars—foremost among them Cecil
Roth, Yitzhak Baer, and Haim Beinart—have offered interpretations of converso
behavior that implicitly or explicitly apply to these cases. And yet writing this book
has had the feel of exploring uncharted territory. This is in large part because
scholars who have depicted judaizing martyrdom, whether at the micro or macro
level, have generally done so in a way that can only be regarded as an interesting
metamorphosis of Jewish martyrology itself.[4] To be sure, these scholars have laid
the foundations for further work on the topic. They have collected and published
many of the primary documents, and examined their facticity.[5] But they have
tended to adopt a view that echoes rabbinic tradition, assuming a timeless affinity
between converso martyrs and other Jewish martyrs, ancient and modern.[6] They
have, moreover, sometimes conflated under the rubric of *martyrdom* a wide range

of behaviors, and projected onto all conversos an imagined readiness for martyr-dom.[7] They have also tended to confine the topic to the sphere of Jewish history, isolating it from the wider context of early modern religious persecution and resistance, and minimizing or denying crypto-Jewish deviations from a mono-lithically imagined rabbinic Judaism. In light of recent scholarly work, much of it cross-cultural, on the phenomenology of martyrdom—particularly in the forma-tive period of late antiquity,[8] but also in medieval and early modern times[9]—a reexamination of crypto-Jewish martyrdom is clearly overdue.

I have tried to analyze overarching themes while at the same time preserving the contours of individual cases. The first chapter sets the stage by briefly examin-ing the historical background of late medieval and early modern Jewish martyrdom in Europe. It then narrows its focus to the main orbit of this book, the Iberian Peninsula, exploring how martyrdom figured in the psychic and intellectual uni-verse of Iberian Jews in the fourteenth and fifteenth centuries. Finally, it looks at how two fateful events brought about a fundamental reorientation of attitudes and expectations among these Jews about sacrifice, dissimulation, and defiant death: first, the mass conversion of Spanish Jews during the riots of 1391; and second, the establishment of the Spanish Inquisition in the late fifteenth century.

The second chapter examines how a distinct pattern of martyrological be-havior crystallized in the late sixteenth century. This pattern developed in the context of interrelated developments in the crypto-Jewish "underground": a) an increasing grasp among judaizers of the limited but real possibilities for action within the sphere of inquisitorial courts and prisons—a grasp that was facilitated by the clandestine oral transmission of prison and martyrdom lore, as well as by the impact of defiant behavior at autos-da-fé and at the stake; b) a growing familiarity with the world of learned, combative Christian opposition to Catholic dogma both in Iberian lands and elsewhere in Europe; c) an awareness of an increasingly powerful and institutionalized ex-converso Jewish diaspora beyond Iberian lands; and d) the ongoing impact of the late medieval *ars moriendi* tradition, which fostered self-conscious attitudes about dying well. This chapter analyzes some of the outstanding traits of the celebrated martyrs, and surveys what we know of an early, partially preserved case. It seeks to penetrate beyond the rhetoric of "truth" and "salvation" used by all sides in the religious battles of the Reformation period, addressing the complex motivations of the educated "*dogmatista*"[10] martyrs.

Chapters 3–6 examine four of the most celebrated and/or best documented of the early modern dogmatista martyrs, in the chronological order of their careers. Each of these careers bears individual scrutiny from the point of view of both the phenomenology of martyrdom and the development of crypto-Jewish theology. What circumstances led each of these men to choose a path of martyrdom? As prisoners, how did they learn to manipulate, humiliate, or control the inquisitors, particularly after choosing a path of martyrdom? How did they construct a consis-tent counter-theology to that of the Church and, in particular, to that of the inquisitors? What written materials did they use and how did they mold that material?

The final chapter analyzes the impact of the careers of the celebrated martyrs in the Portuguese-Jewish diaspora. It looks first at the unanticipated consequences of the emergence of a theological outlook that favored (and indeed required) a high degree of individual autonomy as well as recourse to a "self-evident" reading of the Hebrew Bible. It then examines the posthumous careers of these martyrs, that is, their commemoration in the literature of that diaspora.

On a personal note, let me conclude by saying that writing this book has often been an unsettling experience. The Inquisition was an institution formally invested with power for the explicit purpose of silencing dissent. In that respect, it is alien to the institutional life of modern democracies. But the impulse to maintain power by eliminating criticism is lodged in human nature. Men and women in positions of power in the world of scholarship can still suppress voices they don't want to hear, even if they conceal their actions behind the rhetoric of merit and justice. This is especially so if, together, they are able to create an unacknowledged institutional culture of compliance. To be sure, this volume deals with the past, and it adheres, I hope, to established standards of scholarship. But it is not "just" history.

Acknowledgments

To examine the sources that provided the raw material for this book, I have had recourse to a number of institutions, and invariably benefited from the expertise of their well-trained staffs: the Bodleian Library at Oxford University; the Archivo Histórico Nacional in Madrid; the Biblioteca Nacional in Madrid; the Instituto dos Arquivos Nacionais/Torre do Tombo in Lisbon; the Archivo General de la Nación in Mexico City; the National and University Library in Jerusalem; the Institute for Microfilmed Hebrew Manuscripts in Jerusalem (and its extraordinary living resource Benjamin Richler); the Pattee and Paterno Libraries at Pennsylvania State University (especially their interlibrary loan service); the Huntington Library in San Marino, California; the New York Public Library; the Special Collections division at the Jewish Theological Seminary of America in New York; the library of the Union Theological Seminary in New York; and the Widener and Houghton Libraries at Harvard University.

Thanks to a Visiting Skirball Fellowship at the Oxford Centre for Hebrew and Jewish Studies in Yarnton, England, I was able to spend many hours during the fall and winter of 1997, during the early stages of this project, exploring scholarship on the history and phenomenology of martyrdom. Subsequent travel to foreign archives was facilitated by grants from the Fundação Luso-Americana para o Desenvolvimento and the Fundação para a Ciência e a Tecnologia in Lisbon, as well as from the Research and Graduate Studies Office of Pennsylvania State University.

For their extraordinary hospitality during a memorable stay in Lisbon in 2001, I'd like to thank Pedro Cardim and Roberto Bachmann. I'm also grateful for leisurely conversations during that stay with Rita Marquilhas, Luisa Luzio, José Alberto Tavim, and Bill Donovan. Marco Ferrer, whom I met while he was conducting research at the Torre do Tombo, kindly supplied me with information from that archive after I had left. During briefer visits to Madrid, I profited from conversations with Jaime Contreras, James Amelang, and Harm den Boer. In summer 2003, I enjoyed the resources and collegiality of the Center for Advanced Jewish Studies at the University of Pennsylvania, thanks to the generosity of its director David Ruderman. My gratitude, as well, to Kenneth Brown, who sent me his transcription of Lope de Vera's trial records for comparison with mine, who offered me his advice on some difficult passages in that document, and who provided me with a copy and transcription of documents he obtained in Cuenca relating to the case of Lope de Vera.

I owe a special debt of gratitude to Sharon Mintz, Curator of Jewish Art at the Jewish Theological Seminary, whose incomparable knowledge of the visual riches of the seminary's collections made possible the inclusion in the illustrations of some striking and little-known early modern Inquisition scenes. The maps in this volume were produced by Bill Nelson, with whom it was a pleasure to work silently in cyberspace. I'd also like to thank Lee Sandweiss, my editor at Indiana University Press, for shepherding the book through the early stages of production. My thanks, too, to the readers of the manuscript for Indiana University Press, whose comments and suggestions I've tried to incorporate.

As the project winds down, I recall just how vital to its completion was the support that came from Ruth Wisse and Jay Harris, who made possible a blissfully unencumbered year on a Harry Starr Fellowship at the Harvard University Center for Jewish Studies in 2003–2004. I would also like to express my heartfelt thanks to Janet Rabinowitch, who despite her demanding duties as director of Indiana University Press, and despite the various setbacks this project has suffered, has offered continuing encouragement and advice.

I'd particularly like to acknowledge the many friends, colleagues, and family members whose gifts of wisdom, hospitality, advice, and support transcend easy categories: Mira and Avi Ofran, Margery Davies and Arthur MacEwan, Claire Katz and Dan Conway, Bob and Judy Levy, David Berger, Murray Rosman, my sisters Brenda and Helen Bodian, my brother-in-law Roger Alcaly, my mother, Elinor Bodian, and my uncle Alfred Bodian. As the book goes to press, I'd also like to thank my new colleagues and students at the Graduate School for Jewish Studies at Touro College for providing a warm and convivial environment. Others who belong on this list know who they are, and will forgive me for not extending this paragraph much further.

ABBREVIATIONS

ADC	Archivo Diocesana de Cuenca
AGN Inq.	Archivo General de la Nación, Ramo de la Inquisición, Mexico City
AHN Inq.	Archivo Histórico Nacional, Inquisición, Madrid
ANTT	Arquivo Nacional da Torre do Tombo, Lisbon
BHR	*Bibliothèque d'Humanisme et Renaissance*
FMS	Günter Böhm, *Historia de los judíos en Chile*. Vol. 1, *El Bachiller Francisco Maldonado de Silva, 1592–1639*. Santiago de Chile 1984.
IL	Inquisição de Lisboa
JQR	*Jewish Quarterly Review*
JEEW	Paulo Bernardini and Norman Fiering (eds.), *The Jews and the Expansion of Europe to the West, 1450 to 1800*. New York 2001.
PaP	*Past and Present*
PLC	*Procesos de Luis de Carvajal (el Mozo)*. L. González Obregón (ed.). Mexico City 1935.
REJ	*Revue des études juives*
RHR	*Revue de l'histoire des religions*
SCJ	Martin Mulsow and Richard Popkin (eds.), *Secret Conversions to Judaism in Early Modern Europe*. Leiden and Boston 2004.
TGP	Daniel Levi de Barrios, *Triumpho del govierno popular*. Amsterdam 1683.

DYING IN THE LAW OF MOSES

THE HISTORICAL SETTING

1

Famous acts of martyrdom involve conviction. But they also entail a power struggle. Martyrs "triumph" over their persecutors by refusing to renounce their beliefs
under threat of death. Such acts diminish the persecutor and galvanize fellow
victims of persecution. This, in essence, is the dynamic of martyrdom, stripped of
all the particularities that give the martyr's act power and meaning—the graphic
detail, the culture-specific articulations, the situational drama.

Conceptions of noble death were first elaborated in the Greco-Roman world,
through a fusion of ideas associated with patriotism, philosophy, ritual sacrifice,
and obedience to divine will.[1] Among Jews of the Hellenistic period, such a cluster
of ideas gave rise to a motif that would continue to hold their imagination over the
centuries: the motif of the Jew who prefers to die rather than follow an order given
by a tyrant requiring him or her to violate the Covenant. This motif appears in
three early stories, two in the Book of Daniel and one (in its first known version) in
2 Maccabees. In the first, the tyrant Nebuchadnezzar builds an image of gold and
requires his subjects to fall down and worship it. Three exiles from Judah who are
serving as officials in the Babylonian court refuse to comply, even though they
know they will be punished by being thrown into a fiery furnace.[2] In the second
story, Daniel is required to worship the king himself (Darius), and when he re-
fuses, is cast into a den of lions. The third story, recounted in chapter 7 of 2
Maccabees, is set during the persecutions of Antiochus. An elderly scribe and a
woman with her seven children resist a deliberately provocative order to eat pork,
and willingly suffer dreadful deaths rather than comply.[3]

In each of these morally unambiguous narratives, an edict requiring apostasy
precipitates an act of self-sacrifice by Jews. Such tales had obvious power for a
small people hedged by powerful empires—a people subject to the lure of "alien
gods" and, in certain periods, religious persecution. The message was one of great
simplicity: the Jews were a unique people who served only a single, transcen-
dent God.

This message was conveyed in a narrative framework that exhibited some of
the features that were to become standard in late antique martyrdom stories, both
Jewish and Christian.[4] It squeezed into a single dramatic moment—the moment

when the protagonist had to choose between apostasy and death—the more complex ongoing theological struggle with Greco-Roman culture. It included a pithy dialogue between the victim and the tyrant, and/or a defiant declaration of belief by the martyr, stripping down elaborate theological positions to the antique version of a sound bite. It highlighted the martyr's contempt for the worldly power of the tyrant, as well as his or her heroic attitude to physical suffering and death (to which he or she went in joyful anticipation of reward in the world to come). Such stories offered a cathartic, compressed enactment of the grueling everyday effort to maintain the boundaries of identity and belief while living in a pagan environment.

Even in the early period of Jewish and Christian coexistence under pagan Roman rule, before either group had settled on distinctive terms regarding the act of self-sacrifice (*kiddush ha-shem*[5] and μάρτυς,[6] respectively), there were perceptible differences between Jewish and Christian interpretation of such acts. From the start, Christian theology ascribed inherent sanctity to the martyr's agonizing death: Such a death was *imitatio dei*, indeed, for some, a means of attaining union with God/Christ. Jewish theology, in contrast, placed no such undisputed value on violent death itself. This being the case, episodes of Jewish martyrdom were more likely to raise issues of theodicy (in Hebrew, *tsidduk ha-din*)—that is, justification of the seemingly undeserved suffering that befell the noble and pious persons who became martyrs.

Because of the special theological significance of martyrdom in Christian theology, narratives recounting acts of martyrdom have occupied a more prominent place in Christian than in Jewish literature. Yet as fate would have it, Christians were rarely called upon to martyr themselves after the fourth century. Crusaders who died in battle with Muslims were often regarded in terms of martyrdom, but hardly qualified in the classical sense. More enduringly, the impulse for martyrdom among pious Christians was rechanneled and took expression in new forms.[7] "By the end of the Middle Ages," André Vauchez writes, "the identification of sainthood with martyrdom was only a memory."[8] Identification with Christ could be achieved without bloodshed, through a life of religious commitment achieved in peaceful ways (monastic devotion, extreme asceticism and self-inflicted suffering, scholarship, ecclesiastical leadership, etc.).

Paradoxically it was the Jews, whose early rabbinic theology did not so categorically elevate the value of suffering, who became the persecuted people *par excellence* in medieval Europe and the Mediterranean region. While the vast majority of medieval Jews never faced the actual choice of apostasy or martyrdom (violent death at the hands of persecutors was more likely to come *without* a choice), acts of conscious self-sacrifice came to symbolize the readiness of the entire group for martyrdom. For Jews at the end of the Middle Ages, especially in Christian Europe, even peaceful religious commitment came to be associated with violent death and martyrdom. Jews throughout Europe understood that the very fact that they performed their ritual obligations in communities organized for that purpose made them targets of blood libels and/or mob violence. The assumption that Jews were willing to die a martyr's death became integral to the Jewish collective self-image. It is telling that medieval Jewish exegetes—an argumentative lot—tended to agree about the meaning of Psalms 44:23, "For Thy sake we are killed all day": What could it be but a statement applying to the Jewish people as a whole?[9]

This book analyzes the careers, in life and death, of a number of early modern martyrs whose careers were very distant in time from those of the Jewish martyrs of antiquity. To be sure, their careers were built upon the bedrock of ancient tradition and experience. It might even be argued that their careers signaled something of a Jewish revival of the athletic, quasi-nationalistic character of antique martyrdom, in contrast to a medieval style that tended to emphasize the atoning, sacrificial role of the martyr's death.

Be that as it may, what distinguishes these figures from the classical martyrs, from the point of view of the historian, is the availability of substantial documentary evidence about their lives. Their paths to martyrdom can thus be studied in their human dimensions. We can watch them as they improvised, trying to exploit their limited opportunities to dramatize their vision of the truth. We can watch them vacillating, yielding momentarily, or slipping into depression, as well as performing heroic actions.

Still, reconstructing their experience is a tricky undertaking. These men brought to their task a rich stockpile of images, ideas, and models of behavior. In the chaotic pathways of the imagination, these elements mixed without regard for formal doctrinal boundaries or rules of logic. The martyrs may have vehemently rejected Catholic ritual (including, obviously, the veneration of saint-martyrs). They may have rejected the idea that the martyr achieved perfection, or that God rewarded the martyr with powers that continued to act in his or her physical remains after death. But at a less articulate level, they must also have preserved in memory the painted images of the physical sufferings and fortitude of the early martyrs of the Church, a ubiquitous sight in Iberian churches.

On the other hand, they were men of the Reformation, drawing courage from the Protestant offensive against the Church. They unquestionably had access to information from abroad, at least by word of mouth. In some cases they were acquainted with Erasmus—or even Luther—through books. It is more difficult to determine what they knew, if anything, about the new shapes Christian martyrdom was assuming on English, French, or German soil. Even closer to home, it is hard to ascertain what they knew of the careers of the *luterano* martyrs of the Inquisition in the mid-sixteenth century.[10] But given the likelihood that they had at least some knowledge of heroic Protestant deaths, we must consider the sources and diffusion of lore about these deaths in Spanish and Portuguese lands.

These men, of course, saw themselves as *Jewish* martyrs. All of the men we will examine declared they were "dying in the Law of Moses." But in whose footsteps did they feel they were following? They would surely have been glad to know the martyrdom lore about Rabbi Akiva, Hananiah ben Teradion, and other rabbinic martyrs—figures with whom they would sometimes be associated in poetry and prose in the Jewish diaspora. Yet we can be fairly certain that they were not familiar with these or any other martyrs of the rabbinic period. Still, their careers were an outgrowth of a living oral tradition of crypto-judaizing, transmitted over several generations. Scholars who have analyzed popular belief have amply demonstrated how tenacious and widespread even suppressed forms of folk knowledge can be.[11] Moreover, we are increasingly learning how porous Iberian borders (and even prison walls) were to "forbidden" information. In light of this, there is every reason to wonder whether the celebrated crypto-Jewish martyrs did not know something of the martyrdom lore of late medieval Spanish Jewry. One wonders, too, to what degree they learned from and imitated other crypto-Jewish victims of the Inquisition.

To begin to understand how these men charted their way—and how, after their deaths, interested contemporary Jews reinterpreted their careers—we will have to consider both the immediate human predicaments they faced and the wider cultural environment in which they lived. Examining this environment—or rather, environments—constitutes a particular challenge. We are dealing with a few members of a scattered population, settled in various milieus. We know about them almost nothing except what we find in their Inquisition dossiers. The dossiers do reveal extraordinary things about what these men read and heard, but there is no way to trace the deeper origins of the oral lore. We will therefore have to take a close look at circumstantial evidence. Let us first try to follow, as well as evidence allows, the vicissitudes of defiant death among the Jews and conversos of late medieval Spain and Portugal.

For many lay people familiar with Jewish history, it is the Ashkenazim, or Franco-German Jews, who are associated with martyrdom in the face of persecution, while the Sephardim (Iberian Jews) tend to be associated with apostasy and flight. There are understandable reasons for this view—a view that scholars have helped to perpetuate.[12] Spanish Jewry did not, for one thing, create a literature comparable to the powerful martyrdom literature of the Franco-German Jews. This may be related to the fact that after the violent events of 1391, whose character may have been such as to trigger a less extreme tendency to martyrdom than the Crusades,[13] Spanish Church authorities waged a long, slow, demeaning, but largely nonviolent campaign to bring about Jewish conversion. This campaign crushed the morale of Spanish Jews, without offering them an opportunity for martyrdom. For this and other reasons, Spanish Jews left a legacy in which martyrdom does not figure prominently. This may help explain why scholars have tended to neglect the phenomenon of Sephardi martyrdom.[14]

The very notion of easily generalized differences between "Ashkenaz" and "Sepharad" has come under challenge recently. Scholars have questioned the way these constructs have been used to delineate two absolutely distinct and mutually exclusive cultural modes, fixed in time.[15] This ongoing critique has had various consequences for the evaluation of medieval Spanish Jewry. There were, it appears, more cases than has been supposed of baptism among the Ashkenazim,[16] on the

4

one hand, and of martyrdom among the Sephardim, on the other.[17] The intellectual elite of Ashkenazi society, no less than that of the Sephardim, proved at certain times vulnerable to conversion.[18] Moreover, Ashkenazi martyrdom was never, as Gerson Cohen would have it, an expression of a general Ashkenazi posture of "passivity." As it was among Sephardim, it was a last resort when every form of active resistance had failed. If martyrdom sometimes reflected an attitude of submission (to the will of God), it might at the same time reflect an attitude of defiance (with regard to gentiles). Its expressions (as common sense would suggest) were manifold and unpredictable.

But was it not true that under Muslim rule the Jews of Spain, when threatened, for the most part accepted conversion? Certainly they converted to Islam en masse during one episode of persecution—the Almohad attacks on Spanish Jewry in the twelfth century. But they did so on the assumption that they could revert openly to Judaism when the persecutions ceased.[19] (It should be added that a few *did* choose martyrdom.)[20] In any case, even if we acknowledge an overwhelming tendency to accept conversion in this instance, it does not follow that this was somehow a root "Sephardi" experience that contributed to behavior much later.

In fact, what was true for the twelfth century was by no means the case two centuries later. At the time of mass rioting against Jews throughout Castile and Aragon in 1391, a significant number of Jews from all ranks of society chose martyrdom, some going so far as to commit suicide and kill their children to avoid conversion.[21] It is true that the great majority of those who could not flee or otherwise escape accepted baptism. But their actions were not socially sanctioned within the Jewish community. The conviction that the martyrs had saved the community's honor, while the converts had stained it, is vividly reflected in elegies written in the wake of the violence.[22]

What happened, then, between the mid-twelfth century and the fourteenth century to generate an ethos of martyrdom among some Spanish Jews at the time of the riots? Why were significant numbers of Jews moved to sacrifice their lives rather than convert?

Several reasons have been adduced, none of them mutually exclusive. It has been argued that the Islamic faith of the Almohads was inherently less offensive to Jews than Christianity, since it was manifestly not an expression of "idolatry." Jews living in Christian Spain, in contrast, would have viewed conversion to the dominant faith as an abomination, since Christianity required the worship of a man (not to mention the saints). There was a far greater religious and emotional taboo involved in accepting baptism than in accepting Islam. The threat such an act entailed to a Jew's fundamental self-image created an atmosphere of crisis and horror in 1391 of a kind that had not developed during the Almohad disturbances.

Another explanation for the emergence of an ethos of martyrdom among Jews in Christian Spain is that by the early fourteenth century Ashkenazi culture and its ideals had penetrated Spanish Jewry and modified its attitudes. It is true that Spanish Jews of the generation of the Expulsion apparently knew little of the episodes of martyrdom in the Rhineland at the time of the First Crusade—episodes that were widely commemorated in the Ashkenazi world.[23] Yet one of the post-1391 elegies by a Spanish-Jewish author depicts the recently martyred Sephardim reciting, before their suicide (and/or killing of family members), the benediction used in the ritual slaughter of animals ("*al ha-shehitah*").[24] This arresting use of a benediction that had been used in antiquity for the slaughter of sacrificial animals appears to have been borrowed from Ashkenazi martyrological lore dating from the Crusades period.[25] Given the abundant but haphazard pathways of communication between the Sephardi and Ashkenazi worlds, it is likely that the Ashkenazi ethos of martyrdom had influenced the Spanish-Jewish world by the fourteenth century.

A further argument holds that readiness for martyrdom in 1391 was fueled in part by the Jews' competitive attitude to Spanish Christian culture.[26] As the Reconquest gained momentum in the medieval Iberian kingdoms, and as the gentile population became subject to Christian rule and influence, it became less palatable for Jews to continue on a path that paralleled the Muslim tradition of dissimulation (*taqiyya*). The sacred value accorded by Catholics to the violent death of the martyr—an act lavishly represented in Church art in representations of the crucifixion—stirred a competitive response among Spanish Jews, who did not want to appear less committed than their gentile neighbors.

All of these factors may have played a role in shaping attitudes among the Jews of medieval Christian Spain.[27] The culture of these Jews certainly had its own characteristics, but a relaxed attitude toward baptism under pressure was not one of them. Nevertheless, by the late medieval period, when the Church launched a systematic campaign to bring about Jewish conversions, a certain numbers of Jews began making their way to the baptismal font without the special incentive of violence.[28] The Church's efforts, led by the mendicant preachers, included incitement against Jews (including propaganda featuring blood libels), forced sermons (i.e., conversionist sermons that Jews were required to attend), and efforts to increase restrictions on Jewish life. In the face of this campaign, something more than an ethos of martyrdom was needed to prevent apostasy. The response of the rabbinic leadership was a counter-campaign of anti-Christian polemicizing. The development of Jewish polemics is a chapter in late medieval Spanish-Jewish history that we will have to consider carefully, even if it seems distant to our theme, because in the particular episode of martyrdom that we will explore, martyrdom and polemics became inextricably intertwined.

The need for effective polemics was particularly acute in light of the success of the mendicant orders in educating and deploying Jewish apostates to proselytize among their ex-coreligionists. Such men had the advantage of rabbinic instruction (though not necessarily the best) as well as ecclesiastical training. Their psychological impact was devastating. Nachmanides, perhaps the most eminent rabbinic scholar of his day, knew he was being forced to engage in a very dangerous sport when he was summoned by the king of Aragon in 1263 to participate in a religious disputation with the apostate Pablo Christiani.[29] The terms of such disputations were established by ecclesiastics, who placed out of bounds those issues that put the Church on the defensive (for example, the nature of the Trinity). The very staging of disputations with apostates highlighted the fragility of traditionally powerful ethnic, communal, and cultural bonds among Jews.[30] The fact that some of these apostates rose quite high in the ranks of the Church—indeed, one of them became an influential bishop—further raised the stakes.[31]

The entire picture underwent a drastic change in 1391. In that year, a huge sector of Spanish Jewry underwent forcible conversion. This is not the place to retell the well-known story of this transformation. Suffice it to say that the rioting against Jews broke out in Seville and spread through some of the major towns of Spain—Cordova, Toledo, Madrid, Segovia, Burgos, Valencia, Majorca, Barcelona, and Tortosa. By the time it had ceased, much of Spanish Jewry had been baptized and many Jews had been killed.[32]

The converts became the core of a distinct population of judeoconversos who practiced Catholicism, at least outwardly, alongside the population of unbaptized Jews. In the century that followed, a dizzying series of events unfolded that, among other things, had ramifications for the emergence of crypto-Jewish martyrdom. We will try to provide a brief narrative of these events, highlighting developments that shed light on the much later episodes of martyrdom that occupy us in this book.

Let us look first at the events of 1391 from this perspective. While the vast majority of Jews threatened with violence converted, some of them chose a martyr's death rather than be baptized. The contemporary Jewish sources we possess, though emotional and fragmentary, corroborate each other on this point. (Of course under the circumstances many Jews were clearly killed *without* being given a choice.)[33] There is no way to know the actual extent of martyrdom during the riots. But the significance of such acts is evident in elegies written by stunned survivors.

An elegy written primarily about events in Toledo is revealing. It devotes twenty of its eighty-one stanzas to the martyrs of that city.[34] The structure and contents of these stanzas merit a closer look. While the author first mentions all of those who were killed, devoting a stanza to the men and another to the women (as would be done in their memorialization in the synagogue), the subsequent eighteen stanzas are devoted to eight particular *kedoshim* (martyrs), mentioned by name. They were, in order, the rabbinic scholar Isaac ben Shushan; R. Judah, descendant of the great rabbinic scholar Asher ben Yechiel; Samuel ha-Katan, a relative of both of the latter men by marriage; the poet and scholar Israel al-Nakawa; a cantor named Saul; the latter's brother Solomon; Moses ben Asher, also a descendant of Asher ben Yechiel; and a youth named Abraham ben Ophrit, who suffered a particularly grisly death.[35]

It should be evident at once that these were not randomly chosen figures. The great martyrs of rabbinic literature tended to be scholars and/or powerful pillars of Jewish life. This was certainly related to the fact that traditionally, rabbinic scholars possessed something of the sanctity of the Torah itself.[36] Their deaths were thus a particular blow to the community, an act of sacrilege. Singling out their names among the Toledo martyrs was a way of emphasizing the loss of the community's most precious possessions.

One of the foremost among the survivors of the 1391 massacres was the rabbinic scholar and communal leader Hasdai Crescas, whose son was among those killed. In a letter to the Jews of Avignon informing them of the events, Crescas drew from traditional rabbinic images and concepts to mourn his loss and to vindicate God. Many Jews of Barcelona, he wrote, had sanctified the Holy Name—adding, with shocking abruptness, "my only son among them, an innocent lamb." He continued, "I have offered him up as a burnt offering. I will vindicate the judgment [of heaven] and be comforted with the goodliness of his portion and the pleasantness of his fate."[37]

The image of the martyr as a "burnt offering" is also a theme in the narratives and elegies written by Ashkenazi Jews in the wake of Crusader violence. But in contrast to the Spanish Jews, it became a key element in the idealized self-image of Ashkenazi Jewry for generations to come.[38] It is significant that such an image, though it cropped up in Crescas's letter and in other immediate responses to the riots of 1391, never became a part of the idealized self-image prevalent among Spanish Jews.[39]

There were multiple reasons for this. An important factor was the different fate of the converts in these two contexts. In the wake of the Crusaders' attacks on several major Franco-German Jewish communities, the Jews who had been baptized during the violence were allowed to return to their communities and to the practice of Judaism, and many did. Others assimilated into Christian society. In Spain, in contrast, the converts found themselves in the surrealistic situation of becoming permanent members of a new Catholic community constituted of former Jews. Synagogues were consecrated for use as churches in the midst of what had once been *juderías*, or Jewish quarters. In some cases entire communities underwent virtually instant conversion. In most places, however, the unconverted Jews and the newly converted ones lived cheek-by-jowl on the same narrow streets.

The new sociological configuration was unprecedented in European Jewish history. Under these circumstances (and given the events that would follow), it would have been bizarre indeed if Spanish Jewry had cultivated a collective self-image of heroic sacrifice. Even after the situation began to stabilize, no clear consensus developed among the rabbinic leadership about the status of the conversos. It is true that many of the converts tried to hold onto the framework and rhythms of life as they knew it. Although they were being watched, and could be punished by the local bishop for backsliding, they often continued to maintain Sabbaths, holidays, and dietary laws as well as they could. Their unbaptized Jewish friends or family members might host them at festive gatherings and supply them with unleavened bread for Passover, ritually slaughtered meat, and other ritual items. Yet they were living evidence of the failure to live up to the ideal of self-sacrifice. Since they were not permitted to return publicly to the Jewish community, and were required to comport themselves at least outwardly as Catholics, they remained a vexing reminder of Spanish Jewry's fragility.

This is not to say, as some scholars have wished to believe, that *all* the recent converts tried to hold on to the familiar forms of piety and ritual. There were many New Christians who rather quickly adapted to their new environment and sought to secure their position in it socially and economically. This inevitably meant alienating themselves from members of the remaining Jewish community, particularly as some of them moved into lucrative occupations that were denied to professing Jews. Some of the wealthier among them married into aristocratic Old Christian families.

It is thus not difficult to understand why, despite the redeeming acts of individual martyrs, the latter's example was not defining for the entire community. The author of an elegy for the community of Burgos chose a telling sort of imagery. Borrowing the biblical imagery of the wayward woman, he highlighted the violation of primal sacred boundaries by that city's Jews:

> Her thighs have rotted, her belly swelled,
> She's become a curse amidst a once-tranquil people . . .
> Her righteous men, misled and misleading, have turned against her,
> Her prince [*sar*] has become an enemy [*tsar*], her captains
> Are a snare, like Jeroboam; they beseech the dead one [Jesus], not the Eternal.
> The Levites sing songs of worldly desire, the servants of God praise an idol.[40]

Yosef Hacker has pointed to a certain exegetical shift as evidence that in the late fifteenth century the Spanish-Jewish self-image underwent change, in reaction to the conversions. For centuries, a set of verses in Psalms 44 had been understood to be statements about Israel's steadfast loyalty to God and the Covenant, to the point of readiness for martyrdom.[41] But from about the 1480s, he argues, they tended to be reinterpreted as statements about Israel's *failure* to live up to the ideal.[42] The realities of conversion and drift were such that an idealized self-image was no longer sustainable.

However, human nature—certainly in the collective—does not tolerate self-flagellation indefinitely. It was an important step for the continuation of crypto-Jewish life that the clandestine practice of Judaism by conversos eventually became acceptable to many Spanish Jews. There was, of course, a wish to prevent further erosion. Rejecting erstwhile Jews might serve only to push them firmly toward assimilation into Spanish society. In any case, rather early on, some (by no means all) Spanish rabbis interpreted the presence in their midst of so many baptized Jews in a way that allowed the conversions (and the converts) to be integrated into a larger vision of Jewish history and ultimate redemption.[43] This was a step with important consequences for the subsequent development of crypto-Jewish pride.

A powerful early exposition of such a view came from a prominent rabbinic scholar who had himself converted during the riots of 1391—the remarkable Profayt Duran (Isaac ben Moses Halevi, known as "the Efodi").[44] In a poignant letter of 1394 to the son of a recently deceased Catalonian Jewish leader, Profayt tied the fate of the converts to the fate of the martyrs: the deaths of the latter, he argued, atoned for the nation as a whole—including "that part of the seed of Abraham who were forced publicly to deny their faith and become converts in this great province [Catalonia]." Alluding to Ezekiel's prophecy that God would bring backsliding Jews back into the Covenant (Ezek. 20), he wrote that "if a part of the people has faltered under severe compulsion . . . not for this have they been excluded from the community of the people of the Lord." The existing division, he felt, would soon be remedied, for as it had been prophesied in Deuteronomy 32, "the increase and severity of the affliction shall be an omen that healing salvation is at hand."[45]

The "increase and severity of the affliction" came soon enough, in the years 1411–1416. (Salvation, on the other hand, proved to be in no hurry.) One of the chief deliverers of affliction, from the point of view of the Jews, was the incendiary Dominican friar Vicente Ferrer, who toured Castile and Aragon in these years, accompanied by flagellants, attacking Jews and preaching sermons that Jews were required to attend.[46] Jews sometimes fled as he approached their town, in fear of an angry and violent mob. For many, Vicente Ferrer's visit was a shattering experience, and led to conversion.

In 1412, in the midst of Vicente Ferrer's preaching campaign, efforts were begun to stage an extravagant public disputation. The recently baptized Jerónimo de Santa Fe turned to the anti-pope Benedict XIII (the Aragonese Pedro de Luna, who at this point was recognized as pope only in Aragon) to initiate the event. This "pope" summoned Jewish representatives from all of the communities of Aragon to the papal court at Tortosa, for a disputation that began in early 1413 and dragged on until April of the following year. Following the script fashioned by Pablo Christiani at Barcelona, Jerónimo de Santa Fe sought to prove from the Talmud that the Messiah had already come. By this time, both sides had invested considerable energy in refining their positions. What was novel about this disputation was the large number of Jewish participants, the lengthiness of the proceedings (which kept the leaders of the Aragonese Jewish communities tied up in Tortosa, far from their communities and families), and the level of Jewish demoralization at the outset. The result of this bloodless calamity, from the Jews' perspective, was a new wave of baptisms. To add insult to injury, among the newly baptized were some of the Jewish delegates to the disputation (whose debts during their sojourn in Tortosa nevertheless had to be paid by the Jewish communities that had dispatched them).[47]

To offset the Church's offensive and the new wave of conversions, rabbinic leaders hastened to produce and disseminate Jewish counter-propaganda to as wide an audience as possible.[48] Anti-Christian polemics had been cultivated among Jews for centuries, of course, and the Spanish Jews of the late fourteenth and fifteenth centuries drew from a wide range of sources.[49] But works written in the late fourteenth and early fifteenth centuries revealed new emphases and lines of thought. Their wide dissemination insured that many Jews who were eventually baptized—of particular importance among them the Spanish exiles who settled in

Portugal—departed from organized Jewish life firmly indoctrinated with anti-Christian teachings.

It is natural for polemical works to emphasize those elements of a tradition that provide the most effective ammunition against the antagonist. From a Jewish perspective, the vulnerable aspects of Christian theology were, first of all, its seemingly far-fetched christological exegesis of Scripture, and second, the vulnerability of its dogmas to rationalist criticism. There were two currents of the Sephardi tradition in particular that were mobilized to attack it. First, Jewish polemicists stressed the simple meaning of Scripture (*peshat*), at the expense of more fanciful rabbinic approaches, because it gave them a natural polemical edge in refuting what appeared to be contorted christological readings. Second, they turned to philosophy, which had deep roots in Spanish-Jewish thought, to rebut Christian dogma about such matters as the Trinity, Incarnation, and the Virgin Birth. The philosophical critique of Christianity reached a high pitch of intensity in the late fourteenth and early fifteenth centuries, with polemical works by Abraham Bivach (Bibago), Shem Tov ben Isaac ibn Shaprut, Moses ha-Kohen of Tordesillas, Hasdai Crescas, Profayt Duran, and Joseph ben Shem Tov.[50]

Such polemics were directed at both educated Jews who were in danger of being swayed by sophisticated Christian missionizing, and educated apostates who challenged Judaism on philosophical grounds. While the arguments employed were often technical and required knowledge of philosophical terminology, they were sometimes presented in a pithier, more easily transmittable form. In Hasdai Crescas's *Bitul ikare ha-notsrim* (Refutation of Christian Principles), for example, the author concluded his formal arguments about the doctrine of transubstantiation with some wry remarks:

> Jeremiah has already said: "Can a man make gods for himself? No gods are they!" [Jer. 16:20]. Yet they [the Christians] make him every day. There is no difference between making him by hand or by word, since their priests believe that they make God by word when they say, "This is my body; this is my blood." . . . They bring this God in their hand and lift him up and lower him down and bring him to visit the sick . . .[51]

Still more accessible was Profayt Duran's profoundly sarcastic letter to a friend who had recently chosen to be baptized. In this letter, which was widely disseminated in manuscript, Duran ridiculed his friend for having been awakened to the "truth" of a faith that scorns and contradicts reason.[52] (By all means, he wrote, "don't imitate your fathers, who believed in one single God and utterly rejected any plurality, who said, in their error, 'Hear Israel, the Lord is One!' . . . Not so you! You shall believe that one is three, and three are one!")[53]

Philosophical arguments, technical and less technical, about the impossibility of God becoming a man or entering a wafer no doubt played a role in reinforcing Jewish loyalties. But they were potentially even more powerful for newly baptized

Jews, who found themselves in the actual situation of worshipping before a crucifix and watching a priest declare the wafer they were about to eat the veritable body of Christ. Under the siege conditions they experienced, which would be intensified with the establishment of the Inquisition and the Expulsion, crypto-Jews would have little reason to cling to aspects of Jewish tradition that did not prove themselves useful polemically or defensively, and there is no question that fourteenth- and fifteenth-century polemics—boiled down, to be sure—were instrumental in shaping their version of Judaism.

The late fourteenth century also saw the development of a historicist attack on the Christian tradition that most likely contributed to the formation of crypto-Jewish thinking. It was not new in every respect. Criticisms of the New Testament and of Jerome's translation of the Hebrew Bible—criticisms that suggested falsification in the Christian tradition—had been proposed by earlier Jewish polemicists.[54] But in the 1390s, the Spanish-Jewish scholar Profayt Duran produced a far more elaborate and historically reasoned attack on the post-apostolic Church, *Kelimat ha-goyim* (Reproach of the Gentiles). In his view, the way Jesus interpreted Hebrew Scripture was faulty and ignorant. Still, there was nothing in the Gospels to suggest that Jesus intended that he be regarded as a god, or that he had it in mind to abrogate the Torah. In fact, Duran argued, many of the Church's key teachings had no basis in the Gospels: the Trinity, the Incarnation, transubstantiation, baptism, the institution of the papacy, and the virginity of Mary. These doctrines were human innovations of a later period.

One scholar has argued that Duran's arguments grew out of Jewish exposure to Christian "historicist" attacks on Judaism.[55] Others have argued that Duran drew from contemporary Christian reformist attacks on the Church by the Conciliarists (clergy who argued that a general council of bishops, not the pope, should wield ultimate power) and the followers of Wyclif and Hus, all of whom regarded the contemporary Church as deviating from authentic, early Christianity.[56] It seems likely that both factors played a role. Traditional Jewish polemics had entailed an implicit historicist argument. But by the late fourteenth century, educated Spanish Jews, with close ties to Avignon, must have been aware of the more incisive critiques of the Church emanating from reformist Christian circles. (By the fifteenth century, skepticism about the authenticity of the New Testament text was sufficiently widespread in Spain that Alonso de Espina, in his *Fortalitium Fidei* [c. 1464], listed such a claim as one of the prevalent types of heresy.)[57] But whatever the source of Duran's ideas, the Jewish public was ready for them and they gained wide currency.[58]

Issues discussed so intensely in written polemics were no doubt lively topics of verbal discussion. Occasionally we hear of verbal debates that support our assumption that the sort of written polemics we have discussed passed into popular usage. Abraham Bivach wrote that he argued before Juan II of Aragon that Incarnation was logically impossible because it implied divine imperfection—not perhaps the best example of popular polemicizing.[59] More to the point, Solomon Bonafed wrote that in a debate around 1414 with some conversos who were convinced of the truth of Christianity, he argued that Jews were saved by a faith that, in contrast to Christianity, did not contradict the intellect. (He singled out for ridicule the Christian cult of saints and the sacraments of the Eucharist and confession.)[60] Debates by less erudite figures than these, in the home and in the marketplace, would have been natural.

It is interesting that two Jewish philosophical polemical works dating from this period were reportedly written in the vernacular and only later translated into Hebrew: Moses ha-Kohen of Tordesillas's *Auxilio de la religión* (1379; in Hebrew translation, *Ezer ha-da'at*), and Hasdai Crescas's polemical treatise *Refutation of Christian Principles,* composed in about 1398.[61] Scholars have speculated that Crescas's aim in using the vernacular may have been to reach an audience of converts who could not read Hebrew.[62] But works written in the vernacular were becoming more common in this period among both Christians and Jews. Jews, for example, were contributing to the increasing demand for "romance" translations of the Bible.[63] Crescas thus may have been addressing a non-elite audience of both Jews and conversos for whom a vernacular work was more readable than one in Hebrew.

Skipping ahead momentarily to a later period, when we have the luxury of Inquisition files, we find good evidence of informal polemical discussion among the rank and file of Spanish Jews and conversos. In the words of one scholar, "The many spontaneous conversations of this type reported in Inquisition files may lack theological precision, but they probably reflect much more accurately the actual realities of Judeo-Christian polemics in fifteenth-century Spain than any Latin text."[64]

A striking example of this phenomenon appears in the Inquisition sentence of a Valencian converso cloth merchant named Jaime Ferrer, who was condemned to the stake as a *relapso* and *negativo* in 1485. He had reportedly attended converso gatherings where a practicing Jew read and interpreted Scripture. Ferrer was also accused of possessing a book "that contained many heresies and blasphemies and foul abuses [*improperis neffandissims*] against our Lord Jesus Christ"—most likely a copy of a Jewish polemical treatise. His Inquisition sentence—the only part of his trial record that has survived—singles out his rebuttal of a key claim of Christian missionizing: nowhere, he argued, was it written that Jerusalem had been destroyed because of Jesus' death.[65]

It was such discussions that were to sustain Jewish polemical discourse in Spain and Portugal after public Jewish life disappeared in 1492 and 1497, respectively. That they survived into the seventeenth century (at least in Portugal) is quite likely, as we shall see.

From a Christian perspective, the large-scale Jewish conversions between 1391 and 1414 were a victory for the faith—the achievement of a cherished goal. Yet by the mid-fifteenth century, it became clear that the massive baptism of Jews had not resolved the problem of religious conflict and division in Spanish society. On the contrary, it had created a new and more complex problem. In the environment that had been created, Old Christians began to develop an anti-converso rhetoric that reflected increasing xenophobia, resentment, and suspicion toward baptized Jews and their offspring.[66]

Rising hostility contributed in 1449 to the first outbreak of violence against conversos (a status that had become an inherited one, even for children of a "mixed" Old Christian–New Christian marriage).[67] This episode also marks the first effort to introduce a "purity of blood" statute (it was subsequently revoked). Moreover, it marks the Castilian conversos' introduction to inquisitorial action. Several conversos were arrested, tried, tortured, and sentenced to death at the stake.[68]

There were, however, few prosecutions of judaizing before the establishment of the Spanish Inquisition in the 1480s. This is not to say that crypto-judaizing could be practiced with impunity in the pre-Inquisition period. A papal inquisition existed in Aragon from the thirteenth century, and inquisitors appointed by the pope conducted a handful of heresy trials against judaizers—from the mid-1460s in Valencia, and from the 1480s in Aragon.[69] In Castile, bishops and their ecclesiastical courts had jurisdiction over heretics, a concession the pope granted the king of that realm in 1451. If found guilty, conversos could be burned at the stake. In the rare instances when this actually happened, mendicant preachers were quick to seize the opportunity to stir up the sort of anti-converso sentiment that eventually led to the establishment of a fully institutionalized inquisition.[70]

In this atmosphere, crypto-judaizing came to entail a degree of active resistance and heroism. Indeed, by the second half of the fifteenth century, conditions had been created that made possible not only defiance, but martyrdom as well. Martyrdom in the classic manner, of course, was impossible: a converso did not have the option of demonstrating steadfastness by resisting baptism. But in the new circumstances, a new model of martyrdom emerged: the accused crypto-Jew could choose death rather than reconciliation with the Church by admitting to judaizing and refusing to repent.

The first episode of such martyrdom, to my knowledge, occurred in 1464. Church authorities had obtained information that a converso stockingmaker in Cordova named Juan de Madrid was judaizing. The culprit was seized and led in a procession through the streets of Cordova to a church and up to a platform where, by order of the bishop, he was to take a public oath of penance. Instead of doing this, however, he reportedly took advantage of the occasion to declare before the crowd, "Behold, I have one death to die. It is better to die now and not at another time. I declare that the Law of Moses is the best, and that by it [alone] men can be saved!" He was promptly stoned to death.

The impact of this act on the conversos present was dramatic and it lingered in memory. Twenty-two years later, in 1486, a witness before the newly established Inquisition testified that on the day after the stoning, a prominent converso of Cordova (or possibly a relative of the latter) had been discussing the stoning and declared, "God grant that our souls go where the soul of Juan de Madrid is going!" The testimony about what followed, while not entirely clear, seems to suggest that this witness's declaration stirred local converso emotions to such an extent that it contributed to an outbreak of violence between conversos and Old Christians in Cordova.[71]

The terms in which Juan de Madrid couched his declaration deserve brief attention. He declared his adherence to a Law of Moses as the only law that insured personal salvation. By stressing the goal of personal salvation, he addressed his persecutors in terms that paralleled their own. But he was also presumably expressing his own beliefs. And in this he was not exceptional. There *was* widespread anxiety among Spanish Jews and conversos about personal salvation. This deserves attention because it was not a particularly Jewish way of expressing basic belief—though it did not directly contradict rabbinic Judaism. And the formulation that the Law of Moses was *the only faith in which one could obtain salvation* was unquestionably an appropriation of Catholic usage—one that became a cardinal tenet of crypto-Jewish belief and rhetoric.

Juan de Madrid's act must have stirred admiration not only among local crypto-Jews, but among unbaptized Jews as well. A paradoxical situation had developed: baptized Jews were now in a position to show a degree of steadfastness in their profession of Judaism that was seldom required of unbaptized Jews.[72] This could only have raised the respect in which crypto-Jews were held by their Jewish neighbors—and reinforced a conviction, albeit charged with conflict, that participation in Jewish life was possible even after baptism.

With the establishment of the Spanish Inquisition to prosecute crypto-Jews in 1481, the plight of Castilian conversos became suddenly more precarious. In fact it was much safer, up to the Expulsion a decade later, to be an unbaptized, openly professing Jew. In 1491, the converso Benito García remembered preventing a young Jew from converting. "You see how they burn them, and you want to become a Christian?" he exclaimed. (It was, he remarked, the only good deed he could remember ever performing.)[73]

In the wake of the first auto-da-fé, held in 1481 in Seville, where six persons were burned at the stake, the Inquisition entered a period of rapid expansion. In the next two decades—the most brutal phase of the Spanish Inquisition's activity—conversos condemned for judaizing in Castile and Aragon were burned at the stake in scores, while many others were subjected to confiscations, imprisonment, and public humiliation. Not incidentally, the Jews were also expelled.

In this terrifying early period of inquisitorial activity, trials were hasty affairs and burnings at the stake indiscriminate. Tribunals did not always follow the guidelines that later became standard. Under these circumstances, death at the stake had elements common to death by the mob, or to judicial murder in cases of blood libel. In the eyes of sympathetic onlookers, all of the victims suffered because they were considered professing Jews (whether they were or not). Such suffering made it natural to tap the rhetoric of martyrdom.

The Inquisition, then, played an important role in the crystallization of crypto-Jewish notions of martyrdom. It established a new and powerful frame-work: the auto-da-fé and public burnings at the stake. To be sure, the possibility for converso martyrdom had been created before the establishment of the Inquisition, as we have seen. But now Spanish conversos began to use the term *mártir* in rather free reference to crypto-Jews burned at the stake. The importance of burnings at the stake to the formation of crypto-Jewish concepts of martyrdom can be underscored by a seemingly bizarre fact: well-known judaizers who died in prison before sentencing were never regarded as martyrs,[74] whereas conversos burned at the stake for judaizing were often regarded as martyrs in converso circles *even if they had never actually judaized.*

Let us turn to the kind of rhetoric that was used about these "martyrs" in the first decades of the Inquisition's activity.

Unfortunately, the evidence is scarce. Verbally ascribing martyrdom to victims of the Inquisition was dangerous, even in conversation among friends, since the use of such language was prima facie evidence of judaizing. Nevertheless, Inquisition files provide us with some valuable evidence. Admittedly, denunciations are not a very reliable source of evidence. Still, the documentation taken together points to certain trends.

In 1486, the elderly widow Gracia de Esplugas, of Saragossa, after having been sentenced to be "relaxed to the secular arm" (handed over to civil authorities for burning at the stake, a formality the Inquisition strictly adhered to), declared that she wanted "to be a martyr" (*seyer mártir*).[75] This statement in itself tells us little, but suggests the close association of burning at the stake with the concept of martyrdom.

More revealing are the statements attributed to the Jeronymite friar Alfonso de Toledo, who was accused of judaizing in 1487. He was repeatedly denounced for declaring that "the heretics who were burned were martyrs, as long as they died in the [true] knowledge of God."[76] This judaizing friar (of whom there were quite a few in the 1480s) seems to have regarded as martyrs only those persons burned at the stake who had actually judaized, whether or not they had gone to death defiantly.[77]

In 1511, Constanza Diaz of Almagro was accused of saying about those burned at the stake—perhaps referring to victims of an auto-da-fé in Jaen in 1510—that "they were martyrs and they had gone to glory; and would that her own soul would go where the souls of those who were burned had gone."[78] Perhaps (if these were indeed her exact words) she identified all the victims as judaizers. Even if this were the case, there is no reason to think—as she must well have known—that all judaizers burned at the stake died defiantly. They would have included persons who had confessed and tearfully repented, persons who had refused to confess but were deemed guilty anyway (*negativos*), persons who confessed in the first audience and promptly proceeded to inform on everyone in their circle, and persons who became too depressed and demoralized to resist in any way—to name but some of the possibilities. This does not render Constanza Diaz of Almagro's view anomalous. It is no different from the view that all victims of Crusader violence were martyrs. It reflects the conditions of terror that prevailed, and may have reflected a widely accepted attitude during the early stages of the Spanish Inquisition's operation.

A case several years later supports this supposition. In 1518, a witness testified that a certain Maria Martínez, whose husband had been burned at the stake, had told her that "they [the victims] all followed [my husband], who was like a meek ram leading the sheep to the slaughterhouse . . . that they were all like martyrs [*como mártires*]." Moreover, according to this witness, Maria asserted that her husband was not actually a judaizer. In Maria's words, as reported by this acquaintance, "he [my husband] did nothing except come and go at the tannery, where he had his cell like that of a Jeronymite monk." She claimed that the inquisitors burned conversos just to obtain their property.[79] Perhaps she was trying to protect herself by denying that her husband had judaized—but if she had been taking precautions, why would she call him a martyr, thus opening the door to suspicion about herself? She may well have believed that all victims of inquisitorial violence merited the status of martyr.

The relative freedom with which the term *martyr* was used emerges even more clearly from a set of statements made by Maria González in Ciudad Real in 1511–1512. This woman's husband had been burned at the stake in 1484. At her second trial, González confessed to telling several people shortly after her husband's death about a dream in which her husband came to her at night, appearing to her as an infant of eight or nine months. When she asked him about his transformation he replied, "Woman, I am with the innocents." She responded, "God has had mercy on us, to bring it to pass that being an old sinner you should be with the innocents."

She denied, quite possibly for tactical reasons, having made other damaging statements that were not the unconscious product of a dream. These statements, however, dovetail with the dream and are worth examining. She was accused of saying about her husband "that they have made a martyr of a sinner—that he had died a martyr and as a martyr rose [directly] to heaven," and furthermore "that all those who were burned as heretics by the Inquisition went as martyrs and died like martyrs."[80]

What unites all of these opinions is a non-judgmental perception of the converso condition. Whatever rabbis in Salonika or North Africa may have thought about the status of conversos, the conversos, confronted with the horrifying realities of inquisitorial action, adjusted their perceptions of their behavior in a normal human way. It did not matter to the persons quoted above that the "martyrs" burned at the stake had dissimulated for years or even decades, practicing Catholicism outwardly and lying when necessary about their beliefs. To be sure, leading such a double life was regarded by crypto-Jews as undesirable in principle. In reality, however, it came to be taken for granted as an acceptable way of serving God under the circumstances. Were they not reliving the tribulations of the Israelites in Egypt? The Inquisition had eliminated whatever moral ambiguity was left.

A discussion of converso conceptions of martyrdom in this period would not be complete without considering the place of the "burnt ones" in the apocalyptic vision of the much-studied Inés de Herrara. This young converso "prophetess" from a rural town in Extremadura, a region of Castile bordering on Portugal, had a visionary experience in 1499 that she revealed to a number of local conversos.[81] The conversos of Castile had been living in a state of anxiety for nearly two decades, and Inés's penitential, messianic, and apocalyptic message struck a chord.[82]

Inés's message of impending redemption—she preached that the conversos would soon be transported to the Holy Land, if they would undertake certain penitential practices—came to her during an ascent to heaven. (Such visions of ascent were common in medieval Catholicism. Visions in general were so prevalent in early modern Castile that William Christian has referred to its "culture of visions.")[83]

Of particular interest to us is the centrality in Inés's heavenly vision of the "burnt ones" (*los quemados*) seated on thrones of gold. We do not have testimony from Inés herself. The most elaborate testimony about the vision she reported was given by Juan de Segovia, a cobbler from Toledo. According to his account, the girl's dead mother had taken her by the hand and told her not to fear, because it was God's will that she ascend to heaven where she would see marvelous secret things. A young boy who had died a few days earlier in Herrera took Inés by the other hand, and an angel took them to heaven, where Inés

> saw purgatory and the souls suffering there [on one side], and on the other side she saw others in glory, on thrones of gold, and high above her head in another place she heard much noise (*mucho mormollo*). She asked the angel what was making sounds up there and the angel said, "Beloved of God, those who are making sounds up there are those who were burned here on earth, who are [now] there in glory."[84]

The term *martyr* is not used by any of the witnesses reporting Inés's account of her vision, but it is obvious that the "burnt ones" enjoyed that status. The image of thrones of gold is borrowed from Christian lore, in which such seats were occupied by saints.[85] Inés's conception, like others we have seen, is undiscriminating. She accorded to any person burned at the stake the status of martyr.[86]

Her story is unique, however, in placing the martyrs within a complete moral and metaphysical universe. It is one that both appropriated and subverted the imagery of the auto-da-fé. Even in its relatively undeveloped state around 1500, the auto, with Church dignitaries sitting in a grandstand on one side and condemned heretics sitting on the other, was designed to mirror late medieval representations of the Last Judgment. According to this conception, the heretics were consigned to the flames of hell.[87] Inés's revised picture, in which the "burnt ones" enjoyed the highest place of glory with the angels, is a fine example of crypto-Jewish inversion of Catholic values.[88] It was the condemned crypto-Jews who enjoyed the aura of late medieval sainthood and its heavenly reward. By implication, at least, the inquisitors and their collaborators were consigned to everlasting fire.

By what merit, one might ask, did the "burnt ones" enjoy so unique a place?

Figure 1. *The Last Judgment*. Jan van Eyck and Workshop Assistant. Fifteenth century. The Metropolitan Museum of Art.

Why were they alone there? Why did they not appear in the company of the righteous souls of Jews throughout history?

The splendid isolation of Inés's "burnt ones" probably reflects the provincial thinking of relatively uneducated converso artisans in Extremadura. Conversos *were* the only "Jews" in their milieu. While Inés's messianism drew from Jewish sources, her notions of the afterworld (which included purgatory) were distinctly Catholic, and she did not possess the resources to imagine her subversively construed heaven peopled with anyone but condemned judaizers who had been burned at the stake.

The special glory Inés accorded to those who were burned may also draw indirectly from early modern Catholic thinking about suffering and salvation. Like other conversos of her generation who made burning at the stake *the* criterion for martyrdom, she seems to have shared a late medieval sensibility that elevated patient suffering over human striving. The faceless heavenly chorus of Inés's martyrs does seem evocative of such a sensibility. The appearance of purgatory in her vision (according to two of the witnesses) may throw further light on her thinking. She may have believed that the "burnt ones" escaped purgatory—an aspect of Catholic theology she had unwittingly absorbed—because they had been purged of their sins by their fiery deaths.[89]

Any conclusions to be drawn from the evidence we have presented must certainly be taken cautiously. This evidence comes mainly from rural, non-elite circles. Its importance lies mainly in demonstrating that from an early period, crypto-Jews living under the threat of inquisitorial persecution grasped the potential of their situation for new expressions of Jewish martyrdom.

We cannot trace the development of Spanish crypto-Jewish notions of martyrdom very much further in time. By the time the documentation of Inquisition trials became relatively systematized—that is, by the 1540s—crypto-judaizing among the conversos of Spain was quickly dying out. After the Expulsion in 1492, the remnant of Spanish crypto-Jews was left isolated and without leadership, a fact that surely produced a sense of helplessness and may have triggered desperate hopes of the kind spread by Inés. The crypto-Jews were abandoned not only by the Jews who left Spain at the time of the Expulsion but also, in a more subtle way, by the many conversos in their midst who chose the path of accommodation to Catholic society.[90]

Further compounding the isolation was the fact that there was as yet no vehement attack on the Inquisition from Christian quarters in Europe—no audible voice protesting the cruelty of religious coercion. The crypto-Jews of Spain were, then, in the early decades of the sixteenth century, a dwindling, stigmatized population confronting a Spanish Church and monarchy that were at the height of their power and prestige, with no supportive audience, no vital sources of ideological inspiration to draw from, and little hope for collective release through any kind of action. It is hardly surprising that within a few decades, Spanish crypto-Judaism was essentially extinct. It is true that judaizing reappeared in Spanish lands with the influx of Portuguese New Christians into Spain and Spanish America after

1580. By then, however, expressions of crypto-Jewish martyrdom had undergone considerable development.

Paradoxically, it was among a new generation of highly-educated Spanish conversos who had been absorbed into the Catholic world that trends were brewing that would have a real intellectual impact on the later educated dogmatista martyrs. These men and women were contributing to innovative currents in Spanish religious life. One of these currents would have a long-term impact on early modern Spanish Catholicism—namely the spiritualist movement known as *alumbradismo*. Other currents would survive but, as we shall see, would go underground.[91]

But let us return to the fifteenth century. By 1492, the Catholic Monarchs had put in place extraordinary policies aimed at "de-judaizing" their kingdoms. However, as fate would have it, their ambitions to bring Portugal under Spanish rule soon undermined this very aim, producing a new and significantly different converso problem.

The story of the mass forced conversion of the Portuguese Jews in 1497 has been told many times. Suffice it to say here that dynastic politics convinced the Portuguese monarch to accept the demand of the Catholic Monarchs to expel the Jews of Portugal (in large part comprising the recent Spanish exiles), as a condition for the marriage of their widowed daughter Isabel to King Manuel of Portugal. Although the Portuguese monarch was eager to marry the Spanish princess, he was reluctant to expel a population that provided valuable services to the crown, and he devised a plan to satisfy his future in-laws without sacrificing his own interests: he gathered the Jews of Portugal in Lisbon in 1497 for "expulsion"—and subjected them instead to a mass forced baptism on the spot. According to contemporary reports, Jews were dragged forcibly to churches where baptismal water was thrown on them.

There is good evidence from both Jewish and Christian eyewitnesses that small numbers of these Jews resisted violently, killing their children and committing suicide to avoid baptism. The rabbinic scholar R. Simon Maimi and other members of his family, perhaps unwilling to take this course of action (which was not clearly supported by Jewish law), nevertheless resisted physically; they were imprisoned and beaten, as a result of which the rabbi died.[92] The great majority of the Jews, however, did not take such radical measures to resist. A new population of conversos was created in the course of a few days. Some of the new converts succeeded in fleeing, but the borders were soon closed to converso emigration.[93]

Manuel apparently believed that the new converts would be absorbed into his Catholic population without the use of undue pressure. He promised that for a period of twenty years no inquiries would be made into their religious beliefs, and that no special legislation concerning them or their descendants would ever be instituted.[94] But his expectations were unrealistic. While Jewish life among the conversos went underground—public synagogues disappeared, along with the structures of communal life—the king was in effect giving the conversos license to build the foundations of a crypto-Jewish way of life that would prove tenacious and exceedingly difficult to eradicate. Even several generations after the mass conversions, many Portuguese conversos were involved in judaizing in one form or another.[95]

In 1512, the king extended the period of immunity from prosecution for a further term, to 1534. Royal lenience meant that the new converts enjoyed altogether a period of more than three decades during which they were able to develop and consolidate a crypto-Jewish way of life without significant interference. Unfortunately, the state of research is such that we have only a superficial understanding of the internal development of Portuguese crypto-Jewish networks in the early sixteenth century.

Despite the king's extension of the period of protection from prosecution, by 1515 he was taking the first steps toward introducing an inquisition in Portugal based on the Spanish model. The leaders of the New Christian community—which was not, of course, an organized community but rather a kind of interest group organized for the sake of lobbying—were vigilant from the start, eager to head off the king's plan. A long struggle ensued, beginning in earnest in 1531. Eventually, however—in May 1536—the pope approved the establishment of a Portuguese Inquisition.

Having been given the green light after being constrained for so long, the inquisitors were soon conducting a terrifying campaign against the New Christian population. The brutal trials and burnings at the stake led many conversos to flee (some of them resettling, to the Portuguese crown's dismay, in the pope's own territories, in the town of Ancona). So vociferously did Portuguese New Christians protest the excesses of the new inquisition in the early 1540s that Paul III suspended inquisitorial sentencing altogether in 1544. And so a new round of negotiations began. But at this point, with the Council of Trent getting underway, the pope decided to make the necessary concessions to resolve the issue, and in July 1547 he issued a bull granting the Portuguese Inquisition full powers to prosecute heresy.[96] Quite unwittingly, he thus helped prepare the way for a new form of crypto-Jewish martyrdom.

THE DOGMATISTA CRYPTO-
JEWISH MARTYRS

2

The dogmatista martyrs who are the focus of this book emerged only in the late sixteenth century. For them, the Inquisition—whether Spanish or Portuguese—was a familiar and ubiquitous presence. Few of their contemporaries (if any) remembered a time when it was otherwise. In other ways, too, these men were conditioned by circumstances that were radically different from those confronting the generation of the Expulsion and the forced conversion in Portugal. They had never lived in—or even in the vicinity of—a Jewish community. Their grand-parents' gravestones were located on monastery grounds or in church chapels. In their environment, Latin was *the* language of learning. Personal salvation was a foundational concept in their religious consciousness, as critical in their crypto-Judaism as it was in their parish priest's Catholicism. They had no idea how one worshipped in a synagogue or conducted a Passover seder. In short, they lacked any organic connection to contemporary Jewish life.

Their careers were clustered chronologically in the period between 1579 and 1665. This clustering may be explained in different ways, but it was not mere accident.[1] Nor was it because there had been no crypto-Jews who had chosen to die as martyrs before this time. Converso deaths of a heroic type had occurred, as we have seen, even before the establishment of the Spanish Inquisition, and surely occurred afterward as well, both in Spain and Portugal. But earlier conditions did not lend themselves to the kind of prolonged, staged "combat" between inquisitors and prisoner that mark the careers of the celebrated martyrs. This was due partly to the fact that in the early period of inquisitorial activity in Spain, trials and autos-da-fé were often hasty affairs.[2] The leisurely pace of the trials we will be examining —their records often cover hundreds of folio pages—became possible only at a stage at which the volume of cases had dropped off sharply. But this is not an adequate explanation. The Portuguese Inquisition, in contrast to that of Spain, appears to have maintained a relatively unflagging pace of prosecutions; indeed, there is evidence of acceleration in the seventeenth century.[3] Other factors were clearly involved.

Unfortunately, we have only the sketchiest notion of how crypto-Jewish life in Portugal evolved over time. We can, however, identify some of the major factors and developments that facilitated the appearance of the type of judaizer we will be examining. First, there was the sheer passage of time and, with it, the accumulation of experience. In the decades before the Portuguese Inquisition was established, judaizing conversos in Portugal were able to develop a more-or-less stable, "net-worked," and rooted crypto-Jewish existence, one that was capable of withstanding periodic assaults. As with all groups who endure systematic repression, the crypto-Jews in Portugal became experts in the mode of operation of the regime that victimized them. They built up a stockpile of wisdom, sharing tips, lore, and information in a way that allowed them to anticipate the Inquisition's steps. They were also aided incalculably by the fact that after the early reign of terror in the 1540s, the Portuguese Inquisition, like the Spanish, became a fairly predictable bureaucracy, with elaborate regulations that were usually observed to the letter. (The Portuguese Inquisition operated according to the same methods and procedures as the Spanish, which drew heavily from regulations established by the medieval Inquisition.) Certainly by the 1570s, an intelligent, adult crypto-Jew whose trial had advanced to a certain point could have few illusions about his or her prospects.

Let me give a few examples. A converso who had been tried and reconciled in the past, and who had been arrested again and found guilty of judaizing, would be burned at the stake as a *relapso* whether or not he or she repented. A converso who denied all guilt, but who the Inquisition was convinced had judaized, would in all likelihood be burned at the stake as a *negativo*. A converso who had no prior record and who confessed fully to judaizing, providing details and names of accomplices while expressing profuse repentance, could expect to be reconciled (received back in the Church)—though he or she would also be sentenced to wearing the sambenito for a period, serving a brief prison sentence,[4] and suffering the confiscation of property. Once these realities were clear, it was possible to view martyrdom as a "best" option—that is, as one that would preserve self-esteem and honor (and possibly win one fame), provide a noble outlet for the expression of anger, vindicate one's inner sense of truth, and ensure eternal salvation.

Second, there was the Reformation, which affected crypto-Jews and other Iberian opponents of the Inquisition in multiple ways. By 1521, Lutheran books, translated into Spanish by conversos in Antwerp, were already entering Spain, and despite the Inquisition's best efforts they continued to reach major Iberian urban centers.[5] In 1552, for example, some four hundred and fifty Bibles that had been printed abroad (and were thus prohibited) were seized in Seville.[6] Despite routine searches of ship cargoes in Iberian port cities, forbidden literature inevitably slipped through.

It has too often been assumed that Protestant ideas ceased to play a significant role in Spain after the Inquisition's campaign to suppress *luteranismo* in 1558–1559.[7] As for sixteenth-century Portugal, scholars have scarcely scratched the surface in examining Protestant undercurrents.[8] Yet it should be evident that even the most efficient institutions of repression could not have kept Protestant anti-Catholic propaganda from infiltrating the Peninsula, especially given the large numbers of sailors and merchants from England, France, and Italy who routinely visited Iberian ports. It is true that most cases of *luteranismo* that were prosecuted by the Inquisition after 1560 (except those involving foreigners) involved accused persons who by no means adhered to a fully developed, coherent Protestant belief system.[9] But this should not be taken to mean that heterodox "Protestantish" ideas no longer played a role in Iberian society.

Certain aspects of the Protestant attack on the Roman Church must have resonated keenly with Portuguese crypto-Jews. There can be little doubt that late Spanish-Jewish polemical arguments against Christianity of the kind discussed in chapter 1—arguments that in some ways anticipated the Protestant assault on the Church—had survived among this population in some form, and had perhaps undergone further development. The fact that such arguments were by now being preached openly in German pulpits could only have given new credibility to them. Still, it is difficult to know exactly how Reformation rhetoric influenced crypto-Jewish thinking. An early denunciation recorded by the Portuguese Inquisition in 1540, for example, reports on a New Christian who said to his wife that he didn't need to go to church to see God, because to see bread and wine he didn't need to leave the house[10]—a typically down-to-earth crypto-Jewish witticism about transubstantiation, but one that might well have drawn support from more widespread skepticism about the "real presence" in the host. Likewise, a New Christian was denounced in 1541 for declaring, among other things, that the pope did not have special powers but was like any other bishop. One might wonder whether the accused was a crypto-Jew at all, except that he also allegedly declared his belief in the Law of Moses.[11] Particularly in those fateful years before the Inquisition became active, one can imagine the surprise and satisfaction of Portuguese crypto-Jews as French sailors made sly insinuations about the pope in Lisbon taverns, or as pamphlets smuggled from Flanders declared war on idolatry. While it may be impossible to trace the particular ways in which crypto-Jewish and Protestant ideas dovetailed in heterodox Iberian circles, such a phenomenon was of great importance, as we shall see, in the careers of the dogmatista martyrs.

Once the Inquisition began to prosecute *luteranos* in Spain and Portugal, crypto-Jews must have followed news of the trials with more than ordinary interest. They would have heard about (even if they did not actually witness) burnings at the stake of condemned *luteranos,* including those sensational cases in which the defiant heretic was burned alive. Contemporary crypto-Jews would have paid close attention, for example, to accounts of the English merchant William Gardiner, who became notorious in 1552 when he grabbed the consecrated host from a priest who was raising it in the Portuguese Royal Chapel in Lisbon, and stamped it underfoot. (He was burned alive at the stake soon thereafter, defiant and impenitent.)[12] In fact we have evidence that they did: two New Christians were denounced in early 1553 for having said "that the Englishman who was burned [Gardiner] died a martyr."[13] They would have heard of the *luterano* heretic Bachiller Herrezuelo, burned alive at the stake in Valladolid in 1559.[14] Particularly striking evidence is a remark made by Diego Díaz Nieto, a Portuguese-Jew-turned-judaizer, about a defiant German Protestant who had been burned alive at the stake in Mexico City in 1601. Nieto reported that this man had attacked Catholicism and the Inquisition at length (something he probably learned from the public sentencing); and, he added, he "quite agreed with many of the things" this *luterano* said.[15] New Christians who were active in international commerce and lived in major port cities would probably also have known of sensational burnings of Christian heretics outside the Peninsula, as well—for example, the death at the stake in 1553 of the Spanish antitrinitarian Miguel Serveto (Michael Servetus), who was arrested in Geneva at Calvin's order.

The fact that Christian dissidents were ready to suffer and die to defend their case against the Catholic Church—a case that included objections that had long been a part of Jewish polemics—must have stirred a sense of identification among some crypto-Jews, as we know it did among certain Jews. But the fact that the Christian world was able to produce such heroic martyrs also represented a challenge to a group that survived by trying to maintain secrecy, stirring unconscious competitive feelings and perhaps even a degree of discomfort. That is, the example of defiant Protestant martyrs (and perhaps of defiant Catholic martyrs in Protestant lands as well) may have provided for some crypto-Jews a stimulus to die similar deaths.

Finally, there was the factor of converso migration. Portuguese conversos in particular tended to be a highly mobile population in the early modern period, and found ways to circumvent the sporadic and ineffective efforts of Iberian regimes to contain them. Even within the Peninsula itself, their migratory tendencies were conspicuous. This was especially true after Spain's annexation of Portugal in 1580, when Portuguese conversos began to infiltrate Spanish lands in large numbers, leading to a sudden spike in the number of "judaizers" prosecuted by Spanish tribunals. By the late sixteenth century, Portuguese judaizing had spread throughout the realms and vast overseas territories ruled by Spain.[16] The "Portuguese," as they were known, moved about the Spanish Empire mainly in response to economic opportunities, but their mobility, particularly for merchants, also afforded opportunities to create and maintain ramified crypto-Jewish networks.

Significant numbers of conversos—after the mid-sixteenth century, Portuguese conversos in particular—also fled Iberian lands. Until the mid-sixteenth century, they tended to join Jewish communities originally established by the Spanish exiles in the Mediterranean. After this they began moving north to new commercial centers such as Bordeaux, Bayonne, Amsterdam, Hamburg, and Rotterdam, where they built new Jewish communities or, in some cases, assimilated into the Christian population. The large-scale emigration of conversos to non-Iberian realms proved to have unanticipated benefits for the crypto-Jews who remained behind. Extensive commercial and kinship ties were maintained for generations between the conversos and the émigrés. In the seventeenth century, the well-organized and wealthy Sephardi communities of Venice and Amsterdam provided crypto-Jews in Iberian lands with a degree of moral support, as well as with a powerful tale of crypto-Jewish triumph. As conversos in the Peninsula became aware of an increasingly dynamic and institutionalized "ex-converso diaspora," crypto-Jewish martyrs gained an audience that extended far beyond Iberian lands.[17]

The Inquisition itself not only continued to provide some of the opportunities for dramatic episodes of crypto-Jewish martyrdom, but enhanced those opportunities. Starting in the 1550s, it staged increasingly grand and elaborate autos-da-fé. The experience of being marched out before a jeering throng, wearing a sambenito, and listening to one's public sentencing was intended to be a great humiliation. But for a judaizer with sufficient fortitude, these mass spectacles offered an incomparable opportunity to make a lasting impression on the crowd.[18]

The moment of ultimate defiance, however—the moment that transfixed the crowd and "defeated" the inquisitors—came after the auto-da-fé, when those condemned to death, having been relaxed to the secular authorities, were taken to the *quemadero* to be burned. At this point, the sentence was irreversible. But heretics condemned to death had a last chance to display their contempt for the Church. At the stake, they would be offered a last minute opportunity to make a token gesture of acceptance of the Church (usually kissing a crucifix). They would be rewarded for this act of compliance by being garroted to death before being burned.[19] Those who refused to make this gesture, however, became martyrs in the classic, "athletic" sense: they were subjected to the indescribably agonizing end of being burned *alive* at the stake. Very few condemned people made this choice. Doing so had become, by the late sixteenth century, the hallmark of the martyr.

For the dogmatista martyrs, a defiant death was only the last scene of an extended drama, during the course of which they repeatedly challenged and disparaged the inquisitors. Their psychological ability to sustain this behavior had to do at least partly with their individual temperaments, but it also had to do with evolving new ideas about the locus of religious authority.

Changing historical realities also provided impetus for bold displays of insubordination. Autos-da-fé may have become more spectacular and imposing, but the all-powerful regime they sought to represent was slipping. By the seventeenth century, the Spanish Empire (which included Portugal from 1580 to 1640) was showing obvious signs of weakness. The self-image Spain had cultivated during the reign of Charles V—that of a monarchy with a providential mission, basking in conquest and the possession of a global empire, assured of its moral superiority—seemed more and more phantom-like. The diffusion of the so-called Black Legend, the fierce Protestant defamation of Spain and the Inquisition, contributed to the damage,[20] as did an ongoing financial crisis.[21] In some ways the grand auto-da-fé served as a pseudo victory pageant, a site where triumph was assured—in stark contrast to Flanders or the English Channel. A recognition of the erosion of Iberian power may have had the unacknowledged effect of encouraging the audacity of impenitent dogmatistas.

The Roman Church, of course, was also vulnerable in a new way. In Spain, the Inquisition mobilized itself to respond to the internal Protestant challenge by

Figure 2. Engraving of an auto-da-fé held in Madrid, 1680, from José Vicente del Olmo, *Relacion histórica del auto general de fé que se celebró en Madrid este año de 1680* . . . facing p. 138, signed Gregorio Fosman. The Jewish Theological Seminary. Seated in the stands on the left are ecclesiastical and royal dignitaries; on the right, prisoners who are to be sentenced. The royal box with a canopy can be seen at the center rear, amid the spectators. At the very center of the plaza is the area where prisoners stand to hear

extending its reach to include *luteranos,* and by defining ever more narrowly the bounds of acceptable Catholic belief. Iberian defenders of the faith adopted an increasingly polemical and combative stance toward heresy. It is important to keep in mind that the inquisitors' increasing readiness for theological combat (as well as that of the pertinacious dogmatistas) was fueled by the wider ethos of conflict and confrontation in Reformation Europe. Religious bellicosity was expressed in numerous ways that fell short of actual war—iconoclastic rampages, the dissemination of inflammatory broadsides, public executions of heretics, book burnings, and campaigns to convert the heathens. The lengthy disputations carried on between inquisitors and accused heretics, some of which we shall examine in detail, were an integral part of this confrontational milieu.

In such an ethos, it was not only victory but also the appearance of victory that mattered. Only in this light can we understand the great exertions the Inquisition made to bring about the conversion of condemned judaizers. Francisco Maldonado de Silva, for example, was sentenced to be relaxed to the secular arm in January 1633. But he was not summarily dispatched to the *quemadero,* as he would have been a century earlier. It was only six years—and many conversionist "disputes"—later that he was burned at the stake.

As the case of Maldonado de Silva suggests, the most extravagant efforts to bring about a change of heart were made in cases involving "pertinacious dogmatizers" (*dogmatistas pertinaces*), whether they were judaizers or *luteranos.*[22] The presence in Inquisition cells of self-confident, Bible-literate critics of the Church represented a new kind of challenge—not, as in the late fifteenth century, that of an essentially alien attack on Church doctrine, but that of an all-too-intimate one. From a propaganda point of view, achieving the heretic's humble admission of error was a far more desirable outcome than burning him or her at the stake. As a result, in cases that involved defiant dogmatizers, inquisitorial tribunals were prepared to summon multiple experts (*calificadores*) and to conduct theological disputations behind closed doors that might drag on for months or even years. (The luxury of such long trials was made possible by the dwindling overall number of cases.) This in some ways played into the hands of judaizing proselytizers, whose fame within the prison walls (and to some extent outside them as well) only grew with the passage of time and the intensification of their ordeals.

This is not to say that the Inquisition scored no victories. When after a marathon struggle a "conversion" *was* achieved, it was regarded as a great coup. Take the case of the judaizer Antonio Gabriel de Torres Zevallos in Cordova in 1722, as reported in the official Inquisition account. He had remained "pertinacious up to the time of the reading of his sentence." But upon hearing his death sentence at the auto, he

> repented with such copious tears and acts of contrition that everyone was touched. With death approaching, he voluntarily made loud protestations of our holy faith, testifying to the mercy of God and the Holy Office. He refused to let the executioner kiss his feet,[23] and, ordering his confessor to obey, told him [his confessor] to kiss the

feet of the executioner. He begged to be burned alive (which was not conceded him [since this punishment was reserved for the unrepentant]), holding that this would be little enough pain to atone for his grave sins, and he commended his soul to God, to the great joy and edification of the people.[24]

Similarly, much was made of the purported last-minute conversion (or, possibly, breakdown) of Luis Carvajal, who had followed a path of defiant and self-conscious martyrdom for twenty-two months until he arrived at the stake and witnessed the garroting and burning of his mother and two sisters.[25] A quite different case, but one that held similar propaganda value, was that of Jacob Bueno. Bueno was a Portuguese Jew from Amsterdam who died in 1647 from self-inflicted wounds, apparently a desperate attempt at suicide, in an Andalusian convent where he had been held captive. The Franciscan friars who had held him prisoner sent a letter describing his conversion with great pathos.[26]

On the other hand, cases in which the prisoner did not succumb to pressure and was burned alive as an unrepentant heretic were a great propaganda coup for the Spanish and Portuguese Jewish world. This explains why Isaac Cardoso offered such loving detail about the martyrdom of Francisco Maldonado de Silva, in an otherwise quite abstract work defending Judaism. "The theologians and inquisitorial officers," Cardoso wrote,

> summoned him many times in order to convince him, but he disputed with them by word and in writing. He wrote many treatises in his cell, joining together many old pieces of paper from various wrapped items that he requested, and he did it so ingeniously that they seemed all of one piece. He made the ink from charcoal, the pen out of a chicken bone that he cut with a knife made from a nail, and he wrote in a hand that seemed as if it was printed.[27]

Since burnings at the stake were a very public spectacle, there was little the Inquisition could do to prevent news of a "successful" martyrdom from spreading, except to put its own spin on the event—which usually meant harping on the exceptional power of the devil over the "stubborn apostate." But crypto-Jews preserved and transmitted their own version of events. Not surprisingly, they also sought out information about what had occurred behind prison walls prior to sentencing (the "secret cells" of the Inquisition were rather porous). Pamphlet accounts of the major autos-da-fé, published and hawked in the streets, were rich sources of information. Cardoso gleaned his details about Maldonado de Silva's improvised writing tools from just such an account, published in Madrid in 1640.[28]

More significant for our story than the inevitable literary romanticizing in the Sephardi diaspora was the triumphalist behavior of the judaizing martyrs themselves in their confrontation with the Inquisition. The martyrs had in their favor a theology that was powerfully literalist and untrammeled by the compromises of institutionalized religion. They sensed the opportunities for provocation provided by what J. H. Elliott has referred to, in a narrower context, as "the stockade mentality in Castilian society."[29] Their opponents tended to be members of a clerical bureaucracy, beaten into conformity by the pressures of a career in the post-Tridentine Church. The confidence of the dogmatizers when they appeared before the inquisitors was such that they sometimes entertained fantasies not only of vanquishing but even of *converting* these opponents (or at least shaking their belief). Thus the aspiring martyr Luis Carvajal, burned at the stake in Mexico City in 1596, insisted that he had agreed to debate with learned Jesuits not because he had any doubts about Mosaic Law, but "in order to confound and convert them."[30] Similarly, according to the inquisitors, the prisoner Diogo d'Asumpção, causing "much scandal to those who heard him," tried in 1599 "to teach and persuade the inquisitors, ecclesiastics, and learned men who were trying to guide him in matters of salvation."[31] Such efforts, and the conviction of superiority they imply, reflect a dramatic shift in psychological power relations, contrasted to the situation a century earlier.

The religiously contentious time that helped shape the careers of the celebrated crypto-Jewish martyrs was also a time of widespread debate about the permissibility of disguising one's faith.[32] Among Calvinists, it was regarded as compulsory to declare one's faith openly, even in cases in which this might cost one's life. This anti-Nicodemite position, as it came to be known, could be found across the Christian confessional divide.[33] In the Catholic world in this period, interest revived in the early Christians who had proclaimed their belief demonstratively to the Romans, knowing this would bring them death—surely a response to the dramatic demands of their age.[34] The great Protestant martyrologies of John Foxe and Jean Crespin were naturally not among the foreign books the Inquisition allowed in the Peninsula, but Catholics compiled their own martyrologies. Several such works were published in Spanish in Madrid and Seville, and were in circulation by the late sixteenth century.[35]

Given the intense focus on the manner of one's death and dying in this period (about which more below), along with the intense atmosphere of religious conflict, a great deal was felt to be at stake in living up to the anti-Nicodemite ideal. The unfortunate Italian lawyer Francesco Spiera became a widely known example of how *not* to behave. When Spiera was arrested in 1547 by the newly established Venetian Inquisition for holding heterodox "Protestantish" beliefs, he recanted, and according to the accounts of his life he died six months later believing that this recantation had made his salvation impossible.[36]

Jewish tradition had its own anti-Nicodemite tradition. That is, in certain situations Jewish law required a person to accept martyrdom rather than violate the Law. But among the conversos of the Peninsula, by the late sixteenth and seventeenth centuries, conscious rationalization of crypto-judaizing was hardly needed, and for most crypto-Jews dissimulation entailed little shame or guilt. Diego de Simancas, a late-sixteenth-century Spanish author, noted that the conversos justified their not having chosen martyrdom by citing Deuteronomy 5:33 ("You shall walk in all the way which the Lord your God has commanded you, *so that you may live*"—i.e. live, not die).[37] As Yosef Hayim Yerushalmi points out, this "is indeed a *locus classicus*" for rationalizing nonobservance in dangerous circumstances.[38] But the long-term use of this justification, among crypto-Jews who made no effort to escape to lands where they could practice Judaism in freedom, reflects a process of adaptation. Most crypto-Jews came to feel that the fact that they took risks in order to maintain crypto-Jewish life conferred legitimacy on their condition. Their frequent identification with the Jews enslaved in Egypt was, among other things, an expression of their belief that their plight was an inescapably Jewish one.

A much less classical Jewish source used in crypto-Jewish circles was a verse from the apocryphal Letter of Baruch, justifying the outward practice of idolatry if one believed the truth in one's heart.[39] There is ample evidence that many crypto-Jews who had no resort to this particular source nevertheless relied on a shared conviction that "believing in one's heart" was acceptable to God, under the circumstances.[40]

The strong feelings of guilt felt by some of the conversos who fled the Peninsula and settled in Jewish communities tended to develop only after they had become familiar with normative rabbinic teaching. As the ex-converso Isaac Orobio de Castro wrote in a work composed after he had left the Peninsula and reverted to Judaism in Amsterdam, "We dissembled our faith [in the Peninsula], and although the sin of one who conceals truth or denies it is unforgivable, not all of us were aware that it was in fact our duty to affirm it."[41]

Indeed, some felt it was a virtue to deny one's faith. It was not a religious virtue, to be sure, but one rooted in political resistance to oppression and a sense of personal honor. Thus the wealthy Lima merchant Manuel Bautista Pérez, whom we will meet again in chapter 5, was burned at the stake in Lima in 1639 after refusing to confess (and after urging other accused judaizers to follow the same course of action). The refusal to allow the Inquisition to penetrate his private mental life may have been a natural path of resistance, in particular for a converso whose inner life was uncertain, ambivalent, and prone to skepticism, as may well have been the case with Bautista Pérez. It also appears to have been a matter of honor for this prisoner not to confess (whether falsely or not) to behavior that would have left a stain on the family name: while in prison he sent a coded message to his brother-in-law not to bend under torture, lest the family live in perpetual infamy.[42]

Crypto-Jewish dissimulation fed into Old Christian anxieties about conversos, who in any case continued to be viewed through the prism of anti-Jewish stereotypes. New Christians were greedy; they belonged to a despised people; they were tainting Iberian society with their "blood"; and so on. The fact that they pretended to be good Catholics when in fact they were heretics provided further evidence of their depravity. It reflected their cowardice and deceit. A Spanish inquisitor, writing to the king of Portugal in 1528, alluded to this in his rebuttal of converso arguments that their baptism was invalid because it had been coerced. In fact, he argued, their baptism was not forced at all, because they had been free to let themselves be killed—as perhaps they would have done if they had had the courage of the Maccabees.[43] A similar slur appears in a strongly racialist anti-Jewish report on the conversos submitted to the Portuguese king in 1629 by an assembly of bishops and theologians that met in Tomar, Portugal. Among the "evidence" the report cited to prove the corruptness of New Christian character was the failure of the New Christians (a term used here synonymously with *judaizers*) to live up to the standard of courage set by Eleazar, the Maccabee martyr.[44] The report further discussed a supposed talmudic dictum that permitted Jews to be faithful to Judaism in their hearts while outwardly practicing another religion. The rabbis made this provision, the report concluded, so that Jews might deceive the simple, "or at least to leave ordinary people perplexed and in doubt."[45] Even when they died at the stake, the report went on, they deluded themselves, taking pride in dying as martyrs for a religion they adhered to only in their hearts.[46]

While most crypto-Jews were not ashamed of their behavior—on the contrary, they regarded their cunning and dissimulation as an obvious necessity, like having locks on their doors—it surely rankled to know that Old Christians viewed it as cowardly and dishonorable. Such insinuations no doubt compounded their general feelings of impotence and rage. This being the case, the rare appearance at an auto-da-fé of a person, or persons, who chose demonstratively to "die in the Law of Moses" must have been a heartening—if also horrifying—experience. Crypto-Jewish martyrdom confirmed for them that crypto-Jews, too, had a place in the arena of open theological confrontation and struggle, and that they were as capable of dying heroically as Anabaptists in Flanders or Lutherans in Italy. The fact that crypto-Jewish martyrs had dissembled up to the time of their arrest, and usually for some time after that, did not detract from their glory. To my knowledge, no one with a stake in these matters—inside or outside the Peninsula—ever suggested that dissimulating for much of his or her life rendered a crypto-Jew unworthy of attaining martyrdom.

Each of the crypto-Jewish dogmatista martyrs made the choice at some point to abandon equivocation and openly profess belief in the Law of Moses. This was an important step, but it was only the first one in a complex course of action that required a powerful will, a capacity to strategize as well as to improvise, independence of judgment, and, not least, imprinted notions of how a martyr should conduct himself in life and death. In Luis Carvajal's "Memoirs," composed before his second arrest, we have invaluable evidence of how a person who had embarked on a course of martyrdom self-consciously constructed a "new self," adopting a new name and undertaking an initiation ceremony (self-circumcision) that signaled separation from the past.

Once an accused judaizer chose to profess Judaism defiantly—a course of action that would lead inexorably to death at the stake (barring death in prison)—he embarked on a course of confrontation with the Inquisition of indeterminate length, usually a few years. These years would bring ordeals but also opportunities for action, all of which, experienced in the setting of impending death, would intensify an emerging consciousness of his exceptional power as well as his commitment to a mental archetype of martyrdom. Such a general script was not, of course, unique to this particular set of martyrs. Victor Turner has vividly described such a period in the career of Thomas Becket when, finding himself at a "desperate impasse" with Henry II, Becket was seized, as it were, by a deep-rooted cultural model (of Christian martyrdom), which "came to claim Becket's full attention and to dominate his development from that time forth."[47]

Victor Turner has used the term *root paradigm* to describe a mental constellation that "reach[es] down to irreducible life stances of individuals, passing beneath conscious prehension to a fiduciary hold on what they sense to be axiomatic values, matters literally of life or death."[48] Among the various difficulties posed by Turner's use of this term is his failure to define the specific cultural contours of what he describes simply as Becket's "*Christian* root paradigm of martyrdom."[49] Giving so broad a label to the set of symbols, unconscious impulses, actions, sensitivities to social context, and so on, that constitute—in Turner's view—a root paradigm, dodges the issue of Becket's particular sources of inspiration. In any case, a simple cultural definition of this type will certainly not do for the crypto-Jewish dogmatista martyrs. These figures developed their roles amid a tangled confluence of cultural currents—medieval Catholic, presumed "Jewish," contemporary crypto-Jewish, and "Protestantish," to give a rough classification. The texts, images, and linguistic traditions they drew from did not possess intrinsic coherence. In their efforts to give coherence to the final drama, they drew from a developing general script for the judaizing martyr of the Inquisition. We will follow the articulation of this script more closely in subsequent chapters. For now let me sketch it in broad outlines.

In the early modern period, a person's death was not simply a matter of his or her physical expiration. By the fifteenth century, a preoccupation with the importance of a "good death" had produced a widely disseminated *ars moriendi* literature in both Latin and the vernacular. Works of this genre instructed the reader in detail, with vivid illustrations, how to prepare for death and how to proceed through the final hours of life. They provided warnings about special temptations at the hour of death, and advice about eluding these temptations. Such popular "how-to" books, like those of our own day, offered simple guidelines for achieving a culturally prevalent ideal. While our twenty-first-century self-help literature promises people that if they make an effort they can be successful, attractive, or happy, the *ars moriendi* literature promised that anyone who made an effort could merit salvation and perhaps even escape purgatory. Surely not everyone regarded such manuals as the last word on how to die. But these books did reflect deep-seated anxieties, hopes, and beliefs that even highly sophisticated people entertained in some way.[50]

Contemporary conventions about dying a "good death" helped shape the crypto-Jewish martyrs' roles in a way that would speak to their audience. Their theological ideas might be alien to many of those who watched them—inquisitors, prison wardens, bishops, hidalgos of the old aristocracy, and pious Catholics of the lower ranks. But their comportment might awe even the most firmly convinced Catholics, because it was consistent with ideals they shared. Virtually anyone in early modern Europe who was not a skeptic or a cynic shared the belief that a "good death" was an important goal, both in sealing one's standing in the community and in attaining salvation. For this reason, the fasting and prayer of the martyrs in their cells, their steadfastness in the face of death, their refusal to make even a small compromise to avoid the horrors of death by fire—all of these made a vivid impression on their observers. Even the martyrs' unvarying declaration of faith—namely, that they intended "to live and die in the Law of Moses"—reflected adherence to certain conventions in their environment. This formulation was an adaptation of the standard statement of the pious Catholic, who proclaimed his or her intention "to live and die in the Law of Christ." (This was not, of course, the "good death" the Inquisition hoped for. Heretics condemned to death were escorted during their last day by clerics who sought to help them "die well"—which could only mean, in their terms, as Catholics.)[51]

While the comportment of the crypto-Jewish martyrs had generic qualities reflecting the influence of their milieu, the "Jewish" nature of their careers was highlighted through certain specific acts and rhetorical expressions. Foremost among these was the act of circumcision. The famous martyr Tomás Treviño de Sobremonte, burned alive at the stake in Mexico City in 1649, had a judaizing friend circumcize him around 1635, after his first trial.[52] In cases we will examine more closely, the martyr performed self-circumcision. This act was viewed, among other things, as an act of self-affliction.

Jewish law, it should be said, does not regard circumcision in terms of affliction, much less self-affliction (although the adult circumcision of male converts certainly entails physical suffering). It is a ritual act that symbolizes the Covenant between God and the Jewish people, and is ordinarily performed by a ritual circumciser (*mohel*) on male infants at the age of eight days. But the crypto-Jewish martyrs, while conscious of circumcision as a religious precept incumbent on all male Jews (this was plainly stated in Scripture), were also keenly aware that in their particular environment the act singled them out even among crypto-Jews. It thus possessed theatrical value as a rite of passage, as well as theological meaning as an act of self-mortification and as a kind of ritual sacrifice.[53]

Thus when Luis Carvajal's brother performed the rite, following his younger brother's example, Luis described the event in the following terms (referring to himself in the third person), in a spiritual autobiography that was preserved by the Inquisition:

> His [Luis's] elder brother Baltasar, having long possessed an ardent desire to be circumcised, was moved by the Lord during the time of the solemn Passover [*Pascua de Pan Cenceño*]. The two of them [Baltasar and Luis] went together to the house of a barber and rented a blade from him, which the elder brother of Joseph [i.e., Luis] took in his hands. While they both knelt on the ground, he cut his prepuce and made a great wound. They offered this deed to God, praising and calling upon Him.[54]

The other specifically crypto-Jewish signature act was taking a Hebrew name along with a descriptive epithet. Luis Carvajal renamed himself Joseph Lumbroso; Francisco Maldonado de Silva called himself Eli Nazareo; and Lope de Vera called himself Judah Creyente—to give examples from three figures we will be looking at more closely.

At least one precedent existed for both of these defining acts. The first crypto-Jew known to have performed a demonstrative act of self-circumcision and renaming was the Portuguese converso Diogo Pires. Pires was a young man (but already secretary of the king's council in Lisbon) when the messianic pretender David Reuveni, a Jew of unclear origins, visited Portugal in 1525, stirring messianic excitement among the New Christian population. When Reuveni prudently declined the young courtier's request to circumcise him, Pires circumcised himself and took the name Solomon Molkho. He left Portugal and became a rather learned Jew in Salonica, but after many vicissitudes was burned at the stake in Mantua in 1532.[55] He was widely revered by Jews and conversos of his day, and the memory of his bold act of initiation must have lingered in crypto-Jewish memory in the Peninsula. We have no way of knowing whether Luis Carvajal was consciously imitating Molkho when he circumcized himself in New Spain in the 1580s. But Carvajal's fame undoubtedly publicized the act and helped render self-circumcision a stock feature of celebrated crypto-Jewish martyrdom. One is tempted to speculate that the importance attached to this ritual indirectly helped to establish the arena of crypto-Jewish martyrdom as an overwhelmingly male one.

A very important, but hitherto mostly unstudied, aspect of the martyr's career unfolded behind closed doors, in the audience chambers of the Inquisition. This was the theological confrontation of the impenitent dogmatista and the inquisitors. Happily for scholars, Inquisition regulations required that all interrogations and discussions be recorded—not verbatim, but in great detail—by a notary. This provides us with a rich, if sometimes problematic, record. Once the prisoner decided on a course of martyrdom, he readily gave information under interrogation about how he had become convinced of the truth of "the Law of Moses." While he may have distorted his account for polemical effect, much about these accounts has the ring of truth, and they offer invaluable insight into the religious and intellectual development of the defiant judaizers.

One of the key issues in the verbal struggle between these judaizers and the inquisitors concerned the locus of religious authority. It is on this point that the clashing mental worlds of the two sides come most sharply into relief. For the inquisitors, the "Holy Mother Church" was the ultimate source of religious truth. This phrase evoked a weighty ecclesiastical hierarchy and a chain of authority going back directly to Jesus Christ. The inquisitors' role was not to defend the Church in a new way—indeed, such an effort would have been dangerous—but to convince the dogmatista prisoner of what, to them, was self-evident: namely, that the Law of Moses was "dead," and that by virtue of being baptized, the accused dogmatista was obligated to return to the "Law of Christ." The impenitent dogmatistas, for their part, argued what Jews had often argued in debate with Christians, namely that Christianity's core teachings contradicted the eternally valid teachings of Hebrew Scripture. But the dogmatistas had a certain advantage (if we may call it that) over late medieval Jews who polemicized with Christians. First, since anything was open to debate, and since they were already doomed, they had no need to worry about being judged blasphemous; nor did they need to be concerned about endangering a Jewish community. Second, they did not need to defend rabbinic Judaism, which rarely figured in the inquisitorial debates. They made their case solely on the basis of the authority of Hebrew Scripture—the meaning of which, they argued, was clear and unequivocal to creatures endowed with reason.

The literalist biblicism of the dogmatista martyrs raises a number of questions. If crypto-Judaism was an outgrowth of late medieval rabbinic Judaism (as to some degree it certainly was), how did it evolve in a biblicist direction? Scholars have sometimes blithely assumed that crypto-Jewish biblicism was a simple result of crypto-Jewish isolation from normative Jewish life.[56] But there are several reasons why this is not an adequate explanation.

First, crypto-Jewish ties with rabbinically educated Jews were never entirely severed. A number of conversos who fled the Peninsula later returned, after having spent months or years in a Jewish community. In the early sixteenth century, for example, a converso crops up in Inquisition records who had gone to Fez with his parents. After living there in the Jewish community for sixteen years, he returned to Spain and was reconciled to the Church.[57] A person like this would have been a walking fund of information about "real" Jewish life, if he dared discuss it. We also know of professing Jews who visited Spain (usually on business).[58] Jews living in North Africa also freely journeyed to mainland Portugal.[59] A number of Jews from Fez spent extended periods of time in Madrid.[60] Can we suppose that these persons did not discuss Jewish life with their New Christian business associates?

We know, too, that educated, inquisitive crypto-Jews in the Peninsula had access to literature that offered indirect glimpses of rabbinic Judaism. Yerushalmi's investigations into the sources Isaac Cardoso was able to consult while in Spain set to rest any doubts on this question.[61] Occasionally, too, Jewish works published in Amsterdam and Venice for the ex-converso population were smuggled into Iberian lands. The library of Luis Méndez Chaves, apprehended for judaizing in Spanish America in the seventeenth century, included six such works, all liturgical texts in Spanish published in Amsterdam between 1617 and 1645.[62] Furthermore, we know that crypto-Jewish oral traditions could be quite persistent, surviving over several generations. A woman tried by the Coimbra tribunal in 1583, for example, was able to recite (in Portuguese) a prayer very close to the first benediction recited in Jewish tradition before the *Shema* at nightfall.[63]

How, then, can we account for the fact that the very existence of a post-biblical Jewish tradition had been forgotten among Portuguese crypto-Jews within a generation of the establishment of the Portuguese Inquisition—that by the late sixteenth century the Mishnah and Talmud, as authoritative sources of Jewish tradition, had disappeared altogether from the crypto-Jewish vocabulary?[64]

There may be no way to answer this question definitively. But there seems to have been a transition period in the first half of the sixteenth century, during which the vestiges of rabbinic tradition in crypto-Jewish circles were suppressed, consciously or unconsciously. The loss of the texts and the particular intellectual ambience in which they were studied certainly contributed to an eroding knowledge of the tradition. But there is, I think, another explanation for the disappearance of even the memory of such a tradition. Crypto-Jews could not afford to hold on to an aspect of Jewish tradition that was (and had been for some time) a polemical liability.

The Talmud had been an issue in Christian–Jewish debates at least from the thirteenth century. The Church, with the assistance of Jewish apostates, had attacked it on two grounds: first, because it purportedly contained blasphemies and insults to Christianity, and second, because it was a deviation from, and a falsification of, "true" Judaism, and as such called into question whether rabbinic Jews merited the classic Augustinian justification for their toleration. The mendicant friars who led the Church's attack on the Talmud made extensive use of the fanciful homiletical material of the Talmud known as *aggadah*. This gave them an opportunity to represent post-biblical Judaism as irrational, absurd, and contradictory. Jews reacted in various ways—among them, of course, by accepting baptism.

Nachmanides, whose account of the Disputation of Barcelona offers a model of how to resist the new line of polemical attack, suggested that aggadic material should be taken out of the polemical spotlight by minimizing its authority, at least publicly. At the Disputation of Tortosa, the Jewish delegates followed Nachmanides' lead, arguing that *aggadoth* were like sermons from which no binding conclusions could be drawn.[65] Likewise, as we have mentioned, polemical emphasis was placed on Scripture in its simple sense (*peshat*), which gave the Jews a polemical edge.[66]

If we try to imagine crypto-Jews retaining and transmitting even the memory of a post-biblical tradition, we can quickly discern the problems that would have arisen. Crypto-Jews, like other underground groups, needed powerful slogans and symbolically charged rituals. The memory of an impressively rich but unattainable tradition would only have stirred doubts about the adequacy of their grasp of the "Law of Moses," and eroded their self-image as guardians of the Jewish tradition. Just as importantly, it would have made them vulnerable to the old charge that their interpretation of Scripture was corrupted by absurd rabbinic innovations. By essentially jettisoning any surviving remnant of post-biblical Judaism, they were able to view themselves as fully qualified to defend the true, self-evident interpretation of Scripture.[67]

There is a hint of possible conflict in crypto-Jewish circles around this issue, in a curious letter written in early 1528 by a Spanish inquisitor in Badajoz to the king of Portugal. The letter refers, among other things, to a foreign Jew visiting Portugal a few years earlier who had stirred up messianic hopes among conversos, even across the border in Castile. The figure mentioned was almost certainly David Reuveni, the Jewish political schemer whose arrival in Portugal inspired Diogo Pires to perform self-circumcision. The aim of the letter seems to be to persuade the Portuguese king to take action against unbaptized Jews who were visiting his realm.

Technically, the Inquisition had no jurisdiction over unbaptized Jews, since Church doctrine did not regard them as heretics. However, the inquisitor made an argument that had been used repeatedly in late medieval anti-Jewish polemics, namely that "talmudic" Jews (*talmudistas*, in his words) were indeed heretics, since they deviated from the Law of Moses. In his view, the Church should prosecute them as such—something that had never been done. What is most interesting about his letter is his remark that the *talmudistas* were regarded as heretics by what he called the "true" Jews (*verdaderos judíos*), whom he refers to as Karaites (*carraynes*).[68] This fascinating letter is unfortunately quite unclear, offering enticing clues without a context. Who were these "Karaites" in the Peninsula? Is it possible that the inquisitor's letter reflects theological tensions that developed when some crypto-Jews developed an independent, polemically designed, biblically focused set of beliefs? Could crypto-Jews perhaps even have complained to the Inquisition about "rabbinic" Jewish visitors to the Peninsula, who represented a challenge to the polemical base they were constructing?

We may not be able to answer these questions, but we can be confident that the difficulties crypto-Jews faced in the absence of a traditionally sanctioned and trained leadership encouraged some of them to adopt a more independent approach to theology. This may well have made some of them receptive to contemporary arguments emanating from radical Christian circles, according to which religious authority resided not in the (Catholic) tradition, but in Scripture alone. At least among the defiant dogmatistas, we find a rather close approximation of the argument for *sola scriptura*. On what other terms could they have taken on a highly centralized, institutionalized Church? More generally, what better petri dish could be imagined than that of post-Tridentine Iberian lands for the development of a self-reliant, individualistic theological orientation?

This is not to say that a notion of religious autonomy was pervasive among crypto-Jews. In fact, kinship networks continued to constitute the foundation of much of crypto-Jewish life. Within these networks, conversos often observed the "Law of Moses" in a quintessentially traditional manner, accepting ancestral custom as sacred without critical scrutiny. In this study, however, we are not generalizing about crypto-Jewish religiosity. We are following the careers of a few exceptional men, some of them linked to crypto-Jewish kinship networks and some of them not, but all of them highly educated, inquisitive, and proud. Given their predicament, they were naturally impelled to make independent decisions about the truth.

The final act of the martyr's script was dictated and dominated by the Church, yet offered an opportunity for the judaizing martyrs to undermine the didactic tableau in which they were forced to take part, and to do so before a large audience. Let us follow the ordained sequence of events. In a solemn procession from Inquisition "headquarters" (the prison was ordinarily in the same building as the tribunal) to the site of the auto-da-fé, the sentenced criminals would be seen in public for the first time since their arrest. Their altered status and shame would be symbolized by the sambenitos they wore—garments of infamy, usually yellow. The *relapsos* and impenitent heretics would attract particular attention, since their sambenitos typically bore images of flames and/or devils painted on them, and they wore a conical miter (*coroza*) similarly decorated. A notorious impenitent heretic might also wear a metal muzzle, or *mordaza*, giving him a grim, inexpressive visage. For the crowd, the procession offered a socially sanctioned opportunity to vent its rage at men and women who had been declared outcasts (at least temporarily, in the case of those who were to be reconciled). The criminals might find themselves the targets of insults, taunts, eggs, tomatoes, or worse. Maintaining fortitude under this on-slaught of public humiliation was probably easier for pertinacious heretics than for those who expected to return to the community that was dramatizing their rejection.

The auto-da-fé (literally, "act of faith") was a ceremony organized by an individual tribunal in the central square of the city where a tribunal was active. Inquisitors and dignitaries were typically arrayed in specially constructed bleachers on one side, with the condemned prisoners placed in parallel fashion on the other. The action (the preaching of the sermon and the sentencing of individual pris-oners) took place in the plaza in between, where a pulpit was built. The sermon (often an inflammatory harangue) would be delivered as part of a solemn mass, followed by the sentencing of each prisoner before the pulpit.[69]

The sentences (*sentencias*) would be read out loud in their entirety, even when the number of victims was quite large. These were not "sentences" in the modern legal sense, but rather accounts of the criminal careers of the condemned persons, with punishments stated at the end. The experience of this public assault, after an extended period of confinement, sometimes provoked a prisoner to a pathetic display of contrition, even if he or she had thus far been impenitent.[70]

The culmination of the day's activities, and of the martyr's career, came after-ward, at the *quemadero*. The defiant dogmatista martyr certainly began preparing himself for this occasion long before it arrived. A priest always accompanied a condemned heretic to the stake, offering him the opportunity to kiss a crucifix. The martyr would reject this object, insulting the Church and affirming his per-sonal dignity. In some cases (at least so it was reported), the martyr would shout a final provocative declaration of faith as the pyre was set on fire.

Contemporary accounts often report the satisfaction of the spectators at both the auto-da-fé and the *quemadero*. This was certainly to simplify the scene. Yet autos-da-fé and public burnings were popular and well-attended events, and evi-dently triggered a genuine cathartic response. Maureen Flynn has tried to evoke the impact of an auto on sincere Catholic onlookers:

These acts of faith were vivid reminders of the trial and judgment that spectators believed would confront them all at the end of their days. Watching penitents on stage, they lived through their own apprehensions of the Final Judgment. The Inquisition's trial of sinners rehearsed feelings of fear, awe, and submission that marked the final moments of human destiny. . . . Around the pyre, true believers satisfied desires for vengeance on traitors to their faith at the same time that they empathized with the corporal suffering.[71]

This description is a bit too schematic for comfort. The range of responses was surely greater than this. And there is one type with whom we are concerned who is utterly absent here—namely the converso spectator, whether a judaizer or not. It would be foolhardy to try to describe the various effects such a spectacle might have on him or her.

While hundreds of persons were burnt at the stake for judaizing in Spain, Portugal, and the Iberian overseas territories in the century between 1570 and 1670, only a few became celebrated dogmatista martyrs. Let us digress briefly to consider the numbers, and then sketch their profile as a group.

It is difficult to know even approximately how many persons convicted of judaizing were burned at the stake in this period, or for that matter the overall number of those convicted of judaizing. (The sentence for a condemned heretic was sometimes death, but it was sometimes any number of lesser punishments.) Because records are incomplete, even an exhaustive study using the best of methods will not yield exact numbers of victims for either the Spanish or Portuguese Inquisitions.[72] Still, most scholars today would agree that the Iberian inquisitions were not as lethal as popular wisdom would have it. Overall, it appears that in the period from 1540 to 1700, under 2 percent of those accused for crimes against the faith were burned at the stake "in person" (i.e., not in effigy or after a natural death).

Only a tiny fraction of this fraction were burned alive at the stake. Unfortunately, knowing whether a condemned heretic was burned alive or not is not always possible, since the manner of death is often not indicated in the records for a given case. The data I have collected indicate that in the course of the seventeenth century up to the 1680s, a total of less than twenty-five persons were recognized by name in the literature of the Portuguese-Jewish diaspora as having been burned alive for judaizing.[73] There were certainly more (indeed we know of others), though not by an order of magnitude. The most extensive "catalog" we have of such martyrs—that compiled by Daniel Levi de Barrios—clearly is not complete, suggesting the partial nature of our information.[74]

From early on in work on this project, I was struck by two apparent requirements for celebrated crypto-Jewish martyrdom. All of the famous martyrs were, as we have noted, men. Although a few women were praised in the diaspora literature for having been burned alive at the stake, none of them attained iconic status. This may reflect the internalization of Iberian social mores, according to which upholding public honor was considered a male role. (The need to defend masculine ascendancy in the public sphere may have been particularly acute among crypto-Jewish men, who were denied public leadership roles in their judaizing communities.) In any case, one study of inquisitorial dossiers does suggest that in Spain men were more likely than women to take confrontational, aggressive positions on religious matters.[75]

But what distinguished the famous martyrs was not simply that they were men. They were men capable of engaging in theological disputes with trained theologians of the Church. All of them were highly educated and knew Latin. (It is interesting in light of this that the report of the Assembly of Tomar in 1629 recommended that New Christians not be "permitted to learn Latin or study science.")[76] The dogmatista martyrs' knowledge of Latin (and in one case, Hebrew as well) gave them access to works that might have raised troubling theological questions for a religiously inquiring soul.[77] In fact, then, only a small number of male crypto-Jews possessed the necessary intellectual tools to assume the role of polemical martyr.

I have chosen to present a series of case studies rather than treat the dogmatizing martyrs as a group. Much of the richness of their careers would be lost by treating them collectively. They did not share a single polemical strategy or theological approach. On the contrary, they came from widely differing environments, with access to different crypto-Jewish traditions, and their careers reflect this reality. To present them en bloc would obscure the idiosyncratic ways in which they shaped their thinking and behavior, and would misleadingly suggest uniformity of belief. What they shared was the experience of a common cultural environment and system of repression, and access to varied sources of anti-Catholic thought. It is these that make for the striking parallels in their careers.

The earliest case of such martyrdom that we find described in the literature of the Portuguese-Jewish diaspora is that of a Portuguese New Christian merchant named Diogo Lopes Pinhanços, who was arrested in November 1569, and tried by the Coimbra tribunal. Though his dossier has survived, it is in very bad condition, and breaks off abruptly in the middle of an entry made prior to his sentencing.[78] The information that Pinhanços was burned alive at the stake derives entirely from Isaac Cardoso's Portuguese-Jewish classic, *Las excelencias de los Hebreos*, published in 1679, more than a century after Pinhanços's trial.

Cardoso's reference to Diogo Lopes Pinhanços appears in a chapter of *Las excelencias* devoted to the tenth "excellent quality" of the Jews, namely, their role as "witnesses for the unity of God." In one passage of this chapter, Cardoso abandons the expository apologetic vein in which most of the book is written, and turns to the particular, concrete details of the careers of three judaizers who were burned alive at the stake—Francisco Maldonado de Silva, Diogo Lopes Pinhanços,[79] and Isaac Castro de Tartas.[80] His choice of these three need not concern us here. What is important is that the facts of the careers of Francisco Maldonado de Silva and

Isaac Castro de Tartas, as Cardoso sketches them, are substantiated by their In-quisition dossiers. We might thus cautiously assume that the Pinhanços story has a basis in fact. Let us first examine the main body of Cardoso's account:

> [A] singular event occurred in Coimbra a hundred years ago. They arrested as a Jew one Diego Lópes de Piñancos, in a place near the town of La Guardia [Guarda] in Portugal, in the Serra da Estrela, and, from the time he was taken, he began to announce that he was a Jew, and wished to live and die in the Law of Moses. He was brought before the Inquisition, and although they brought in theologians to convince him, he always remained firm in his resolve. . . . To this day, in the Convento de la Cruz in Coimbra, he is painted, among others being burned, with two demons at his shoul-ders, and with the name of Diego Lópes de Piñancos. And elderly Old Christians used to relate that they themselves had seen him, and had been present at the event.[81]

The last sentence indicates that Cardoso (who was born in the same region in 1603–1604) had oral sources for this story and, given his intellectual gifts, proba-bly conveyed fairly accurately what he had heard. It thus comes as a surprise to see what the Pinhanços dossier reveals, despite its poor condition. Pinhanços was, it appears from this document, raised in a crypto-Jewish environment. He belonged to an extended family of crypto-Jews from the little town of Pinhanços, in the bishopric of Guarda, whose members were arrested in late 1569 and accused of typical acts of judaizing, such as fasting (including "o jejum de setembro"—the fast of September, or Yom Kippur), preparing food for the Sabbath in advance, and eating unleavened bread on Passover.

Initially, from his first audience, which was held some time before January 25, 1570,[82] up to at least April of that year, Pinhanços confessed to having abandoned Catholicism for a period of twelve or thirteen years. He confessed to acts of judaizing, and implicated other family members. He "begged pardon and mercy, and promised from that point on to be a very good Christian." Diogo Lopes, it seems, did not proclaim his loyalty to the Law of Moses "from the time that he was taken."

Initial confessions, however, were not atypical of men who later became de-fiant martyrs. Moreover, the geographical detail and dates given in the dossier seem to confirm Cardoso's information. But what the dossier subsequently reveals is a story that bears no resemblance to Cardoso's. In his testimony of April 10, 1570, Pinhanços suddenly revoked his denunciations of other members of his family, saying he had denounced them only because his nephew—who was being held in another cell—had smuggled a note to him saying that he, the nephew, had already implicated those family members (and probably Diogo Lopes himself). Now, he said, he was telling the truth—namely that the relatives he had denounced had not judaized with him.

Such a statement was inherently unconvincing. If Pinhanços's nephew had smuggled the message he described, he would have done so to establish a strategy for the family. He may have reasoned thus: if all the family members who had been arrested followed the same course of action—confessed, denounced everyone else, and repented—the tribunal would not be able to trap them in a web of contradictions, and their sentences would be relatively mild. If these family members had never judaized, as Pinhanços now claimed, why would the nephew have sent a message recommending such a strategy, since members of the family would not have a common story to confess? The only rationale for Pinhanços's revocation the tribunal could have hypothesized was that he experienced anguish at having denounced loved ones.

The nephew, when interrogated about the message, found himself in a predicament. Taking the chance of compromising his own credibility, he denied sending any such note. When Diogo Lopes was again interrogated on June 16, he may have sensed that the inquisitors believed he was lying to the tribunal in order to protect family members—in itself a serious offense. At this point, when asked "in what law and what belief he lived in," he gave the startling answer that he "believed in God." Under the circumstances, it was a provocative reply.

For the period between June and October, the surviving record is silent. We next encounter Diogo Lopes at an audience of October 16 that he had requested. The reason for the request, he said, was that when he had appeared before the inquisitors the day before (in an audience whose record has not survived), they had questioned whether he was of sound mind. He wanted to assure them that he was very much in his right mind (*em muito seu cizo e entendimento*). He then stated that his family had deceived him into believing in the God of Heaven ("*Deus dos ceos,*" a crypto-Jewish term). It was true that up to this point he had always believed there was a God in heaven. But now, he continued, he no longer believed this, because he had never seen God, and one need not believe what one could not see. Furthermore, he did not believe in Jesus Christ, nor had he ever believed in the teachings of the Church. (Presumably it had been similar statements made on the previous day that had raised the inquisitors' doubts about his sanity.) The inquisitors warned him that he was speaking foolishly and that he should seek pardon and mercy. He replied that he was perfectly sane, and that he did not have to believe what he could not see.

He was summoned for an audience three months later, on January 19, 1571. He was reprimanded for his remarks at the previous audience and encouraged to confess and beg pardon. He replied that he had "no faith or law," that it was all a lie, that there was no God in heaven and that he had never believed in Jesus Christ. He also suggested (as he had in the previous audience) that they should punish him.

In a subsequent audience (the initial lines of the entry noting the date have not survived), the inquisitors tried to convince Diogo that natural reason (*juizo natural*) required that one believe in a God who created the world. Diogo countered with a barbed question. How could he believe that the consecrated host was God, when he could see it was made of flour? He declared that just as he did not have to believe that the host was God, he did not have to believe there was a God.

At an audience ten days later, inquisitors again tried to convince him of his error, to no avail. After that he may have had no contact with the inquisitors until an audience he requested on April 23. When asked why he had requested the audience, he said he wished "to retract everything that he'd said and confessed to concerning the salvation of body and soul," and to ask "for death." He declared that he no longer wanted to live. He regretted everything he had ever done to achieve salvation, and everything he had done in the name of God that his family had deceived him into believing—his crypto-judaizing, that is. He emphasized, however, that he had never in his life believed in Jesus Christ or in the Church.

The final surviving record of an audience is dated April 25, 1571. The prisoner again requested death. He reiterated that he rejected the Catholic faith and the law of God and all of Christian doctrine, and it was in this state of mind that he wanted to live and die. On May 29, he was declared a "pertinacious heretic." The entry mentions that he had "been sent theologians and priests [*padres theologos e religiosos*]" in an effort to convert him. We learn something of what transpired in this effort from the testimony of two Jesuit preachers on May 30. They recounted that they had taken the prisoner to the chapel of the Inquisition. When they had knelt and prayed to the crucifix, urging the prisoner to do likewise, Diogo responded that if they wanted to pray, they should go ahead and do so, but he himself had no reason to, and did not want to kneel. The Jesuits told the tribunal they found him to be sane, and declared him a "professing pertinacious heretic and apostate."

The final entry, for August 9, breaks off in mid-sentence during the testimony of an Old Christian witness who had just told the inquisitors that Diogo Lopes "must be about thirty years old."

There was, then, a turning point in Diogo Lopes Pinhanços's trial, but it did not lead in the direction of crypto-Jewish martyrdom. Once he had declared his lack of belief in God—any God—he never once referred to the Law of Moses or indicated any attachment to Judaism. Had a conversion to materialist skepticism taken place during his imprisonment? Or had he harbored a skeptical outlook for a while, even while practicing crypto-Judaism with his family (a perfectly feasible possibility)?

Regardless of precisely when Pinhanços became a conscious skeptic, it is obvious that at a certain point in his trial he chose to die a defiant death as a skeptic. But let us recall Cardoso's statement that in his own day "elderly Old Christians" who had been present at the auto-da-fé believed he died steadfast in the Law of Moses. Of course, we are deprived of information about the later stages of his trial and burning, and cannot exclude the possibility that Pinhanços abandoned his skeptical position for a judaizing one. But it is more likely that crypto-Jews who knew Pinhanços's family, who witnessed his death, and who had not been privy to his revelations in secret audiences assumed that he had died a martyr in the Law of Moses. Was there anything in the painting Cardoso apparently saw in the Monastery of Santa Cruz in Coimbra, depicting Diogo Lopes Pinhanços "with two demons at his shoulders," to suggest the particular kind of heretic he was?

Despite its anomalous aspects, then, Diogo Lopes's trial still belongs to our story. He conformed to the type of the "dogmatista judaizing martyr" in the sense that he argued with inquisitors and theologians and refused to be swayed by them. Moreover, he seems to have been remembered as such a martyr—and presumably served as an example of martyrdom for future generations of Portuguese crypto-Jews.

There is no such ambiguity about the deaths of the four men whose careers will be charted in the following chapters. I have not, however, chosen them because they offer the best examples of the defiant polemicizing judaizer. Their choice has been dictated by several factors, chief among them the nature of the documentary evidence.

Only three of the four clearly conform to the pattern of having chosen to be burned alive at the stake. The exception is Luis Carvajal, who appears to have been garroted before being burned (although the record is not entirely clear).[83] I have included Carvajal for two reasons: first, because he openly chose the path of martyrdom shortly after his second arrest and maintained that posture until very close to the end, and second, because we have a wealth of documentation on his career. On the other hand, I have not included the celebrated martyr Tomás Treviño de Sobremonte, despite the fact that we possess his dossier, because this figure denied judaizing throughout his trial and chose to die defiantly as a Jew only after his sentencing.[84] Four other celebrated martyrs were not (or could not) be included: Isaac de Castro Tartas, burned alive at the stake in Lisbon in 1647, whose voluminous dossier is virtually complete[85] but who spent many years in his youth in the Spanish and Portuguese Jewish community of Amsterdam and was thus conditioned by direct experience in both a Jewish and an anti-Catholic Protestant environment; and three figures tried in Cordova and burned alive at the stake in 1655 or 1665, whose trial records have not survived.[86]

Let us turn, then, to the dossiers—large volumes bound in leather, their pages sometimes worm-eaten but more often ravaged by acidic ink from the notaries' pens—and try to discern something of the human dynamics of martyrdom in the historical context we have sketched.

A CONQUISTADOR'S NEPHEW IN NEW SPAIN

3

Luis Rodríguez de Carvajal was born in 1566 in Benavente, a town in Castile near the Portuguese border.[1] Both of his parents were New Christians with some ancestral roots in Portugal. The family moved to Medina del Campo in 1577, where Carvajal's father engaged in retail trade to support his growing family. Luis was the fifth of eight children at the time; a ninth would be born two years later. When Luis was "about fourteen years old," according to his testimony before the Inquisition, his older brother Baltasar initiated him into the family's crypto-Judaism, teaching him "the Holy Law that God gave to Moses on Mount Sinai." The initiation took place on Yom Kippur (or rather, on the day the family observed as Yom Kippur, namely the tenth day after the new moon in September)—an extremely important occasion among crypto-Jews.[2] Luis's brief account of the Yom Kippur disclosure leaves the reader with the impression that he had no inkling of judaizing in the family prior to this date.[3]

Three years later, Luis and his family immigrated to New Spain. The impetus to make this move came from Luis's maternal uncle, also named Luis Carvajal, who had recently returned to Castile after a decade of entrepreneurial and military activity in New Spain.[4] Now a powerful man, he prevailed upon the crown to grant him a charter to govern an expanse of territory north of the Valley of Mexico that he had staked out and surveyed (it possessed silver mines), and that he had begun to "pacify" (it was populated by a group of tribes known as the Chichimeca).[5] The territory was to be called the New Kingdom of León. The charter granted the new governor the right to take one hundred persons with him. Shortly thereafter, the elder Luis Carvajal obtained an additional document exempting the entire entourage from genealogical investigation.[6]

With his plans thus in place, the governor visited his sister's family in Medina del Campo in the spring of 1580 to persuade them to return with him to New Spain. Martin Cohen speculates that one of his motives for doing this may have been his anxiety about their judaizing. Writes Cohen,

> Having the rest of his family and his friends with him in an isolated region where his power was all but supreme would give him two . . . advantages: it would reduce the

chances for the discovery of their Judaizing practice, and it would give him repeated opportunities to bridle such practice. But if anyone in his entourage did become involved with the Inquisition, Don Luis would certainly be in a better position to protect himself in the New World than in the Old.[7]

By now the governor was familiar with conditions in Spanish America, which offered a relative haven to the heterodox. Unfortunately, it is difficult to know for certain whether he knew of the family's judaizing.

In any case, one suspects that the governor had personal and social reasons for taking his sister's family with him. He was estranged from his wife (who stayed behind in Castile) and had no children. Who would care for him in his old age, and who would inherit his "kingdom"? Before departing from Spain, he tried to settle these issues too, appointing his nephew Luis as his heir and successor. (This did not mean, though, that his nephew would inherit his title as governor, which was not hereditary.) In so doing, he bypassed the latter's older brother Baltasar (whom he appointed, however, to be treasurer of the new domain).

The family probably had financial reasons to agree to the governor's proposition. Medina del Campo (as indeed all of northern Castile) was in economic decline in the 1580s. Moreover, the family now had five daughters, for whom dowries would have to be provided if the young women were to make acceptable marriages. In the Americas, where eligible women were in demand, the burden might be less onerous. Certainly there was no shame in relying on a successful relative, and Governor Carvajal had the worldly skills to help the family adjust to a new environment. He had already helped one of his sister's sons, Luis's brother Gaspar, enter a Dominican monastery in New Spain.[8]

In an effort to overhaul the family's image to conform to his new grandeur, the governor also arranged for some name changes before the family's departure for the Americas. "Rodríguez," the surname of Luis's father, was dropped from young Luis's name (as well as from that of other family members), and he became "Luis de Carvajal."[9] The change was probably motivated partly by the governor's wish to get rid of a name that suggested New Christian origins. But it might also have been an expression of his wish to stake a claim on the future of young Luis.

The émigrés left Seville for the Americas on June 10, 1580, on the ship *Nuestra Señora de la Luz,* which the governor owned. Sailing in a convoy, they were at sea for more than ten weeks. Such an interlude naturally invited intimacy among the passengers. When young Luis fell ill, he was attended by a prominent Portuguese physician, Manuel de Morales. It may have been at this time that Morales became known to Luis and other members of his family as a learned crypto-Jew.[10]

The impact of Manuel de Morales's instruction and example on the Carvajal family can hardly be exaggerated. It is unfortunate that we do not know more about this key figure. He and his family left New Spain a few years later, in 1584, apparently making their way to an openly practicing Jewish community outside the Peninsula. (A sailor testified in 1589 to having heard from a fellow sailor that

Morales was living in the Venetian ghetto, wearing a yellow hat.)[11] Morales was tried in absentia by the Mexican Holy Office in 1590, and burned in effigy at an auto-da-fé in 1593—the same auto-da-fé at which Luis Carvajal and members of his family were sentenced after their first trials.[12] His Inquisition dossier has survived, but since Morales and his family were fugitives and did not testify, it fails to provide even basic information about Morales's earlier life. We do have one enticing piece of information from Luis's testimony, however—namely, that Morales's father-in-law had been burned at the stake in Lisbon for judaizing.[13]

One thing is certain: During the four years Morales was in New Spain, he invigorated crypto-Jewish life there and transformed the thinking of Luis Carvajal. Under the physician's tutelage, Luis's crypto-Judaism changed from an inchoate, textually unanchored array of beliefs and practices to a reasonably coherent and well-articulated one. Luckily, the Inquisition dossiers of members of Carvajal's family supply us with some evidence about this pivotal figure's thinking and pedagogy.

Luis himself revealed almost nothing about Morales in his testimony, and the Inquisition did not pursue the matter with him.[14] Other members of the family were more forthcoming. While it is difficult to discern anything distinctive about Morales's teachings from the testimony of Carvajal's mother, Francisca, at her trial in 1589,[15] the testimony of her daughters is another matter. Luis's sister Catalina, who would have been about twenty-five years old at the time, confirmed under interrogation Morales's role as an educator of the family. A "certain person in Mexico," she was informed in one of the charges against her,[16] had taught her and strengthened her in the observance of the Law of Moses. He had written a book by hand, which described at length the "commandments and precepts" of the Law. (This little book was to have wide circulation among the crypto-Jews in New Spain.)[17] He had given that book to someone who had read it to Catalina and others in the family, "and it is known that the person who gave this other person the book of these precepts has left this country for a *judería*" where Judaism was practiced openly. Catalina responded by identifying this "certain person" as the physician Licenciate Morales.

A certain person close to her, she was then charged, went from Mexico City to the province of Pánuco to teach the Law of Moses to her and to others close to her. Subsequently she ceased eating pork, animal fat, food prepared with animal blood, and fish without scales. Moreover, she began beheading fowl in preparation for cooking. Catalina responded that "this [charge] was true," adding that "before Licenciado Morales strengthened and instructed her brothers in the observance of the Law of Moses, they had not observed it so perfectly [*tan perfectamente*], nor did they dare to."[18] It is possible that Morales not only expanded their knowledge of Jewish observance, but introduced the concept of observing the Law "perfectly" (*con perfección*), a phrase that Luis was to use repeatedly.

Further revealing testimony about the teachings of Manuel de Morales was provided by Luis's younger sister Mariana, then eighteen years old. She stated that in Medina del Campo her family had "never done anything properly"—meaning that the family's crypto-judaizing was uninformed and faulty. But after they came from Spain to the province of Pánuco, she said, the physician Licenciate Morales gave instruction to her brothers Baltasar and Luis, and "there was more clarity in these matters [*ovo en estas cosas mas claridad*]." In Tampico, where they settled after the voyage, Baltasar and Luis taught other members of the family what Morales had taught them at sea. The brothers were then able to perform the rituals they had learned from Morales without his help, she said, whereupon she erupted into a colorful litany of his holiday teachings. These included keeping the Fast of Esther, "fasting three successive days, eating eggs and fish and meat and cheese only at night, to commemorate the fast that Esther fasted so that God would liberate her people from the indignation of Haman," and observing the Fast of Judith for two successive days, because God had liberated Judith and the Jewish people from Holofernes when they lived in the city of Betulia. The family also celebrated Passover (*la pasqua del cordero*) which fell in the Holy Week and lasted seven days, refraining from work on the first and last day and reciting prayers of praise to God for having liberated his people from the captivity of Egypt, eating unleavened bread, "and not using tortillas of maize in place of unleavened bread"—apparently their previous practice—because it was unleavened bread that "the Children of Israel brought out of Egypt, because they were in a hurry and it did not have time to rise."[19]

Mariana's description reveals a number of things. Morales's crypto-Judaism was profoundly bibliocentric. Thus the three-day fast of Esther, rather than the one-day rabbinically ordained Fast of Esther. Thus a Fast of Judith—unknown in rabbinic law. Thus, too, the seven-day observance of Passover, with two festival days, rather than the eight-day rabbinic observance of Passover outside the Land of Israel, with four festival days. It is also obvious from these descriptions that Mariana had read (or at least had heard someone read) texts that described the origins and significance of these holidays.

The importance of textual sources emerges elsewhere in Mariana's confession as well. She stated that during the time she observed the Law of Moses (she was now claiming to be penitent), she believed that the Messiah had not come and that Jesus Christ was not the Messiah—and she believed this because her brother Luis found it to be so in the Bible. Before the coming of the Messiah, she added, Elijah and Enoch would have to come to prepare the way, a piece of knowledge Luis had discovered in the prophecies of Esdras "which he [Luis] had memorized, Licenciado Morales having told him where to find them in the Bible."[20]

As the testimony suggests, the creed Morales taught was not based, as was much of the judaizing in Iberian lands, on orally transmitted traditions that relied on ancestral authority.[21] Morales placed a singular value on written texts. He provided his protégés with manuscript copies of critical texts prohibited by the Inquisition: the Ten Commandments in Spanish translation, crypto-Jewish prayers and hymns in Spanish, and, to a few, a complete Spanish translation of the Book of Deuteronomy.

The importance Morales placed on possessing the biblical text in the vernacular is striking. Bibles in Spanish (along with other Protestant propaganda) first began circulating in large numbers in the Peninsula in the 1550s, when Protestant refugees from Spain began printing them in Geneva, Frankfort, Antwerp, Lyon, and elsewhere. These books were smuggled into Spain and Portugal by sea.[22] Initially the danger was less the translated text itself than the glosses, which emphasized such Protestant teachings as *sola fide* and opposition to the Roman Church's "idolatry." Eventually, however, the Spanish Inquisition suppressed all vernacular Bibles—even going so far as to suppress copies of books of hours that had been printed in the Spain, because they contained biblical passages in the vernacular.[23] The Portuguese Inquisition acted similarly, with its own Indexes.[24] This policy was justified early on by the Spanish theologian Alfonso de Castro, a participant in the Council of Trent: he regarded vernacular translations of Scripture as an important "source of heresies" and as more damaging even than the reading of pagan philosophy.[25] In reality, of course, entirely preventing the reading of the Bible in the vernacular was impossible. As the case of Manuel de Morales shows, an educated, motivated man in the Peninsula could make his own translations from the Vulgate and circulate them in manuscript copies.

Morales taught the members of his circle in New Spain to rely on a literal reading of key biblical proof texts to "see for themselves" the falsifications of the Church, in a way that prepared them to engage confidently with orthodox Catholic believers. One senses that under Morales's tutelage, Luis learned to engage his faculties actively in the enterprise not merely of perpetuating, but of "discovering" the Law of Moses.

But let us return to our narrative. When in the summer of 1580 the émigrés' ship landed at Tampico, just south of the territory the elder Luis Carvajal now governed, Luis was still ill. He had to be carried ashore, where he continued to be attended by Morales.[26] Meanwhile, the governor busied himself with the many practical tasks enumerated in his charter,[27] as well as with unanticipated difficulties, including a Chichimeca offensive against the Spaniards, a series of financial setbacks, and obstacles put in his way by the viceroy.[28] If the family had expectations that the governor would provide for their welfare, they were soon disillusioned. Indeed, for several years after their arrival they lived in Tampico on the verge of poverty.

In an untitled work that we will refer to as his memoirs, composed between about 1591 and 1594, Luis Carvajal devotes an early passage to this period of adjustment to life in a tiny colonial port city. Somewhat disappointingly, he dwells mainly on a meteorological event—a hurricane from which Luis and his brother Baltasar barely escaped alive. This seemingly accidental event, however, establishes the dominating motif of the entire work. From the start, the author promises to enumerate the miraculous acts of deliverance God has performed for him, opening with the words "Of the grave dangers [*De gravísimos peligros*]" before launching into a winding and untranslatable sentence. It is clear, then, from the start that we are dealing with divine history, not with a chatty diary. And it is a history that

begins in Tampico. While Luis briefly offers the facts of his birth and early education, the story he really wants to relate begins in New Spain.[29]

The governor's absence provided ample opportunity for Luis and other family
members to enliven their miserable existence with Morales's teachings. The crypto-
Jewish fervor Morales aroused, however, also stirred some wishful thinking—a
recurring theme in Luis Carvajal's life. Luis's father Francisco, his sister Isabel, and
his brother Baltasar all made careful overtures to the governor and Gaspar in a
attempt to being them into their religious orbit. (Perhaps they also entertained
hopes that a judaizing senior Luis Carvajal would take greater interest in their
welfare.) Their efforts, however, were repelled—quite violently by the governor,
who among other things dismissed Baltasar from his post as treasurer of New León.
Luis did not become involved, and when the governor tested him on his theological
loyalties, he replied with reassurances of his Catholic orthodoxy.[30]

Luis and his father Francisco left Tampico for Mexico City in the late summer
of 1583. They (along with Baltasar) were supporting the family as itinerant merchants in the silver mining towns, selling *cosillas*—household items such as blan-
kets, shoes, raisins, printed fabric, and preserves,[31] as well as Indian slaves.[32] They
would purchase goods imported from Europe in Mexico City and transport them
by pack train, selling them at a profit in places where money was abundant but
amenities scarce.[33] But the following February, Francisco fell ill with a terminal
disease. He was tended to during the six months he languished by his judaizing
cousins Catalina de León and Gonzalo Pérez Ferro, whose home was a meeting
place for other members of the network.

After his father's death, Luis rejoined the rest of the family in Tampico. Here
he managed to buy a printed copy of the Vulgate from a local cleric (who also
apparently knew how to turn a profit on scarce commodities). Morales departed
from New Spain around this time, but he left behind his intellectual imprint, and
Luis took up the task of discovery on his own. With a Vulgate in hand, he devoted
himself to studying the Jewish Scriptures (which for him included Apocrypha)
while occupied as a merchant in the mining town of Pánuco, near the northern
frontier entrepôt of Zacatecas.[34]

The impact of his Bible reading appears to have been explosive. In his memoirs (written in the third person), he recorded his most electrifying moment, which
occurred while he was reading the Book of Genesis for the first time.[35] "In the
course of his assiduous reading [of this Bible] in the solitude [of Pánuco]," he
wrote, "he came to understand many divine mysteries; and one day he happened to
read Chapter 17 of Genesis where the Lord commanded Abraham to circumcise
himself." Reading the passage carefully, Carvajal was struck by "those words that
said that the soul who went uncircumcised would be blotted out of the book of the
living."[36] Terrified, he immediately sought out a place where he would not be
discovered and, "with burning desire to be inscribed in the book of life, which is
impossible without this holy sacrament [*este sacramento santo*]," he circumcised
himself with scissors.[37] What Luis certainly wanted to convey in his rendering of
the episode was that he was not moved to action by someone else's example or by

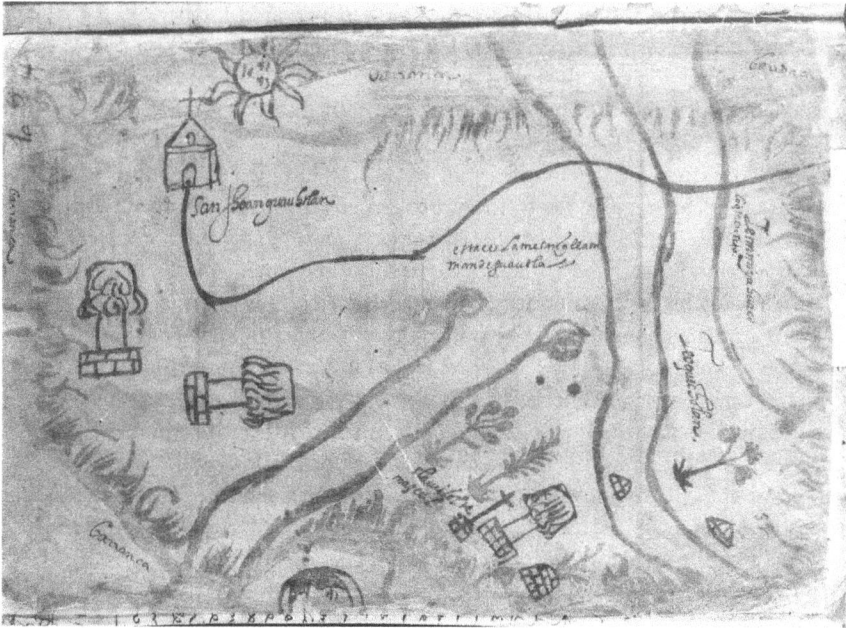

Figure 3. Anonymous map of a village in the Pánuco region, New Spain, 1593, with pictographic elements. AGN, Tierras, vol. 1871, exp. 1, fo. 32. Archivo General de la Nación, Mexico City.

simple knowledge of the precept (of which he must have been cognizant), but by his encounter with the authentic scriptural source.

Remarkably, Carvajal resorted to another passage from Scripture to reassure himself that his surgical effort, though slightly imperfect, would nevertheless be acceptable to God. In this passage, Solomon states that his father David "had it in mind" to build the Temple, but desisted after God said to him, "You did well to consider building a house for my name; nevertheless you shall not build the house, but your son who shall be born to you shall build the house for my name."[38] This passage would not, for most early modern Bible readers, have suggested a theological point with important practical implications. For Carvajal, however, it had particular resonance. The fact that God credited David for his mere intention to carry out the plan implied authority for the belief that it was sufficient to perform precepts "in one's heart."[39]

It is revealing that hand-copied notebooks figure prominently in Luis Carvajal's valuable memoirs. (The memoirs were seized after Luis's second arrest and were preserved by the Inquisition.)[40] Whether or not Luis and his brother were as incessantly occupied with Bible reading as his memoirs suggest, it is significant that he chose to portray the two of them in this way.[41] It is also significant that one of Luis's sisters possessed a booklet that he had prepared for her, with his own translations of passages of Scripture, Psalms, and other texts.[42] This would reinforce the impression that the ethos of the Morales circle was one that encouraged unmediated access to Scripture for all.

About a year after his self-circumcision,[43] Luis left Tampico to join his uncle in the San Gregorio Mountains far to the north, where silver mines had recently been discovered. He remained there for about one and a half years, occupied with military action against the Chichimecas and the settlement of new territory. His memoirs, which are not a narrative of his experiences but a spiritual testament, are not very revealing about this activity. He chose to report about his daytime exploits only the episodes of extreme danger he faced "in that war-torn land" among "the Chichimecas and savage enemies," and his deliverance from them by a benevolent God.[44] But his daytime exploits were accompanied by nighttime adventures of another kind. It was in this period that Luis read and reflected on the pseudepigraphical apocalypse known as the Fourth Book of Ezra, integrating his understanding of its messianic message into his theology.

Despite the mercantile efforts of Luis and Baltasar, their family was still living in poverty in Tampico. But early in 1586 the situation improved, with the marriage of twenty-one-year-old Catalina and twelve-year-old Leonor to wealthy Portuguese New Christians, Antonio Díaz de Cáceres and Jorge de Almeida, respectively. Shortly after the wedding of these two, Mariana, fourteen years old, was engaged to her mother's cousin Jorge de León (who had been arrested but released by the Lisbon Inquisition).[45] The family moved to Mexico City while Luis was still at the San Gregorio mines, but he left the mines to join them, arriving in Mexico City in mid-1586. He was delighted to find his mother and sisters no longer in the threadbare dresses he remembered, but wearing gold jewelry and dressed in velvet and silk (for which he thanked God).[46]

Later that year, another abortive effort to proselytize within the family circle produced results that would eventually be disastrous. When the governor's adjutant Felipe Núñez, a New Christian relative of the governor's estranged wife, visited the family in late 1586, Luis's widowed sister Isabel took the opportunity to inquire into his beliefs. (It is not clear whether this was a spontaneous act on her part or one that had been discussed in advance with other members of the family.) The captain quickly declared his loyalty to Catholicism and the matter was dropped. For the moment, at least, the family was safe, since Felipe Núñez had no incentive to denounce a close relative of the governor.

After a year in Mexico City, the family was again on the move, leaving for the silver mining town of Taxco where the two new brothers-in-law were conducting business. Baltasar and Luis remained based in Mexico City, but continued to travel about the mining districts—to Temazcaltepec, Sultepec, Pachuca, Taxco, Mixteca, Oaxaca, and other towns—selling their wares and making contacts with other crypto-Jews. Such itinerant trade appears to have been an occupation favored by Portuguese crypto-Jews in New Spain—perhaps partly because a life of wandering in and out of mining towns made it easier to observe Jewish rituals without being detected.[47] It was apparently not uncommon to "escape" even these towns to the safer environs of local Indian villages. Luis reported, for example, that the September before his second arrest, he had observed Yom Kippur in a small Indian village near Pachuco, while on the road. He was able to perform ritual immersion in a nearby river beforehand, and to fast for three successive days—which he did because he was "not sure on which of the days [Yom Kippur] fell."[48] There is ample evidence that in outlying villages, baptized Indians managed to evade Church supervision, observing their customary rituals as they pleased.[49] Judaizers may have felt safe spending a brief period in such villages from time to time.

This was the sunniest period in the brothers' life in New Spain. At a time when many of the family's financial burdens had been relieved by their brothers-in-law, they were finally making good profits themselves. And they were meeting with some of the most intriguing personalities of the crypto-Jewish underground in New Spain.

From the judaizer Antonio Machado, who had been a patient of Manuel de Morales, the brothers also obtained access to a new text of considerable value. Morales had acquired the text from the New Christian Francisco Rodríguez, who had lived as a Jew in Italy but whose poverty drove him temporarily to New Spain. When Rodríguez returned to Italy, he left Morales with this hand-written booklet, which contained religious verse ("couplets, *redondillas,* and *octavas* in praise of the Law of God"), a Spanish translation of Deuteronomy, and Spanish translations of prayers "recited in synagogues."[50] Luis and Baltasar borrowed the booklet on a visit to the dying Antonio Machado and copied it.[51] It was soon integrated into their judaizing practice. It may have been from this booklet that Luis gained his knowledge of the first lines of the Shema in Hebrew (presumably in transliteration).[52] In any case, Luis expressed his pleasure in possessing prayers "which the wise and chosen people of His church [*iglesia*] recite to invoke His name and worship Him in the synagogues of the Israelites."[53]

Religious poetry from this and other sources was an essential feature of the family's crypto-Jewish practice. During her trial, Luis's sister Leonor recited a number of pieces of such poetry that they were in the custom of reciting on the Sabbath eve, written in pure Castilian.[54] It is conceivable that these were Luis's compositions.[55] But one of the poems she recited, an especially long one that the family sang on Sabbath mornings—it is described as a summary of "all of the Law of Moses," and perhaps served as a substitute for the Torah-reading—is peppered with Portuguese words, and is possibly from the booklet brought from Italy.[56]

Italy seems to have been the main (but not exclusive) channel of contact with the normative Jewish world. Luis heard about the Ferrara Jewish community from Ruy Díaz Nieto and his son Diego, who had lived there as Jacob and Isaac Nieto.[57] Luis's brother-in-law Jorge de Almeida had also spent some time in his youth as a Jew in Ferrara.[58] Luis also had contact with Juan Méndez, a confectioner in Mexico City, who discussed with him how he had lived among Jews in North Africa.[59] Caravajal became acquainted, too, with the Portuguese New Christian Jorge Díaz,

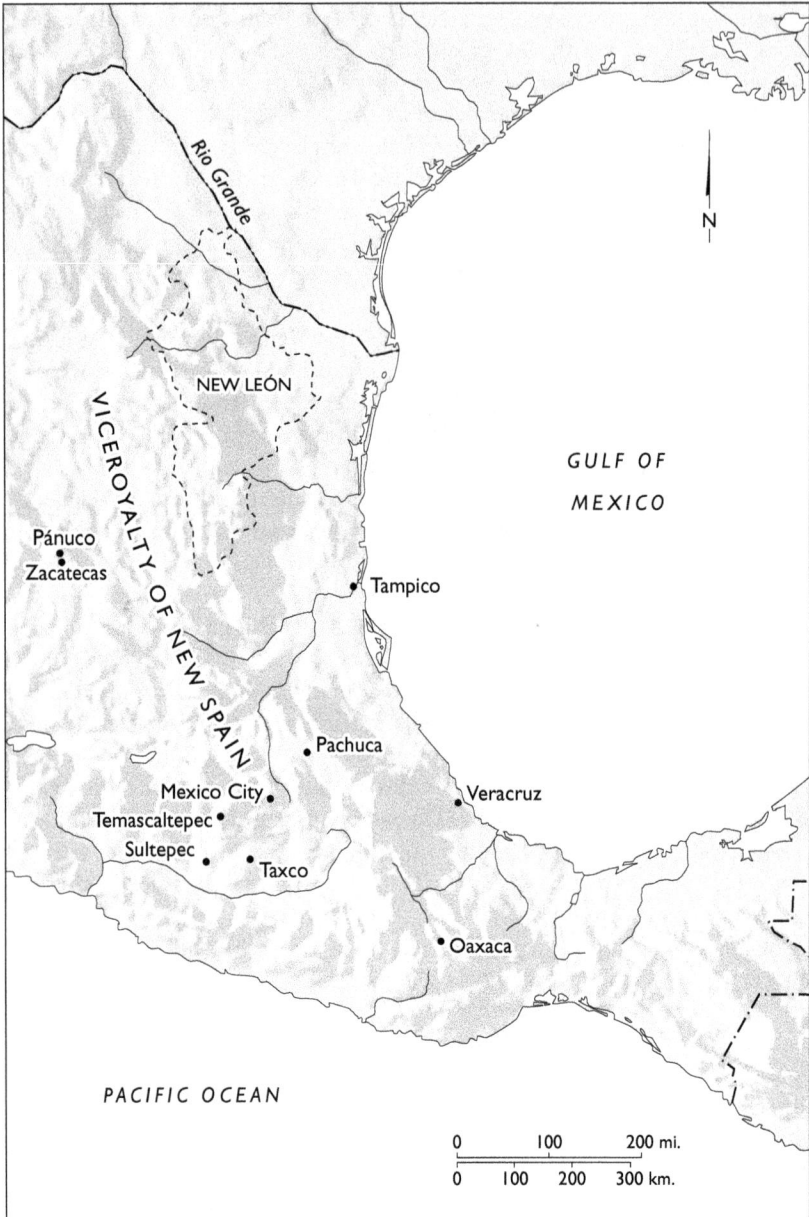

Map 1. Late-sixteenth-century Mexico, with locations important to the career of Luis Carvajal.

a goldsmith, who had lived for a time in the Venetian ghetto and had visited other Jewish communities abroad. The two men discussed how they might flee New Spain and settle in a Jewish community, "after earning some money."[60] Luis never succeeded in doing this, but his brothers Baltasar and Miguel did, and it is hardly an accident that they settled in Pisa. Luis's awareness of a "Jewish people" outside Iberian lands—one that had formerly been mainly an abstraction—must have become more concrete in this period. Yet it did not seem to put a stamp on his crypto-Jewish thinking.

Let us consider this issue briefly. The "common sense" explanation for the biblicism that is so prominent a feature of the Morales–Carvajal circle is that the Bible was the only available source of knowledge about Judaism in Iberian lands.[61] We have already questioned this assumption. But Luis Carvajal's contacts with New Christians who had lived in Jewish communities highlights the problem. He expressed obvious delight about "our brothers who live in freedom to observe the Law."[62] He cherished the rabbinic prayers in translation that he had obtained through Francisco Rodríguez. And he and Baltasar planned to escape to a Jewish haven abroad. It seems implausible that Luis should have believed that the Jews of the diaspora observed Jewish law according to the method of Bible consultation he used. Is it conceivable that he had heard nothing of the talmudic erudition of the rabbis? Did none of the visitors from Italy ever mention that the Fast of Esther was observed for only one day in Jewish communities? Had he never asked about the source for the crypto-Jewish practice, followed in his family, of changing one's clothing before the Sabbath—a practice for which there was no apparent biblical source? And if it is true, as he testified, that he owned and had read a copy of Luis de Granada's *Introducción del símbolo de la fe*, had he not read the chapter of that book, rich in detail, titled "On the Lies, Falsehoods, and Nonsense of the Talmud"?[63]

It seems almost certain that Luis was, in fact, aware of aspects of post-biblical Judaism. Even if Diego Díaz Nieto, who was born and raised in the Jewish community of Ferrara, maintained a cautious distance from Luis, he was in close contact with other judaizers in his circle and had an extensive knowledge of rabbinic Judaism as it was practiced in Ferrara (including rabbinic teaching on the Fast of Esther).[64] We can only speculate about Luis's apparent lack of interest in rabbinic elaboration of the Law. It may be that he was so heavily invested in the crypto-Jewish creed he had adopted, with its particular polemical power in the struggle to achieve certainty about the "error" of Catholicism and the "truth" of the Law of Moses, that he could not afford to think in other channels. And yet this rigidly dichotomized religious outlook did not prevent him from turning to Catholics and Catholic texts for religious information.

Interesting in this respect is Luis's acquaintance with a remarkable spiritual figure in the Iberian Catholic world, Gregorio López. López had come to New Spain in his youth, in 1564, and settled as a hermit in Chichimeca territory. Little is known of his early life, but he apparently had no formal ecclesiastical training. He came under suspicion of the Inquisition as a *luterano* because of reports by visitors, who noted the absence of religious images in his hut, his failure to attend mass, and his general orientation toward a life of religious interiority.[65] He was fortunate to emerge from the investigation unmolested.

Gregorio López's radical asceticism, his saintly behavior toward people from all ranks of society (including Indians), and his unconventional thinking brought him considerable fame. Interestingly, he was beatified (though not canonized) after his death. López's commentary on the Book of Revelation reveals the learned hermit as a millenarian who anticipated great suffering and martyrdom in a final battle against idolatry.[66] His insistence on the incorporeality of God and his hostility to the worship of images contained an implicit criticism of the doctrine of the Eucharist and of saint worship. He was widely known for his interest in, and knowledge of, the Bible. It is clear even from the testimony that was gathered to support his beatification that he took a particular interest in the Old Testament, which he chose to read from a historical perspective that would have gratified a crypto-Jew as much as it would have aroused the attention of an inquisitor.[67]

Given the importance Gregorio López placed on sacrifice and martyrdom, and his bibliocentric, individualistic theology, Luis's attraction to him is not surprising. But Luis seems to have felt that a special spiritual affinity tied him to this man. When Luis was imprisoned for the second time, he asked his cellmate (who turned out to be a spy) to go to visit Gregorio López after he was released from prison, in order to tell him that he (Luis) had chosen the path of death, and that he was joyful—singing and dancing—at his approaching death. He added that he knew this news would give much joy to Gregorio López.[68]

Luis's attraction to Gregorio López is but one indication of the slippery boundaries between crypto-Judaism and radically inclined heterodox Catholicism in Iberian lands. In fact, much of Luis's piety and notions of spiritual discipline derived from sixteenth-century Iberian Catholic sources. His Jesuit schooling in Medina del Campo probably exerted a strong and enduring influence. Moreover, all of the "Jews" he knew were raised in an environment permeated with the images and rhetoric of Catholic religiosity. How could he have known the different inflections and rhythms of an actual Jewish environment?

Sometime late in 1588 or early in 1589, other members of the family moved back to Mexico City from Taxco. Luis and Baltasar were by now planning their escape from New Spain to a place where they could live openly as Jews. They were collecting debts and liquidating their assets.[69] Even at this late point—or perhaps particularly at this point—they decided to try to persuade Gaspar to join them. With this in mind, Baltasar visited Gaspar at his Dominican monastery in Mexico City, testing the waters twice in an oblique exchange that both of them understood very well. Gaspar seems to have been quite clear in his rejection of Baltasar's feelers.[70] Yet Baltasar later made another visit to Gaspar, this time accompanied by Luis.

This time, according to the memoirs, Luis led the conversation. His effort began with a disingenuous question. Was it true, he asked, that God himself

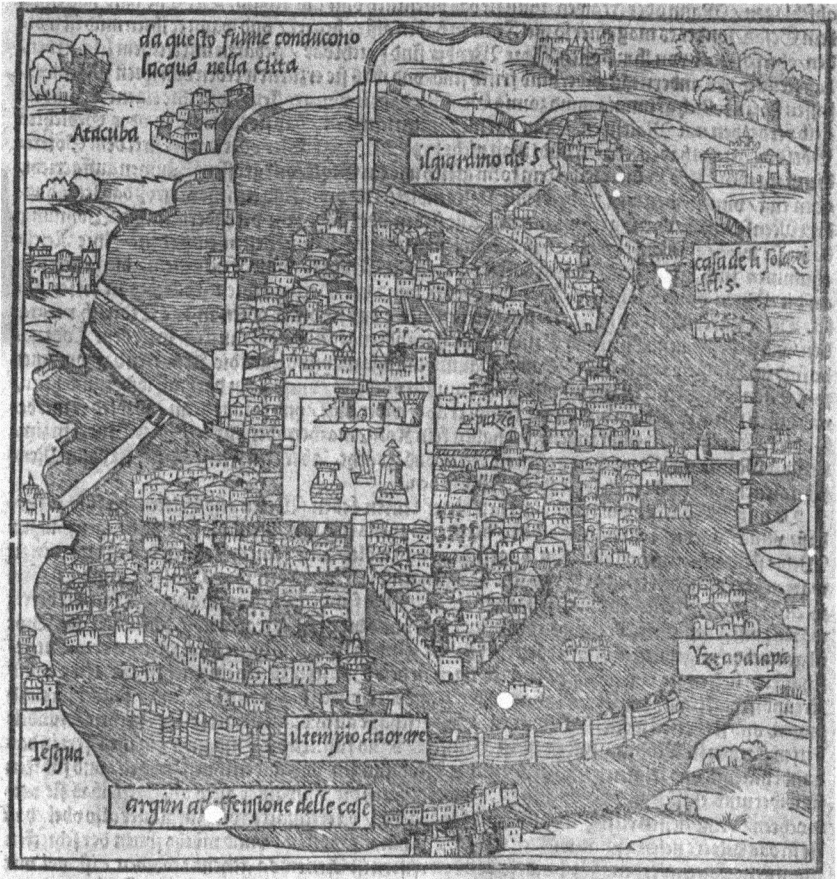

Figure 4. Bird's-eye view of Mexico City in the late sixteenth century. From an unidentified German edition of Sebastian Münster, *Cosmographia Universalis* (1597 or later). The Library of Congress.

inscribed his commandments on the Tablets of the Law? Gaspar opened a Bible to the relevant passage in Exodus (presumably Exod. 32: 15–16) and showed it to his brother. This affirmation gave Luis the opportunity to remark that if this were so, the Law of Moses must be the Law one must observe. Gaspar surely understood precisely what was being hinted at. He replied that while it had once been the Law, it was now superseded.

At this point Baltasar intervened, citing another prooftext—this time from the New Testament: "The Gospels themselves relate that your Crucified One[71] said, 'Do not think that I came here to annul the laws or the prophets and their holy and truthful prophecies!' for thus he said, 'Surely it is an easier thing for the sky or the earth to disappear than for an iota or dot of his holy law to pass away or be changed.'"[72]

Gaspar was not swayed (although Luis assures us, in typical polemical fashion, that he was confounded). Still not ready to concede defeat, Luis suggested that Baltasar and Gaspar spend a few days studying together. Gaspar declined, explaining, according to Luis's account, "that his law forbade him to inquire and to increase his knowledge."[73] It seems unlikely that Gaspar actually made this exact statement. Luis attributed it to him, most likely, for a didactic purpose, situating Gaspar in an ethos in which knowledge *was* viewed with suspicion and anxiety, in contrast to the ethos of Scripture-searching espoused by Luis.[74]

Late in 1588, the stunning news arrived that Governor Carvajal had been arrested by the viceroy. The nature of the charges was not clear, but a long history of friction between the governor and the viceroy suggests a probable motive. At once the precarious structures of secrecy that had allowed the family to function in New Spain began to crumble. With news of the governor's arrest, Felipe Núñez hurriedly left the Kingdom of León for Mexico City. No doubt terrified by his own vulnerability, in light of Isabel Carvajal's overtures to him three years earlier, he went before an inquisitor and denounced Isabel, taking pains to distinguish between her behavior and that of the governor, who was, he said, "an exemplary Christian."[75] A few days later, on March 13, 1589, Isabel was arrested on charges of judaizing and was imprisoned in the Flat House (*la Casa Chata*), as the inquisitorial prison in Mexico City was popularly known. After Isabel's testimony quickly revealed that the governor had known of, and failed to report, judaizing in his family, the elder Luis Carvajal was transferred from the royal prison to the inquisitorial prison. On the day of his transfer, Gaspar, too, was arrested on charges that he knew of Isabel's judaizing and had failed to report it. Luis and Baltasar fled to Veracruz, taking their young brother Miguel with them. Luis, however, soon returned to Mexico City to try to protect his mother. On the night of May 9, he and his mother were arrested. Baltasar went into hiding. In December, acting on testimony extracted from Isabel under torture, the Inquisition arrested Leonor, Catalina, and Mariana, and interrogated the ten-year-old Anica.

Throughout his imprisonment and trial, over the course of almost ten months, Luis tried to minimize the damage to himself and his family. He at first denied having anything to confess, blaming the governor for making false accusations out of enmity. Luis was soon faced, however, with detailed accusations that were based on testimony from Isabel, Gaspar (who revealed his conversation with Luis at the monastery), and the governor. Though the witnesses who denounced him were not named—a standard practice of the Inquisition—Luis would have known immediately that imprisoned family members were incriminating him. For our purposes, the most interesting of the eight formal accusations against him was the third:[76]

> In order better to fulfull the obligations of the Law [of Moses] and its observance, he [Luis Carvajal] has devoted himself to reading and is well read in the Old Testament

and the Prophets, which he cites—especially Isaiah—whenever the occasion presents itself. Whereas if he heeded and considered these prophecies with the proper care and devotion, eradicating from his heart the obstinacy he has inherited from his ancestors, he would clearly see that they have all been fulfilled in our Lord Jesus Christ, the true Messiah; and he would cease living miserably in his vain and perfidious hopes, believing that he [the Messiah] has not yet arrived.

The simple fact that Luis Carvajal busied himself with the Old Testament constituted the heart of this accusation. The polemical tenor of the accusation, heaping calumny on the defendant at the very outset of his trial, is striking, given the fact that the document was for internal use only.

Luis, who was required to reply to the accusations on the spot, took the path of many inquisitorial defendants and essentially denied all the charges. To the specific charge concerning his biblical researches, he responded simply "that he was not well read in any prophet, and denied it."[77] This stance served to limit the immediate follow-up interrogation, and gave Luis a chance to consider his strategy.

A week and a half later, having decided on a course of action, he requested an audience—something all prisoners might do. When he appeared before the inquisitors, he immediately launched into a performance that was recorded by the notary with great pathos:

Falling to his knees, striking his chest, and kissing the ground with many tears, he said that he had sinned, and as a sinner he asked for mercy, and weeping copiously he said, I have sinned, mercy, mercy! And when they ordered him to get up and sit down, he said that God had inspired him—though he deserved to be condemned for his guilt—to struggle these recent days with the demon that had not let him confess.[78]

Luis proceeded to confess at length. He placed responsibility for the family's judaizing squarely on his father (who was now dead). His father, he said, had been taught to judaize by an uncle who lived in Portugal, but who had visited the family in Spain. (He was also dead.) He admitted to buying a Bible for six pesos from a cleric named Juan Rodríguez in Pánuco. For his wish to own a Bible, however, he blamed his father, who had said to him "that everything he [his father] had taught him about the Law of Moses was written in the Bible." Perhaps anticipating a medical examination of his private parts, he added that his father had also told him Jesus was circumcised.[79]

Of his immediate family members, Luis denounced only those whom his denunciation would not appreciably hurt: Baltasar (who was in hiding) and those he knew to have been arrested, namely his mother, Isabel, Gaspar, and the governor. Concerning Manuel de Morales, he volunteered only that his father had said the Portuguese physician's family were judaizers, and claimed he had never spoken to Morales about religious matters.[80] Luis seems to have thus successfully prevented a widening of the scope of the inquisitors' inquiry—perhaps applying a family strategy that had been worked out in advance.

In his account of his first trial in his memoirs, Luis mentioned his behavior in the audience chamber only briefly, explaining that fear had caused him to conceal and deny his true beliefs.[81] He dwelt almost entirely on his thoughts, feelings, and experiences within the confines of his cell. These, however, were critical experiences, and reveal his dawning consciousness that he was a person especially singled out and blessed by God.

This budding awareness is reflected in the account of two dreams he had while in prison. In the first, God ordered Solomon—the biblical King Solomon—to take a flask, fill it with the "sweet liquid of divine wisdom," and give it to him, Luis, to drink.[82] Awakening, Luis interpreted the dream as "a light that God deigned to give him, so that he might keep the Law of Moses and understand the meaning of sacred Scripture." The dream made such an impression on him that in its aftermath, he renamed himself Joseph Lumbroso.[83] Adopting the name Joseph after such a dream, by a person so sensitive to portents, may reveal, among other things, Luis's hopes that despite finding himself in prison his fortunes, too, would eventually be reversed. Taking the name Lumbroso (a reference to light) was directly connected with the message of the dream, as well as with Luis's growing conviction that religious knowledge, far from being a monopoly of the Church, was a gift from God granted to exceptional individuals.

At his second trial, when he related the experience of the dream, Luis recalled that when he had awakened "he was so consoled that he did not feel the oppressiveness of his imprisonment as he had before."[84] The cells of the Mexican Inquisition were perhaps no more unpleasant than other prison cells of the time. But the adobe walls and earthen floors, which absorbed the waters of the lake bed on which Mexico City was built, made them exceedingly humid.[85] A single candle was distributed to each cell at night, offering minimal illumination.[86] In his dream Luis had swallowed an elixir that removed him from these harsh realities, producing, as it were, a light from within.

The second dream came to him after he had endured the excruciating experience of hearing his mother's cries under torture, sounds that reached his cell.[87] He recounted that he

> saw the Lord sending him a man, distinguished by the God-fearing fortitude of his nation, who carried a large, beautiful sweet potato in his hands, which he showed him [Luis], saying, "See what a lovely and beautiful fruit this is." . . . He let [Luis] smell it and, praising the Lord who creates all, he said, "Truly it smells good." Then he divided it in two and said, "Now it smells even better."

He was then, he recounted, informed of the interpretation of this dream: "Before your mother was imprisoned and broken under torture, she was fragrant, for she was a sweet-smelling fruit before the Lord. But now that she is torn with tortures, she exudes the aroma of fortitude before the Lord."[88]

Luis appears to have had a remarkable stroke of good fortune—which he no doubt took as evidence of his special relationship to God—in the Inquisition's choice of a cellmate for him. This man, Francisco Ruiz de Luna, was a Franciscan friar of Old Christian ancestry who had been arrested for performing sacraments both in Spain and in the Americas with false papers of authorization.[89] When the inquisitors transferred the friar to Luis's cell in late June or early July 1589 (on condition that he not reveal that he was a cleric), it was certainly with the intention that he would inform on Luis, thereby obtaining leniency in his own case. Luis should have been aware that this might be the case. But he also had a strong impulse—no doubt strengthened by the solitude of prison—to disseminate his beliefs. (This is a trait, we might mention, that he shared with other dogmatista martyrs, who tended to proselytize not only among conversos but among Old Christians as well—a striking indication of their expansive attitude, in contrast to the ethnic exclusivism more typical of crypto-Jews.)[90]

The friar, as it turned out, had some heterodox leanings of his own—not, clearly, such a rare occurrence. (The fact that he had administered sacraments with false papers of authorization obtained in Italy might suggest that he was not overawed by the mystique the Church cultivated around these acts.)[91] Indeed, Luis recalled that it was the friar who opened the way for theological discussion. While the friar was seeking warmth near the fire—probably a charcoal brazier used for cooking[92]—he took his cross, placed it near the flame, and remarked to Luis that if he left it too close to the fire "it would burn like any piece of wood."[93] This was a heretical statement (or *proposición*, in the language of the Inquisition) that he may have felt he could safely share with an accused judaizer.[94]

The cellmates began to discuss theology. Presumably, they also pledged not to reveal each other's beliefs to the inquisitors. Neither informed on the other, and as a result the friar was sentenced only for his unauthorized administering of sacraments[95]—despite the fact that after his conversations with Luis he was actually converted (in some fashion) to the Law of Moses. This was not, as it turns out, a figment of Luis's active imagination, as we shall see.

What transpired between Luis and the friar to bring about the latter's conversion can only be conjectured. According to Luis, a conversation began that lasted for "over eight days," during which Luis related to the friar "some of the holy stories" and instructed him in the basics of Jewish dietary law. As Luis tells it, the friar was persuaded by his arguments—and, wrote Luis, overwhelmed by his awakening, supposedly cried, "Would that I had been enlightened (*alumbrado*) in the truth of God . . . while I was still in the monastery, where there are open libraries with the Holy Scriptures and many other good books!"[96]

For whatever reasons, the inquisitors did not pursue Luis's case very rigorously. His cellmate's testimony that he, Luis, was behaving like a good Christian may have deflected interest from him. Perhaps his performance had been convincing. In any case, his trial was essentially over by August 1589. However, it was not until the following February that he heard his sentence at an auto-da-fé held in the cathedral of Mexico City, where his mother, his uncle, his sister Isabel, and several other members of their judaizing circle were also sentenced. Francisco Ruiz de Luna, Luis's former cellmate, appeared there, too, and received a punishment of six years' service in the galleys for performing mass without authorization.[97] (Gaspar, like other clergy who were condemned by the Inquisition, was granted a private auto, so as not to embarrass the Church.)[98] Luis's sentence consisted of the confiscation of his goods, abjuration, and confinement for a period during which he would have to wear the sambenito. He was dispatched to serve his sentence at the Hospital de los Convalescientes de San Hipólito in Mexico City, a shelter for the insane.

Baltasar, who had been in hiding during Luis's imprisonment, now felt free to leave New Spain, and escaped with his younger brother Miguel. The brothers returned to Spain with the fleet and then, in November 1590, departed for Italy where they settled, as we have mentioned, in the Jewish community of Pisa, taking the names David and Jacob Lumbroso.[99]

In May 1590, Luis was temporarily released from the hospital to visit his mother and sisters. He was especially chagrined, as he reported in his memoirs, to find that his mother and sisters, chastened by their experience with the Inquisition, were eating prohibited foods out of fear of the Inquisition, "on the bad advice of some friends." Luis urged them to desist, using an argument that suggests that he had read 2 Maccabees while in Pánuco and that it had left him with a strong impression. By his third-person account,

> Joseph intervened to stop them . . . and held up to them the example of the saints who had consented to be torn into pieces through cruel torments rather than eat foods prohibited by the Lord or even pretend they ate them.[100]

He thus explicitly urged his mother to follow the example of the Maccabee martyrs —including the elderly Eleazar, who had refused even to feign eating pork.

Luis returned to the hospital, and his mother resumed eating what she liked for about a year. But by a happy twist of fate (or divine intervention, as Luis believed), Luis was transferred to the Franciscan Colegio de Santa Cruz de Tlatelolco, a school founded in 1536 by Antonio de Mendoza, the humanistically inclined first viceroy of New Spain, for educating the sons of Indian aristocrats. There Luis served as a secretary and copyist for the highly educated Fray Pedro de Oroz, who had arranged the transfer. With his Jesuit education, intellectual attainments, and fine handwriting, Luis was an exceptionally well-qualified penitent. He tells us nothing of the Indian students at the school (he did not share Gregorio López's interest in the indigenous peoples), but he was delighted to find at his disposal a library of considerable richness.[101] Notably, he discovered a translation of Maimonides' Thirteen Articles of Faith in a sixteenth-century biblical commentary by the Dominican Jerónimo de Azambuja, known as Jerónimo Oleastro. (He promptly copied it.)[102] He also took advantage of the ready supply of paper, pens, and books to make copies of important passages from the Prophets, and prepared at least one copy of Psalms in Spanish translation, perhaps using a breviary.[103]

It was during his time at the colegio that the friar who had shared Luis's cell, Francisco Ruiz de Luna, was rearrested, a fact recorded by Luis in his memoirs.

The renegade friar, he wrote, had "smashed an idol"—perhaps a crucifix—in the galleys to which he had been condemned. Luis was terrified the friar would denounce him. But in his memoirs he reported that the friar had stood firm against inquisitorial pressure—something he'd learned, he wrote, from a dream his mother Francisca had reported. According to her dream, the friar affirmed his "Judaism," stating that "what I believe and confess is the truth, and everything else is a lie and deception of the devil." Although the friar was tortured (according to the dream), "God allowed him to bear it all with great confidence and patience."[104] What we know for a fact is that he was tried for judaizing, and though reconciled on March 25, 1591, he was sent for a further ten years of galley duty.[105]

Sometime in 1593, Luis was released from his "captivity" at the colegio, partly as a result of the lobbying of his brother-in-law Jorge de Almeida in Spain. He was given license to beg for charity, and letters of introduction, since he was still wearing a sambenito and was unable to make a living. Traveling among Franciscan monasteries, he was able to raise money, and took the opportunity to visit judaizers, as well as Gregorio López. Finally, in the fall of 1594, he was informed that he had obtained a decree of rehabilitation, again with help from Jorge de Almeida, and was allowed to remove the sambenito. But it was not a moment for celebration. On the same day, Manuel Gómez Navarro and Manuel de Lucena, with whom Luis had recently stayed in Pachuca while collecting alms, were denounced to the Inquisition for judaizing, and were arrested eight days later. Shortly thereafter, Luis wrote that he and his family

> had one of the worst scares they'd ever had, from which the Lord in his infinite mercy freed them in two hours. But he [Luis] will not write about what happened now, because he is still in the lands of captivity—though on the verge of escaping (with God's help) one of the most dangerous captivities the people of our nation have ever endured. Indeed, by the singular goodness of our Lord, he and his family have lived in no less danger than the holy Daniel in the lion's den.[106]

With this premature expression of gratitude, the narrative breaks off abruptly.

By November, Manuel de Lucena's resistance had been broken. He was testifying before the Inquisition about (among other things) Luis Carvajal's continued judaizing. On the basis of this testimony, Luis was arrested in February 1595 (his mother and sisters were arrested shortly thereafter).[107] He was transferred into the custody of the warden of the prison, Gaspar de los Reyes Plata, an unsavory character who was notoriously corrupt.[108] When searched, Luis was found to be carrying three books, titled, in Latin, *Psalms, Prophets,* and *Genesis.*

As a *relapso,* Luis's future was grim. At his first audience, on February 9, he denied having done anything contrary to the teachings of the Church. But a week earlier he had already begun talking very openly to his cellmate, Luis Díaz, an unscrupulous priest who had a record of winning the confidence of arrested judaizers and informing on them. Luis, in great need of signs and wonders (and no doubt remembering his experience in converting his friar cellmate during his first imprisonment), revealed a great deal of incriminating evidence to Díaz, which the latter reported to the Inquisition before Luis had even been summoned to his first audience.

At his first audience, Luis denied any guilt. But he was tipped off afterwards about Díaz, and realized the severe damage that had been done.[109] After considering his options, he requested an audience. The logic of his situation—he knew he would not escape the stake this time—was now driving him to adopt the standard of martyrdom that he had cultivated as part of his image for years. At the audience, he began to recount at length—without remorse—his entire career of judaizing, while trying not to implicate others. He believed in the Law of Moses, he announced, and had believed in it since his adolescence in Medina del Campo. His belief, he said, was founded on the commandments that could be found in Exodus 19 and Deuteronomy "6 or 7" (actually, 5). At this point the inquisitor asked him if he could recite the Ten Commandments. Seizing the opportunity for provocation, he requested permission to do so on his knees, "since he would have to mention the sacred name of the Lord our God who created heaven and earth." The inquisitor quickly cut him off, ordering him to recite the commandments as he was, in his seat.[110] Such was his bravado at this point that it apparently took three officers of the tribunal to prevent him from kneeling.[111] Luis proceeded to recite the commandments in Spanish translation, but with a slight twist: as the notary dutifully tried to record, he prefaced the first commandment with the opening Hebrew words of the Shema.[112]

Three days later, when summoned to an audience, he recited the thirteen articles of the Jewish faith he had already disclosed having discovered. Again he requested to perform the recitation on his knees—a request that was again denied. At his interrogation the following day, he was asked whether he intended to persevere in the Law of Moses. He replied "that he intended to live and die in it."[113]

The tempo of Luis's trial is unusual. Between February 9 and March 3, he appeared at nine audiences. He may have been defiant, but he was offering information, and the inquisitors wanted to reap the harvest. In the meantime, Luis Díaz revealed to the tribunal where Luis had hidden his memoirs (something Luis had disclosed in the hope that his cellmate, after being released, would send the book to his brother in Pisa).[114] The Inquisition promptly retrieved the incriminating work and on February 25 presented it to Luis before interrogating him about the persons mentioned in it. He avoided implicating anyone still vulnerable to arrest, and insisted that his mother and sisters had not resumed judaizing after their reconciliation.[115]

Overconfident as he frequently was about his powers, Luis not only confessed to judaizing, but also sought to persuade the inquisitors of the truth of his beliefs. (A warden reported overhearing Luis boasting to Luis Díaz "that he could convert the inquisitor Dr. Lobo Guerrero within two hours if he had him in his prison cell.")[116] He voluntarily recounted in earnest detail his self-circumcision, as well as the dream that led him to rename himself Joseph Lumbroso. And he repeated his intention of living and dying in the Law of Moses.[117]

The inquisitors were trained to be suspicious of dreamers and visionaries, and took clinical note of Luis's revelations. But they moved on to the heart of the matter: What were his reasons for rejecting the Church in favor of the Law of Moses? It was a striking characteristic in Luis that he was able to move effortlessly from his world of personal symbolic discourse to one of clearly reasoned, well-defined theological principles. This is not to say that he had a sophisticated theological outlook. He did not. But he was able to identify and focus on core issues about which he possessed a polemical arsenal, attacking the Church's positions with "common sense" readings of Scripture and with arguments whose unvarnished simplicity made up for what they lacked in sophistication.

He responded to the inquisitors' question about his reasons for rejecting the Church with a nine-point statement that he had clearly formulated in advance. In the course of laying it out, he cited biblical passages that proved, in his view, that the Jews were God's people and were obligated to fulfill the commandments, that Jesus was a false prophet, that the Jews' exile and punishment at the hands of their (Christian) enemies was a result of their backsliding—and not, by implication, a result of their rejection of Jesus—and, finally, that God's promises to the Jews would eventually be fulfilled. It was not a systematic presentation, by any means. Luis cited as a reason for his beliefs, for example, "everything that David wrote," and then went on to cite specific psalms as additional points. It was, however, a rather good digest of passages that could be used for polemical effect, and he must have made an impression on the inquisitors by quoting his prooftexts verbatim in Latin.[118]

The inquisitors did not try to address Luis's points, either one by one or in general terms. Rather, they asked him if he would like to meet with learned clerics, who would convince him of his error and blindness and convert him to the Law of Christ. Luis replied that he was not in error, but that he would like to hear what these learned clerics had to say about the points he had made. If they convinced him of his error, he would convert. If not, he would die in the Law of Moses.[119]

The inquisitors also inquired about Luis's reading of works that dealt with the Old Testament. Luis mentioned four books, all of them Iberian Catholic devotional works.[120] There was *Espejo de Consolación*, by Fray Juan de Dueñas. This work, loosely organized as a moral guide, gave rather detailed accounts of episodes in the lives of Old Testament heroes (and villains). It was used by crypto-Jews in Castile as "a sort of lives of the saints *a la judaica*," to quote one scholar.[121] Luis no doubt took particular interest in the abundant material on the life of Joseph. There was *Guía de pecadores* and *Introducción del Símbolo de la fe*, both popular devotional works by the Dominican Fray Luis de Granada (1504–1588).[122] Luis told the inquisitors that he and his brother-in-law Jorge de Almeida read "quotations from the authorities and material about the Law [of Moses]" in the latter book, *Símbolo de la fe*, which quotes many passages from the Old Testament in Spanish translation. (Luis added that "they laughed a lot at Fray Luis [de Granada], saying that this drunkard wrote these things about the Law of God, without understanding [that Law]."[123] But this may have been an effort to deflect institutional interest from Catholic works that inquisitors had begun to regard as crypto-Jewish aids.)[124]

Let us pause for a moment to consider Luis's Catholic reading and the spiritual universe it reflected. His reading of these texts may have been subversive, as he suggested, at least consciously. At the same time, however, there was much in these works that resonated with Luis. They were conduits for the Reformation piety known as the *devotio moderna* that had swept Europe. This sort of piety had assumed particular contours in Spain, under the sway of such figures as Teresa of Ávila and Ignatius Loyola.[125] It gave Luis much of his religious vocabulary and sensibility, and even colored his dreams.[126]

To give but one example, in his defiant confessions during his second trial, Luis repeatedly praised the conduct of certain judaizers in his circle by saying they observed the Law of Moses *con perfección*.[127] Such an aim reflected a transfer of sixteenth-century Catholic spiritual values to a Jewish enterprise. It was not a perpetuation of attitudes prevalent in late medieval Jewish life. While Jewish tradition strongly encouraged a person to make every effort to be punctilious in the observance of precepts, it did not recognize the possibility of "perfection." Luis's idea reflects the assimilation of a discourse of spiritual perfection found among the Franciscan mystics, the so-called *alumbrados* (who were sometimes referred to as *perfectos*), and other exponents of sixteenth-century Catholic piety. His notion of "observing the Law of Moses *con perfección*" is a variant of the Spanish spiritualists's "loving God *con perfección*." He referred to himself as a *siervo de Dios* (servant of God), a term used in the contemporary Iberian Catholic world for a person devoted to following a path of spiritual perfection. (Gregorio López was routinely mentioned with this epithet.)

Until further research is done on the topic, we will have little idea of the degree to which wider patterns of crypto-Jewish experience are reflected in Luis's writing and speech. It is suggestive, at least, that the notion of observing the Law of Moses *con perfección* appears in other trial records involving crypto-Jews of New Spain in Carvajal's time.[128] In any event, the religious culture of Luis Carvajal and his circle was a crypto-Judaism that had, not surprisingly, mutated over time, preserving many old constituents, but gaining revitalization from an infusion of Reformation elements present within the Iberian world. It is noteworthy that although the Inquisition actively repressed *alumbrados* and *luteranos*, and was suspicious even of such figures as Teresa de Ávila and Luis de Granada, the inquisitors interrogating Luis Carvajal, bound by rigid institutional definitions and presuppositions, did not link Luis's heterodoxy with these subversive currents.

Also striking is the way the Inquisition ignored or overlooked Luis's ideas about religious authority. This is evident in his defense of his interpretation of Scripture. It is true that he at several points asserted the existence of a self-evident "true" reading of the text, accessible to anyone. According to his reading, such verses as "All his precepts are trustworthy, they are established for ever and ever" (Ps. 110), or "You shall not add to the word which I command you, nor take from it" (Deut. 4:2), constituted empirical proof, as it were, that Christianity was in error.[129] To argue in the face of such verses that the Law of Moses was no longer valid, he argued, was as if to say that the sky had fallen or the sun had ceased to shine.[130] The Church was trying to prove "that snow is not white and that there are no nights, only days."[131] This kind of starkly dichotomized thinking is reminiscent of the language of the pamphlet wars. (As one Netherlands pamphleteer put it, "Truth and falsehood are as much at odds as Belial and Christ, and hence there is as little in common between the Reformed teaching and Roman fantasies as there is between white and black.")[132] Such blunt claims were part of a polemical and rhetorical strategy, and a response to the escalating language on both sides of the Reformation divide.

What made Luis's path of martyrdom psychologically possible was his assimilation of new notions of authority almost certainly emanating not only from crypto-Jewish, but from *alumbrado* circles.[133] The experience of religious exaltation was, for the *alumbrados,* a sign of being touched and illuminated directly by God. This meant, among other things, that *alumbrados* lived in absolute certainty that they could read Scripture in freedom without committing dogmatic error. The early *alumbrado* Isabel de la Cruz, for example, insisted to inquisitors that "as long as she retained this love of God she could not be deceived, and that she could not err as long as she remained in this love of God and her neighbor."[134] Similarly, Pedro Ruiz de Alcaraz stated that "the love [of God] was so deeply rooted in him that it was impossible [for him] to give false interpretations of Sacred Scripture or to err."[135] As José Nieto has put it, "The reading and exploration of the Bible had opened [Ruiz de Alcaraz] to a new world, where God is present in the life of His people without the sacramental or hierarchical structures and systems of the Church."[136]

It is not clear whether Morales taught this point of view, which could have been absorbed by Luis in other ways.[137] In any case, its importance cannot be overstated in Luis's career, since it gave him the confidence to confront inquisitors and calificadores in the certainty that they were wrong and he, despite his limited Jewish education, was right.[138] Indeed, he cited Scripture to express his sense of invulnerability and his obligation to engage in confrontation, citing Psalm 119:46: "I will also speak of thy testimony before kings, and shall not be put to shame."[139]

One might argue that reliance on Scripture in the fashion of Luis Carvajal was only natural in a population with roots in Iberian Jewry. Of course it is true that rabbinic Judaism, in contrast to Catholicism, encouraged all of its adherents (at least adult males) to engage in innovative interpretations of Scripture. But it did so in a highly controlled fashion. A person was free to arrive at an unmediated interpretation so long as it did not contradict basic tenets of belief. But such a reading had no authority, and was not likely to be valued. Authority was vested in persons who had undergone extensive training in rabbinics, a form of study that enmeshed Hebrew Scripture in later legal and homiletic texts to such a degree that

Scripture lost its spare, independent existence. Moreover, where observance was concerned, interpretation was vested entirely in the hands of trained rabbis. For a layperson to draw independent conclusions about the observance of Jewish law from reading the Hebrew Bible was unthinkable. It is of course true that under the conditions in which crypto-Judaism emerged, independent reading of Scripture became a necessity. But the *justification* for such reading, in Luis Carvajal's case, was couched in a rhetoric that was profoundly *alumbradista*.

The first phase of Luis's second trial came to an end within a month. At the final audience, on March 3, Luis embellished his declaration of intent to persevere in the Law of Moses with a speech, heavy with pathos, in which he asserted that he would "imitate the holy zeal of Mattathias [the Maccabee], who in the hour of his death said to his sons: 'My sons, be zealous in the Law of God and give your lives for the Holy Covenant of our fathers.'"[140]

After the intense month-long effort of the first phase of the trial, in which Luis found himself in the spotlight, he was left to the isolation and misery of his cell. (His cellmate, no longer useful now that Luis knew of his collaboration with the Inquisition, had been removed.) The solitude was relieved to some degree by a system of communication with his mother and sisters that he began to establish two weeks after his arrest. The warden, Gaspar de los Reyes Plata, apparently offered to serve as a go-between. He probably received clandestine payments from the Carvajal prisoners (or someone acting on their behalf). The warden proved to be duplicitous, however—a possibility of which Luis was probably aware. In February, the warden showed the inquisitors one or more avocado pits on which Luis had scribbled half-legible messages for his sister Leonor. Realizing the potential value of such exchanges, the inquisitors agreed to provide Luis with pen, ink, and paper.[141]

In late May and early June of 1595, Luis was writing almost daily to one or two of his sisters (particularly Leonor) or to his mother.[142] He did not expect his sisters or mother to reply regularly in writing, but they sometimes responded by sending objects as an indirect means of communication.[143] For the most part, Luis's letters are safe expressions of encouragement and affection, written in a tone of some desperation.[144] He did, however, try in one message to convey that while he had confessed his own judaizing, he had been consistent in claiming the women's innocence. Although he praised them as "martyrs," he did not expect them to defend themselves polemically, and was probably anxious that if they began confessing they might eventually break down and accept Catholicism. Or perhaps he was understandably indulging in wishful thinking, hoping that despite the women's status as *relapsos* they could avoid the stake.

The twenty-two charges in the *acusación* against Luis were read to him in an audience of June 10, 1595, more than four months after his arrest. The most painful moment during the reading of the charges was likely the discovery that the

Inquisition possessed good evidence that his sisters and his mother had confessed to having judaized after their reconciliation.[145] He was forced to admit that he had not testified truthfully on this matter—an admission to withholding evidence that suggested he had much more to tell (something the inquisitors already believed).

The charges against him concerning his beliefs were formulaic and mechanical.[146] To most of them, Luis simply responded that they were true. (He objected, however, to being likened to "a dog returning to its vomit.") On the charge of insulting and blaspheming Christ, the Virgin, and the pope, he denied making some of the particularly inflammatory remarks about Jesus attributed to him. He did not, however, deny remarking to some persons that "they should see how God became moldy in the host." Nor did he deny asserting that Jesus "was born among shepherds and had disciples who were lowly and vile, not kings and princes, and was crucified between thieves."[147]

Regarding Luis's mystical experiences, the *acusación* assumed a mocking, amused tone. One senses that the inquisitors felt that this, at least, was an area in which they possessed superior rhetorical and polemical strength. The *acusación* reads,[148]

> He is so intoxicated with the observance of the Law of Moses that he spends all day thinking about it. And since it is natural for men to dream about what they think about, or because the devil who blinds and deceives him leads him so to dream, he has dreams which he says are revelations of God, gifts and favors that He gives him. He regards events and accidental things . . . as miracles. One day when a constable [*alguacil*] with a basket of bread came to his house because they had no money [the municipal corregidor had ordered it to be sent to his mother and sisters because they were poor], they [Luis and his family] thought the man was the *alguacil* of the Inquisition, and when they saw who actually was coming they counted it a miracle and a blessing from God . . .—a matter that is laughable, revealing how ignorant [*deslumbrado*] of the truth he is.

To this Luis replied

> that one should recognize the blessings of God and, acknowledging them, recount them. The men of Sodom laughed at Lot when he said that fire and brimstone were descending from heaven.

The next charge continued in the same vein:

> He has taken this foolishness [*estas boberías y desatinos*] and written a manuscript book which he wanted to send to his brother Baltasar Rodríguez . . . (who is at this time judaizing in the *judería* of Rome), and to his other brother Miguel . . . (who is judaizing in Salonica, near Constantinople [*sic*], and is now a great rabbi . . . and doctor in the Law of Moses), so that they should know the miracles and marvels God had visited on him, his mother, and his sisters here [in New Spain].

And the next:

> And delighting in Jewish names . . . he named himself Joseph Lumbroso and gave his
> reason for doing so: That when imprisoned five years ago by the Holy Office, he had
> dreamed of a flask full of a very precious liquid, and that God had said to Solomon,
> "Take a spoonful of this liquid and put it in the mouth of this young man," and that
> when Solomon had done this he awakened, and was so consoled that from then on he
> was not so oppressed by his imprisonment. He understood that the dream was a light
> from God, who wanted to give it to him so that he could observe the Law of Moses and
> understand Scripture, and thus he called himself Lumbroso—all of this the foolishness
> [*desatinos y disparates*] of the Jews who defend the Law with chimeras, dreams, swin-
> dlings [*embaimentos*], and fantasies.

Luis's hostility to and contempt for the Inquisition was probably aggravated
now by anger and humiliation as the inquisitors mocked him. Whatever illusions
he had harbored about impressing the inquisitors with his spiritual qualities must
have been shattered. And it now appeared that, despite his best efforts, his mother
and sisters would not be spared. Given his role in inducing them to return to
judaizing after their first trial, he must have been burdened by guilt as well as grief.

But to capitulate at this point was unthinkable. It would have required him to
lose his belief in himself as a superior person who possessed special spiritual
powers—by now an integral part of his personality. In any case, doing so would not
save his life. Luis's state of mind is not ours to know, but his predicament—
concrete and emotional—left him few good choices. At the end of the day's two
audiences dealing with the *acusación*, he announced that he longed for death, "not
by base strangulation [*no como vil ahorcado*]," but "alive, in the fire, with greater
glory." He would go to his glory, he proclaimed, "like the blessed martyr Eleazar,
and Salomona and her seven holy Maccabee children."[149]

The tribunal allowed Luis to languish in his prison cell for four months. He
was then summoned, on October 30, to a series of three meetings over two days
with two Jesuits—*personas doctas*—whose role it was to dissuade him of his "errors
and blindness." Since these discussions were not part of the trial strictly speaking,
they were not recorded. The Jesuit fathers did state, however, that they had shown
Luis "many authoritative passages of sacred Scripture." At the end of each audience, Luis stated his intention to remain in the Law of Moses.[150]

Summoned to an audience a month and a half later, Luis said he had vowed to
God that even if they offered to make him King of Castile, he would not reject the
Law of Moses. The Law of Moses had been given "for all eternity." (Some of his
remarks at this point were not recorded by the notary, as the inquisitors deemed
them "offensive to the Law of Jesus Christ.") If he had consented to have discussions with learned theologians, he went on, it was not because he had doubts about
the truth of the Law of God, but "in order to confound and convert them."
Ordinarily, he signed the written statements of an audience "Luis de Carvajal." On
this occasion, however, he signed "Joseph Lumbroso, slave of the Great Lord of
Hosts [*esclavo del Altísimo A. Salvaoth*]."[151]

Luis's exalted, even grandiose, view of himself may suggest an underlying fear of failure. Ever since his thinking had been transformed under the influence of Manuel de Morales, he had drawn on moments of good fortune to support his view that God had singled him out and blessed him with miracles. His letters to his sisters and mother are full of expectations of the miraculous. No doubt he still hoped for divine intervention. But his reliance on miracles to sustain his beliefs (including his belief in himself) was proving a point of weakness, one that may have led to an undermining of his will as the crushing realities of his situation closed in on him.

Certainly the experience of the torture chamber had a corrosive effect on Luis's morale. From February 8 to February 14, 1596, he was subjected to two episodes of torture and repeated threats of additional ones. The inquisitors' aim was to obtain information about other crypto-judaizers in New Spain. Luis was unable to withstand the pain, and in the course of this week Luis informed on more than one hundred people. The transcripts of the sessions in the torture chamber are distressing to read, not only because Luis's cries of pain are recorded, but because he systematically betrayed the entire network of his judaizing associates and family members.[152]

However, inquisitorial procedure required that testimony given under torture be ratified by the prisoner at a subsequent audience. When Luis appeared before the tribunal for this purpose, he took the opportunity to say that everything he had said in the torture chamber was untrue, and had simply been an attempt to spare himself further torture. Such a statement was certain to lead to new sessions of torture, but he argued that he would "prefer to die from torture than go to hell" (for his lies). He signed the entry for this audience "Joseph Lumbroso."[153]

As he was being led back to his cell, Luis broke away from his guard and threw himself through a window or over a low wall onto a courtyard below. This seems to have been a desperate attempt at suicide, which would have left his testimony unratified and technically unusable, and at the same time would have relieved him of the shame of his humiliating capitulation under torture. But once again fortune eluded him, and he survived. The injuries to his legs, however, were severe enough that more than two weeks later he was visited in his cell rather than summoned to the audience chamber.[154]

The following day, exhausted and bedridden, Luis requested an audience with the inquisitor Lobo Guerrero—explicitly asking that the latter not be accompanied by the second inquisitor, Alonso de Peralta, "the sight of whom caused him to tremble." The request was granted, and Lobo Guerrero came to his cell, where Luis ratified everything he had said in the torture chamber. This time he signed "Luis de Carvajal."[155]

After Luis's desperate jump, two non-judaizing prisoners were assigned to his cell to provide a kind of suicide watch. It seems good evidence of Luis's recovering confidence that one of them was soon judaizing. This was a tailor from Danzig or Hamburg, Daniel Benítez, who was charged with being a *luterano*. Luis's creed may have been particularly compelling to someone who had already rejected much of traditional Christian teaching, and who was acquainted with the Protestant doctrine that held Scripture to be the sole authority for establishing Church teachings. In any case, at some point Benítez was discovered performing what were said by the Inquisition to be Jewish rituals, and singing "Jewish songs" in his cell. Under torture, he confessed that he had been converted by Luis Carvajal.[156]

Because of the injuries Luis had sustained—and perhaps because of his suicide attempt—the tribunal feared that Luis might die before he could give final confirmation of his testimony. At an audience held in his cell, he ratified a list of the scores of persons against whom he had testified.

With this, the Inquisition had no further use for him. Four days later, on February 23, a *consulta de fe* was held to decide his fate. Seven officials, including the two inquisitors and the two Jesuits who had debated with him, voted unanimously to sentence Luis to be relaxed to the secular arm. As was the case with other prisoners, Luis was not informed of this vote.

From late June through mid-August, Luis requested a series of audiences at which he offered further testimony about judaizers. It is not clear what he hoped to gain. Perhaps he was trying to sound out the inquisitors, who had ignored him for months. Among other things, he asked to be allowed to discuss matters of salvation, alone in his cell, with "*personas doctas.*"[157]

The request was granted. On August 24, he met with two Augustinian friars, *calificadores* of the Inquisition, for three and a half hours. As in his first set of debates with theologians, the proceedings were not recorded, except to note that at the end of the session he declared that he wanted to live and die in the Law of Moses.[158]

It must have been quite clear to the prisoner that his time was running out. He set about writing what he called his final will and testament—a spiritual testament—which he presented to the tribunal on September 12.[159] It opens with a lofty prayer praising and petitioning his Creator, a prayer that strongly reflects the influence of the first part of Luis de Granada's *Introducción del Símbolo de la fe*. Although he stated that he wanted to reaffirm in God's presence the truths in which he lived, before his death, this was clearly not his only motive. Toward the end of the document he stated more candidly that the testament was his "final answer . . . to the [inquisitorial] charges against me." It was indeed a polemical response, not a summary of his core beliefs. He did not, for example, include in his elaboration of eight "truths" his very strong belief in the salvation of the righteous, a belief that was shared by Christians.[160]

His first two "truths" require no comment. He believed in one God, and he believed in no others. His next was a polemical response to the Inquisition's contention that the Law of Moses was "dead." He cited some of the "thousand places" in which God had proclaimed the eternity of this Law, quoting the Vulgate imperfectly but to the point.[161] Not only was the Church's teaching about the abrogation of the Law of Moses contradicted by the Hebrew Bible, it was also contradicted by the Gospels: Had not Jesus said, "Think not that I have come to abolish the law"? Had he not declared, "Till heaven and earth pass away, not an iota, not a dot, will pass from the law"?[162]

The cataloging of his beliefs gave Luis an opportunity to return to a passage of Scripture that had marked a turning point in his career. With some redundancy (he had already stated his belief that the Law of Moses was eternal), he asserted his belief that the "sacrament" of circumcision was eternal. He quoted the verse that had, by his account, precipitated his self-circumcision about twelve years before: "The soul of the man who is not circumcized will be obliterated from the list of the living: Gen. 17."[163]

And then comes this: "I believe that Christ, the true harbinger of the end of days [*futuro siglo*], the prince of peace, the real son of David, the holder of the scepter of Judah, light to the gentiles and beloved of God, has not yet come." He continued,

> And even if he has been born, the redemption of the people of God and of the world has not occurred. For it is clear from all the holy prophets . . . that when he [the Messiah] comes by a miracle of God, all the loyal people of Israel, wherever they are scattered, will be revived and gathered in from the four corners of the earth, . . . by miracles greater than those the Lord performed when he redeemed us from Egypt. . . . [With the coming of the Messiah] Israel shall cease to be in captivity; the wars, sins, and idolatries of the world will cease; people everywhere will be converted to the knowledge of the true God; and men will be restored to their original state of innocence.

He continued in this apocalyptic vein, arguing that the fourth empire whose collapse Daniel prophesied was the Roman Empire—Christendom—which was about to collapse. The evil Antiochus, who persecuted the Jews, had prefigured the kings of Spain and Portugal "from whom have proceeded the inquisitions and persecutions of the people of God, as well as the blessed martyrs who are the faithful and true Jews who die for their faith [in the Law]." Both of these notions merit brief elaboration.

The identification of the fourth beast with Christendom had a long history among Jews, and did not occur to Luis from a simple reading of the text. Someone —perhaps Morales—had provided him with this link to Jewish exegetical traditions. It may also have been Morales who suggested the notion that the crumbling "feet of clay" of Christendom could be seen in contemporary divisions "among these heretics: English, French, and the rest"—a sign of the fall to come. The identification of Antiochus with the kings of Spain and Portugal, on the other hand, was of more recent vintage, and may conceivably have been the personal interpretation of an aspiring martyr who identified with the Maccabees.

In a particularly poignant passage in the final section of the testament, Luis acknowledged fears about his own weakness. Given the questions that later arose about events around his death, it is worth examining. He opened with a formulaic declaration of his intention to die as a martyr, hoping that he might "imitate the holy zeal of Hananiah, Azariah, Mishael, and Matathias." But, he continued, "I do not trust myself, since I am only flesh and of frail nature." Still, he wrote, "[I declare that] just as I have placed a mother and five sisters in danger for this faith, I would give away a thousand [lives], if I had them, for faith in each of His holy Commandments."

How, in fact, did Luis Carvajal die?

There seems little doubt that he was garroted before being burned, after a spectacular auto-da-fé involving sixty-six prisoners, held in the *plaza mayor* of Mexico City (today the Zócalo) on December 8, 1596.[164] (The now thirty-year-old Luis would have seen among the condemned his mother and his sisters Isabel, Catalina, and Leonor,[165] clothed in sambenitos that indicated they were condemned to death.)[166] The question is how he actually behaved. The day after the auto-da-fé, the chief constable and three of his lieutenants testified as follows: Luis, as he was being taken to his execution, "demonstrated signs of having converted. He took a crucifix in his hand and spoke a few words by which it was understood that he had converted and repented. Thus, on arriving at the *brasero* which was situated in the marketplace of San Hipólito, he was garroted until he died and his body was consigned to the flames, burning until he was reduced to ashes."[167] Such behavior, of course, need not reflect a sincere conversion.

A Dominican friar who accompanied Luis to the stake, Alonso Contreras, also wrote an eyewitness account that is, however, highly tendentious and unreliable.[168] It was dated December 9, 1596—the day after the auto—but it was undoubtedly written later.[169] Its aim was to "prove" that Luis was genuinely repentant.[170] The apparent reason for writing such an account was to quiet rumors in Mexico City that Luis had made a gesture of kissing the crucifix only in order to be spared a horrific death, *and that he had made defiant gestures afterward.* The author took the opportunity to write a self-serving and fictionalized account, according to which he himself, accompanying Luis to the stake, brought about the heretic's sincere conversion. (It is testimony to the man's character that he also complained of being kicked by the horse carrying Luis and of getting dust in his eyes.)

The feat had been achieved, the friar claimed, by quoting to Luis a verse—Lamentations 4:20—which Luis said he did not recognize. The friar took a Bible, which he opened to the verse in question and (on his way to the stake!) Luis became engrossed in the entire chapter, describing the destruction of Jerusalem and the defeat of the Jews. Luis was, according to the friar, suddenly "enlightened." This ludicrous claim—Luis had consistently viewed these events as fulfillments of prophecies in the Hebrew Bible—would not have been convincing to crypto-Jews living in Mexico City. But many of those crypto-Jews, if they had not been burned at the stake, were already serving sentences.

Like all of the dogmatista martyrs, Luis Carvajal followed a profoundly personal path. His emotionalism, his lively imagination, and his certainty that he possessed exceptional spiritual powers were key features of his religious profile. He was

HOMME qui vâ être Brûlé par arrest de L'INQUISITION.

Figure 5. Image of a condemned prisoner in a sambenito painted with flames and devils. From Bernard Picart, *Ceremonies et coutumes religieuses de tous les peoples du monde* (Amsterdam 1723), vol. 2, p. 96. The Jewish Theological Seminary.

instinctively drawn to Iberian *alumbrado* currents that helped shape his personal grasp of the divine. But he also inhabited a wider milieu in which radical biblicism had become the versatile foundation for creeds of various types. Though driven underground in Iberian lands, they thrived in some unexpected quarters. That the crypto-Jewish physician Manuel de Morales and the marginally Catholic hermit Gregorio López were both among Carvajal's mentors in New Spain speaks volumes about the changing contours of crypto-Judaism by the late sixteenth century.

A MONK OF CASTANHEIRA

4

Three years after Carvajal was burned at the stake, a young Capuchin monk in Portugal, Diogo d'Asumpção, was seized by the Inquisition.[1] This curious and tormented figure had little if any Jewish ancestry. He was born in the port town of Caminha, near the mouth of the Minho River in northern Portugal, where his father was a customs inspector.[2] Frei Diogo had fled his monastery in Castanheira, outside Lisbon, on the eve of the day of São Lourenço, and was seeking passage to the Netherlands or France or elsewhere, "to live as he liked, in freedom," as he later confessed.[3] He does not seem to have been fleeing a severe outbreak of plague, which was waning by the time of his flight.[4] Initially he sought out a New Christian merchant named Gaspar Boccarro, who was living about a quarter of a league (about a kilometer) from the monastery, to be supplied with nonclerical clothing and money.[5] The latter referred him to a local Old Christian *fidalgo* named Diogo de Sousa[6]—something he probably did in order to get this dangerous visitor off his hands. The fugitive went to see the fidalgo, who was a complete stranger,[7] at his estate a few kilometers away in Cadafais, on August 11, 1599.

The friar who approached Diogo de Sousa, saying he had been sent by Gaspar Boccarro,[8] was about twenty-five years old, dressed in a Capuchin habit of coarse woolen cloth, with a beard and a tonsured head. The friar asked that they withdraw to a place where they could speak privately. He was very thirsty, he said, and asked for water.

The fidalgo must have been astonished by what transpired. Frei Diogo said he wished to confide "many things" to him, asking him on his word of honor as a nobleman not to reveal them. He began to pour out his heart, revealing a fierce, bold, and rather wide-ranging critique of the Catholic Church.[9] The fidalgo listened carefully.

Frei Diogo said he deeply repented having become a friar, which he had done eight years earlier. He had by now come to the conclusion that "everything among the friars is a pack of lies, falsehoods, and deceptions." He added that he "could demonstrate [this] with documents he carried with him," promptly drawing from his habit three or four small notebooks into which he had copied passages from books in the monastery library, whose titles he did not mention. (He was also carrying a closed cloth sack full of other papers, which he said were the monastery regulations drawn up by the friars; he had stolen them, he said.)[10]

Frei Diogo then began to read passages in Latin from his notebooks to support his views. When the fidalgo said he didn't know Latin, Frei Diogo seized the opportunity to attack the Church which, he said, recorded its doctrines in Latin to prevent the laity from knowing them. He proceeded to translate the passages into Portuguese. The term *Christ*, Frei Diogo said, meant *anointed king*. Many kings of the Old Testament had been anointed. Jesus, however, had never been anointed king. It was because Jesus had expropriated this title that he paid as he did on the cross. Nor had Jesus been named Immanuel, the name Isaiah had prophesied would be given the Messiah.[11] The early Christians had attributed this name to him post facto. The "law of Christ" had been invented by the rabble around Jesus, and adopted by ignorant gentiles who did not know what God had commanded in the Book of Deuteronomy, namely, "that His words were not to be misinterpreted, nor were they to be given any sense but the literal."[12] Christians treated Scripture "like a nose of wax you could push this way and that."[13] Moreover, their innovations defied reason. Aristotle had declared that a living being could generate only another being of its own kind—a horse another horse, and so on. How was one to believe that God could be transformed into a piece of bread? What was more, the theologians of the Church could not even agree among themselves. They were divided by "great controversies," the Franciscans following Duns Scotus or Domingo de Soto, the Dominicans Thomas Aquinas.[14]

The friar, emboldened by the fidalgo's attentiveness, ventured onto more risky ground. Mary had given birth not only to Jesus, he said, but to his brothers, and she must therefore have had sexual relations with Joseph. The fidalgo was so scandalized at this statement that, he reported, he was tempted to draw his dagger and stab Frei Diogo to death on the spot—which he would have done had the visitor not been a cleric. He succeeded, though, in maintaining his composure, "neither contradicting him nor approving what he said, in order to hear everything." The friar, encouraged, took from his habit a small book bound in vellum, which he said was "about the sacraments," and mockingly read a passage in Latin that specified what was to be done in a case when a rat happened to eat a consecrated host. In such a case, "they" (not specified) caught the rat if they could, burned it, and threw the ashes into the sacrarium (*sacrario*), a drain for disposing of sanctified material that no longer had a use. The friar repeated the words "if they could" pointedly, adding, "And if they couldn't, God would be running about in the body of a rat!"[15] It is easy to understand why this conversation, which continued at length, was recalled by the fidalgo in detail.

It had been a long time, the friar said, since he had recited the hours with devotion. To pray in earnest, he recited the psalms of David. (This was his first suggestion of a judaizing tendency.) He was well aware that his deviation from the Church's teaching and practice was an egregious error from a Catholic point of view. But he arrogated to himself the right to do so on grounds that were gaining increasing acceptance in sectarian circles in Europe. God, he said, had granted him reason (*juizo e entendimento*) to understand these things. He was therefore obligated to seek his salvation; to do otherwise would be a sin. The conclusion to which his reason had led him, in conjunction with his reading of Scripture, was that the Law of the Jews had never been abrogated. Anyone who understood this and failed to act accordingly, he said, faced damnation. He proceeded to praise the saints and prophets of the Jews, mentioning Moses and Aaron in particular, and holding them up to the "miserable wretches" the Church had turned into saints. The apostles, as he saw it, were all relatives of Jesus, dishonorable men "who hid among rocks and were full of lice."[16]

Frei Diogo was troubled by the soteriological contradiction, as he saw it, between the Old and New Testaments. According to the Hebrew Bible, God had offered a means for men to atone for their sins, namely the sacrifice of animals. If goats sacrificed on the altar could atone for sins in the time of the Temple, he reasoned, why could not such sacrifices have atoned for the death of Jesus, who was subject to the Law of the Jews? And if Jesus had been subject to the Law of the Jews, as Scripture reveals he was, how could he have created a new Law that utterly contradicted the Law by which he lived? It seemed to the friar that if the Law of Jesus (whatever it was) had been good, the Jews would not have killed him. But what the Church *called* the Law of Jesus, he asserted, was not the Law that Jesus professed. For if it were true that Jesus had instituted baptism as a means of cleansing one of one's sins, why did St. Paul have Timothy circumcised?[17]

To support his belief that Jesus had not instituted baptism as a sacrament, Frei Diogo turned to an unexpected authority. Martin Luther, he maintained, held that "whoever invented the sacraments was an enemy of Jesus."[18] This statement was not by any means, however, an endorsement of Martin Luther. On the contrary, Luther and the Reformers were Christians, by which, he said, he meant gentiles. Thus, "because they had no foundation in our Law"—here, if we can rely on the notary's record, we are confronted with a striking suggestion that Frei Diogo identified personally with the Law of the Jews—"they fashioned new sects in order to gain fame." Many people, he said, referring to monks and priests who could read Latin, knew these things, but in order to eat and stay alive they suffered in silence.

Frei Diogo then asked the fidalgo for financial aid and for some old clothes. His plan was to go to Setúbal, where he would embark for England or the Netherlands.[19] He had by now become somewhat calmer, the fidalgo reported. But he continued to unburden himself. He turned at this point to a problem that had been stirred anew among Christians as a result of the overseas discoveries. If the Law of Christ were good, he said, it would have to be accessible to everyone. Yet it was not available to Africans (*negros*) and to other peoples in a multitude of lands. Even from a very technical point of view it was inaccessible: since these lands lacked consecrated bread and wine, the Eucharist could not be performed there even for a hypothetical believer.

The monologue continued. The Church taught that as Jesus grew older, he grew in wisdom. But if he were God, he would have had no need to grow wiser. (The fidalgo noted with indignation that when speaking of "Christo Nosso Senhor," the friar said only "Christ" or "Jesus," and when speaking of "Nossa Senhora" he said simply "Maria.") The first Christians, Frei Diogo said, possessed only the *Pater noster* as a prayer, but successive popes added new prayers of their own making. While on the subject of fabrications, he reiterated the Reformation cliché that there were so many Holy Roods that the supply of wood was in danger of running out. He dwelt mockingly on the miracles attributed to a certain piece of stray wood that an obliging ferryman (*barqueiro*) had provided to an old woman to satisfy her great longing for a piece of the cross.

St. Francis had written, he continued, that Portugal would never become subject to Spain. (He did not need to explain to the fidalgo that Spain had forcibly annexed Portugal in 1580.) Just as this prophecy was "a lie," so were all the rest. When St. Francis died, he was buried in a certain place (the fidalgo could not remember the place Frei Diogo named), and only afterwards was his body moved to Assisi. Yet a certain abbot in Assisi claimed that he had seen St. Francis alive and bearing stigmata. How could this be if St. Francis had been buried elsewhere? A cardinal who had recounted this story himself called it a "tall tale," pointedly asking how it was, if St. James ("Santiago," the patron saint of Spain) had been killed in Jerusalem, that his body had ended up in Galicia?[20]

The friar ended his discourse (at least as the fidalgo reported it) in an apocalyptic vein, asserting that Christendom would suffer great persecutions in 1601. When he had finished speaking, Diogo de Sousa, who had been planning a course of action as he listened, did what he could to keep Frei Diogo in his house, bringing him food and suggesting that he take a siesta. As soon as the friar was asleep, the fidalgo wrote to the superior (*guardião*) of the friar's monastery of Santo Antonio in Castanheira, asking him to come immediately. The superior, suffering from a bad leg, sent two other friars. Diogo de Sousa met them in a house outside his estate and reported what Frei Diogo had said. He advised them to follow him to his estate, where he would stay with Frei Diogo while waiting for them.

Frei Diogo must have been awake, and heard the friars enter the fidalgo's home. He panicked and hid under a bed. When the friars entered the room, the fidalgo gestured toward the bed. The friars dragged out their pitiful colleague, tied him up, and took him back to the monastery, where he was placed in the monastery's "jail" (*tronco*). On the following day, August 12, the fidalgo wrote an account of the previous day's extraordinary events and sent it to the Lisbon tribunal, sealing it with his coat of arms. He concluded it with the dubious assertion that Frei Diogo was "as much a Jew as those in North Africa." He then went to the monastery and spoke personally to the superior, who advised him to go to the Inquisition in Lisbon to denounce the fugitive under oath. Meanwhile Frei Diogo was taken to Lisbon, where he was transferred to a secure cell in that city's monastery of Santo Antonio.[21]

Some days later, a deputy inquisitor (with a notary to record the session) conducted an initial interrogation of Frei Diogo in his Lisbon monastery cell.[22] The friar claimed to be an Old Christian "without any New Christian ancestry."[23] He could not, however, deny the heresies he had elaborated so vividly for the fidalgo. He decided to confess that he had held these ideas (which he presented in a tamer fashion than he had before the fidalgo), but now rejected them and repented. He explained why he had been driven to hold these ideas. (The events involved would crop up in later testimony by his superiors and a peer in the Capuchin order). About a year earlier, some of his peers had been ordained to celebrate mass. He had apparently been passed over. Feeling humiliated and badly treated, he had become disillusioned in his belief, and in this state of confusion the devil easily seduced him.

During this time he had done some reading that had intensified his feelings of alienation. He had borrowed a book from Frei Jeronimo de Jesus, a friar in his monastery, which was identified later in the trial as a work by Fray Marcos de la Camara. This work sought to resolve the apparent contradictions between certain verses of Scripture. If we try to read between the lines, it would seem that Frei Diogo, in his discontent, rejected the author's efforts at harmonizing, which struck him as forced and lame. He "discovered," as he put it, that the "sacraments" of the Law of Moses were still valid, and that the Virgin, after giving birth to Jesus, had had sexual intercourse with Joseph.[24] He reported that he had also read the *De Sacramentis* of Francis de Vitoria, an influential Dominican theologian at the University of Salamanca in the first half of the sixteenth century, and that this work had raised doubts in his mind about the sacraments of baptism and ordination. In the *Summa Silvestrina*—a popular guide for confessors that is listed in a nineteenth-century inventory of the Castanheira monastery library's holdings[25]— he learned, he said, that God's Law did not become obligatory until it was accepted by the people. He stated that about a month earlier he had come to the definite conclusion that the Law of Christ was false, because the majority of people in the world had not accepted it. He could thus "adopt whatever Law he wanted to live in," and was beginning to incline to the Law of Moses. While living in these "errors" (as he now presented them), he had decided to flee to the Netherlands or France.

But, he said, he now rejected his erroneous ideas. His awakening had occurred suddenly, in an illumination from God, about a week after his capture and incarceration. Once God had "opened the eyes of his soul," he had determined to return to the Catholic faith and remain loyal to it. He begged pardon and mercy for his sins and, dropping to his knees, said he was ready to undergo any penance. However, assuming that the notary's record is reasonably accurate, Frei Diogo's confession was very general, and did not reflect an enthusiastic endorsement of the Church's teachings.

Two days later, Frei Diogo was again questioned in the Lisbon monastery cell.[26] Understandably nervous about his situation, he wanted to supply some details he had failed to mention in his previous testimony, and to stress how scrupulous his observance of the Catholic faith had been up to the time of his disillusionment. He had entered the Capuchin order eight years earlier at the Lisbon monastery, he related, and had been professed after serving for a year and a day as a novice. He also gave an account of his lineage, highlighting his family's respectability on both sides.

The inquisitors decided that Frei Diogo's testimony was partial and untruthful, and that the prisoner was confessing only because he knew he had been denounced. Frei Diogo was formally transferred to the jurisdiction of the Inquisition, though he remained in the monastery until October 25, when he was moved to the inquisitorial cells. And the Inquisition opened an inquiry into his genealogy.[27]

On August 27, several days after Frei Diogo's initial interrogation, the dutiful fidalgo appeared before the Lisbon tribunal, affirming the testimony he had given in his letter and adding some details.[28] Interestingly, when he was asked whether he could affirm that Frei Diogo believed in the Law of Moses, he preferred not to commit himself. Perhaps the fact that the question was asked signaled doubts on the part of the inquisitors, or perhaps looking back on the episode more coolly it was no longer so clear to him. But he was quite clear in his conviction that the fugitive had not been hallucinating, and that, on the contrary, Frei Diogo had been entirely in his right mind (*em todo seu siso perfeito sem perturbacāo do juizo*). The inquisitor asked him if Frei Diogo "was a New Christian, or what ethnicity (*casta*) he was." The fidalgo replied that he only knew what he had heard from the friars at the monastery—namely, that Frei Diogo was the son of a sister and uncle of Pero da Costa, and that it was presumed he was a New Christian.

Frei Diogo apparently fell ill after his transfer to the Inquisition prison, as a result of which he was summoned for his first audience before the tribunal only on November 24.[29] The inquisitor who would take the major responsibility for his case, Manuel Álvarez Tavares, was convinced that someone had indoctrinated Frei Diogo in his heretical ideas. It was easy to suppose that this prisoner was doing what many others did, that is, trying to conceal the identity of mentors and like-minded associates. It was also hard to divine how Frei Diogo could have arrived alone at views that were so radically at odds with his conditioning in childhood and as a young adult. There was nothing exotic about his rage when his peers were granted a privilege he was denied; but was it conceivable that this disappointment alone had led him to reject the Law of Christ?

Frei Diogo persisted in maintaining that no one had taught him, and that his doubts had crystallized as a result of reading perfectly orthodox, and not terribly wide-ranging, books.[30] He reiterated his distress at the fact that different Church authorities held contradictory opinions—something he could certainly have learned from his reading. But the inquisitor, unconvinced, noted that "the books he [Frei Diogo] mentioned do not teach that the Law of Moses is still today the Law in which one can be saved." Frei Diogo was admonished to give a complete confession and name the persons who had "taught him that Law."

The task of determining Frei Diogo's lineage was handed over to the Coimbra tribunal, which had responsibility for the region in which Frei Diogo's immediate ancestors had lived.[31] Thorough investigations were carried out in Aveiro and Coimbra. They yielded consistent results on two points: first, that Frei Diogo was descended entirely from Old Christians on his mother's side, and second, that on his father's side he had one New Christian great-great grandparent named Bernaldo Dias, who had been baptized as an adult (*baptizado em pee*), presumably in 1497. The effort expended in this investigation—six witnesses in Aveiro and eight in Coimbra were selected for their advanced age and good reputation, and in some cases were questioned at length—reveals the Inquisition's eagerness to obtain a religio-ethnic "explanation" for the friar's heterodoxy.[32]

Frei Diogo languished in his cell during the winter months while the Inquisition gathered genealogical testimony. On April 6, 1600, he was granted an audience at his request. In such cases the inquisitor routinely asked the prisoner why he had requested an audience, and typically the prisoner would reply that he wanted to "unburden his conscience" with some new information. Frei Diogo, however, said that he wanted to make some points in his own defense.[33] This was either naïveté or impudence on his part. There *was* no defense for heresy, no argument that could mitigate its severity. The inquisitor's brusque reply was that he was not there to respond to the prisoner's arguments. At this, Frei Diogo stood up "with great anger" and asked the inquisitor, in Latin, "What is the name of God?" The inquisitor told him to calm down. But the agitated prisoner began quoting from the Bible (the notary did not record his quotations), insisting that "Scripture could not be understood in any other way [than his]." The inquisitor concluded that Frei Diogo was not in his right mind just then, and ordered the warden to take him to his cell.

The following day, Frei Diogo was summoned to appear before two inquisitors and two deputy inquisitors.[34] He was again asked why he had requested an audience the previous day. He now said that "he had nothing to ask of the tribunal" because the inquisitors couldn't even tell him the name of God. An inquisitor asked him his reason for asking them this question. Frei Diogo was silent. An inquisitor asked if *he* knew the name of God. He replied in Latin, "'I am the God of Abraham, the God of Isaac, the God of Jacob, and this is my name forever, for all generations,'"[35] which was "what God had told the people of Israel." Since the inquisitors didn't even know this, he added, how could he be expected to listen to them? (The notary noted that he said this "with much anger, standing up and gesturing with his hands.")

After the inquisitors succeeded in calming Frei Diogo down, they began to ask him directly about his beliefs. He no longer made any effort to protect himself. Asked whether he shared the beliefs of the people of ancient Israel, he replied in the affirmative. Like them, he was awaiting the Messiah. He added that when the inquisitor had said during a visit to his cell that he, Frei Diogo, would soon leave these cells, he was prophesizing, because the Messiah was coming very soon, and would take him out of there. Now Frei Diogo's anger was rekindled, and the inquisitors sought to calm him down by saying that they only wanted to lead him on the right path. Furious, he got up again and made an insulting remark about the Inquisition. When he was told to get on his knees, he said, "You can't order me to do that, because I don't owe obedience to this tribunal." He sat down, still agitated. He was admonished "with great kindness" and led back to his cell.

On the following day, April 8, an inquisitor named Manoel Correa, who had not been present at any of Frei Diogo's prior interrogations, visited the friar in his cell, posing as a cleric who had come to help and console the prisoner. When he asked Frei Diogo about his spiritual state of mind, the friar responded that he was "much better, because he had been enlightened by the Lord in the true Law, which was that of the Jews, in which he was now living."[36] Questioned further, he said that he had been a friar for eight years, in all of which time he had been indifferent (*frio*). The inquisitor understood him to suggest that he had been vacillating all that time.[37] How and where, the inquisitor asked the prisoner, had he been enlightened? Frei Diogo replied that when he was reading the passages in the *De Sacramentis* of Francis de Vitoria dealing with the Old and the New Law, God "showed him inwardly [*mostrandole interiormente*]" that there can be only one eternal Law of God, and that what people call the New Law is a law made by men. He then proceeded to quote "a multitude of verses [*autoridades*] from Psalms" to support his contention that the people of Israel were God's only chosen people. When the inquisitor responded that he, the prisoner, was either mad or malicious, Frei Diogo said it was "they" who were in error and ignorant. They didn't even know the name of God, which was "the God of Abraham, Isaac, and Jacob." He then launched into a furious monologue, peppered with verses from the Psalms.

The inquisitor tried to persuade Frei Diogo of his error. In the many, many instances in which such efforts were made, one is struck by the absence of anything close to real dialogue. Frei Diogo was raising fundamental issues about the sources of religious authority, about hermeneutical certainty, about textual authenticity, and about the problem of choosing between multiple religious "truths." He was claiming the right (indeed, obligation) to examine religious tradition critically. The inquisitors who questioned him, and the clerics who were sent to talk with him, all wished to convince him he was in error. But they refused (or were unable) to meet him on his own ground. To be sure, it would have been difficult to have had a reasoned debate with so obstreperous a critic. Yet it is striking that, given the concerted efforts that were made to convert this lone heretic, none of the men who sought to convert Frei Diogo took the offensive in any consistent way. How did the friar know he had been enlightened by God, and not by the devil? What prevented him from concluding that the Old Testament was not also a human fabrication? If persons with Jewish ancestry had superior understanding, why did the ancient Israelites whore after false gods and revile their own prophets? And so on.

Manoel Correa responded to the friar's aggressive assertions by cautiously reiterating key Church doctrines of which the friar was fully aware: that the Messiah had come long before, that he was the son of God, and that he had introduced the Law that Christians professed. Frei Diogo cut off his visitor by stating categorically that the coming of the Messiah was near, and that the Messiah was not the son of God, but fully human. The inquisitor asked Frei Diogo whether he perhaps believed that he himself was the Messiah. Frei Diogo responded cryptically, saying only that the Messiah was near. He added, however, that it was not only about the Messiah that the Church was wrong. The doctrine of the Trinity in effect posited the existence of three deities, thus contradicting the scriptural prohibition of worshiping multiple gods.

The inquisitor did not choose to reply to this sally. He concluded the meeting by saying that he did not think Frei Diogo was insane, but that the devil had seized him, and that it was malicious of him to continue in his error despite the time that had been given him to reflect. In a revealing further remark, the inquisitor noted that the Inquisition had even generously given the prisoner a mantle for warmth![38] Frei Diogo responded that he was not insane, nor did he have illusions about himself. He was a Jew and had the faith of a Jew.[39]

Five days later, Manoel Correa was asked by the tribunal to visit Frei Diogo again, this time in the company of another inquisitor, Gaspar Ferraz, a Jesuit.[40] Correa found the prisoner in a quieter mood. There ensued a fascinating dialogue worth reconstructing at length. (I have taken the liberty of changing the indirect speech of the dossier to direct speech in some of the long exchanges, to facilitate reading.)

Asked how he was, Frei Diogo said he was much consoled and enlightened by God, because he had been blind before, but now, in prison, he had received many consolations and manifestations (*illustracões*) of God. Asked if he prayed, he said yes, he recited psalms from the breviary, but without the Gloria Patri, because there was no Trinity.[41]

Asked where he had studied, he said that as a child he had studied in Braga, where he had learned Latin.[42] He added that he had practiced Catholicism devoutly, "but in blindness." He denied having been taught any of his present beliefs either by his parents or siblings, who were sincere Catholics, or by other friars. Everything, he said, had come to him as an illumination from God. Asked whether he had New Christian origins, he now said that he understood his mother was a New Christian and his father an Old Christian. (It is hard to interpret Frei Diogo's apparently erroneous placement of the "New Christian" component of his ancestry on his mother's side.) Asked what books he had read, he answered that he'd read books that quoted verses from Scripture—verses that Catholics "did not want to learn or understand." Catholics followed a New Law that the popes and Church councils, failing to understand Scripture, had fabricated.

> INQUISITOR: The New Law was not invented by men. It came from God, being given by the Messiah, as promised by the prophets. The Messiah declared he was doing this in the Gospel when he said, *non veni solvere legem sed adimplere* ["I have come not to abolish the Law but to fulfill (it)," cf. Matt. 5:17].
>
> FREI DIOGO: The Messiah has not come. If people choose to believe me, they will understand the truth.
>
> INQUISITOR: So you, then, are the Messiah?
>
> FREI DIOGO: It's you who said this.
>
> INQUISITOR: If you are the Messiah, why haven't you liberated your people, and why are

you not equipped like a king, and why don't you perform miracles, and do the other things that the Messiah whom the Jews await must do?

FREI DIOGO: Because you don't want to hear and you are all blind, but I am the Messiah, though I didn't know this before I was imprisoned. Before, I prophesied without understanding. But afterward I understood.

The inquisitor asked Frei Diogo what things he had prophesied. The friar cited three "signs" that he had been given of his future messianic role. The first is rather cryptic. When he had been angry with his superior, he said, he had written an anonymous note to him that posed the question, in Latin, "Who sucks honey out of the rock, and oil out of the flinty rock? [cf. Deut. 32.13]," after which he wrote, "Christus Dominus."[43] The second "sign" was something he had presumably heard, or believed he had heard, from his mother. When she was pregnant with Frei Diogo, she had gone on a pilgrimage, during which another woman had offered her own child in exchange for the child Frei Diogo's mother was carrying. His mother reportedly replied, "I don't want to give you this child I'm carrying, because he will one day be a servant of God [servo de Deus]." Finally, the friar said, he discerned his own name in Scripture. "Diogo" was the Portuguese form of the name "Jacob." He had also found his mother's name, Oliveira, meaning "olive tree," a frequent image in Scripture. And he'd found his father's name, "Velho," which was the equivalent of the Latin senestus or venerabilis. Was Frei Diogo taunting his visitor with new "Christological" discoveries? Such "signs" from Scripture are suspiciously similar to a sort of exegesis Frei Diogo ridiculed.

INQUISITOR: How can you be the Messiah if, as you say, your father is not a member of the nação [i.e., a New Christian] and if, as you say, your mother is blind to the truth [cega]? And how can you be the Messiah when you are poor and incarcerated, trembling with cold, and scorned by everyone?

FREI DIOGO (quoting in Latin): "I would rather be a doorkeeper in the house of my God than dwell in the tents of wickedness" [Ps. 84:10].[44] I have endured many sufferings and persecutions while a monk [na religião], having been scorned by everyone, left behind [in rank] by others who entered [the order] after me, going from kitchen to kitchen [begging, as a Capuchin friar], and three times imprisoned.[45]

Frei Diogo said he consoled himself, however, by reciting verses from the Psalms concerning the blessings God had bestowed on the Israelites who observed his Law.

INQUISITOR (with sarcasm): Oh, look at the many gifts God has given to this Israelite people, the guardian of his Law! In sixteen hundred years he has done nothing [for them], as they wander about the world dejected and exiled, without a Law or sacrifices or priests. It certainly looks as if [they have] done something evil, for God to forsake them so. So many years!

FREI DIOGO (in Latin): "A thousand years in thy sight are but as yesterday when it is past" [Ps. 90:4]; "The Lord builds up Jerusalem; he gathers the outcasts of Israel" [Ps. 147:2].

INQUISITOR: This [verse] alludes to the time long ago when the Jews returned from Babylonia. But let us suppose it alludes to something in the future. If so, it is to the end of the world, the time of judgment, when the Jews will convert, and the celestial Jerusalem will be filled with converts!

FREI DIOGO (according to the inquisitor, "very serenely"): Well, there will be no judgment, nor resurrection of the dead.

INQUISITOR: Frei Diogo, we understand Scripture this way [i.e., that there will be a final judgment and resurrection], and the Jews do not deny this either. I hope God will enlighten you in the true faith in which you were raised. May you be commended to Our Lord.

FREI DIOGO ("very serenely and with gravity"): Such prayers will not be heeded by God, because everything the Church asserts is a lie, such as the claim that St. Francis had wounds, and the things they say occurred to other saints—it's all a fiction.

With this, the inquisitor and his companion withdrew.

The inquisitor, Manuel Correa, recognized that this prisoner fit no familiar type. He had very little New Christian ancestry and had not declared himself a martyr. In a subsequent overall evaluation of the two interrogations he had conducted, he concluded that Frei Diogo did not seem to have the "malice characteristic of a Jew," because he spoke candidly and sincerely. Nor did he seem to be insane, "even when he spoke of his Judaism," because he spoke coherently, citing appropriate verses from Scripture. Confounded by this novelty, the inquisitor sought some precedent, some historical analogue that would "explain" it. He recalled such a "case" being discussed in a classic guide to the monastic life, the *Conferences* of the fifth-century monk John Cassian.[46] In a passage that dealt with "discretion"—in the sense of a person's capacity to distinguish between a good spirit and an evil spirit that had entered him—the author related a vivid story about a monk who had ended up having himself circumcised.[47] In Cassian's work, the story is told by an anchorite monk named Moses, in a fictional dialogue. Let us take a look at this story:

> It would take a long time . . . to tell the story of the deception of the monk from Mesopotamia who maintained an abstinence that few in that province could imitate. Hidden alone in his cell, he had practiced this for many years, and in the end he was deceived by diabolical revelations and dreams that, after so many labors and virtues, in which he had exceeded all the monks living in that place, he fell wretchedly into Judaism and the circumcision of the flesh. For after the devil, wishing to draw him by frequent visions to believe in future deceptions, had, like a messenger of truth, revealed things that were perfectly true, he finally showed the Christian people along with the leaders of our religion and faith, the apostles and martyrs, as dark and repulsive and all evil-looking and deformed. And on the other hand there were the Jewish people with Moses, the patriarchs and the prophets, bounding with the greatest joy and shining with a splendid light—all to persuade him that if he wished to share in their dignity and blessedness he should hasten to be circumcised.[48]

At first glance, it would seem that this story was suggested to the inquisitor by the simple theme "monk becomes Jew." But there seems a good deal more to it than that. For the inquisitor, it was axiomatic that Judaism was the "deformed" faith. The only explanation for a friar's attraction to such a faith was some hidden, sleight-of-hand trick of the devil. Such a view defused the real challenges inherent in Frei Diogo's harangues, allowing Correa to continue secure in his own rigidly defined moral and aesthetic universe.

Eleven days later, on April 24, Frei Diogo was again questioned in his cell by Manoel Correa, who was accompanied by another inquisitor.[49] He was asked whether, in his opinion, the religious orders had a basis in the Gospels. He replied that they were the "inventions of men." In one of their few offensive efforts, the inquisitors proceeded to note that Jews also had "orders." The Levites, they said, were a case in point. Frei Diogo was uncharacteristically silent. It is hard to know why he did not make the obvious rejoinder, namely that God, not men, had given the Levites their special status. The inquisitors may have touched on an area where his biblical knowledge was weak. (His overall biblical repertoire, despite his virtuosity in quoting psalms, seems to have been quite limited). In any case, the inquisitors did not pursue or return to this point, perhaps because higher-ranking inquisitors than Manoel Correa understood that this was less than a clinching argument. As would be the case from this point onward in reports by the various people who would speak to Frei Diogo—inquisitors, fellow friars, and cellmates— Manoel Correa and his companion declared that Frei Diogo was sane.

Two and a half months passed before Frei Diogo was again summoned to an audience, on July 7, 1600.[50] He took the prescribed oath to tell the truth, with a slight change in established procedure—the record notes for the first time that he placed his hand not, as was routinely done, on the Gospels, but on a breviary (the book from which he recited psalms). He had most likely refused to swear on the Gospels (though he had done so at least once at a previous audience).[51] He swore "by the God of Abraham, the God of Isaac, and the God of Jacob" to tell the truth. He then announced for the first time (at least in the written record) that he had chosen the path of martyrdom, that he was a Jew, and that he intended to die as a Jew.

Asked if he understood what he was saying, Frei Diogo replied, in Latin, "God is known in Judah, and his name is great in Israel."[52] Perhaps to underscore his refusal to swear on the Gospels, he asserted that "the evangelists did not write what they heard from God, but what they heard from St. Peter and St. Paul, and did not attain the wisdom of God. And who were St. Augustine and St. Jerome to interpret the wisdom of God?" At this, the inquisitor asked him who *he* was to say such things about St. Augustine, St. Jerome, and the evangelists. He replied, in Latin, "I am thy servant, the son of thy handmaid."[53] He added that St. Augustine had been under the sway of the devil when he said the Messiah had come, but that he, Frei Diogo, was subject only to God, being a Jew and keeping the Law of the Jews. He added that God had not revealed Scripture to St. Augustine because he was a gentile, and had revealed it only to Jacob and Israel because God "declares his word to Jacob, his statutes and ordinances to Israel."[54]

He was asked what Jewish precepts he observed and what prayers he recited. He said that he recited psalms from the breviary, without the Gloria Patri; the Pater Noster, "which is a prayer given by God"; and prayers from "the Testament of God" (the Old Testament). By way of illustration, he recited selectively from the Ten Commandments, "You shall have no other gods before me, you shall not take the name of the Lord in vain, remember the Sabbath day to keep it holy."[55]

He said that he kept the Sabbath and tried to fast according to the Law of Moses.[56] On Fridays, he ate nothing. On Saturdays (sábado, in Portuguese) he ate the midday meal and supper in the evening. This is an important detail. Knowledge of the sunset-to-nightfall boundaries of the Sabbath was common in crypto-Jewish and converso circles. If Frei Diogo had been in contact with crypto-Jews, it is unlikely that he would have been oblivious to this basic characteristic of Sabbath observance. Yet his own testimony, in conjunction with the later testimony of his prison companions, shows clearly that Frei Diogo did not know about the sunset-to-nightfall cycle of days according to the Jewish calendar. This fact lends support to his own insistence that he had had no crypto-Jewish mentor. If Frei Diogo had arrived at the conclusion that Saturday-Sabbath observance was incumbent on him on the basis of a literalist reading of Scripture, he was by no means alone among non-Jewish religious dissidents in the early modern period.[57]

Yet the inquisitors continued to pursue the question. Once again the friar denied having had teachers. The inquisitor argued that it was not possible for him to be a Jew without someone having taught him. He asserted that only God had taught him, adding tartly that it was enough to see what the apostles and popes had done to be converted to the Law of Moses. It is perhaps indicative of the ways in which certain Reformation pathways of thought independently echoed others that Frei Diogo, in making this comment, was uttering a thought that went just a step further than a remark Martin Luther had expressed in the period just after his break with Rome.[58]

Frei Diogo spent most of his time not before inquisitors, but in his cell. He may have been kept in isolation at first, but by late summer 1600 he was not alone. The first testimony against him by a cellmate—it was the first of a series of denunciations—was given on September 11, 1600. An Old Christian prisoner, Pero Domingues, requested the audience.[59] He had been arrested for "committing excesses in the exercise of his duties" as a guard in the inquisitorial prison in Coimbra. In coming forward with information, he was undoubtedly angling for advantage, which raises questions about the reliability of his testimony. But when we examine his testimony in light of the testimony of other cellmates, and in the context of the dossier as a whole, much of it has a ring of authenticity.

About fifteen days earlier, Pero Domingues reported, he, together with two other prisoners, a Frenchman named Miguel Siguet and a New Christian named Tristão Dias, both of whom had been his cell companions, were moved, along with "a young friar in the Capuchin habit whose name he did not know," to another cell—one that was, apparently, within shouting distance of a New Christian named Antonio Gomes. Such moves were not only common, but part of a considered strategy on the part of the Inquisition. The regulations of 1552 laid down the basic principles of placing prisoners together, with the aim of minimizing collusion. A prisoner who did not need to be isolated should be placed with other prisoners, the regulations held, but these prisoners should be from other regions, and charged with different crimes. A *negativo*—a prisoner who denied committing the crime he or she was charged with—should be placed with prisoners who had confessed. Prisoners should not be placed with relatives. Prisoners who had just begun to confess should not be moved. And so on.[60] These rules made for frequent moves as new prisoners were admitted, older ones changed their status by confessing, and others were released.

One day shortly after the move he mentioned, Pero Domingues had heard Frei Diogo calling out to Antonio Gomes. The two prisoners were discussing Antonio Gomes's son, who was at the time in the Coimbra inquisitorial prison. Frei Diogo was trying to persuade Antonio Gomes that his son, who had apparently made some impetuous remarks revealing his judaizing sympathies, was not crazy, but was a "prophet of God," and that he, Antonio Gomes, was lucky to have such a son. Whereupon Frei Diogo began to expound his belief in a coming messianic age when there would be peace, as well as his conviction that the Law of Moses (unlike the Law of Christ) was the one true Law given by God. This set off something of a religious debate. The Frenchman, Miguel Siguet, admitted that the Law of Moses had indeed been the Law of God, but that it had been valid only until the coming of the Messiah, and was now superseded by the Law of Christ. Frei Diogo replied that they (presumably his prison companions) were not learned (*não erão letrados*), nor were the inquisitors. He proceeded to enumerate his basic beliefs, by now familiar to the reader. Pero Domingues tried to implicate the two New Christians who were listening to Frei Diego's monologue, insinuating that they were sympathetic to what they heard because they failed to object. (He presumably knew that both were *negativos* accused of judaizing.) Moreover, he said, another New Christian in their part of the prison, Pero Gomes, also a *negativo*, told Frei Diogo that "he had been very glad to hear the dispute that he [Frei Diogo] had engaged in the other day." The informer said he did not know what this dispute was, but noted that Frei Diogo and Pero Gomes were on very friendly terms and shared secrets that he, Pero Domingues, did not understand.

Eleven days later, Miguel Siguet, an Old Christian merchant from Rouen, was granted an audience, at which he testified against "a young Capuchin friar whose name he did not know." Siguet's testimony is certainly self-serving. He presented himself as the only prisoner in the group who consistently sought to rebut Frei Diogo's heresies. But it is also quite detailed, and much of it has the ring of truth.[61] Siguet gave some particularly interesting testimony about Frei Diogo's vision of the messianic future. God had declared that in the days of the Messiah there would be general peace "between Moors and whites and blacks [*negros*]," there would be no more war, and "all the nations of the world would recognize and worship God." Since none of these things had occurred with the coming of Jesus—indeed, no nation had recognized Jesus in his lifetime, and he had been hanged between two thieves—it was clear that the Messiah had not yet come. The informer noted that Frei Diogo supported his theological arguments by quoting Scripture in Latin, which no one in the group apparently knew. He may have done this to impress his prison mates with his greater learning, and one suspects that it did not endear him to his companions.

At one point prior to their move in late August, Siguet reported, Frei Diogo had performed an act that seems to suggest his continuing intention to follow a path of martyrdom. Someone had written an inspirational inscription on the prison walls that read, "For one's country, honor, and property—fight! For Christ—die!" Frei Diogo had taken a bone and scraped away the word "Christ," writing in its place, using soot produced by candles, the word *"Deus* [God]." Siguet reported that he had objected to this act, declaring that "whoever fails to recognize the Son fails to recognize the Father." The friar reportedly replied that he would take the trouble to answer him if he, Siguet, knew Latin.

When asked about Frei Diogo's balance of mind, Siguet averred that the friar was perfectly sane. Although he sometimes spoke with anger, Siguet said, he understood this to be caused by "his great affection for the Law of Moses."

The inquisitors were expected to visit the prisoners in their cells from time to time, but such visits were rarely noted in the dossiers. However, a visit to the cell where Frei Diogo was being held together with Miguel Siguet, Pero Domingues, and two other Old Christians, on October 25, 1600, merited comment. When the friars entered the cell, Frei Diogo was wearing his cloth cowl (*barrete de pano*), which he failed to remove. The inquisitors ordered him to remove it, but he refused, saying that he paid reverence only to God. The inquisitors retorted "that God has ordered men to pay reverence to their superiors as well." He responded with some verses from Psalms that were not recorded. The inquisitors, turning the focus to the question that continued to trouble them, asked him how a person "raised on the milk of the Catholic Church, and a professing friar, could be a Jew." He replied, in Latin, "I have gone astray like a lost sheep"—alluding to his days as a Catholic—"seek thy servant, for I do not forget thy commandments."[62] No one, he said, had taught him to be a Jew. The inquisitors did not reply to this, but ordered two of the other prisoners to remove Frei Diogo's cowl.[63]

In December, Frei Diogo's prison companion Pero Domingues again asked for an audience. He was ready, for whatever reasons he had at the moment, to report the actions of Frei Diogo since his previous testimony in September. It is remarkable that he still did not know the friar's name, but identified him as a Capuchin friar, tall, thin, and without much beard. He reported a quarrel that had broken out concerning the doctrine of the Trinity between Frei Diogo and another prisoner, Miguel Fernandez de Luna, a Castilian Old Christian. Frei Diogo had become furious at the newcomer's unyielding attitude. Pero Domingues, Miguel Siguet, and an Old Christian prisoner accused of bigamy, Antonio Gomes Gorião, came to the Castilian's defense, telling Frei Diogo that he was a heretic and that if they had not been in prison they would have killed him for uttering such heresies. Frei Diogo responded with a torrent of blasphemous statements "for more than an hour." Such scenes were occurring repeatedly now, perhaps with provocations from both sides. The simmering tensions between Frei Diogo and his prison mates must have made life in prison more unpleasant than it already was, if not intolerable.[64]

About a week later the Castilian prisoner, Miguel Fernandez de Luna, testified against Frei Diogo.[65] Fernandez de Luna had been arrested in Tangiers (then under Portuguese rule) and brought to the Lisbon inquisitorial prison in mid-September, along with his wife and children, for trying to flee to Muslim North Africa, and was trying to convince the inquisitors to expedite his trial. Frei Diogo, who was by now regarded with general hostility by his companions, provided convenient material for a denunciation. Like Pero Domingues and Miguel Siguet, Miguel de Luna did not know the friar's name—because, as he put it, "he had never heard him called by name, nor did he [Frei Diogo] give or want to give his name when asked." According to Miguel de Luna's account, two months earlier he and Antonio Gomes Gorião had been transferred to the cell of Miguel Siguet, Pero Domingues, and the friar. On the first day he had spent in this new company, at supper, he began to pass the time with his companions discussing life in Tangiers. Among other things he had witnessed there, he related, he had seen openly professing Jews, and he noted "how abased [abatidos] they were." We can assume that by this time, the Castilian had already heard from Miguel Siguet and Pero Domingues just what the friar was doing in an inquisitorial prison, and what they thought of him. It seems probable that the Castilian's remarks about the Jews in Tangiers were thus a provocation aimed at Frei Diogo. In any case, Frei Diogo was stirred to reject the accepted Christian theological implications of Jewish subjugation. He declared that even if the Jews were abased, this condition would come to an end when God sent the Messiah, as he had promised, to govern the world. (He added, for good measure, that this scenario would not bring the world to an end, nor would it be accompanied by a Final Judgment.)

Having engaged Miguel de Luna polemically, Frei Diogo now asked the Castilian his trademark question, namely, how he invoked God's name. The Castilian replied that he invoked him as "God the Father, God the Son, and God the Holy Spirit, three 'persons' but one single God." At this, he reported, the friar became extremely irritated, and insisted that God should only be invoked as the God of Abraham, the God of Isaac, and the God of Jacob. Despite all of his and his companion's efforts to correct the friar, the Castilian said, the heretical Capuchin continued in his errors.

Half a year passed before another cellmate, the Old Christian Antonio Gomes Gorião (the accused bigamist), testified against Frei Diogo, with whom he had by now spent nine months in prison. His testimony reveals nothing we do not already know, with one exception. He reported that Frei Diogo (whom he knew by name) claimed to be the son of a Jewish woman from the line of David, and that his father was a relative of the kings of Portugal. Whether the friar had said this in a moment of grandiosity, or whether he had asserted it more consistently—or for that matter, whether he had said it at all—is impossible to know.[66]

We hear virtually nothing until almost a year later, when Frei Diogo was summoned to an audience on June 20, 1602.[67] He placed his hand on a breviary and swore "in the name of the almighty redeemer of the world, the God of Abraham, the God of Isaac, and the God of Jacob." At this audience, and indeed from this time on, he showed little of the impulsive anger he had shown in earlier audiences, and answered the inquisitors' questions with lucid statements punctuated by verses from Psalms. The inquisitor still believed the friar was withholding key information, and pressed him again about his ties to other persons. Once more Frei Diogo insisted that only God had taught him, offering a verse from Psalms (as always, in Latin) as a prooftext indicating that such isolated conversion was possible: "Give ear, O my people, to my teaching; incline your ears to the words of my mouth!"[68] He argued that just as God had given the Law to the Jews ("my people," as this verse puts it), he had given it to all the nations, as he made clear in a similar but different verse, "Give ear, O heavens, and I will speak; and let the earth"—*all* the earth—"hear the words of my mouth."[69]

Such an argument, however ingenious, was not likely to persuade a Portuguese inquisitor for whom direct illumination by God (or from Scripture) was a dubious claim even for a believing Christian. He asked Frei Diogo once more how it could have happened that a child of Christians, raised among Christians, could become a follower of the Law of the Jews, interpreting Scripture in a non-Christian spirit. It was true, Frei Diogo replied, that he had been born "a gentile and a son of gentiles." It was true that his father had no Jewish ancestry (though his mother had some), and that his parents had taught him to worship idols and believe in falsehoods, in the manner of "gentiles who are Christians." But God had converted his soul in the way Scripture describes when it declares, "He restores my soul, He leads me in paths of righteousness for his name's sake."[70] He, Frei Diogo, had come to understand Scripture as he did because that was how God had taught him how to understand it, just as Scripture says, "Thy word is a lamp to my feet and a light to my path."[71]

The inquisitor abandoned this line of questioning and turned to an issue that would play a part in the friar's eventual condemnation at the auto-da-fé. He wanted to know if, at the time of his early interrogations when he had confessed and expressed penitence, the friar had done so falsely, concealing his continued adherence to the Law of the Jews.

Frei Diogo's reply to this question may throw some light on the development of his thinking. At the time he expressed penitence, he said, *he was not yet a Jew.* Only afterward, when he was incarcerated in the inquisition cells, was he enlightened by God and became a Jew.

Given the friar's attacks on Christian doctrine from the moment he began to bare his soul to the fidalgo Diogo de Sousa, and his rejection of the authenticity of the New Testament, it is understandable that the inquisitor was not satisfied with this response. If it was true that he was not yet a Jew, he asked, why had the friar said he was, even before he entered the inquisition cells, and indeed even before he was arrested?

Frei Diogo replied "that he had *never said before he was incarcerated in these cells that he was a Jew* [my emphasis]." It was only true that he had criticized the sacraments and other aspects of Church tradition, as his confession indicated. But never, he insisted, had he said he was a Jew.

For Diogo de Sousa and the inquisitors, who naturally turned to the conventional taxonomy of heresy to identify Frei Diogo's beliefs, the friar must have seemed from the start to fit the category of "judaizer," at least in some ways, and this tentative conclusion must have been reinforced by his later behavior. But Frei Diogo saw things otherwise. A close reading of his early statements, along with his declaration to Manoel Correa on April 8, 1600, that he had been enlightened (as well as his subsequent actions), suggests a more complex story. When he fled his monastery, he had been in a state of confusion, not one of changed conviction. It was true that he no longer believed what the Church had taught him to believe. It was true that he believed that the Old Testament in its literal sense was the revealed word of God. But (however we are to understand this) he did not yet believe in "the God of Abraham, the God of Isaac, and the God of Jacob." It was only with his illumination experience, it appears, that he reestablished a relationship with God—only now it was with "the God of the Jews."

But to return to the audience of June 20, 1602, Frei Diogo may have been reconstructing his state of mind correctly when he said that at the time he confessed and expressed penitence he was not a Jew. But tracing the development of Frei Diogo's heretical beliefs was not the business of the inquisitors. Whether he had been a Jew or not, his confession was a false one, because he had not been a believing Catholic, either. The modern reader is thus left to speculate about the process by which the friar came to identify so fiercely with Judaism. The inquisitor moved on to the typical conclusion of all audiences with pertinacious heretics, urging him to abandon the "illusions of the devil" and return to the faith in which he had been baptized. Frei Diogo responded that the water with which he had been baptized did not have the power to save, that he was a Jew and would die a Jew. And he urged the inquisitors to convert to the Law of God, which was the Law of the Jews.

The summer passed without further interrogation. But the pace of the trial was about to pick up.

On September 3, 1602, a little more than three years after his initial arrest, Frei Diogo was summoned to an audience.[72] When he swore on a breviary, he said was doing so "by the words of God that were in that book, not those [added by] Augustine." (This was the formula he would henceforth use in taking his oath.) He appears to have been self-possessed, direct, and clear. He was asked if he recalled having confessed his sins to the tribunal and asking for pardon. He said he did, but that at that point he had not been enlightened [*allumiado*] as he was now in the

Law of Moses, in which he would live and die and be saved. When he was asked if he would like to see a priest to enlighten him, he repeated that he had already been enlightened, that he had no need for a priest. They could send him one if they wanted to, he said, but he acknowledged only God as his master.

Asked if he wished to be a Christian and observe the faith of Christ the Redeemer and obey the supreme pontiff, Frei Diogo replied that the Roman Church was not the "Church of God," because the Church of God was in Jerusalem and had been established by God, not by Constantine. For "unless the Lord builds the house, those who build it labor in vain" (Ps. 127:1).[73] And he did not want to obey the pope since to do so would be to ignore the advice of Scripture: "Put not your trust in princes, nor in a son of man, in whom there is no help" (Ps. 146:3).[74]

The inquisitors pressed: Who had taught him? Again, he said no person had taught him; his parents and relatives had taught him only lies and falsehoods and idolatry. He was admonished and taken to his cell. The inquisitors made a note that in this audience Frei Diogo had been calm and very sound in his mind.[75]

Having been admonished three times, and having more than satisfied the inquisitors that he was a pertinacious heretic, Frei Diogo now faced a new stage of his trial. The tribunal proceeded to draw up the *libelo*, the Portuguese equivalent of the Spanish *acusación*.[76] In early November, this document—a lengthy, detailed, fourteen-article summary of the evidence against him—was read to the prisoner. In conformity with the regulations, it concluded with a preliminary sentence that was subject to change if he showed a change of heart. He was declared an "apostate heretic . . . obstinate and pertinacious" who had incurred the penalties of excommunication, confiscation of his goods (a rather empty formality in the case of a Capuchin friar), dismissal from his order, denial of all ecclesiastical privileges, and relaxation to the secular arm.[77]

As was the rule, Frei Diogo was asked to respond on the spot. Ordinarily, a prisoner at this point would have just been confronted for the first time with the evidence the tribunal had gathered against him or her. In the case of Frei Diogo, however, there could have been little in the *libelo* that he did not expect, or that troubled him. He had already declared himself ready to die in the Law of Moses. And, unlike Luis Carvajal, he had not been lying to protect loved ones (if indeed he had any "loved ones"). The *libelo* was simply a summary of everything he had openly professed to believe, and of actions he had openly performed (including both his Jewish ritual observance and his "insolent" behavior toward the tribunal).

It may be recalled that at this point in Luis Carvajal's trial, the defendant for the most part tersely affirmed the accuracy of the accusations. Frei Diogo, however —with what might seem to be a striking obliviousness to the realities of his case— seized the opportunity to further expound his views to the inquisitors. He began by announcing that he contested all the accusations against him. As he proceeded to speak, however, it became clear that he did not deny the accuracy of those accusations. Rather, he denied the Inquisition's fundamental notions of criminality.

To the charge that, having been baptized, he had apostatized, "he confessed that he had been baptized and anointed with chrism," but he asserted that baptism "was nothing but being washed with a bit of water; that it was not a sacrament and did not save one's soul." After a while, the notary stopped recording Frei Diogo's words, noting simply that he "responded with many remarks to each article" of the *libelo*, entering into discussion of issues "about which he had not been specifically asked." Put more bluntly, Frei Diogo was preaching to the tribunal rather than defending himself against the charges. In an attempt to force him to focus his response, the inquisitor ordered that he be given a copy of the *libelo* and some paper, and asked him to respond in writing to each of the articles after returning to his cell. He was also asked to choose as a *procurador*—an inquisitorial official who served as an "adviser" to the accused—one of two persons named by the tribunal.[78] Frei Diogo replied that God was his *procurador*, and rejected both candidates because they did not adhere to "the Law of God that God gave to Moses."[79] (One of them was assigned anyway. Predictably, the friar did not cooperate with him.)

On November 6, 1602, Frei Diogo was summoned to an audience to respond verbally to the *libelo*, because he had failed to write down his answers to the charges. His verbal response is recorded in seventy dense pages of the dossier. Between the lines, we glimpse the sort of bizarre episode that sometimes resulted from the Inquisition's scrupulous adherence to regulations. Over the course of six audiences between November 6 and November 12, Frei Diogo "responded" to each of the articles of the *libelo* in lengthy discourses supported by verses from Scripture. The inquisitor interrupted him neither to question him nor to comment; there was little he had not heard before. Frei Diogo talked to his heart's content, and the notary dutifully recorded his statements.

On November 18, Frei Diogo was summoned to an audience.[80] He must have realized that his trial was drawing to a close, but made it clear that he was not open to invitations to return to the Church, and remarked pointedly that the inquisitors "had not been able to contradict him on any point."

There is a way in which, as we have noted, this remark was not unjustified. During the inquisitors' interaction with Frei Diogo, they never addressed the theological issues he raised head-on, but rather approached him as if his ideas were self-evidently erroneous. However, the friar's remark may also reflect his unrealistic interpretation of why they had listened in silence as he laid out his "case" in response to the *libelo*. That is, there was misunderstanding on both sides. It may be true that the inquisitors were not able to distance themselves enough from their own beliefs to address Frei Diogo's contentions directly, but it may well be that Frei Diogo did not have the social intuition or maturity to understand why they behaved as they did.

Whatever the case, the inquisitor soon turned to a different line of questioning. The tribunal still found it difficult to believe Frei Diogo had become "a Jew" on his own. The friar repeated that he had had no human mentor. "My father and my mother have forsaken me," he quoted (with a verse that perhaps expressed not only his theological alienation), "but the Lord will take me up."[81]

The inquisitor asked the friar if he would like to speak to a learned cleric, who might be able to remove his "doubts." The friar retorted that he had no doubts, and that he had no wish to speak to a priest who would tell him only falsehoods.

The inquisitor became more aggressive. Frei Diogo may have learned Psalms from his breviary, he said, but he didn't learn Jewish *ceremonies* from a breviary. Who, then, had taught him these ceremonies, and with whom had he communicated on this subject? Frei Diogo replied that the breviary did not contain information about Jewish ceremonies, but the Bible did.[82]

This brings us to an important question. Was Frei Diogo's observance of "the Law of God" based entirely on his reading of Scripture?

In fact, the friar's Jewish practices included a number of standard crypto-judaic customs that he could not have derived from the Bible. He fasted on Fridays—a crypto-Jewish custom with no basis in Scripture.[83] On that day he also cleaned his oil lamp and inserted a new wick. On Saturdays he wore a clean shirt, when he had one. He recited psalms without the Gloria Patri. All of these practices were common in the crypto-Jewish environment; some had rabbinic roots but none of them is to be found in Scripture.

Yet there are also indications that Frei Diogo was not familiar with some common crypto-Jewish practices. He did not, as we have seen, know that the Jewish calendar day began at sunset and ended at nightfall the following day. When he fasted on Friday, he did so *until Saturday.* Moreover, he knew nothing of Jewish holidays—even the most frequently observed of them among crypto-Jews, namely Yom Kippur, Passover, and the Fast of Esther. Much of his terminology, too, was alien to crypto-Jewish rhetoric—for example, his repeated claim to be "a son of the Church of Zion [*filho da igreja de Sion*]," or his preference for the term *the Law of God* over the conventional crypto-Jewish term, *the Law of Moses.* These facts would seem, in conjunction with other evidence from his dossier, to support two conclusions: first, that Frei Diogo was not a committed "judaizer" prior to his arrest; and second, that his disillusionment with the Church arose from a potent mix of professional jealousy and attentiveness to anti-Catholic and humanist currents in contemporary Europe.

These facts would also seem to support the conclusion that while Frei Diogo had at least two New Christian prison mates who were accused of judaizing, these companions were either falsely charged or were simply too prudent to give instruction to a person like Frei Diogo. Let us suppose it is true that one of these New Christians removed the fat from his meat—a crypto-Jewish practice—as an Old Christian prisoner reported in a denunciation. It may then also be true that Frei Diogo, as reported, followed his example. But denunciations of fellow prisoners were of dubious reliability, particularly when they were as generic and vague as this one, and were not supported by the testimony of others.

How, then, if Frei Diogo had not been taught by crypto-Jews, did he learn the non-biblical Sabbath practices that he himself admitted to performing? And why did the inquisitors not confront him with his non-biblical practices, when he claimed to have learned them only from the Bible? The most obvious explanation is that the kind of "judaizing" practices Frei Diogo observed in prison were widely known in Iberian society. Information about judaizing (not always accurate) was disseminated in various ways—through rumor, gossip, and jokes; through auto-da-fé sermons and sentences that were read aloud at autos-da-fé; and through the edicts of faith that were read to parishioners to enable them to recognize "Jewish" acts.[84] Given this situation, it seems unlikely that the inquisitors were troubled by the fact that Frei Diogo *knew* about basic Jewish practices. The piece of the puzzle that eluded them was his *motivation*, which seemed impossible to explain in the absence of crypto-Jewish family members or tutors.

Frei Diogo, then, almost certainly knew about certain crypto-Jewish practices without ever having wittingly met a crypto-Jew. He may have absorbed lore about these practices in such a casual way that he himself was unaware of possessing extra-biblical Jewish knowledge. Yet it is likely that this previously inconsequential lore played a significant role during that pivotal conversion experience in prison that he described as his "illumination"—a moment in which the destructive forces that had been unleashed by his anger and his uncompromising nature were creatively redirected, allowing him to overcome feelings of loathing about Judaism, bringing him back into intimate contact with God, giving order to a shattered theological universe, and providing him with a new religious community (if only imagined) that rendered his ancestral "stain" a virtue.

Frei Diogo was not called to an audience for another two months. Finally, on January 21, 1603, he requested one.[85] The entry is unclear; perhaps his train of thought was unclear. He alluded to a previous session and the opportunity he had had to formulate written responses, but then began to expound on the way Scripture associated God's word with wisdom, quoting a series of verses including some from the apocryphal Book of Wisdom, "Set your desire on my words, long for them and you will be instructed. Wisdom is clear and unfading."[86] He regarded these verses, apparently, as new "evidence" to persuade the inquisitor that a straightforward reading of the Bible (i.e., Old Testament) was sufficient to illuminate a person in the truth.

The inquisitor may have thought that Frei Diogo, who had adopted a pious, not a belligerent, tone, was fishing for an opportunity to reconcile his beliefs with those of the Church. While naturally not disputing that Scripture was the revealed word of God, he guided the friar by explaining that the true precepts of God were given "by the mouth of God incarnate, who is the Messiah promised in the Law, Christ our redeemer." He gave a rather long speech about God's mercy and the many miracles performed in the name of Jesus Christ. (On this subject he mentioned that no Jew while still a Jew had ever performed a miracle, while many Jews who had converted to Christianity had performed miracles.)

The inquisitor was soon disabused of any hopes that Frei Diogo had experienced a change of heart. The friar's immediate response to the inquisitor's benevolent speech was that "everything preached by the Church of Rome was a fraud [*fingido*], and that God hated fraud and falsehood," quoting some appropriate verses by way of demonstration. Yet he soon turned to "all the questions" of the tribunal that he had been asked to answer in writing. The inquisitor cut him short and ordered the prisoner taken to his cell.

The reader of Frei Diogo's dossier cannot help but be astonished by what appears next, beneath the entry for this session, beside the signature of the inquisitor, Manuel Álvarez Tavares. In the place to the right of the inquisitor's signature where the friar invariably signed his name as "frei dº dasumpcão," in a neat, crabbed hand, he signed this time "Christus Dominus."[87] When the scandalized inquisitor saw this (perhaps informed by the notary), he ordered Frei Diogo to return and sign "in the manner he usually did." The friar at first refused. Then, however, appearing to assent, he took the pen in hand. But he "complied" in his own way. After the words "Christus Dominus" he wrote, "who is the very same Frei Diogo d'Asumpção [*q he o mesmo frei dº dasumpcão*]."

The inquisitor's understanding of this action may reflect psychological insight. But it could also reflect a tactical decision. He minimized the scandal by noting that earlier in the trial, in one of his many provocative remarks, Frei Diogo had declared that "every saintly man is Christ." Yet in this case the friar had not written *Christ*—a word that he routinely reduced to its literal, quotidian meaning—but "Christ our Lord." This, then, was either the revelation of a profound delusion, or a bizarre expression of blasphemy and contempt for the tribunal. We can only speculate why the inquisitor chose to see it as the latter. He concluded that Frei Diogo was driven to this act by the anger he felt (the inquisitor had seen it) when he was cut short and ordered sent back to his cell, rather than be allowed to hold the tribunal captive to his pronouncements. Of course it may be that the inquisitor sensed a dynamic in the chamber that is lost to a reader of the opaque dossier entry. But it may also be that he wanted to make sure that new questions did not arise about the prisoner's sanity.

From late 1602 through the spring of 1603, the Lisbon tribunal collected evidence about Frei Diogo's behavior during the years when he was in the Capuchin order. Three friars who had known him presented testimony. Their statements are worth examining in some detail for the light they throw on Frei Diogo and the motives of the people around him.

The first piece of testimony was a written statement by Frei Diogo da Conceição, the superior of the Capuchin monastery in Lisbon, the monastery in which Frei Diogo had resided when he entered the order.[88] This septuagenarian offered a narrative that was also, it would seem, an attempt to offer some kind of explanation for Frei Diogo's apostasy. Frei Diogo had entered the monastery in July 1593, along with Frei Jeronimo Fagundez, a childhood friend, who was now pursuing higher studies at a *colegio* in Coimbra, and Frei Pedro de Piedade. The three young men had served their year as novices, he recalled, and prepared to take their vows. They were told that if at any time it should be discovered that they had any New Christian, Muslim, or heretical ancestors, their status as "professed" monks would be nullified. At the time, the information in the monastery's hands showed Frei

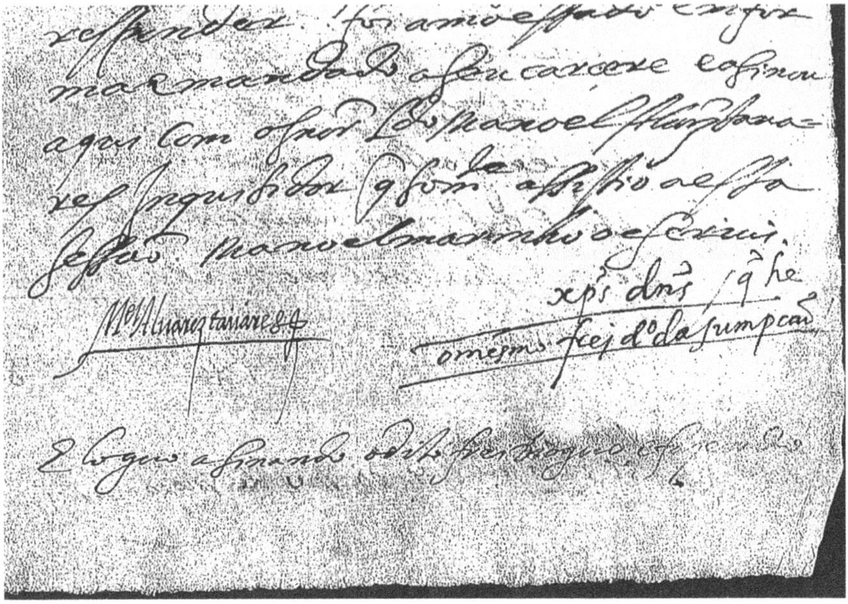

Figure 6. Signature of Diogo d'Asumpção, "Christus Dominus," ratifying the notary's record of an audience on January 21, 1603. ANTT, Inquisição de Lisboa, processo 140, fo. 181r. Arquivo Nacional de Torre do Tombo, Lisbon.

Diogo to be free of any such ancestry. (Inquiries into "purity of blood" by the orders were not, however, always rigorous.)[89] After taking his vows, he spent three or four years in the monastery, then transferred to the Castanheira monastery. He was well behaved and respected there. Serving in the infirmary, he cared for the ill with "much charity and love," and received the orders of *epístola* and of *evangelho*.[90]

The elderly friar then sketched the events that, as he saw it, had brought about a change in Friar Diogo. A young friar named Frei Francisco das Chagas, who like Frei Diogo was a native of Viana de Caminha, had entered the order some time after Frei Diogo. He must have known from local gossip about Frei Diogo's "impure" lineage, and at the monastery he called Frei Diogo either *judeu* or *cristão novo*—the old cleric could not remember which. This accusation was apparently ignored by the authorities, since Frei Diogo was not dismissed from the order. Subsequently, about a year and a half before Frei Diogo fled the convent, both Francisco das Chagas and Jeronimo Fagundez received the order of *missa*, permitting them to celebrate mass. Frei Diogo did not receive the *missa*, despite the fact that he was two or three years older than Frei Jeronimo.[91] Angered, he asked (or more likely demanded) that he also be ordained to celebrate mass. But, the deponent wrote, it was not the rule in the order to grant ordination on request, and the petition was denied. Frei Diogo complained publicly and appealed, but to no avail. This was the background, Frei Diogo's former superior implied, to the friar's flight from the monastery. After Frei Diogo was returned to the monastery and incarcerated, he, Frei Diogo da Conceição, ordered a certain Frei Miguel to speak to Frei Diogo. When they met, Frei Diogo said he repented what he had done and wanted to confess. Frei Diogo da Conceição had also spoken to Frei Diogo and admonished him. He could thus state that Frei Diogo was then, as he had always known him to be, of sound mind.

Another elderly Capuchin named Frei Belchior, a member of the governing hierarchy of the order (he was the definitor of the province of Santo Antonio), was interrogated about Frei Diogo's behavior prior to his flight.[92] At the Capuchin monastery in Lisbon, he had met Frei Diogo when the young friar, serving in the infirmary, had cared for him during an illness, and had known him since. Frei Belchior's testimony was quite similar to that of Frei Diogo da Conceição. It seems possible that these two senior members of the Capuchin order had discussed how they would present the case before the Inquisition. Frei Diogo's apostasy was, after all, a sensitive matter: it reflected badly on the order, and as leaders of the order they had a strong interest in depicting it as an isolated case, a sudden aberration in a friar whose behavior had not previously shown any signs of deviance.

Like Frei Diogo da Conceição, Frei Belchior stressed that Frei Diogo had always been a conscientious friar, of perfectly sound mind. As such, he had been granted the orders of *epístola* and *evangelho*. But, Frei Belchior added, pointing to the same series of events that Frei Diogo da Conceição had singled out, a change had come over him. He related how Frei Francisco das Chagas had called Frei Diogo *christão novo* or *judeu* (he, too, could not recall which), and how Frei Diogo had become agitated (*se inquietara*) after Frei Francisco das Chagas and Frei Jeronimo Fagundez were given the promotion he was denied—that is, permission to celebrate mass. While it was true that Frei Diogo was of sound mind, he testified, he tended to be "impatient and choleric." He recalled that at the time Frei Diogo was about to be transferred from the monastery cell to the inquisitorial prison, he, Frei Belchior, had met with him, along with a few other friars. Frei Diogo, understanding that he was about to be handed over to the Inquisition, began to behave inappropriately, uttering mocking words and making faces. When the friars told him to cease behaving this way, however, he complied.

The third of Frei Diogo's monastic colleagues to testify was Jeronimo Fagundez, whose promotion, along with that of Frei Francisco das Chagas, had triggered Frei Diogo's rage. He now went by his spiritual name, Frei Jeronimo de Jesus, but there is no doubt that these are one and the same person.[93] In January 1603 he sent an unsolicited letter to the Lisbon tribunal from Coimbra, where he was studying at a Franciscan *colegio*.[94] He was, he said, a childhood friend of Frei Diogo from Viana de Caminha. He had studied Latin with Frei Diogo in Braga and had taken the Capuchin habit with him at the Capuchin monastery in Lisbon. He and Frei Diogo had done their novitiate together, were professed together (i.e., took vows), and began their advanced studies (*artes*) together. But then Frei Diogo had "become blinded by the deceptions of the devil [*por engaño de demonio o cegou*]."

Frei Jeronimo recalled having reproved his friend for "certain offenses he had committed against the perfection and purity of the order" (*contra a perfeição e pureza da religião*)—offenses that were known to the entire monastery, but that did not involve matters of faith (presumably he was alluding to the rage Frei Diogo had shown when he was denied the privilege of celebrating mass). Because he knew Frei Diogo "better than anyone in the province"—he had known him for fifteen or sixteen years, he wrote—and because Frei Diogo "believed no one loved him as much as he did," the ambitious young friar asked the tribunal to grant him an opportunity to visit with him alone, in order to persuade him to behave properly (as he had succeeded in doing many times before, he wrote, when others had failed).

He described with lengthy pathos the pain Frei Diogo's apostasy had caused him. He had wished to help, but feared that this wish might appear presumptuous. However, he had fallen very ill, and suspected the illness was punishment for his failure to act on Frei Diogo's behalf. He was therefore asking the tribunal to allow him to meet with Frei Diogo alone "for as long as this spiritual battle might last," a service he offered "for the honor of God and with zeal to save that soul."

After reading this letter and reflecting on the circumstances surrounding the passing over of Frei Diogo (including the charge of impure blood), one begins to wonder whether perhaps Frei Diogo *was* caught in a web of lies and hypocrisy around the issue of his advancement. Frei Jeronimo's self-serving letter does, in any case, throw Frei Diogo's vituperation into a somewhat different light. Could this calculating and self-absorbed young friar really believe that Frei Diogo would be glad to see him?

The inquisitors, whatever their considerations might have been, responded favorably to the request. Frei Jeronimo de Jesus appeared before the tribunal on March 26, 1603, having been granted permission to make the trip by his superior (who happened to be Frei Diogo da Conceição). Frei Jeronimo reported that he had known Frei Diogo's parents very well (his mother had since died), and had always assumed them to be Old Christians. Diogo's father, Jorge Velho Travassos, was from Cantanhede, where he had been a merchant for some period. He had moved to Viana de Caminha after being appointed to an office in the custom house (*alfandega*) in that town. It was only after entering the Capuchin order that Frei Jeronimo heard some of the monks say that Frei Diogo's father had New Christian ancestry (*tinha raça de christão novo*). Once while he was at the Capuchin monastery in Lisbon, he had heard Frei Francisco das Chagas, who now lived in a convent in Viseu, call Frei Diogo a New Christian. Both Frei Jeronimo and Frei Diogo had left the Lisbon convent some three and a half years after they had been professed, during an outbreak of plague, and had gone to the monastery in Castanheira.

While he was at the monastery in Castanheira, Frei Jeronimo continued, he had bought a book for his uncle, Baltasar Vaz Fagundez, the vicar-general of Vila

Map 2. Early-seventeenth-century Portugal, with locations important to the career of Diogo d'Asumpção.

Real. This was a certain work by Marcus de la Camara, published in Madrid in 1587, that dealt with apparent contradictions and difficulties in Scripture.[95] Frei Diogo had asked Frei Jeronimo if he could borrow it, and Frei Jeronimo had agreed. "He almost didn't want to return it," Frei Jeronimo remarked, "but he did."

Echoing the testimony of his superiors, Frei Jeronimo stated that it was generally believed that Frei Diogo had fled the monastery because he did not receive permission to celebrate mass. He asserted that as long as he had known him, Frei Diogo had been "a very Christian man" and had been devoted to healing the sick. He said Frei Diogo had always been of sound mind for as long as he had known him. It was true that he angered easily, but Frei Jeronimo understood this to be a family trait, because the members of Frei Diogo's family "were all bold and impudent [animosos e atrevidos]."

On April 3, Frei Jeronimo de Jesus met with Frei Diogo, and reported briefly to the Inquisition.[96] As might be expected, nothing had been accomplished.

But Frei Jeronimo had more to say. On April 15, after he had returned to Coimbra (and, one suspects, discussed the matter with Frei Diogo da Conceição), he wrote a letter to the inquisitor, adding some details to what he had reported after his visit to Frei Diogo's cell.[97] He mentioned, for example, that Frei Diogo had told him that the book by Marcos de la Camara was a "stupid book" (libro parvo), because God had no contradictions. But he seems to have had another reason for writing the letter.

He opened the matter delicately. "There is only one thing," he wrote, "that I would advise you—not to be giving you counsel, for I well know with whom I'm speaking, but just to express my view." When he, like so many before him, had asked Frei Diogo who had indoctrinated him, Frei Diogo responded that God had. There was nothing new in this. But Frei Jeronimo added that

> without a doubt he told me he did so in dreams, because God was accustomed to talking to his [cherished ones] in this way, as in the case of Joseph. From this and other hints [conjecturas], I inferred that without doubt the devil spoke to him in dreams. In the monastery he was accustomed to speak in his dreams, very loudly and with great vehemence. Indeed I once chastised him sharply, saying that he should never become a confessor, because he would reveal the confessions [he had heard, in his sleep]; and he became very angry at this.

If it was true, as he believed, that Frei Diogo was possessed by the devil, then "the most efficacious remedy, from what he knew" was exorcism.

It seems rather likely that there was more behind this letter than loving concern for a childhood friend and fellow friar. After all, Frei Diogo had been arrested in August 1599, but Frei Jeronimo had waited until January 1603 before contacting the Inquisition. One suspects that fear of scandal was behind the sudden flurry of activity, beginning with Frei Diogo da Conceição's letter of December 1602. Reading the entire series of letters and spoken statements, one is struck by the fact that no one at the monastery seemed to have had an inkling that Frei Diogo was harboring heretical thoughts, despite his general impulsiveness and despite the fact that the presumptive "cause" of his apostasy—his denial of permission to celebrate mass—had occurred a year and a half before his flight. Implicit in the inquisitors' badgering of Frei Diogo for information about his mentors was the unspoken question, What *else* was going on within the Capuchin order? Frei Diogo himself had claimed, in his outpouring of discontent to Diogo de Sousa, that many of his colleagues believed as he did, but maintained their silence for reasons of expedience. But the issue of possible theological ferment among the friars was avoided by the Capuchin witnesses.

This is not to say that the "master narrative," so to speak, of the Capuchin witnesses had no basis in fact. It may very well be—indeed, it seems altogether plausible—that the combination of (mostly) unarticulated racial discrimination, career frustration, and envy of his favored peers stirred Frei Diogo to question and then to attack the foundations of the institution that had injured him. What seems suspicious is the apparent effort to contain the potential damage by focusing on the particularities of Frei Diogo's personality, ancestry, and experience (not his theological ideas), and the suggestion that the problem could be resolved through an exorcism. It may be, too, that even as late as the turn of the seventeenth century, the early scandal of the Capuchins—the defection of their great preacher Bernardino Ochino in 1542 to the Protestant movement—remained a source of insecurity, and encouraged something of a siege mentality among the leadership when heterodoxy emerged in their ranks.

Amid the pages of testimony by outside witnesses—remarkably few in number—there is an undated memorandum by a certain Frei Paulo Foreiro, probably in the role of *qualificador*. This theologian had been summoned to examine Frei Diogo and to assess the nature of his crime or crimes.[98] As he discovered in his meeting with the friar, this was no easy task, not only because Frei Diogo's beliefs fit no clear-cut category, but because the prisoner unleashed the full measure of his wrath on the visitor.

The report is a curious blend of analysis and description. It opens with the conclusion that Frei Diogo was a "heretic of the Jewish perfidy," but immediately qualifies that straightforward conclusion by noting that the friar adhered to "the error of the Saduccees" insofar as he denied the resurrection of the body. Yet he was not a true Saducee, because he did not deny the immortality of the soul as the Saducees did.

It was also an "error of Judaism," the theologian continued, that Frei Diogo claimed to be Christ and the Messiah. When he had said this was not possible in light of what Scripture taught, Frei Diogo became "impatient" with him and refused to justify his own position. He did argue, however, that Lisbon was at the center of the world, and that Scripture stated that "God would bestow salvation and redemption at the center of the earth." Such a statement bears consideration. Frei Diogo, we have already seen, was adept at bringing to play in his mind, in the process of creating a reasonably coherent personal theology, very diverse materials, including several perfectly orthodox post-Tridentine Catholic works. His effort to defend his status as Messiah—his claim that Lisbon was the "center of the world" where the Messiah would appear—may reflect the impact on his fertile, absorbent mind of a particularly Portuguese form of messianism known as Sebastianism. An important aspect of Sebastian messianism was, like that of the friar, the expectation of world peace. A Sebastian element in his thinking might also help to explain the genealogical claim he had earlier made to his Old Christian cellmate Antonio Gomes, namely that Frei Diogo's mother was descended from King David, and that *his father was a relative of the kings of Portugal*—perhaps a more meaningful statement than one would have thought.[99]

Like others who had testified, Frei Paulo Foreiro found that the prisoner was of sound mind. His *impaciencias e furores* were not capricious, but occurred when he was shown clearly to be in the wrong.[100] He had become confused and ashamed (*corrido*), for example, when Frei Paulo showed him a passage in Jeremiah that he, Frei Diogo, had claimed did not exist. When the theologian had admonished him to conduct himself with more control and respect, he responded that there were things that could not be suffered and that he could not reply to with less vehemence. He asked for the warden (presumably to take him back to his cell), saying that no one had angered him or scandalized him more than he, Frei Paulo Foreiro.

Given his *furias* and *disputas,* Frei Paulo wrote, one might be persuaded that he was insane (*alienado*)—particularly since he was given to saying that he was the Messiah and Christ, and that God revealed himself and spoke to him. Yet this did not persuade him that Frei Diogo was insane. He believed, rather, that the devil had reached him. He, the devil, had not turned him into a demoniac, but had rather deluded and persuaded him of his heretical ideas. God, he wrote, often permitted this to happen to persons who had sinned, who were alone for a long period, and who had become susceptible to the "enemy." He himself knew of cases in which such persons had lost their belief in God. In Germany and England, where people were corrupted (*estragado*) and exposed to the devil, it happened frequently that they were persuaded of heretical things; some even became atheists.

But he also believed Frei Diogo had been indoctrinated by a person or persons in his Jewish beliefs and in his understanding of the Old Testament. The apostate defended the Law of Moses "not like a fool," but like a person trained in principles, quoting verses that were not in the breviary. He also spoke like a person trained in principles in his attack on the Catholic faith and the monastic life, which made it probable that in these matters, too, he had been taught by someone. Yet in his attack on the Church, he seemed more like a *luterano* than a Jew. Frei Paulo resolved the problem raised by the apparent lack of consistency in Frei Diogo's views: Ultimately, he wrote, the devil was Diogo's schoolmaster for both these heretical inclinations. He concluded that Frei Diogo was "essentially a Jewish heretic" who held "many other adjunct errors."

One is struck by Frei Paulo Foreiro's efforts to arrive at a "diagnosis" in this case without ignoring the apparent contradictions, in light of the accepted taxonomy of the Inquisition. Frei Diogo's uncontrolled rage, and his belief that he communicated with God, might suggest that he was not of sound mind. But in his thinking he was entirely coherent. Frei Paulo made a distinction between the raving demoniacs, who might be cured by exorcism, and the great majority of "heretics" in the Europe of his day, in whom one could detect the subtle machinations of the devil only in their theology. He did not ignore the elements of *luteranismo* in Frei Diogo's thinking, but hastened to draw a clear distinction between those aspects of his thought that were "Jewish" (his adoption of the Law of Moses and his reading of the Old Testament) and those that were "*luterano*" (his attack on the Church and on the monastic life). However inadequate his analysis may seem from a modern historian's point of view, it reveals an empirical honesty and intellectual sophistication rarely displayed by functionaries of the Inquisition.

On May 16, 1603, Frei Diogo was again summoned to an audience.[101] He was solemnly advised that if he would return to the Church, the tribunal would deal with him mercifully. Even if Frei Diogo had believed that such "mercy" would save him from the stake—he was surely not so naïve—it would have been an act of sheer psychic self-destruction for a person with such a brittle personality to capitulate. His self-esteem was now entirely bound up with his role of resistance and martyrdom.

He replied that "the only counsel he took was from God, who ordered that he should continue to observe the Law of Moses. And he was observing it because the Lord had ordered him to observe it, as it is written, 'Thou hast commanded thy precepts to be kept diligently.' "[102]

The inquisitor urged Frei Diogo to waste no time in returning to the Church, "because if he did not do so, he would be castigated with the full rigor of the law, which in this case is very great." Frei Diogo declared that he would remain "a Jew," and was immediately ordered to be taken back to his cell.

A month later, in an audience of June 16, he was offered the same opportunity. When he rejected it, the notary proceeded to read the lengthy charges against him. This was not a repetition of the *libelo;* this time the names of the witnesses and other identifying details were supplied.[103] He was asked if the contents were accurate. He said they were. He was asked if he wanted to challenge them or to see his *procurador*, and he declined.

On July 3, six inquisitors signed the *sentença*. Frei Diogo was found guilty of apostasy and heresy. He was sentenced to be defrocked and relaxed to the secular arm.[104] The document was sent for approval to the *Conselho geral*—the highest governing body of the Portuguese Inquisition. It was approved, but with two stipulations: Frei Diogo, when he was taken to the auto-da-fé, should be muzzled, and "his *sentença* [which would be read publicly at the auto] should mention that he has New Christian ancestry [*que tem raça de christão novo*]."[105] It is surprising that Frei Diogo's ancestry was not mentioned in the original document. The *Conselho geral* was no doubt anxious to include a piece of information that could "explain" the culprit's malfeasance.

On July 10, Frei Diogo was brought from his cell and was informed of the verdict against him of "heresy and apostasy."[106] He said he had nothing to say.

Figure 7. Image of the burning of heretics at the stake in Lisbon in 1682. From Bernard Picart, *Ceremonies et coutumes religieuses de tous les peples du monde* (Amsterdam 1723), vol. 2, p. 64. The Jewish Theological Seminary. Picart's image is copied from "Auto-da-fé no Terreiro do Paço" (Lisbon, c. 1682), printed by Michael Geddes, an Anglican cleric who spent the years 1678–1688 in Lisbon, where he himself was harassed by the Inquisition.

On Friday, August 1, 1603, Frei Diogo was notified that he would be relaxed to the secular arm after the auto-da-fé that would take place two days later, on Sunday, August 3. His hands were immediately tied—presumably to prevent him from trying to take his life—and he was assigned two Jesuit priests who would stay with him to console and try to convert him.

From this point on, Frei Diogo's voice is not heard from the pages of the dossier. We have no key to his thoughts as he was taken, muzzled, to the auto-da-fé held in the central plaza known as the Terreiro do Paço (today the Praça do Comércio), overlooking the Tejo River. The viceroy Christoção de Moura was present, along with a large crowd, to view the dramatic event at which 153 penitents were sentenced and seven persons relaxed to the secular arm.[107]

One wonders whether Frei Diogo took some degree of pleasure in hearing his lengthy *sentença* read. As a summary of his heterodox "career," it was reasonably accurate, although it did not spell out Frei Diogo's convictions about how Scripture should be interpreted. (It stated only that he had recited "a great many verses and passages of Scripture, which he understood badly.")

The reading of the *sentença* undoubtedly played a role in establishing Frei Diogo's posthumous reputation among crypto-Jews and Portuguese Jews. One passage in particular stands out. Efforts had been made to persuade him, it stated, by

> many important, virtuous, and learned *religiosos* of his own order [*religião*], as well as others of other orders, yet he remained in his errors. . . . And he said that he had no need of *padres* to guide him, because he did not follow the doctrine of men, but of God, and that he had been enlightened. Always obstinate and pertinacious, he remained in his Judaism and apostasy, defending his errors and wanting to persuade the persons with whom he spoke, as well as the above-mentioned *religiosos,* whom he said had strayed from the Law of God.[108]

Presented thus, he was the very model of the dogmatista martyr.

The tribunal appears to have accepted Frei Diogo's claim that he had not adhered to "Judaism" prior to his imprisonment. This may have been in part a face-saving gesture on behalf of his order. While his "Judaism" was mentioned in the narrative part of the *sentença*, it was notably absent from the final paragraph giving the verdict and sentence: he was found guilty of being a "heretic" and a "pertinacious apostate," but not of being a *judaizante.* Nor was he explicitly judged to be a *luterano.* He was, however, condemned for his "false opinions and *new heresies* [*falsas opiniões e novas herejias*]"[109]—a clear allusion to his "Protestantish" opinions.

The final, brief entry in the dossier tells us nothing about events at the *quemadero*, beyond the comment that Frei Diogo "died by being burned alive."[110] We can be sure, however, that he had been given the chance to make a gesture of contrition, which would have allowed him to be garroted. He was apparently combative to the end.

Five days after the auto-da-fé, a certain Francisco Fernandes, described as "half New Christian," appeared before the Lisbon tribunal to make a confession. At the time of the auto or just afterwards, he had been staying at an inn. Some other travelers, discussing this noteworthy event, made some remarks about the judaizers who were burned at the stake, in particular "the Capuchin friar who was burned as a Jew," and expressed approval at this mode of punishment for such people. Fernandes, who had perhaps downed a glass or two, retorted that "it was truly a shame to see such a holy friar burned alive," and that "God would have mercy on this friar and on the others who were burned." As for those who remained alive, he added (presumably referring to accused judaizers who had confessed, repented, and been reconciled to the Church), "God would illuminate them and give them knowledge of the truth so they would not be damned."[111]

A Franciscan friar, Frei Antonio d'Abrunhosa, was denounced in December 1603 for remarks of a different kind about the burning of the celebrated heretic. He criticized the Inquisition for what he saw as an act of unwarranted cruelty. In his opinion, "the friar they burned in the last auto-da-fé [i.e., Diogo d'Asumpção] was crazy [*doudo*]."[112]

Did Frei Diogo arrive at his beliefs alone, relying on a few unlikely works of impeccable Catholic orthodoxy?

The apostate friar may well have taken the path he did by himself, at least in a social sense. There is no evidence that he had contacts with crypto-Jews before or during his imprisonment. There is no evidence that other members of his family were suspected of judaizing (he had six living brothers, one of whom was a priest, yet none of the four who were living in Portugal was summoned to testify before the Inquisition.)[113] His denial that he had been instructed by other persons may or may not have been true, but there is no evidence that he had mentors, crypto-Jewish or otherwise. It is true that his life was commemorated by Jews outside the Peninsula, that a judaizing confraternity was founded in his memory in Coimbra,[114] and that other judaizers in the Coimbra area also apparently venerated his memory.[115] But his posthumous fame among conversos does not prove that he had connections to a crypto-Jewish network in his lifetime. The fact that he turned for help to a stranger who happened to be a New Christian (and evidently *not* a crypto-Jew) seems good evidence to the contrary. In fact, it may be misleading to call him a crypto-Jew at all.

Yet Frei Diogo was clearly *aware* of crypto-judaizing. In Portugal at the time, crypto-Jews were virtually the only "networked" group disseminating a compelling counter-Catholic teaching. The very existence of such opposition to the Church may have given plausibility to the idea that the true Law of God was that of the Old Testament. Entertaining this idea may also have been piqued, in a paradoxical sort of way, by the insult he suffered when he was accused of being a "Jew" or a "New Christian" by a fellow novice. (He may not have known until then about the ancestral blemish his family sought to conceal.) But his developing convictions about "the Law that God gave the Jews" were a logical extension of his thinking, not yet a concrete possibility for living. Taking the radical step of becoming a judaizer may have been a leap that required a deepening of his crisis, perhaps involving his overcoming lingering negative associations concerning Jews and Judaism.

In any case, although he was reevaluating Judaism in a positive light at the time he fled the monastery, he was not seeking to flee to a Jewish community. He told the fidalgo that he wanted to flee to England, France, or the Netherlands—to a place, as he said, where he could "live in freedom." The remark is eloquent for what it is missing. What religion did he intend to practice? If Judaism, why didn't he say so, since he was speaking with such abandon? And if Judaism, why flee to England, France, or the Netherlands? In 1599 there was as yet no Jewish community in the Netherlands, and Judaism could not be openly practiced in France or England.

One wonders whether, had Frei Diogo reached the relatively free soil of northern Europe, he would have joined the Protestant ranks, as other Iberian clerics had done,[116] or (more likely) associated with a group of radical sectarians. Certainly he could have found a place among people who shared his convictions that "it was not necessary to petition saints, but only God; and that the popes and councilors did not understand Scripture, creating and following human laws and calling them divine; and that the [holy] orders were not [divinely ordained] orders, nor was the mass a sacrament, nor was the sacrament of communion more than bread; . . . nor was a man obligated to confess to another man but only to God, and that everything [else] was the invention of men." Outside Iberian lands, moreover, no one would have cared that he had a distant Jewish ancestor. In such circumstances, he would not have felt so intense a need to create an idealized identity around this socially degrading aspect of his genealogy.

At the time of his flight, Frei Diogo suggested that other friars shared his criticisms of the Church. As he put it (in the notary's third person), "The monasteries don't have the sanctity they seem to outsiders to possess, and some friars in the monasteries hold the same ideas that he [Frei Diogo] does. But in order to continue eating and drinking in the monasteries, and so as not to disturb themselves, they don't reveal [their thoughts] as he has."[117] It is true that during this interview Frei Diogo was feigning penitence and seeking to minimize his own transgressions. Yet Diogo de Sousa remembered him making very similar comments during the friar's unrestrained outpouring at the fidalgo's estate.[118]

How are we to understand such statements? Was the Capuchin monastery in Castanheira a breeding ground for religious discontent and controversy? Or was Frei Diogo exaggerating for effect? Unfortunately, the eighteenth-century chronicle that devotes a chapter to this institution offers no clues.[119] In general, the religious landscape of sixteenth-century Portugal has not yet been delineated by scholars in more than a skeletal fashion. The monasteries, as elsewhere in Europe, were in a state of great decadence. But the Capuchins in Portugal appear to have maintained a relatively high degree of discipline, and were not associated with the kind of corruption prevalent among the Conventual Franciscans, a less rigorous branch of the Franciscan order. Indeed, they were regarded as being in the vanguard of Catholic reform in Portugal, as elsewhere. Interestingly, in view of Frei Diego's claims of having been enlightened by God, they were also known to be prominent in illuminist circles in Portugal. But existing scholarship gives us too vague a picture of Frei Diogo's monastic context to draw even tentative conclusions about his cryptic remarks.[120]

The many denunciations of people in sixteenth-century Portugal for expressing "Protestantish" notions like those of Frei Diogo attest to the fact that such ideas were widely known, even among people who did not defend them. Like crypto-Jews, Iberian critics of the Church developed formulaic, concrete aphorisms and sayings that were intended to deflate the Church's regime and give them the satisfaction of secret rhetorical triumph—a feature of dissident discourse in all repressive societies. Frei Diogo seems to have been more familiar with anticlerical, antisacramental rhetoric than he was with crypto-Jewish rhetoric—though it is risky to draw conclusions in this realm.

It is worth noting that in his exposition of his beliefs to the fidalgo, Diogo d'Asumpção echoed a statement attributed to a Portuguese Old Christian two generations earlier. Frei Diogo stated that the Law of Christ could not be good because the Eucharist could not be performed for the *negros* and other peoples in lands that lacked consecrated bread and wine. We learn that this idea was in circulation from a denunciation of 1545, in which Fernão de Pina, a fidalgo and man of letters, was accused of stating, among other things, that if the Catholic doctrine of the Eucharist were true, "there would be no God in those places that lacked flour, priests, and wine."[121] Frei Diogo's claim that Jesus was a fraud and an imposter was one with a very long history, and could have come from radical currents in Portugal that were isolated from crypto-Jewish sources, though crypto-Jews may well have contributed.[122] Perhaps as scholars continue to sift through the vast evidence, Frei Diogo's barbed rhetoric will prove to have deeper roots in Portuguese society than we can detect today.

The Lisbon inquisitors concluded (many times) that Frei Diogo was entirely sane. The criterion they repeatedly applied was that of verbal coherence. He was able to speak to the point. He was not a raving lunatic. This obviously does not mean that he was a well-adjusted person. The question of his psychic makeup is important because this book deals not only with judaizing heresy but with martyrdom and its dynamics. What, if anything, we need to ask, did the friar's emotional economy contribute to his remarkably unswerving path of resistance?

He unquestionably had what might be called today "problems with relationships." His effort to put his life on a new footing was ill considered and desperate. But when he fled the monastery, had he lost touch with reality? Was he psychotic when he suggested that he was the Messiah? Did he consider the consequences of what he was doing, or was he driven by unbridled rage?

The inquisitors seem to have raised the question of Frei Diogo's sanity in part because they could not grasp how a monk of his training and background could come to hold such wildly erroneous and unclassifiable ideas. This supposition, at least, we can dismiss out of hand. If passionate and daring religious thinking was a sign of insanity in early modern Europe, then Europe was being transformed by madmen. Frei Diogo was certainly not a great original thinker. But the questions he asked were among the most pressing in his day, and his solutions had a resolute logic about them.

Moreover, if I can be excused for venturing into the psychiatrist's territory, there was, given Frei Diogo's personality, a healthy, adaptive aspect to his conversion to the "Law of Moses." The inquisitorial prisons were notorious for the high incidence of psychosis among their inmates. Even among those who did not become psychotic, despair and depression were common. Given Frei Diogo's fragile sense of self and his fractured religious universe at the time of his flight, his arrest and long imprisonment could certainly have led to psychic deterioration.

Frei Diogo's embrace of the Law of Moses, by his own account, took place in April 1600, under profoundly stressful circumstances. He had been incarcerated for more than seven months. He knew the Inquisition possessed damning evidence against him. When finally summoned to an audience, he antagonized the inquisitors, and in effect revealed that his earlier contrition had been feigned. The restoration of his faith at about this juncture—a uniquely constructed faith compatible with his intellectual and emotional rejection of Catholicism, his literalist reading of Scripture, and his growing identification with his Jewish ancestry—would seem to be no mean psychic and intellectual feat.

There is a way in which Frei Diogo's career resembles that of other early modern skeptical rationalists who overcame their doubts through Scripture-reading and an experience of illumination or conversion.[123] The seventeenth-century British scholar Samuel Hartlib, for example, described such a dynamic in the life of John Dury, a contemporary Protestant millenarian. The great René Descartes, he related, was "discours[ing] with Mr. Dury, complaining of the uncertainties of all things." Hartlib wrote that Dury had himself been

> in great straits once in these very particulars. He could find no certainties almost in any thing, though he was able to discourse as largely of any thing as any other. Yet solidly and demonstratively he knew nothing; till he betooke himself to the Scriptures and lighted upon an infallible way of interpreting them.[124]

Despite his liminal existence and isolation from the philosophical and scientific environment to which Dury and his associates belonged, Frei Diogo's path bears a resemblance to theirs. The resources available to Frei Diogo for his investigations were infinitely more limited, and he probably never engaged in conversation with anyone who had a clear grasp of the crosscurrents into which he had tapped. But his conclusions were compelling for the same reasons that similar conclusions were compelling to perplexed souls throughout Europe. We will encounter another such case in chapter 6.

On the other hand, Frei Diogo *was* a troubled person. The testimony of witnesses suggests that he had had an uncontrollable temper long before he fled the monastery. His anger was undoubtedly exacerbated by his career frustrations, which may have been due to discrimination. But discrimination may not have been the cause, or the sole cause, for his denial of permission to celebrate mass. His understanding of emotional life—his own and that of others—was quite limited, and he inevitably antagonized people. Deeply intolerant of ambiguity, he seemed able to "read" the world only ideologically. It is not credible that such a person was a paragon of monastic devotion before the events that, according to the Capuchin witnesses, triggered his flight.

Because of his emotional frailties, Frei Diogo projects a less heroic and charismatic *Gestalt* than other figures we are examining. He showed no interest in attracting admirers or in creating an impressive persona. Not only did he not give himself a Jewish "spiritual name," but he apparently refused to disclose *any* name to his cellmates. On the occasions when he created drama around himself, he did so mainly by scandalizing people, not by engaging in acts that excited awe or sympathy—self-circumcision, for example, or the telling of powerful dreams. And he disparaged his cellmates for failing to understand the Latin verses he recited, rather than trying to engage their interest by citing Scripture in a language they knew.

He did, however, fit the model of the dogmatista martyr exquisitely in his verbal sparring with the inquisitors. The inquisitors may have concluded that there was no point in directly and fully challenging him, since this had the effect only of throwing him into a fury. But it seems doubtful that his beliefs would have been shaken even if the inquisitors had pursued effective counter-arguments. Despite Frei Diogo's verbal aggressiveness, his real prowess was in solitary psychic and intellectual work: in arriving, virtually alone, at a system of belief that satisfied the very diverse demands of his personality and life circumstances. In this respect, Frei Diogo's exaggerated need to live by an uncompromising, dogmatic system, removing himself from the realm of everyday give-and-take, no doubt contributed considerably to his capacity for martyrdom. Indeed, in the end, he was entirely invested in the theology he had constructed—for most people, a rather bleak existence; for Frei Diogo the only possible one.

A CONVERSO SURGEON IN THE VICEROYALTY OF PERU

5

In 1639, more than a generation after Frei Diogo d'Asumpção's death, the converso physician Francisco Maldonado de Silva was burned alive in Lima as an impenitent judaizer. During his twelve years in prison, he engaged in lengthy disputations with theologians summoned by the Inquisition. His dramatic career made a great impression on the ex-converso diaspora, further elaborating the emerging image (and self-image) of the celebrated judaizing martyr.[1]

In terms of identity formation, Maldonado's childhood had been a wrenching and bewildering one. His father, Diego Núñez de Silva, was a crypto-Jew from Lisbon, a surgeon by profession.[2] As was true of quite a few other Portuguese conversos, he had first immigrated to Brazil and then made his way via Río de la Plata to the silver mines of Potosí in the Viceroyalty of Peru (at the time this territory included most of Spanish-ruled South America).[3] He may have castilianized his name in Peru to obscure his Portuguese origins, which Spaniards invariably associated with Jewish ancestry.[4] It is not clear whether he arrived in Peru before or after an inquisitorial tribunal was established in Lima in 1569.

In Potosí, Diego Núñez practiced medicine and fraternized with other Portuguese New Christians. Some time before 1579, for unknown reasons (perhaps influenced by the first penancing of a judaizer by the Lima tribunal in 1578),[5] he moved south to the small town of San Miguel de Tucumán. This town, in what is today northern Argentina, had been established at a major pass out of the Aconquija mountains as a strategic center to safeguard the roads to the plains.[6] The entire region of Tucumán was at the time developing as a vital source of food for the boomtown of Potosí, which was located in mountainous terrain not suitable for agriculture. A number of Portuguese New Christians settled there, perhaps in part because it was only in the early seventeenth century that *comisarios* of the Lima tribunal had begun to function in the region.[7]

The province of Tucumán was a frontier area, with European women in short supply. Now in his thirties, Diego contracted a marriage with the daughter of a local Old Christian *encomendero*—a member of the tiny Spanish rural elite who were granted the right to exploit Indian labor. As an *encomendero* in the Tucumán province, making his livelihood from the sale of his crops and livestock, Diego's father-in-law was probably not a man of impressive wealth or social status. He and his daughter, Aldonza Maldonado, presumably knew of (or suspected) Diego's New Christian ancestry. But Tucumán was a world away from Seville or Madrid. In a place where the overwhelming majority of the population was Indian, with a growing mestizo population, customary social barriers between Europeans were instinctively relaxed. It is certain that Aldonza and her father knew nothing of the groom's ancestral orientation to the "Law of Moses."

If Diego Núñez de Silva had hoped to find his fortune in the Americas, he was soon disillusioned. Driven to look for more profitable work, he uprooted his family numerous times, moving from town to town in the Tucumán province. But while he may not have thrived in his practice, he had ample opportunity in this region to develop contacts with other Portuguese New Christians. Beginning in the 1580s, the towns of Tucumán and Rio de la Plata became points along a route for contraband traffic that stretched from Potosí to Buenos Aires—a route that was opened and developed primarily by Portuguese New Christian merchants. Many of these merchants had entered New Spain illegally from Brazil. They used the route to transport untaxed silver from the Potosí mines to southern Brazil and then to Lisbon. In the opposite direction, they transported contraband European imports and slaves. The Spanish government sought to drive them out, perceiving their activity to be a threat to both the treasury and the faith. But its efforts were largely fruitless. Records indicate that Portuguese New Christians continued to constitute a significant minority in the Tucumán orbit.[8]

Between 1579 and 1592, five children were born to Diego Núñez de Silva and Aldonza Maldonado. Francisco Maldonado de Silva, the subject of this chapter, was the youngest. While Francisco was still a young boy, his father sought to inculcate crypto-Jewish beliefs in his eldest child, Diego, who was about seventeen at the time. This would have been around 1596. We do not have sound evidence about young Diego's real beliefs, but he clearly acquiesced to his father's instruction. In practice, this meant mainly assuming a heavy burden of silence in the presence of his mother and younger siblings.

The Lima tribunal had only recently begun seriously rounding up and prosecuting suspected judaizers, virtually all of them Portuguese.[9] In December 1600, a number of accused judaizers were sentenced at an auto-da-fé in Lima. Among them were two men who had been in contact with Núñez de Silva in Potosí, and who in the course of their trials confessed that they had judaized with Diego Núñez de Silva: Pero Gómez Piñero, a native of Lisbon who had been arrested in La Plata, and Gaspar de Lucena.[10] Diego Núñez de Silva must have heard about their sentencing. All three men were reconciled, which meant that they had given sufficiently detailed confessions about their judaizing to satisfy the inquisitors. Diego must have wondered about his safety.

In fact his arrest came not long thereafter, in San Miguel de Tucumán. His erstwhile companions had testified that Diego Núñez de Silva played a role in the Potosí judaizing circle as an expounder of crypto-Jewish doctrine. He had read them passages from the Bible (presumably translating them from Latin, which he

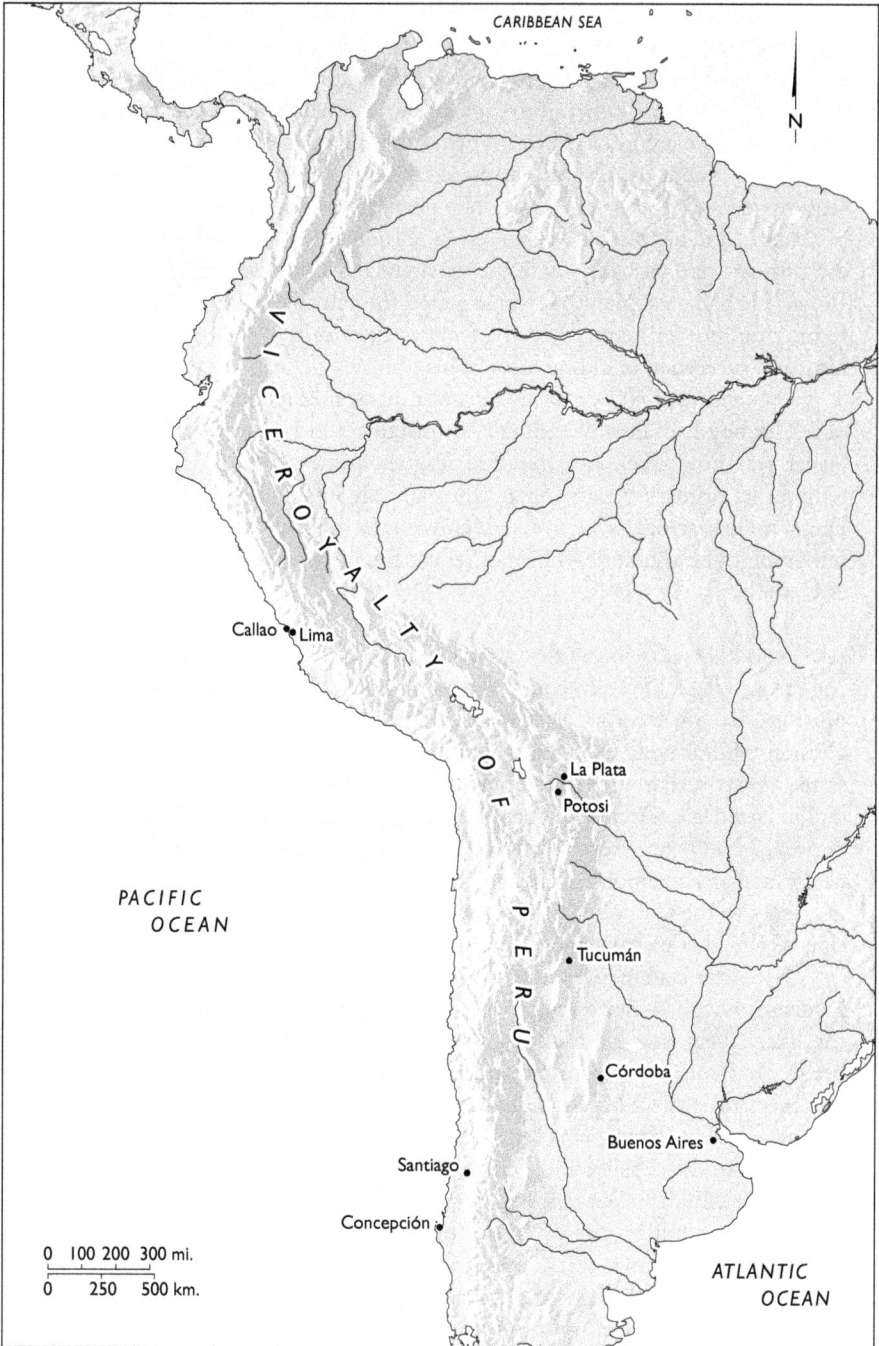

Map 3. The Viceroyalty of Peru in the seventeenth century, with locations important to the career of Francisco Maldonado de Silva.

knew) to offer proofs that Jesus was not the Messiah, and that the Messiah had not yet come. Diego was, then, according to this testimony, the kind of dogmatista with which we are concerned, who sought to anchor crypto-Jewish belief with prooftexts from Scripture. Diego's role in the "textualization" of crypto-Judaism in the Potosí circle is confirmed by his own subsequent confession.

When Núñez de Silva was arrested, at about age fifty-three, his property was sequestered as a matter of course. The property proved to be so meager that the prisoner had to be fed at the expense of the Inquisition. (What moveable goods he did possess were probably auctioned to finance his transportation under guard to Lima.) He had presumably not yet acquired the valuable books he later bequeathed to his children—or he may have had advance notice that the tribunal was seeking him, and succeeded in hiding most of his library.

At the time of Núñez de Silva's arrest, his son Francisco was about nine years old. The boy had already endured an unstable and impoverished existence. His father was now taken five hundred leagues away to Lima, leaving the family without its primary breadwinner. One can only imagine the anguish of an intelligent nine-year-old who was suddenly confronted with the discovery that his father might be a "heretic." His mother continued to raise him and his three sisters as Catholics.

At Diego Núñez de Silva's first audience in May 1601, the prisoner immediately began to confess. He crafted his confession, however, to implicate as few people as possible. By his account, he had developed doubts about the teachings of the Church while having engaged in a solitary reading of the Old Testament about sixteen years earlier. He denied having had contact with other judaizers. And he had judaized, he stated, for a period of only about ten months. Even during that period he had been anxious that perhaps he was in error, and therefore had never performed any ceremonies. He had finally realized his error, and returned wholeheartedly to the Catholic faith. He even purchased a book by Dionysius Carthusianus to further instruct and strengthen himself in the faith.[11]

The latter statement is of some interest. After the arrest of his erstwhile co-judaizers, Diego Núñez de Silva would certainly have tried to prepare a defense in the likely event that he, too, was arrested. The claim that he had judaized only briefly in Potosí did not exculpate him, but might have served to lighten his sentence and protect his son Diego. Such a claim would be supported by the fact that after he left Potosí he had married an Old Christian woman. He may actually have gone to the expense and trouble of acquiring a book that would corroborate such a story. But the fact that he claimed to have tried to strengthen his Catholic faith with a work by the prolific fifteenth-century Flemish mystic Denys van Leeuwen, better known as Dionysius Carthusianus, tells us little.

In fact, Núñez de Silva may have been exploiting a work that he had actually acquired for subversive aims. As we have seen, it was not unusual for Iberian judaizers, lacking access to Jewish books, to make use of Catholic works, either to glean from them information about Judaism or to borrow from their universe of pious expression. It is true that the works of Dionysius the Carthusian are not among those that routinely surfaced in the confessions of judaizers.[12] Since we do not know which of this author's many works (if any) Núñez de Silva read, or how he made use of it (if he did), we can only analyze the possibilities. One of them, certainly, is that this judaizing surgeon had gotten hold of the learned Carthusian's commentary on the Five Books of Moses in order to explore it for "Jewish" insights.

Diego Núñez de Silva's effort to depict himself as a lone judaizer was of course futile, given the testimony against him. He must have realized this fully at the point in the trial when he was read a summary of that testimony (in keeping with the Inquisition's policy of secrecy, the names of the witnesses were withheld). He immediately revised his story, and admitted to judaizing with other New Christians during the ten-month period that he had mentioned.

Six days later, however, having mulled over what he had learned, he requested an audience in order to admit to further guilt. Though it was true, he said, that he returned to Catholicism after ten months, he had subsequently met the New Christian Gaspar de Lucena and judaized with him for about two years, until Lucena was arrested (he had correctly identified one of the witnesses against him). During these two years, he said that he had read the Bible to other judaizers "according to its Jewish interpretation," and had observed fasts, the dates of which he and his fellow judaizers tried to determine according to the new moon. (Incidentally, according to one or two of the witnesses against him, Diego Núñez de Silva and his companions had also engaged in "ad hoc" fasting. They had observed a day-long fast that they broke at nightfall, in typical crypto-Jewish fashion, with a meal that included fish, as an act of supplication for a very down-to-earth purpose: namely, to bring Diego luck in his effort to obtain a post at a hospital for Indians.)[13]

Núñez de Silva also confessed that he had taught his eldest son and namesake the Law of Moses. He related the rather unusual circumstances of the initiation. He recalled that when the young Diego was seventeen or eighteen, he found him crying and complaining of pain from a fracture. The injured youth must have cried out for divine assistance in terms that would come naturally to a Catholic. This apparently had a sufficiently disturbing effect on the crypto-Jew from Lisbon that he took the opportunity to tell his son that he "should commend himself to the God of heaven as a Jew." He added that what the Church taught about Christ was foolish and fabricated (*cosa de burla; fingido y compuesto*), and that the youth should observe the Sabbath if he could—in his heart, if he could not observe it actively. He should mention nothing to his mother and sisters, or to anyone else.

The fact was, Núñez de Silva told the inquisitors, he was not sure his son had taken his counsel to heart, because the boy's mother was a pious Old Christian and, as he reasoned, "the nurture of the mother is more powerful than the instruction of the father." To further persuade his son, he told him that there were many Jews in the region who observed the Law of Moses, but they did so secretly out of fear of the Inquisition. He taught him to pray as a Jew to a single God, replacing supplications to the Trinity with supplications to "Almighty God [*Dios todopoderoso*]." The youth dutifully memorized a prayer but, the father said, he was not sure he had ever actually "prayed as a Jew." His son, he explained, was "a somewhat incapable boy, of limited understanding." The defendant may well have drawn this unflattering picture of his son to minimize the latter's culpability, but there may have been some truth to the words.[14]

A familiar of the Inquisition was sent to Chile to arrest the junior Diego, who was now twenty-three,[15] and bring him to Lima. He first appeared before the tribunal on May 29, 1602. He said he did not know his *casta y generación*—that is, whether he had any Jewish ancestry—but that his father was Portuguese and his mother Castilian. Nor did he know why he had been arrested. At a second audience, which he requested, he asked to know the reason for his arrest so that he could respond. In reply he was told that if he would honestly unburden his conscience he would not need to know the reason for his arrest.

At this point the young man capitulated. He begged for mercy, alleging that it was only out of fear that he had withheld information from the tribunal. His father, he confessed, had instructed him when he was about seventeen or eighteen years old, explaining that he should not believe in Jesus Christ, that he should believe in one almighty God, and that everything the Church said about Jesus Christ was "a falsehood and a lie." His father had further instructed him to tell no one, not even his mother. However, he testified that his father had prevailed on a Portuguese crypto-Jew who was a guest in their home, the *bachiller* Álvaro Núñez, to "reveal himself" to his son and encourage him to hold fast to the Law of Moses.

At first the young Diego denied having taken to heart his father's teaching. But once he was presented with the *acusación* (which included a summary of the testimony against him), he admitted to having abandoned the Law of Jesus Christ and adopted the Law of Moses, in the observance of which he had kept the Sabbath and recited some prayers and psalms in Spanish that his father had taught him. He now expressed repentance and promised "to live and die in the Holy Catholic Faith." It is noteworthy that he did not make the argument commonly made in cases like this, namely that as a minor he was forced to follow his father's instructions, even though he had never truly believed in the Law of Moses. This may suggest that he had in fact accepted his father's teaching and was now genuinely repentant.

Both father and son were reconciled at an auto-da-fé held in Lima on March 13, 1605, the Lima tribunal perhaps not knowing that a general pardon of judaizers on trial had been issued in Spain on January 16, 1605.[16] The Portuguese New Christians who were reconciled and sentenced in the Lima auto of 1605 later sought their freedom and the return of their confiscated property when they learned of the pardon, and the Suprema agreed to their claims, but the Lima tribunal, situated well beyond the Suprema's effective control, proved reluctant to comply.[17] The father was sentenced to the confiscation of his meager property, to wearing the sambenito, and to serving six years in prison; the prison term, however, was commuted to medical service in Callao, a port town outside Lima.[18] The son was sentenced to wear the sambenito for a year, and to undergo instruction in Catholicism at a monastery.[19]

The auto-da-fé, while offering release from prison, must have entailed considerable mental suffering for Diego senior. His friend and colleague Álvaro Núñez, whom his son had denounced, was among the persons sentenced at the auto; he, too, was reconciled.[20] Another of his fellow judaizers in Potosí, Gregorio Díaz Tavares, was sentenced to be relaxed to the secular arm. The background to the condemnation of this man bears closer scrutiny.

Díaz Tavares had once been a broker on the exchange in Lima, but having gone bankrupt he had become a miner, and thus found his way to Potosí and the circle of judaizers there. After he confessed and demonstratively expressed repentance, the tribunal decided to reconcile him. He was released from prison and confined only to the city of Lima. Some months later, however, when he was visited by the warden of the Inquisition, it appears that Díaz Tavares felt strongly impelled to drop his charade. He told the warden that if he were to appear then at an audience, he would declare, "Señor, I do not believe in the Cross, nor need one believe in it. I have been a Jew since birth, the child and grandchild of Jews." He was promptly rearrested. In ensuing audiences, he openly and unashamedly recounted how he had been instructed from a young age in the Law of Moses, and how he had observed that Law, in which "he wished to live and die." Although he briefly changed course and feigned repentance, he soon resumed a defiant posture. He refused to swear by anything but "the God of Abraham and Israel." Two calificadores were summoned by the Inquisition to persuade him of his error, meeting with him in four audiences. But he was "so shameless and impudent that he tried to preach the Law of Moses to the theologians, and refused to listen to what they were teaching him about the Law of our Lord Jesus Christ." He was sentenced and burned at the stake—possibly alive, although we have no evidence of this.[21]

In the context of the legacy of martyrdom available to Francisco Maldonado de Silva at a later date, it is of interest that Díaz Tavares, though he never became a celebrated martyr in the Portuguese-Jewish diaspora, displayed some of the signature behaviors of the dogmatista martyr. Maldonado's father would have learned of this behavior when the sentencia was read aloud at the auto-da-fé where his own relatively light sentence had already been read.

At the time of the release of his father and brother, Francisco was about twelve or thirteen. During the years his father had been in prison, his mother had raised him as a Catholic. He later testified—under circumstances in which he had no reason to hide the truth—that in his childhood he had been a believing and conforming Catholic. Yet it could not have been quite so simple. As the son of an imprisoned judaizer, he undoubtedly endured public slights, and must have experienced private confusions.

In 1610, when he was about eighteen, Francisco left his mother and sisters in Tucumán and went to join his father in Callao, where the reconciled judaizer was completing his term of service as a physician. This major step was almost certainly a practical one. It was customary for a physician to train a male child in his profession. But the intellectually eager Francisco also probably welcomed the opportunity to study medicine at the Universidad de San Marcos in nearby Lima.

Francisco's later testimony about his reunion with his father conceals as much as it discloses. He stated that when he first joined his father, he studied medicine with him but conformed to Catholic practice. About a year after his arrival, however, he studied a book in his father's library that was to have a profound effect on him. This was *Scrutinium scripturarum*, a conversionist work by the fourteenth-century baptized Jew Pablo de Santa Maria, addressed to his former coreligionists.[22] It is conceivable that the many unanswered questions in his family history impelled him to open this book, or that his father steered him to it without being explicit.[23] The title itself—from John 5:39, "*scrutamini scripturas*," that is, "search the Scriptures"—may have been alluring to a youth who had probably not, up to that time, had any direct access to Scripture.

The structure of the first part of the work—a dialogue between Paul, the Christian, and Saul, the Jew—allows Saul to ask some pointed questions: for example, how a Law that had been given to the Jews "forever" could be abrogated, or how Christians could obey the first injunction of the Decalogue (the prohibition of worshipping graven images) while worshipping the crucifix. These key points in the long history of Jewish anti-Christian polemics appear to have had a revelatory effect on Francisco. Having read "some questions that Saul had asked in defense of the Law of Moses, which Paul had replied to in defense of the Law of Jesus Christ," as he later testified, he found himself dissatisfied with the replies of Paul. He turned to his father, asking him "how it was that Christians worshipped images, when the first commandment of the Ten Commandments was to worship not images, but only God."

His father replied, according to his testimony, that it was exactly on this point that the Law of Jesus differed from the Law of Moses, which God had declared directly (*por su misma boca*) on Mount Sinai. In the course of breaking his long silence, Diego Núñez de Silva revealed to his son that he had actually never abandoned his Jewish beliefs. He had allowed himself to be reconciled, he related, only because he feared death. After this disclosure, the curriculum Francisco was studying with his father broadened to include instruction in the Law of Moses. Following a pattern we have seen in other cases, Diego Núñez de Silva encouraged his pupil to read the Bible on his own.[24] Father and son must also have had conversations about the elder's experience of judaizing in Potosí. It seems inconceivable that Núñez de Silva did not discuss, among other things, the defiant career of Gregorio Díaz Tavares.

Francisco had planned to leave Callao for Tucumán to find more lucrative work as a surgeon; but in the wake of his surprising discoveries he decided to remain in Callao. He practiced medicine with his father there until his father's death in 1616. Francisco also studied medicine at the university, receiving the degree of *bachiller*.[25] It may have been there that he came in contact with a young man named Tomé Cuaresma, a Portuguese physician about whose judaizing Francisco became aware, as we shall see. There is no evidence that he had contact with other Portuguese crypto-Jews at the university (or for that matter elsewhere), but it is certainly possible.

The death of his father, while no doubt a crushing blow, allowed Francisco to move to Santiago de Chile, where there was great need of physicians.[26] He took his father's library with him, including the *Scrutinium scripturarum*.[27]

The name Francisco Maldonado de Silva is mentioned for the first time in official records when, on April 12, 1619, he was listed as one of the two licensed physicians in Santiago in the minutes of the municipal council.[28] On December 20 of that year, he was appointed "chief surgeon" of the Hospital of San Juan de Dios, a post that had fallen vacant.[29] He now had a steady source of income—certainly a welcome circumstance after years of financial instability.

Among Francisco's patients in Santiago was an Old Christian hidalgo, Don Cristóbal de la Cerda y Sotomayor, who had arrived in Chile in 1618. He had been sent to Chile in 1617 to serve as a royal colonial administrator in Santiago. As fate would have it, however, his ship was captured by pirates on the voyage, leaving the family robbed of its fortune and Don Christóbal ailing. After a long recuperation in Lima, he was sent to Chile, where he served as interim governor from 1619 to 1621 before finally taking up the position of colonial judge (*oidor*). It was presumably during one of Francisco Maldonado de Silva's visits to the *oidor*'s home to treat members of the family that the doctor met his future wife, Isabel de Otáñez, a relative or orphan who had been taken in by Don Cristóbal and his wife and was being raised as a member of the family.

A marriage between the son of a reconciled judaizer and an Old Christian woman of reasonably high social rank would have been unlikely, had Francisco not become successful in his practice since arriving in Santiago. His wife's dowry (which was to become an issue between Isabel de Otáñez and the Lima tribunal, known for its venality) throws some light on the negotiations that preceded the 1622 wedding. Don Cristóbal provided his charge a modest dowry of clothing and linens assessed at 326 pesos, as well as 250 pesos in cash. Francisco contributed 300 pesos in cash (a tenth of his wealth, he stated), with a commitment of no less than 1,800 pesos in case of his death or the termination of the marriage.[30]

It is striking that Francisco repeated his father's act of marrying an Old Christian woman who knew nothing of his crypto-Jewish commitments. It may be that he refrained from contact with crypto-Jews as a matter of caution, drawing from his father's unhappy experience. As we shall see, he seems to have lived quite outside the orbit of the Peruvian Portuguese New Christian network that would come to light with a wave of arrests in the 1630s. Naturally, it is possible that romantic interest played a part in bringing about the marriage, although given contemporary social norms it would be foolish to make such an assumption. In any case, Francisco Maldonado de Silva seems to have chosen to follow his father's example, in the years after his reconciliation, of total dissimulation and religious self-sufficiency.

Sometime after Francisco's marriage, his sisters Isabel and Felipa joined him in Santiago. Isabel was now a widow. She had been married to an Old Christian *encomendero,* and was left with a married daughter. Felipa was a Jesuit *beata,* that is, a lay sister who took a vow of chastity and devoted herself to prayer and good works.[31] (As a *beata* without individual property, she was probably quite poor.)[32] By the time the sisters joined their brother's household, Francisco Maldonado had achieved what must have appeared to be a comfortable creole life, with a family compound and a domestic staff of several slaves.[33]

Privately, he must have suffered intense isolation. This may help to explain an extreme step this otherwise prudent man took three years after his marriage, while his wife was absent—though as we shall see, other events may have prompted him to action. Taking lodgings where he could be alone (as he later testified), he circumcised himself with a razor, finishing the surgical operation with a scissors.[34] This should not automatically be regarded as a sign that he was embarking on a course of martyrdom. Nor, however, should it be dismissed: It certainly signaled a readiness to take new risks as a judaizer. We do not know precisely when the self-circumcision was performed. But it was not long after, in December 1625, that he decided to break his silence within the family circle.

Can these developments have been precipitated by the death on December 21, 1625, of the judaizer Manuel Tavares, a cousin of Gregorio Díaz Tavares who had been burned at the stake at the 1605 auto where Maldonado's father and brother were reconciled? Tavares, also known as Manuel Fonseca, was a forty-one-year-old surgeon at the time of his death, and had a long history of entanglement with the Inquisition. He had first been sentenced for judaizing by the Mexican tribunal in 1601, but fled to Lisbon and then to Livorno. Arrested by the Lima tribunal in 1608 and again in 1618, he admitted under torture that he had indeed judaized, that moreover he had been circumcised in Livorno, and that his true name was David. He became extremely defiant, insulting the inquisitors and arguing his beliefs using traditional Jewish polemical criticisms of Catholic doctrine. He said he wished to be burned as a Jew, and the Inquisition indulged his wish.[35]

Did news of the sensational death in Lima—no doubt a topic of conversation among the residents of Santiago de Chile—cause an inner crisis in Maldonado that he sought to resolve through action?

In any case, it was in December 1625, that he took a trip with his sister Isabel to some baths "six leagues from Santiago" on a pretext that gave the two of them leisure and privacy. According to Isabel's later testimony,[36] Francisco told her that he was now commending his future to her hands.[37] He proceeded to announce "that he was a Jew and observed the Law of Moses."

Isabel was evidently terrified. She asked how he could say such bad things, "since he knew the Holy Office burned Jews and took their haciendas." She sought to persuade him "that the devil had deceived him, because the law that Christians observed was the just and good law of Grace." He replied by saying it was the Christians who would be damned, "because worshipping images was idolatry and God had long ago commanded that one must not worship images of wood." To say that a virgin had given birth to Jesus, he continued, was a lie; Mary had just been a woman married to an old man, a woman who had become pregnant and gave birth.

As for Jesus, he was only a man who ate and drank and attended wedding feasts (*andaba en bodas*).[38] Francisco also told her that he had not confessed for a year, because he believed a person needed to confess only to God, not to another man.[39]

Isabel returned to Santiago in a state of great anxiety. In an effort to do something about the situation, she placed a note in Francisco's room urging him to turn away from "such bad thoughts" and pleading with him that he must not, under any circumstances, believe what he had said. Francisco responded by handing her a note and asking her to reply to it within three days. She testified that she accepted the note so as not to offend the brother who was supporting her financially, but that she burned it without reading it. She then related everything that had passed between Francisco and her to her sister Felipa, who wept, she later testified, to hear such things about her brother. Perhaps at the urging of her sister, who as a *beata* was a rigorous defender of the Church's discipline, Isabel revealed what had transpired to her confessor. At this point the die was cast. Her confessor ordered her to make a statement about her brother's behavior before the commissioner of the Holy Office in Santiago.

It seems intriguing that eight months or so passed before the sisters carried out their duty. But they overcame whatever hesitations they had, and on July 8, 1626, both Isabel and Felipa testified (separately) before an officer of the Inquisition in Santiago.[40] Isabel related the events that had transpired at the baths and in their aftermath. Felipa related what she had heard from Isabel. She also added that in retrospect she recalled behavior in her brother that suggested he had been observing the Law of Moses—particularly his excuses, on occasion, for abstaining from eating, and his donning of a clean shirt on several Friday nights. The sisters' testimony was immediately sent to the Holy Office in Lima, which ordered Francisco's arrest.

The meager information we possess about the period between Francisco's abortive effort to convert his sister in late 1625 and his arrest in the spring of 1627 is nonetheless significant. Francisco Maldonado seems to have made a rather sudden move from Santiago to Concepción de Chile. (In any case, he left Santiago before he could collect some debts there.) In Concepción he took up residence with his wife, his wife's brother Antonio Yáñez de Zurita, his daughters, and four slaves. One wonders where his sisters went, but they were no longer with him. Despite the precariousness of his situation, he seems to have attempted to resume a normal life. He had brought his books and medical instruments with him; he bought a house and found employment at a local hospital; and he was even apparently proceeding with plans to enlarge the house.[41]

Francisco was arrested in Concepción de Chile on April 29, 1627. He was taken to the local convent of Santo Domingo where he was placed in a cell. He could not have been entirely surprised, and must have already considered his possible courses of action after capture.

If we may pause for a moment to consider his wife's predicament, however, we will be faced with the harsh side not only of the Inquisition, but of the martyr's resolve. There is no reason to think Francisco's wife had the slightest clue that her husband was a judaizer. If Maldonado had not confided in her before his disastrous conversation with his sister (which he surely did not), he certainly would not have done so afterward. This Old Christian woman—who was pregnant with her second child, a son her husband would never see—faced not only the incarceration of her spouse, but the loss of the family's livelihood and property (the latter was promptly inventoried), as well as its honor.

The following day, Maldonado was visited by the commissioner of the Holy Office in Concepción, Fray Martín de Salvatierra, who was also the provincial of the monastery. In a town with a European population of only one hundred or so persons, the prisoner presumably knew his interrogator. Francisco took the first opportunity to indicate the path he was choosing: he refused to take an oath "in the customary way, with a sign of the cross and in the name of Dios Nuestro Señor," insisting rather on swearing simply "to God [*a Dios*]." This would have been a sign of Maldonado's intention to pursue a course of martyrdom whether or not he was following patterns set by others. But he may well have heard from his father how Gregorio Díaz Tavares, whose sentencia Diego had heard read aloud at the time of his own sentencing, had refused to take the usual oath of a Catholic.

At least judging from the record, Maldonado's dramatic gesture was greeted with bureaucratic indifference. The commissioner proceeded to question him about property that may not have been inventoried and debts that had not been collected.[42] Shortly afterward officials were dispatched to Maldonado's house, where the prisoner's wife was required to exhibit the items he had mentioned, including records of debts owed him by patients.

On May 2, Francisco Maldonado was visited again in his cell, this time by Diego de Uruña (or Urvina), a friar who had apparently known Francisco for some time.[43] According to the friar's testimony, the prisoner appealed to his friendship, asking him to keep secret what he was about to say, namely, that he had observed the Law of Moses for many years; and that because he viewed his sister Isabel as "capable and intelligent," he had tried to persuade her to observe the Law in which their father had died—an effort that, he said, had been his own downfall. The friar, upset by the chain of events the prisoner had set in motion, responded by saying that Francisco must have lost his mind. Francisco insisted that he was sane, and "that he intended to live and die in the Law of Moses, because Christ the son of Joseph was not the Messiah, because his mother was not from the house of David." A discussion ensued, in which the friar cited passages from Scripture to try to convince him of his error. The prisoner, he reported, told him his response was very learned, and had caught him unprepared, but that he intended to die in the Law in which his father had died—at which the friar, "muy escandalizado," left the room. On another occasion as well, the friar tried to convert the prisoner with passages from Scripture. The prisoner replied "that there was no passage in all of Scripture that said there were three divine persons." The friar, aware of the prisoner's family history, took a different line of reasoning, arguing what he had no doubt had long assumed—namely that the prisoner's father had repented and died a good Christian. The prisoner replied that his father had only feigned repentance out of fear of torture and death.[44]

Some of Francisco's possessions were sold to finance his transport to Santiago and then to Lima, and to maintain him for a period in prison. He left, under guard, for Santiago—a trip of about twenty days—with some clothing and furnishings that he would need in his cell, and two mules. In Santiago, where he was housed in an Augustinian convent, he was again questioned, this time by a calificador of the Inquisition. He took the opportunity to make a more fully articulated statement of his intentions, declaring

> that he knew there was only one God, . . . who had given his Law to Moses at Mount Sinai, [a Law] which he guarded in his heart and must be ready to die for, it being the Law of his forefathers, and given that God could not change, nor could his Law. . . . And he hoped God would rescue him from the tribulations his sister had brought upon him, she being the one who had denounced him to the Holy Office, for he had not communicated [his beliefs] to any other person.

He added that he had observed "the holy and immaculate Law of Moses" secretly, out of fear of the Inquisition.[45]

From Santiago he was sent by sea, under arrest, to Lima, where he was transferred to the inquisitorial prison. It had been almost two months since his arrest.

His first audience was held a month later, on July 23. Once again he was asked to take an oath on a cross. After "hesitating a little," according to the notary, Maldonado launched into a solemn declaration, stating: "I am a Jew, señor, and profess the Law of Moses, and for it I will live and die, and by it [alone] I will swear. And if I must swear, I will swear by the living God, who created the heaven and the earth, who is the God of Israel."[46] It was a classic statement of the martyr's intention, disdaining the tribunal's power as well as its claims of religious authority.

After giving his name and age—he was now thirty-five years old—he was asked to explain why he refused to take the oath. He replied that the Law of Moses prohibited swearing by alien gods (*dioses agenos*), and that the God worshipped by the Christians was Jesus Christ, whom he did not recognize as a god. Questioned about his genealogy, he stated that everyone on his father's side of the family—"his grandfather and all his ancestors"—had been "*judíos*" and died in the Law of Moses. All of his mother's family, on the other hand, had been Old Christians. He recounted how he himself had lived as a Christian until his conversion to the Law of Moses when he was with his father in Callao. It was true that after that he had continued to go to mass and confess, but "only as a ruse, not because he thought it necessary for the salvation of his soul." When he confessed to a priest, he did so in his mind as if he was confessing to God, and he only confessed offenses that were also "against the Law of Moses." He was asked to make the sign of the cross and recite the standard Catholic prayers. Initially he refused. On reflection, however, he decided to demonstrate that he knew how to do these things, and complied—

probably using the technique of mental reservation that he had described using during confession. He was given his first admonition.[47]

At his second audience, four days later, at which he was given a second admonition, Maldonado gave an account of his judaizing practices.[48] The report of this audience in the trial summary sent to the Suprema—the only evidence we have—is lamentably meager. Nevertheless, a sketchy picture emerges of a practice constructed on the basis not of traditional lore but of the biblical text. He observed the Sabbath, he declared, because God had so commanded the Jews in the book of Exodus (the summary notes that he recited the appropriate Latin passage from memory, presumably Exod. 20: 8–11).[49] There follows a brief summary of crypto-Jewish prayers Maldonado proceeded to recite—prayers that may have been a regular part of Maldonado's Sabbath service. Two of the three that are mentioned were of biblical origin. One was a chapter from Psalms—Psalm 74, a prayer for collective deliverance, distinctive in its repetition of the plea for God to save his people for the sake of his name, which his enemies revile.[50]

The second biblical text that served as a prayer for Maldonado was chapter 32 of Deuteronomy, which begins, "Give ear, O heavens, and I will speak; and let the earth hear the words of my mouth" (again, the summary notes that at the audience Maldonado recited the passage verbatim).[51] This song of Moses is not a prayer in the ordinary sense of the word. It might, however, have served as a kind of credo, since it gave eloquent expression to the four core biblical themes of Israel's chosenness, Israel's backsliding, God's chastisements, and God's ultimate faithfulness to the covenant and to his people.

The third prayer mentioned is "a very long prayer that begins, *Domine deus omnipotens, deus patrum nostrorum Abrahan, Isaac y [sic] Jacob.*" This is not a psalm, nor is it a passage from the Hebrew Bible. If we look at the elements (Lord God almighty, God of our fathers Abraham, Isaac, and Jacob), it appears at first glance to be an approximation of the opening benediction of the standard Jewish *amidah* prayer. If this is the case, one would suspect two possible sources: either it had been preserved for generations in Maldonado's family, or it had been transmitted to his father (or directly to Francisco) by New Christians who had lived in Jewish communities in Italy or elsewhere. In either case, however, we would expect the prayer to be in Spanish or Portuguese, not in Latin. In fact, this prayer, too, has been gleaned from the Bible, though not from the rabbinic Bible: it is the first verse of the apocryphal Prayer of Manasseh, which after the Council of Trent was included with 3 and 4 Esdras in the appendix to the Vulgate, thus becoming a Jewish source for diligent crypto-Jews.[52] The Prayer of Manasseh itself, which is sufficiently long that an inquisitor might well regard it as "very long," is, in contrast to the other prayers Maldonado recited, deeply personal and penitential in character.

Some days later, the Inquisition recorded testimony about Francisco Maldonado de Silva from a María Martínez, a mulatta slave born in Portugal who was accused of witchcraft.[53] She reported that while she had been detained in the house of the *alcaide* of Lima, after her arrest, some bailiffs had brought a prisoner from Chile to the house. According to her testimony, during the two hours she spent with him there, the prisoner spoke freely to her about his crypto-Jewish beliefs. He told her, she said, that he did not believe in Christ and that worshipping images was a form of idolatry. Glancing at a cross she wore around her neck, he stated that he did not "believe in it"; that "Christ was a piece of wood"; and that if Christ was indeed what the Christians believed, "it [the cross] would shine." He said that he was from one of the two tribes of Israel that were kept in a terrestrial paradise, waiting for the end of the world, which would come soon so that God could unite them (with the rest of the Jewish people), and that they would be greater in number than before. He said the Inquisition had given his father only the light sentence of wearing a sambenito because he told the tribunal he believed in Christ, but this was a lie he told for the sake of his children. In fact, he didn't believe in Christ, only in (the one) God and in the future coming of the Messiah. He himself, Francisco Maldonado, was a Jew facing excommunication and death at the stake, and he didn't care if the whole world knew. He said that those who were burned to death didn't die, because God kept them alive forever. And that was what he would say to this tribunal when they summoned him. He further said that he ate no pork. He said he had fasted for forty days in devotion to the Messiah promised by the Law, for the sake of a sister of his, after which he had taken her into his home. After a year in which she had resided with him, he had told her about his fast for her, and how one must believe in the true Messiah. But she had responded with silence, and a few months later denounced him. The prisoner from Chile had also asked her about a man named Tomé Cuaresmo, saying he was "of his blood" (a New Christian), and that his father, Diego Núñez, had said Cuaresmo was a very good man.[54]

It is hard to know what to make of this testimony. The Inquisition did not need it, since more reliable witnesses had already testified and the prisoner was already incriminating himself before the tribunal without any inhibitions. María Martínez may have offered it freely while she was confessing to witchcraft, seeking to lighten her sentence by denouncing a person who meant nothing to her. That Maldonado de Silva would have disclosed his judaizing to her is not so difficult to believe, given his decision—apparently made months previously—to take the path of martyrdom. He would want, presumably, to make as many people aware of him as possible. What actually transpired between the accused witch and the accused judaizer is impossible to know. What we have is probably her unreliable understanding of what he said, as recorded by the notary.

After his second audience, Maldonado began to request audiences on his own, establishing a pattern according to which he was able to exercise a degree of control over the tribunal. At an audience he requested on August 5, only nine days after his second audience, he told the tribunal that two years earlier he had performed the precept given by God in Genesis 17 ("which he related by heart," the scribe added), namely circumcision. To do so, he had found lodgings where he could be solitary in Santiago while his wife was away. He had performed the operation with a razor, completing it with scissors. He also discussed the fateful conversation he had had with his sister. Among other things, he said he had told her that Jesus and his followers were condemned because they had violated God's precepts, and that the Law of Christ had first been adopted in Rome because the Romans were strongly inclined to idolatry. He told her that the doctrine of the Trinity was false, because there could be only one God, in conformity with what Moses taught the Israelites in his song "Give ear, O heavens" (*Audite celi* [*sic*])—the same chapter 32 of Deuteronomy that Maldonado had recited to the tribunal while discussing his crypto-Jewish prayers.[55] He had also tried to persuade his sister to observe the Sabbath, as well as the fast of expiation of "the tenth of December" (presumably a scribal error for "September").[56] The fasts, he had told her, should be accompanied by physical afflictions, as God commanded in Deuteronomy.[57] These afflictions, he said, consisted of wearing a hair shirt (*çiliçios*), sleeping on the ground, refraining from eating meat, and not eating at all during the day, until a star was visible at night. (It is noteworthy that the inventory of Maldonado's sequestered belongings included a hair shirt—a standard piece of equipment among contemporary Catholic ascetics.)[58] In his conversation with his sister Isabel he had, he said, cited many verses (*autoridades*) from the Psalms and Prophets, which he had copied in a very small hand on two pages (in Latin), and which he recited to her in Spanish. But his sister, not persuaded, told him he was going to end up "in the Inquisition," which would have him burned at the stake. He replied, he said, that if he had a thousand lives he would give all of them for the Law of Moses.

It is unfortunate that we have only summaries of the original records of the accounts given by Francisco and his sister Isabel of this crucial encounter between them. We can speculate, however, that Francisco had requested this audience in order to give his own version of the story, knowing that Isabel must have depicted his behavior in a light that he would consider unflattering, given his self-image as a martyr. In his own account, he highlighted his readiness for suffering and death. It is significant that he chose at this time to give an account of his self-circumcision.[59]

Five weeks later, on September 13, 1627, Maldonado was summoned to an audience where he received his third admonition. We are told about his behavior only that "among many blasphemies he uttered against our holy faith, he said that his father had taught him that Jesus Christ . . . had learned the art of magic, with which he had deceived some ignorant people." He also apparently spoke of the little booklet—presumably the one that had been discovered by agents of the Inquisition[60]—in which he had recorded the "festivals of Moses and some prayers . . . that he had copied from the *calendario* of Genebrardo on the psalms." The work he was referring to was by the sixteenth-century German Benedictine Gilbert Génebrard, whose *Psalmi Davidis vulgate editione, calendario Hebreaeo, Syro, Graeco, Latino . . .* was printed in Paris in 1577. It is probable that this was the volume noted as "*Salmi Davidis*" in the inventory of Maldonado's books sequestered by the Inquisition.[61] This work would have been particularly valuable to a crypto-Jew like Maldonado, because it listed the Hebrew calendar of festivals and fasts by the name of the Hebrew month. Yom Kippur is listed, for example, as "*Tizri 10—Ieiunium expiationis. Levit. 23 ver. 27.*"[62] The volume also contained the Psalms with a commentary that incorporated rabbinic sources, citing, for example, David Kimchi and Abraham ibn Ezra, and using Hebrew terms, which were also transliterated.

On October 5, Francisco was summoned to hear the *acusación* against him and reply to it. He "confessed" to all of its clauses. He added that he had recently observed the "fast of expiation" (*ayuno de la expiación*) that had fallen on September 10—not for one day, as required, but for four, neither eating nor drinking (during the day), so that God would pardon his sins. Such behavior would probably have been reported to the tribunal, but he wanted to be sure they knew. This unsolicited confession is evidence that the fast was not only an act of piety, but an act of resistance aimed at impressing the inquisitors. It was certainly in this spirit that he asked to speak to "learned persons," with whom he could discuss what he had confessed.[63]

This request was a sly hint that he might be vulnerable to persuasion of his "error" by learned theologians. To achieve the conversion of so learned and pious a figure as Maldonado de Silva would have been quite a victory for the Inquisition. The Inquisition acceded to the request, giving Maldonado a Bible "and everything he wanted" to prepare. Francisco Maldonado was soon debating a panel of high-ranking theologians for the Inquisition (calificadores), comprised of a university-educated cathedral canon, an elderly Franciscan theologian, a Dominican professor of theology, and a Jesuit, "*maestro* of all the learned men in this realm."[64] Over the course of two days in October 1627, he discussed his "doubts and difficulties" with these men. But he was toying with them and perhaps playing for time. At the end of this long discussion he declared that he wanted to die in the Law of Moses.[65]

By now he appears to have been exquisitely aware of the power he wielded within the constricted orbit of the prison and tribunal. He had succeeded in putting the Inquisition on the defensive: it was up to them to prove the truth of Catholic doctrine. Four more "*conferencias*" were held with theologians between January 13 and November 16, 1628.[66] Prior to these, Maldonado was given a Bible and four sheets of paper, in order to elaborate his arguments for the calificadores he would debate. He returned the sheets covered with his comments, in a very small hand. Unfortunately they have not been preserved. The trial summary gives almost no information about the proceedings, except to note that the prisoner declared at each one that he intended to live and die in the Law of Moses.[67]

The trial would seem to have been approaching its conclusion. On November 17, a day after Francisco Maldonado's fifth debate with theologians summoned for the purpose, he was presented with the *publicación* of the testimony against him. He readily "confessed" to all of the testimony against him. In view of Francisco's defiance, the "advocate" appointed by the Inquisition to represent him resigned.

The winter passed with no activity deemed worth reporting by the inquisitor who drafted the trial summary. In early April 1629, the prisoner was given an audience at his own request. He asked to be given a New Testament, a Bible, some paper, and "the chronicle of Fray Alonso Maldonado," which he requested "so that he could see the interpretation of the hebdomad—the 'seventy weeks'—of Daniel, which he had always insisted had not yet been completed."[68] This work by a fifteenth-century Dominican author had probably been cited by the calificadores during their disputation with Maldonado about the "seventy weeks."[69] If so, they did so in an attempt to convince him of the Church's interpretation of Daniel 9: 24–27, namely that Gabriel's prophecy to Daniel had prophesied the crucifixion of the Messiah 490 years after Ezra left Babylonia.

It was only on August 22 that an audience was arranged with theologians. While the previous such meetings are referred to in the summary as *conferencias*, they are referred to from this point as *disputas*. In this sixth "dispute" over the prophecy in Daniel, the judaizing prisoner was certainly at a great disadvantage. While the *Chronica universal* of Alonso de Maldonado alluded to Jewish interpretations—which it was the author's aim to refute—it did not lay them out. Provided only with the Vulgate translation of this difficult prophecy, Maldonado de Silva may well have been confounded. According to the summary of the trial, the prisoner "was left not knowing what to respond" during this dispute. Be that as it may, the session, which lasted three hours, did not alter Francisco's declared intention to live and die in the Law of Moses. Of the seventh "disputation," held on October 25, 1629, at the behest of the prisoner, the summary notes only that it lasted two and a half hours, and that Francisco Maldonado remained "pertinacious."

The summary is silent about what happened in the next two years, except to say that the prisoner repeatedly asked the inquisitors to summon theologians "so that he could discuss with them the salvation of his soul." Finally, on October 21, 1631, three Jesuit theologians were summoned for the eighth "disputation," meeting with the prisoner for three hours along with the inquisitors. On this occasion, the prisoner recited "a long harangue in Latin verse, in which he discussed the stability of the truth and the enduring quality of the Law of the Moses [as demonstrated] by the [scriptural] words *aeternum*[70] and *sempiternum*." The Jesuits told him that these words did not signify eternity in the sense of unending time (*duración perpetua*), and showed him verses to proved this. He considered these "frivolous explanations."

Two months later, in December 1631, a ninth "disputation" was held, about which we know no particulars. Francisco subsequently requested "many audiences" with the inquisitors, at which he asked for paper "to write down his doubts." The inquisitors indulged his requests, and the prisoner wrote "many booklets" that were shown to the theologians assisting the Inquisition, and then put in his dossier.[71] A tenth and an eleventh "disputation" were held, in October 1632 and January 1633, respectively. The calificadores finally concluded that the prisoner was requesting these meetings "more to make an arrogant display of his ingenuity and sophistries than out of a desire to convert to our Holy Catholic Faith."[72]

Not long thereafter, in early 1633, the inquisitors ruled that Maldonado should be relaxed to the secular arm, with confiscation of his goods. Like other prisoners, he was not informed of the sentence. But he undoubtedly sensed the inquisitors' increasing indifference to his case. At some point he undertook a fast of eighty days, "during many of which he ate nothing, or, if he ate anything, it was small amounts of cornflour and water," and under this regime he declined so much that he became "skin and bones." His many bedsores made him unable even to turn over in his bed.

This was apparently not the first or last fast that Maldonado de Silva kept in his cell.[73] Lacking the original Lima file, we are left in the dark about much of his behavior in prison. We thus do not know when, during his long imprisonment, he began to call himself "Eli Nazareo" and to use this name to sign the notary's record of the audiences at which he appeared. It is only from the following brief passage in a printed account of the auto-da-fé composed after his death—an important document we will return to—that we learn that his change of name was accompanied by a change of behavior:

> He let his beard and hair grow, like the Nazirites,[74] and changed his name from Francisco Maldonado de Silva to Heli Nazareo. And he used it when he signed his name, writing "Heli Nazareo, unworthy servant of the God of Israel, alias Silva."[75]

The biblical passage that describes the Nazirite vow[76]—presumably the only source Maldonado had to inform his behavior—does not prescribe fasting. It does, however, call for self-denial in the realm of ingestion, since it calls for refraining from the drinking of wine. It is possible that this passage suggested to Maldonado a way of further dramatizing his self-transformation. That is, it might at least partially explain his rationale to begin an extended period of fasting—a step that would have "made sense" to his audience since fasting was so much a part of the repertoire of religious abstinence in Spanish culture. He was perhaps drawing from Spanish practices associated with persons who were associated with the term *siervo de Dios*, in order to create a comparable Jewish role.

In any event, after ending his eighty-day fast, Maldonado gradually recovered. He began insistently requesting an audience with the calificadores—in order, he said, to resolve the doubts he had articulated in the notebooks he had turned over. Perhaps the inquisitors believed that the physical crisis he had weathered (which made an evident impression on them and probably on others in the prison) reflected a spiritual crisis and a readiness to rethink the merits of the Law of Christ. Astonishing as it may seem in light of the fact that he had already been sentenced, his request to meet with the calificadores was granted. The calificadores were called on June 26, 1634, for a twelfth dispute, which lasted three hours.[77]

Some time after the twelfth dispute, Francisco Maldonado succeeded in planning and executing an escape from his cell. Prison discipline in Lima being shockingly lax,[78] he was able to fashion a rope from corn husks and lower himself from a window, gaining entrance to nearby cells. There, according to the notary's bland record of events, "he persuaded the inmates to follow his Law." It is hard to know what to make of this remark. Maldonado, too, testified that he had converted two of the prisoners. He did, at least, persuade two inmates—neither of whom had

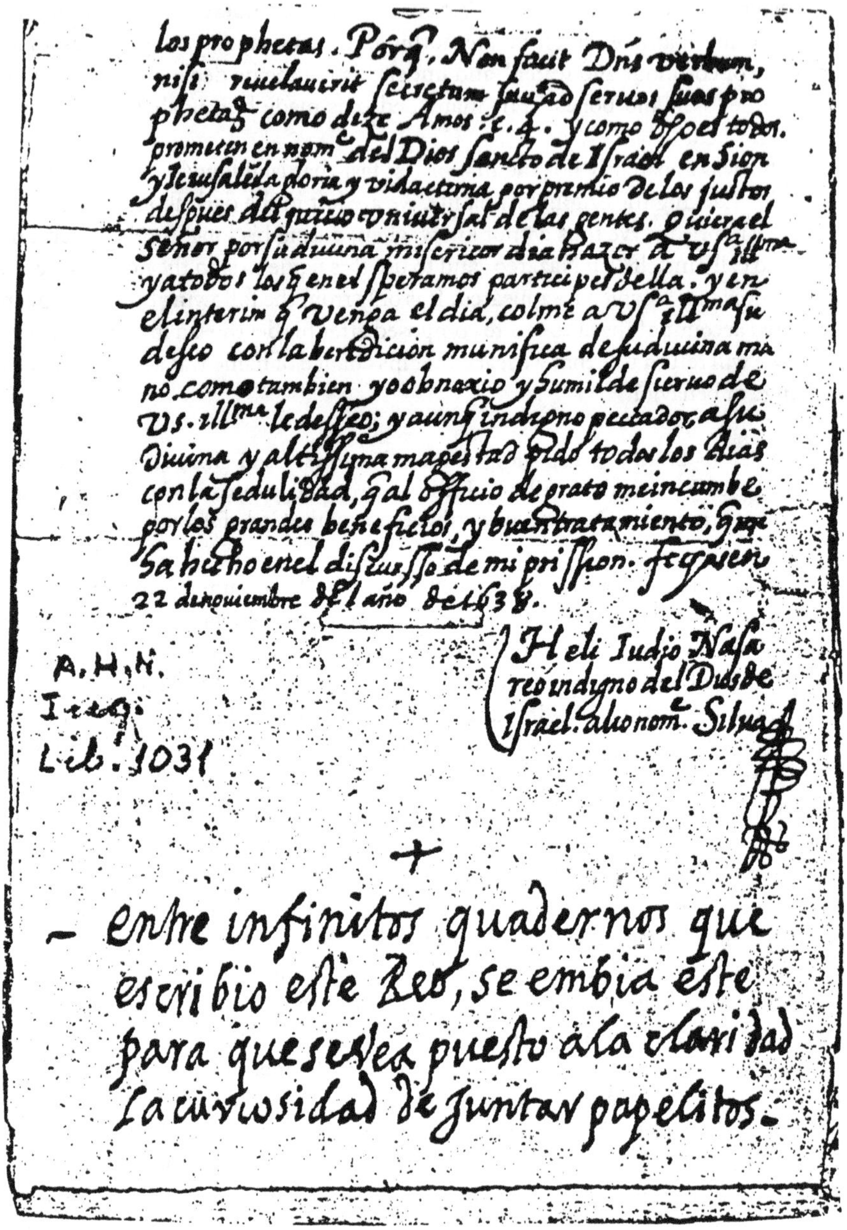

los prophetas. Porq. Non facit Dns verbum,
nisi revelaverit secretum suum ad servos suos pro
phetas como dize Amos c. 3. y como todos
prometen en nome del Dios santo de Israel en Sion
y Jerusalem la gloria y vida eterna por premio de los justos
despues del juizio universal de las gentes. Quiera el
Señor por su divina misericordia hazer a V. Sa. Illma.
y a todos los q en el speramos participes della. y en
el interim q venga el dia, colme a V. Sa. Illma. su
deseo con la bendicion munifica de su divina ma
no como tambien yo obnoxio y humilde sierno de
V. S. Illma. le desseo; y aunq indigno peccador, a su
divina y altissima magestad pido todos los dias
con la sedulidad, q al officio de grato me incumbe
por los grandes beneficios, y buen tratamiento, q me
ha hecho en el discurso de mi prission. fecha en
22 de noviembre del año de 1638.

Heli Iudio Nasa
reo indigno del Dios de
Israel. alias nome Silva

A.H.N.
Inq.
Lib. 1031

+

— entre infinitos quadernos que
escribio este Reo, se embia este
para que se vea puesto a la claridad
la curiosidad de juntar papelitos.

Figure 8. Francisco Maldonado de Silva's signature to a letter written during his imprisonment, signed "Heli Iudio Nasareo." Archivo Histórico Nacional, Madrid.

been imprisoned on charges of judaizing[79]—to accept copies of a letter in Latin that he had written to "the synagogue of the Jews in Rome and its environs," to deliver after their release.[80] The copies of the letter to the Jews of Rome were either found in a search or handed over to officers of the Inquisition. Fortunately for scholarship, they were sent to the Suprema with the summary of the trial, and were thus preserved.

Maldonado was surely by now a figure of some notoriety among the prisoners, and this escapade must have gained him further attention. When summoned to an audience, he declared that he had been motivated to make the escape and contact other prisoners by his zeal for the Law of Moses.[81] Such a declaration seems to be a genuine reflection of his regimented psychic life. In contrast to Luis Carvajal or Diogo d'Assumpção, Francisco Maldonado sought to keep his emotions entirely under wraps, projecting an image of himself as a person whose only sentiments were pious. This image is vividly reflected in his letter to Rome.

It is not clear why he chose to address the Jews of Rome rather than, say, the Jews of Venice or Amsterdam. There may have been symbolic value for him in the fact that he was addressing a community of Jews who lived in the shadow of St. Peter's. Or he may have wanted to address a Jewry that he imagined played an active diplomatic, intercessory role on behalf of Jews throughout Christendom. Either way, the address he chose seems to suggest the point of view of a man who still saw the world as dominated by papal Rome, and who was scarcely aware of the great upheaval that had been set off in Wittenberg more than a century earlier.

He introduced himself to his readers as "Heli Nazareo de Dios"—Eli, a Nazirite of God. By 1634, then, at the very latest, he had adopted this name and had taken the Nazirite vow (as he understood it). The attitude he adopted toward his intended Jewish audience was characteristically grandiose, defiant, and aggressive. While briefly apologetic about having lived for years as an outwardly compliant Catholic, he presented himself for the most part as a model of uprightness and self-sacrifice, worthy of attention and emulation. In this, he drew from a widespread self-image among his generation of crypto-Jews.[82] He believed, he wrote, that his obligation as a Jew extended beyond simply adhering to the Law of Moses. Being a Jew required him to "attack the impious with the truth"—to go on the offensive and confront the Church and the Inquisition polemically. "Since the day I was arrested," he wrote, "I have promised to die fighting for the truth with all my power by refuting the enemies of [God's] Law, as well as by observing [this Law] up to the very altar of fire that they are (so I gather) preparing for me."[83]

After briefly describing the fate of crypto-Jews in the Iberian Peninsula and his own incarceration, he offered, as it were, the material for his martyrology. He described how he had presented to the tribunal and its associates (*esos pérfidos*) more than two hundred arguments, to which, he said, they were unable to respond. (He was presumably referring to the material in the two manuscript books he had composed in prison, which he later handed over to the Inquisition.) "So pray for me to the Lord, dear brothers, that he should give me strength to suffer the torment of fire: for death is near, and I have no one to help me but God. Without doubt, I await eternal life from him and the speedy salvation of his people." There follows a lengthy passage of advice and encouragement. "Choose for yourselves life, beloved brothers; observe the Law of the Lord so that you may return to the land of your fathers."

He also sought in this letter to transmit to the wider Jewish world the theological solutions he had arrived at in reply to three arguments made by the calificadores—arguments that "at first glance appear difficult." The first made use of the passage in Haggai 2:7–9, in which God declares to the prophet (in the language of the Vulgate) that "yet one little while, and I will move the heaven and the earth . . . and *the desired of all nations* shall come, and I will fill this house with glory." The calificadores expounded a christological interpretation of this verse, to demonstrate that "the desired of all nations"—the Messiah—had come before the destruction of the Temple ("this house"). Maldonado's "solution" is not really of interest, since the calificadores' argument was based on a translation that any educated Jew (not to mention many a humanist) would not have accepted: in the original Hebrew, *ḥemdat kol ha-amim* was a reference to the treasure the nations would bring to the rebuilt Temple.

The second argument drew from Psalm 109,[84] in which the psalmist, understood to be David, opens with the words "Dixit Dominus Domino meo," or "The Lord says to my Lord"—evidence, according to the calificadores, that God was speaking to his son Jesus. Maldonado's argument was that this psalm might have been written by another prophet, and wrongly attributed to David "by a scribal error, or intentionally, by Christians." Or, he wrote, if it was in fact written by David, it was to be read aloud by the people in the messianic days when he would rule as Messiah, and so he referred to himself—but only metaphorically—in the third person as "Dominus." That is, the psalm as a whole could be read as a prophecy about the messianic days when David would be exalted over all the kings of the earth (an interpretation that had in fact been used in medieval Jewish polemics). As with the verse from Haggai, Maldonado was handicapped by his reliance on the Vulgate. Jews had argued on the basis of the Masoretic text, which reads, "The Lord said to my lord [*adoni;* i.e., my *human* lord]."[85]

One would like to know Maldonado's reply to the third difficult point, namely the Church's classic argument that the Temple in Jerusalem was destroyed as a punishment of the people who killed Christ; that the Temple has not and will not be rebuilt; and that the savior must thus have come. Unfortunately, the letter breaks off at this point.[86]

It seems striking that Maldonado fails to attack the Church at what would seem to be its most vulnerable points in the seventeenth century. From this correspondence and a further letter he addressed to an inquisitor, which we will discuss below, it appears that Maldonado's arguments for the truth of the Law of Moses rested entirely on medieval Jewish anti-Christian polemics. He evidently had no inkling of early modern humanist and Protestant attacks on the authority of the Vulgate, the traditions of the Church, and the pope. He also seemed quite oblivious to the erosions of the Church's claims in light of the Reformation and the fragmentation of Christendom. This cannot be explained simply by the colonial context in which he lived, far from the centers of Reformation innovation. A number of foreign Protestants were active in the Viceroyalty of Peru, even in interior regions, and they were not always discreet, as dossiers of the Lima tribunal reveal.[87]

After his final dispute on June 26, 1634, the Lima tribunal had more pressing business than arranging theological disputes with a prisoner who had already been sentenced to be relaxed. In August 1634, the Portuguese New Christian merchant Antonio Cordera was denounced to the Inquisition, a denunciation that led to the Lima Inquisition's most intense and lethal phase. The episode came to be known as the "Complicidad Grande"—a term that is accurate at least quantitatively. Between 1635 and 1639, nearly one hundred persons were taken into custody and tried, the majority of them men of Portuguese New Christian origin who were accused of judaizing. There were so many arrests that the inquisitorial prison could not house the prisoners, and the tribunal had to rent some nearby houses.[88] The Complicidad Grande arrests resulted in the sentencing of no less than sixty-three persons for judaizing. Ten of them were burned at the stake in 1639 alongside Francisco Maldonado, whose arrest predated theirs by many years.[89] Scholars have been inclined, for good reasons, to believe that behind the "Complicidad Grande" arrests and convictions lay a complex amalgam of anti-Jewish stereotypes, political paranoia, and financial concerns, rather than real evidence of judaizing.[90]

There is a curious brief passage in Maldonado's trial summary, which states that before the arrests of the first Complicidad Grande prisoners in 1635, "God caused this prisoner [Maldonado] to become [temporarily] deaf as a result of his eighty-day fast," thus rendering him unable to communicate with—and stir up trouble among—the host of newly imprisoned New Christians. The passage was added to the trial summary only later, after the auto in 1639 at which the condemned judaizers of the Complicidad Grande and Maldonado de Silva were sentenced.[91]

In July 1638, Francisco's wife, Isabel, arrived in Lima, having made the long trip from Concepción de Chile to ask the tribunal to restore her dowry from the family property that had been sequestered at the time of her husband's arrest. She presented her petition on July 15, claiming some of this property as hers alone according to the terms of her dowry. (The Inquisition's seizure of property that belonged to third parties during sequestration was not unusual, and it was the responsibility of the third party to prove his or her right to the property.)[92] Isabel asked to have the sequestered property, including the house in Concepción and two male slaves, sold at auction and the sum that was due her paid from the proceeds—as soon as possible, she added, "because I am poor and am suffering much need." In her petition she noted the long journey she had undertaken, and begged the tribunal to act with mercy and justice.[93]

The tribunal declined her petition after hearing the counterclaims of the officer in charge of sequestered property (*defensor de bienes*), stating simply that she had already been provided her due. On August 17, Isabel sent a second letter of petition (which she presumably had drawn up for her by a legal expert), along with a copy of her marriage contract (*carta de dote*). Her firm and aggrieved letter sought to prove that she was entitled by law to what she was requesting.[94] The two male slaves who had been seized, it argued, should be sold at auction, lest they die or escape to another country. Two hundred pesos of the proceeds should be given to her as part of her dowry. The letter also asked that she be given the use of the small house (*casita pequeña*) and plot of land in Concepción that the tribunal had sequestered.[95] Faced with the evidence she produced, the inquisitors finally acceded to her request.[96] But Isabel de Otáñez had to wait a year before the slaves were sent to auction, and she received the sum of 200 pesos only after she became a widow.[97] Then, after the rest of the property was sold and Maldonado's expenses in prison paid—expenses that may well have been inflated—she received another 325 pesos.[98]

On November 12, 1638, when preparations were already in progress for the spectacular auto that would be held in January, the tribunal finally acceded to repeated requests from Maldonado de Silva, and arranged for a thirteenth debate with some calificadores. The tribunal's calculations may have included the remote hope for a last-minute conversion. Three "very learned Jesuits" debated with the prisoner for three and a half hours. If he had suffered from deafness, he had clearly recovered.

Given Maldonado's investment in his martyrdom, it is almost unthinkable that he would have changed course at this point. And he did not. In fact, he seized the opportunity to make a dramatic gesture. Rising from his seat before the Jesuit calificadores, he drew two crude manuscript books from his pocket, which he had produced in his own hand in his cell. Given that he was permitted neither paper nor ink, this disclosure must have come as a small bombshell. One of the books was made up of 103 folio sheets; the other, more than 100. They were signed with the words, "Eli the Jew, unworthy [servant] of the God of Israel, otherwise known as Silva [*Heli judio indigno del Dios de Hisrrael, por otro nombre Silva*]." The prisoner offered, with no little irony, an explanation for why he was handing them over, using the formulaic statement used by prisoners when they confessed to crimes, namely that he was doing so to clear his conscience (*por descargo de su conçiençia*). He was very learned in Sacred Scripture, he said, and his doubts had not been resolved by the calificadores.[99]

It is worth digressing a moment to offer the tribunal's account of how Maldonado produced these "books" and other writings:

> He wrote various tractates, some of which were burned [at the stake] with him, dedicated to the *Señores Inquisidores Apostolicos* of this kingdom, and said that they were refutations of Fray Luis de Granada's *Símbolo de la Fe*.[100] . . . With old paper used to wrap some things that he had requested [presumably to eat], he joined the pieces together so cleverly that they seemed to be a single sheet, and fashioned the pages of these tractates. Using a pen made with a chicken bone, cut with a nail he made

into a knife, and ink made from charcoal, he wrote in a script that looked as if it had been printed.[101]

This description, from Maldonado's sentence at the auto-da-fé, was immortalized in a printed pamphlet we will discuss below. It thus became public knowledge, and part of the martyrological lore about Francisco Maldonado de Silva.[102]

The prisoner continued to manipulate the tribunal by invoking his "rights" to the very end. On December 1, he requested and was granted an audience. But this Wednesday in December was not an ordinary day in the secret cells. The slaves (*negros*) who worked for the Inquisition, performing menial labor in the prisons, had been locked up. This measure was taken to prevent them from witnessing a solemn occasion taking place in town, and thus from reporting it to the prisoners.

The familiars of the Inquisition had assembled on horseback, followed by Inquisition officials and municipal officers. As the trumpets and kettledrums struck up, these figures paraded through the main streets of the city, attracting a crowd wherever they went. A crier pronounced a formal notice, first in the square of the Inquisition and then in front of the viceroy's palace, that an auto-da-fé would be held in the main square of the city on January 23.[103] According to the sympathetic chronicler, the large crowd "gave thanks to God and to the Holy Tribunal for holding so grand an auto, for thus they anticipated it would be, given the many arrests that had been made." Once this preliminary ceremony was over, the tribunal called on Juan de Moncada, "who for fifty years has served on these occasions for the Inquisition," to oversee the preparation of the sambenitos, corozas, effigies, and green crosses that would be used at the auto. A "secret" workshop to produce these articles (which indirectly provided information about the fate of the prisoners—information that family members would have been desperate to receive) was set up in the home of the warden.

Nevertheless, Francisco Maldonado was granted the audience he requested. Since the inquisitorial notary attended the procession, the audience must have been held after the ceremony. Maldonado was perhaps not unaware of what was stirring, since from his cell he might have detected the absence of the slaves, and must have heard the drums and trumpets. In any case, he again presented a written document. It was a five-page letter he had composed on November 22, which he asked the tribunal to show to the calificadores. If the latter could convince him that his points were erroneous, he said, he would submit to the Catholic faith. On the ninth and tenth of December, two "very long disputations"—the first lasted an entire day—were held. They would be the last. Maldonado, the notary remarked, "remained as pertinacious as ever."[104]

This letter survived because the inquisitors in Lima sent it, along with the trial summary, to the Suprema in Spain. (They explained that they wanted the authorities to see how Maldonado had "created" sheets of paper by joining together small scraps, perhaps wishing to demonstrate that they had not negligently allowed him to obtain sheets of paper.)[105] The letter is superficially (perhaps caustically) respectful, addressing the inquisitor as "Ilustrissimo Señor." He had already, Maldonado wrote, replied to all the matters raised by the calificadores in the two books he had handed over, but he wanted to clarify two points.

The points he focused on were central to crypto-Jewish polemics in general: first, that Jesus was not the Messiah prophesied in Scripture, and second, that the Trinity contradicted both Scripture and reason. The calificadores had undoubtedly heard his arguments before. What Maldonado wished to do, one would guess, was to present the most streamlined final case he could for the truth of the Law of Moses.

That Jesus was not the Messiah, he argued, is proved by three different ways in which Jesus's life contradicted Old Testament prophecies about the Messiah. First, the messiah was to have been named David, not Jesus.[106] True, a califi-cador had argued earlier in reply that in Scripture, personal names were used as patronymics, so that Jesus, being a descendant of David, could be understood to have had the name David. Maldonado rejected this argument, probably as sophistry. But even if it were so, he continued, they could not explain away two fur-ther contradictions. First, there was no evidence, even in the Gospels, that Christ (this was the term Maldonado used) was a descendant of David, "as I have proven in the two books I gave to your honor [the inquisitor]." Moreover, even if Jesus was a descendant of David, he had not become a king as had been prophesied, nor had he brought eternal peace, or possessed any other of the characteristics of the Messiah.

These were arguments that any Bible-literate crypto-Jew might have used. It was when he turned to the issue of the Trinity that he revealed the impact of medieval philosophy on his thinking. He noted that one or more of the cali-ficadores had made the following argument: "God, to know himself and under-stand himself and comprehend His divine essence, formed a conception of himself, and by this act He was conceived [*ay concebido y concibiente*]; but what God con-ceives cannot be an accident, thus it must be substantiated. This substance, how-ever, cannot be the same person as God [*el mismo suppuesto de Dios*], for this would imply a contradiction which philosophers regard as absurd.[107] Therefore it entails the existence of another person [*supuesto o persona*], who is the son of God." Maldonado disputed this, citing Thomas Aquinas and Nicholas Lyra. For God, he argued, there can be no distinction between action and essence. As Aristotle argued, to understand and to will are sterile in the sense that they produce nothing. But, Maldonado continued, adopting the basic nominalist position, even if we argue that this generalization holds true only for mortals, but not for God—that is, that God is able to do what he chooses by simply willing it—in fact, there are many things that God *could* do that he has not done and will never do. There is thus no validity to the argument that God engendered from his own essence a coeternal son of equal potency. "Aside from the fact that there is no place in Scripture that states [that] this [happened]," Maldonado wrote, "natural reason holds such en-gendering to be impossible and absurd." A son cannot be coeternal with the father: he must come into being after the father who produced him. As Nicholas Lyra stated, Maldonado went on, adding, "and I have heard other theologians say [this]," even God cannot engender himself. Learned Christians have argued that the production of a son is a necessary result of divine perfection; but if this were so, one would have to infer that God created himself, as an expression of his perfection. If he were incapable of doing so, he would not be God, being imperfect. He further cited Pablo de Santa Maria ("Burgense") as having stated in his *Scrutinium scripturarum* that only material, corruptible beings could engage in the act of generation; a perfect, divine being could not. Finally, Maldonado argued, if God were a trinity of persons, he would not have hidden this phenomenon from his people, the Israelites, for as he said to Moses (Deut. 29:29): "The secret things belong to the Lord our God; but the things that are revealed belong to us and to our children forever, that we may do all the words of the law." Nor would God have hidden such a thing from Moses, to whom he entrusted the teaching of the existence of one, single God—a teaching repeated many times in Scripture. Moses and the prophets would simply have been lying if, knowing that God existed in three persons, they taught the Israelites that he was one and without peer.

At this point Maldonado moved to a rhetorical mode. One senses that he was aware that this was his final statement. I will quote at length these last passages of the letter.

From everything I have said, it can be concluded that God is One and unique and of a single person, as demonstrated in the reasonings [*razones*] and unambiguous verses [*authoridades*] of Holy Scripture, [according to which] there is none other than he, the true God of Israel who took his host out of Egypt with such wonders and miracles. Thus one must adopt his faith and no other, and observe the law that he gave to Moses, which is the true one, in order to merit from his divine hand the reward of glory and eternal life which he promised on Mount Zion for all his prophets. For it is not probable that the reward for the just must be in heaven, as Christian scholars teach—[a notion] which I have confuted in the last debate I had with the calificadores under the pretext of [my] having doubts. They did not respond with a single word, as your honor is witness, from which I infer that they accept my truth. For as the common proverb puts it, "Silence is consent." Not for lack of wisdom (for they are exceedingly learned), but out of prudence, so as not to contradict a truth so manifest, following the counsel of Ecclesiastes [Sirach], chapter 4: "Never speak against the truth," and chapter 5, "Be meek to hear the word, that thou mayst understand, and return a true answer with wisdom. If thou have understanding, answer thy neighbor: but if not, let thy hand be upon thy mouth, lest thou be surprised in an unskillful word, and be confounded."[108] From which your honor can see how vain are the hopes for reward among those who toil in the Christian law and faith, for they [that law and faith] have no basis in Holy Scripture [*S. Sra. Canonica ni agiographa de los prophetas*]. For "Surely the Lord God does nothing without revealing his secret to his servants and prophets," as Amos said in chapter 4,[109] and as all the prophets have promised in the name of the Holy God of Israel glory and eternal life in Zion and Jerusalem as a reward for the righteous after the universal judgment of the peoples. May the Lord grant his divine mercy to you, Ilustrissimo Señor, and to all those who hope to share in it. Meanwhile may the day come that you be showered with the blessings of his munificent hand, as I, your helpless and humble servant, desire. . . . Written on 22 November 1638.

Heli Judio Nasareo unworthy [servant] of the God of Israel, alias Silva.[110]

While Francisco Maldonado was debating theological issues with the calificadores, construction of the "set" for the approaching auto-da-fé was proceeding in Lima's main plaza. We know about the construction of the grandstands and other necessary structures (which took two masters and sixteen African slaves fifty days to erect) because the process was recounted in excruciating detail by the priest Fernando de Montesinos, who was appointed by the Lima Inquisition to write an account of the auto-da-fé.[111] Montesinos's chronicle is the only source we possess about the lavish auto. It was written, among other things, to sell to the public at a profit; but it was also a transparent piece of boosterism for the Inquisition. In so far as the details can be corroborated with Inquisition material concerning the prisoners, it is factually correct. This is not surprising, as many people had witnessed the auto and the Inquisition granted the account its imprimatur.

Tedious as the account may seem to the modern reader, lingering as it does on matters of costume and drapery, it does convey the image the authorities hoped to project when they staged the auto. Montesinos achieved this by providing sumptuous visual detail and by underscoring the presence of dignitaries, officers, and soldiers. He offered a detailed description of the procession of the participants, including the prisoners, from the Inquisition compound to the site of the auto on Sunday morning, Saint Ildefonso Day, January 23, 1639. While he focused on the orderly pomp of the civic display, however, he did allow Francisco Maldonado de Silva to surface briefly in a description of a moment that introduces a note of disharmony:

> First came the crucifixes [taken from the churches of Lima], accompanied by the priests and sacristans, in large numbers. After them came the penitents [who had been sentenced] for minor crimes, the witches, and the bigamists. Then came the judaizers in their sambenitos. Those among them who were to be given lashes had thick ropes around their throats. Finally came those who were to be relaxed in person, wearing corozas and sambenitos [that were painted] with flames, as well as various kinds of demons, serpents, and dragons, and carrying green crosses—with the exception of Licenciado Silva who, being rebellious, refused to carry one. All the others carried green candles.[112]

It seems evident from the way Maldonado de Silva was mentioned—"Licenciado Silva"—that he had become a notorious figure who needed no introduction. Certainly the prisoners designated to be relaxed would have attracted the greatest attention, especially if their sentences had indeed been kept secret from the public. Maldonado de Silva would probably have been immediately recognizable to the crowd, particularly if his hair and beard were still uncut. Further distinguishing him from the other prisoners were the two books he had so painstakingly written, now strung around his neck.

AVTO
DE LA FE
CELEBRADO EN
LIMA A 23. DE ENERO
DE 1639.

AL TRIBVNAL DEL SANTO OFICIO
de la Inquificion, de los Reynos del Perù, Chile,
Paraguay, y Tucuman.

POR EL LICENCIADO DON
Fernando de Montefinos, Presbitero,
natural de Offuna.

CON LICENCIA DEL ILVSTRISSIMO
feñor Inquifidor General, y feñores del Confejo de
fu Mageftad, de la Santa, y General
Inquificion.

En Madrid. En la Imprenta del Reyno,
año de 1640.

Figure 9. Frontispiece of Fernando Montesinos, *Auto de la fe celebrado en Lima 23. de enero de 1639* (Madrid 1640). Houghton Library, Harvard College Library.

But he was by no means the only prisoner to attract attention. Eyes must also have sought out the powerful Portuguese New Christian merchant Manuel Bautista Pérez, reportedly known by the Peruvian New Christians as the *Gran Capitan*, and one of the wealthiest merchants in the New World. Montesinos's account depicts him as having been able to exercise a degree of leadership even within the prison. By means of secret communications, he successfully convinced his brother-in-law and fellow prisoner Sebastian Duarte—who had confessed (or "confessed")—to revoke his confession, and as a result Sebastian Duarte died a negativo.[113]

Maldonado de Silva seems to have been isolated from this group—and not, as the Inquisition would have us believe, because of a bout of temporary deafness. His arrest came in 1627, eight years before the first "Complicidad" arrests, and well before many of those arrested had even arrived in Peru. During his trial he gave information about the judaizing of only one person, namely his (deceased) father. His sisters were the only other New Christians to testify against him. Even if some of the others who were sentenced for judaizing in 1639 were in fact judaizers (as is surely possible), he appears to have known none of them personally. He had only heard *about* one of them from his father—the now elderly surgeon Tomé Cuaresma.

By contrast, there were many ties—kinship as well as commercial—binding those arrested as part of the "Gran Complicidad." In prison, neither those who accepted what may well have been Manuel Bautista Pérez's advance tutelage to remain negativos nor those who confessed and were sentenced as reconciliados had reason to wish to be associated with Maldonado de Silva. Bautista Pérez (even if he was in fact a judaizer) may have regarded Maldonado's flamboyant judaizing as dangerous and, ultimately, as meaningless. Maldonado's independent course is given striking expression by his solitary refusal to carry the green cross in the procession. Most likely he was not, and never had been, intimately connected to a network of judaizers, or even of Portuguese New Christians.

Let us return to the events of January 23, 1639. At three o'clock in the afternoon, after the reading of the sentences, a violent windstorm suddenly struck Lima. According to the account of Montesinos, it was "so severe that long-term residents of this city affirmed they had seen nothing so strong in many years." The wind, Montesinos reported, tore the canopy over the grandstands (*tablado*) just above Francisco Maldonado de Silva's head. Maldonado, "looking at the sky, said, 'The God of Israel has made this happen, so that he can see me face to face from heaven.'"[114] Inevitably, this story became part of the mystique around Maldonado de Silva. Whether or not there is a grain of truth in it—and of course something like it may actually have happened—it reinforces an image of Maldonado as a man who faced death, as he lived much of his life, alone with his beliefs.

At the close of the auto-da-fé, the eleven accused judaizers who had been sentenced to death were turned over to the secular arm—that is, the civil authorities. They were taken to the *brasero* outside the city. Sensational as this finale to the auto was, Montesinos did not describe it in his account. The defiant negativos, insisting on their loyalty to the Church to the end, would have been garroted before being burned. From the final entry in the trial summary, we learn that Francisco Maldonado, in contrast, was burned alive at the stake, along with the two books around his neck.[115]

Unlike the other dogmatista martyrs discussed here, Francisco Maldonado de Silva seems to have had no inkling of humanist and Protestant attacks on Catholic post-apostolic traditions. One wonders about this gap in the awareness of a man who was deeply driven to search out weaknesses in the Church's positions. One possible explanation may be that Francisco Maldonado de Silva avoided making contacts with other judaizers or theologically unorthodox persons. Such a path of caution may have been urged upon him by his father, who had adopted this path after he was reconciled.

Yet his father (and mentor), prior to his own arrest, had had fairly extensive contacts with judaizers in Potosí. Even if Potosí in the late sixteenth century was a post-Tridentine Iberian town, it was a boom town that drew together men from widely diverse backgrounds. Indeed, among the various Portuguese men sentenced along with Maldonado de Silva's father for judaizing was a miner named Antonio Rodriguez de Leon, "of Bayonne."[116] It hardly seems possible that news of the Protestant assault on the Church had failed to reach this circle.

Even within the Peruvian orbit, people must have been aware of manifestations of Protestantism. Surely judaizers would have taken an interest in the Lima tribunal's prosecution of luteranos. The claims of defiant luteranos who were burned at the stake in the 1570s and 1580s must have been widely known, if only because of the publicity the Inquisition itself gave them when their sentences were publicly read at autos-da-fé. One thinks of the case of Mateo Salado, arrested in 1571 and burned at the stake in 1573, who asserted that Erasmus and Martin Luther were "enlightened saints of God [santos alumbrados de Dios]."[117] Then there is the case of Juan Bernal, a tailor from the Low Countries who was burned alive at the stake in Lima in 1581 as an openly pertinacious luterano. Bernal refused to take an oath on a crucifix, attacked Catholic belief in the intercessory power of priests and saints (which he regarded as a form of idolatry), and generally rejected Catholic tradition as a human invention.[118]

Yet there is no evidence that the judaizers in Diego Núñez de Silva's circle derived theological support from arguments of luteranos. In the absence of evidence, it would be foolish to infer that they must have done so simply because we have evidence of such cross-fertilization in Mexico, Portugal, and Spain. In sum, we cannot exclude the possibility that crypto-Jewish circles in the Viceroyalty of Peru—in contrast to circles we have encountered elsewhere—stayed within the perimeter of crypto-Jewish polemics, relying principally on what Nathan Wachtel has described as a "cult of memory."[119]

Certainly Maldonado's reading of books—or more precisely, what we know of his reading—reflects no access to innovative currents of Reformation thinking. Among the fifty-seven titles listed in the (admittedly incomplete) inventory of his possessions drawn up by the Inquisition in 1627,[120] only one work can be said with confidence to have shaped his polemical thinking: Pablo de Santa María's *Scrutinium scripturarum*. This late medieval work, written in 1432–1434 by the former rabbi Solomon Ha-Levi of Burgos more than forty years after his conversion to Christianity,[121] sought to remove the basic theological obstacles to the Jewish reception of Christianity—obstacles of which, as an apostate, the author had particular insight. He clearly recognized that the Jews' strongest polemical edge was their insistence on a straightforward, if not strictly literal, interpretation of the biblical text. Santa María therefore sought to build a defense of Christianity that was structurally similar to contemporary Jewish polemics, deploying biblical prooftexts that were persuasive in their simple sense.[122] When Maldonado de Silva read this work—at least this is what he reported to the inquisitors—it seemed to him that the Jewish position was simply stronger than the Christian one, from a bibliocentric perspective that he took for granted. Given the central role Santa María's work played in his judaizing career, by his own account, we may wonder whether Maldonado's text-based crypto-judaizing did not constitute simply a development of late medieval Jewish polemics.

We will come back to this. But let us for a moment take a look at the rest of what we know of Maldonado's library.[123] Unfortunately, it is difficult to identify definitively many of the books listed in the inventory of his sequestered goods, because the inquisition official who drew up the list often itemized these books in the most economical way possible—sometimes indicating nothing more about a volume than an author's last name. It is evident, though, that the library was mainly a professional tool for someone in medical practice. Some of the medical works are canonical, such as the *Prognostikon* attributed to Hippocrates, as well as unidentified works by Vesalius, Galen, and Dioscorides. Others are contemporary practical medical manuals in Spanish, such as a work listed as *Verdadera medicina, cirujía y astrología*. A more general interest in natural history is reflected in a work on "The Properties of Rocks" and a work by Pliny, most likely Pliny the Elder's *Natural History*.

Striking in this inventory, when compared with many contemporary libraries, is the lack of works in humanistic fields. There are no texts in history, philosophy, or geography. True, there are at least two literary works: a volume of the comedies of Lope de Vega, and the unremarkable, popular emblem book *Emblemas Morales* of Juan de Horozco y Covarrubias (Segovia 1589). But overall, the scanty representation of nonscientific, nontheological works in the inventory of Maldonado's books suggests that Maldonado (and his father) had a rather limited interest in secular humanistic studies.

The inventory does not yield much in the field of theology, either. Despite Maldonado's theological inquisitiveness, the list reveals only three items that were (or might have been) important to his religious formation. Two of them have already been mentioned: *Scrutinium scripturarum* and a "*Salmi Davidis*"—the latter possibly being the work by Gilbert Génebrard that Maldonado mentioned during his trial. The third, however, is worth a moment of consideration. *De los nombres de Cristo* is a work by the controversial theologian Fray Luis de León, whose converso background and unconventional piety landed him in prison for five years. David

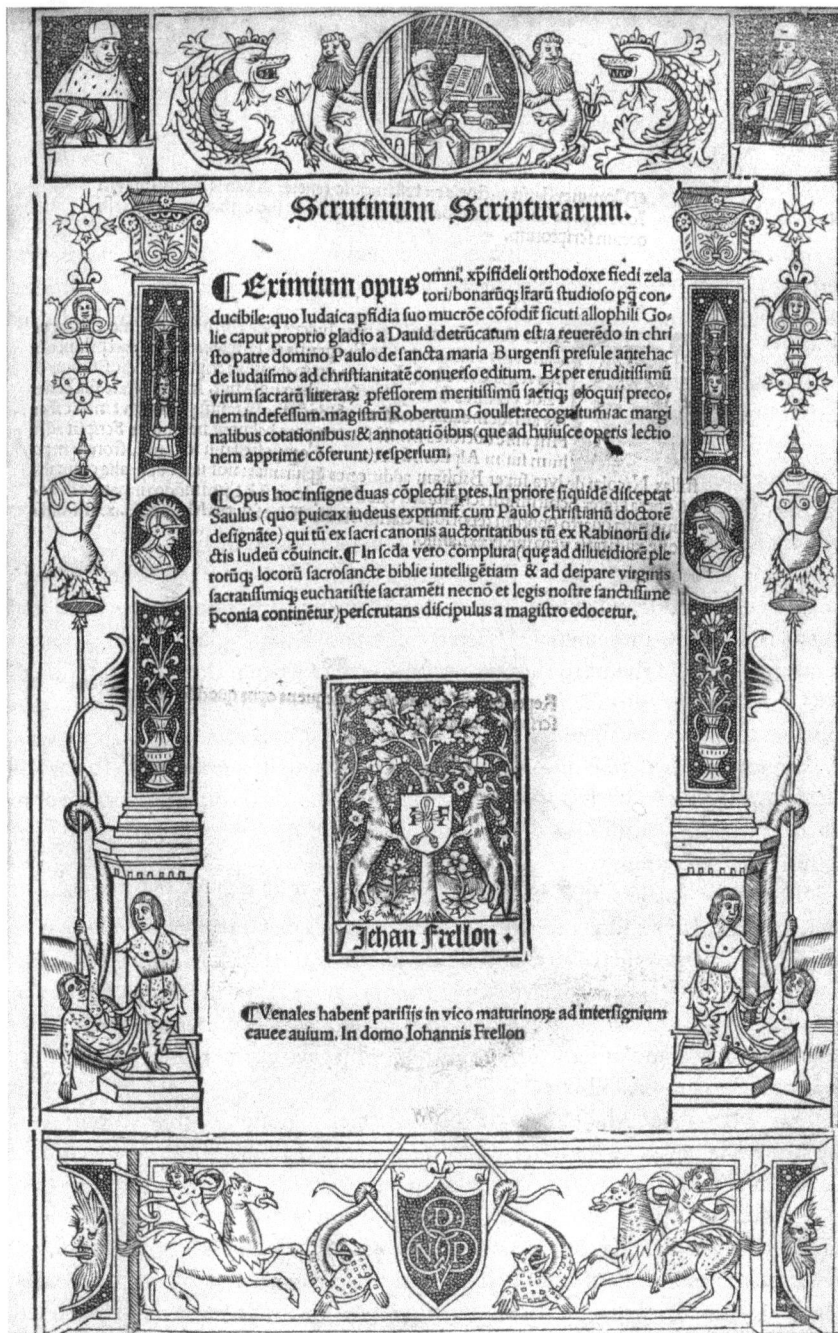

Figure 10. Frontispiece of Paulus de Santa Maria, *Scrutinium Scripturarum* (Paris [1513?]). The New York Public Library.

Gitlitz has postulated that this work "may have been attractive to Judaizers because of its abundant citation of Old Testament material."[124]

But Maldonado de Silva did not need such citations. A discussion of his reading would be incomplete without noting a book that is not listed in the inventory, but that was surely the most important single work in his theological formation: namely, the Vulgate Bible. Maldonado's ability to cite biblical passages verbatim in Latin—and to construct his beliefs around them—leaves no doubt that he had studied the Vulgate very carefully, and probably owned a copy.[125] In his efforts to arrive at a proper understanding of this text, he was presumably aided by another work listed in the inventory, a book listed only as "Ambrosio Calepino." This would have been a copy of the Latin dictionary by the fifteenth-century Augustinian monk of that name.[126]

Everything we have hypothesized thus far suggests that Francisco Maldonado de Silva (along with his father) was driven to a bibliocentric judaizing theology without recourse to the Reformation attack on Catholic tradition. He may, however, have been familiar with a Reformation spirit of interiorized belief through Luis de León's work and at least one other Catholic source. It may be recalled that when Maldonado presented his secretly composed theological writings to the inquisitors, he told them (so they wrote) that he had written them in refutation of Luis de Granada's *Introducción del Símbolo de la fe*. It is possible that this book was supplied to him by the inquisitors, with a request that he respond to its arguments. We cannot know whether his prison writings were actually a response to this work, since they were destroyed. But it is also possible that he had read this work prior to his arrest, taking an interest in its focus on biblical texts even if he rejected the author's interpretations.

It may be recalled that Luis de Carvajal was also drawn to the sixteenth-century current of Catholic spirituality to which Luis de Granada gave expression, with its asceticism, interiority, and biblicism. It is true that Maldonado, unlike Carvajal, does not appear to have drawn from what we may call the "vocabulary of interiority." Yet it is certainly possible that Maldonado read and was inspired by Luis de Granada and other Catholic authors who gave expression to a powerfully personal religious sensibility.

But what about Maldonado de Silva's "athletic" notion of martyrdom? Was the strident language of his letters to the synagogue of Rome simply a reflection of his personality?

It was, surely, that too. But it seems highly likely that he had heard stories—not only from his father, but from people around him who disseminated news of sensational events—about crypto-Jewish and *luterano* martyrs of the Inquisition who had dramatized their defiance. It was crypto-Jewish patterns that most likely led him to perform two of the signature acts of crypto-Jewish martyrdom, that is, self-circumcision and the adoption of a Hebrew name. The fact that we cannot connect the dots to specific episodes is perhaps a reminder of how much we do not know about what was done in crypto-Jewish circles, and about what further revelations may be hidden in Inquisition files.

We can speculate, at least, that Maldonado de Silva may have known of the career of Luis Carvajal through his father, who maintained ties with a crypto-Jewish network up to his arrest in 1601. (I infer this from the fact that Álvaro Núñez was a guest in the home of Maldonado's father around 1596, the year Carvajal was burned at the stake, or some time thereafter.)[127] But Diego Nuñéz de Silva undoubtedly had stories of defiant crypto-Judaism to relate to his son that came from closer at hand as well. In 1595, when he was in Tucumán province, two Portuguese conversos were burned at the stake in Lima as defiant judaizers. One refused to speak a word to the inquisitors after he confessed under torture, and was reportedly burned alive. The other admitted he had practiced the Law of Moses for eight years and wanted to die in it.[128] In 1600, a Portuguese converso being tried in Lima likewise insisted that he would die in the Law of Moses, "in which his fathers and ancestors had died," and was burned at the stake.[129] Moreover, as we have mentioned, a man whom Maldonado's father had instructed in the Law of Moses, Gregorio Díaz Tavares, was burned at the stake just after the auto in 1605 at which Diego Nuñéz de Silva was reconciled, after having engaged in disputations with inquisitors. And as we have noted, the timing of Maldonado de Silva's self-circumcision and "declaration" to his sister Isabel came in close proximity to the burning at the stake of the defiant judaizer Manuel Tavares, who had been circumcised in Livorno and had adopted the name David.

There were publicly known precedents in the Peruvian sphere, then, for many of Maldonado's key actions. But there is one striking act in his career for which we know of no precedent—an act that was particularly expressive of the militant and masculine self-image of a dogmatista martyr: that is, taking the Nazirite vow. Not only was this act not part of the repertoire of the crypto-Jewish martyr, but taking the Nazirite vow had also become very rare in the wider early modern Jewish world.[130] Yet Maldonado de Silva's vow became part of the mystique around his career in the lore of the Portuguese-Jewish diaspora. Unique as it may have been, it resonated among his admirers; and a closer look suggests that it was, in an indirect way, tailored to appeal to a seventeenth-century audience.

It was not the vow *per se* that made a mark, but the association of this vow with the biblical Nazirite Samson, who in Reformation Europe had become a celebrated dramatic figure. Indeed, as one scholar has put it (albeit in the English context), "Allusions to the Samson story are ubiquitous in the seventeenth century, in both low-brow and high-brow culture, among Royalist apologists and Puritan pamphleteers. Now Charles I invokes the Samson legend—and now John Milton."[131] The early modern development of this story throughout Reformation Europe, Catholic and Protestant, drew on an ancient Christian tradition that associated Samson with the figure of the suffering Christ. The fact that rabbinic tradition rather shunned the figure of Samson did not inhibit the converso imagination, either in the Iberian lands or outside them.

Indeed, a few years after Maldonado de Silva's death, the converso author Antonio Enríquez Gómez—at the time living as a crypto-Jew in France—wrote an epic work about the biblical Samson.[132] The impulse to write this work may well have been triggered by Maldonado de Silva's career, of which Enríquez Gómez was certainly aware. At the same time, the work belonged to an Iberian literary universe in which Samson figured prominently. In fact, only a few years before Enríquez Gómez composed his *Sánson Nazareno,* two Spanish authors made Samson the protagonist of their works.[133]

The possibility that Enríquez Gómez was at least partly inspired to write his *Sánson Nazareno* by Maldonado de Silva is reinforced by the fact that he used the imagery of Samson in a long poem memorializing the judaizing martyr Judah Creyente (alias Don Lope de Vera), burned at the stake in 1644—a figure who will be the subject of the next chapter. In the poem, titled "Romance al divin mártir Judá Creyente, martirizado en Valladolid por la Inquisición," Enríquez Gómez associated this martyr's strength with Samson's physical prowess. He praised him as a "soldier of the ancient army of Sinai" who "recalled the bravery of the powerful Maccabees,"[134] and had the martyr view himself as resembling "that other Samson, bound to the columns of the temple, dying in order to live, though the Philistines regret it."[135]

As unaware as Maldonado may have been, then, of Reformation rhetoric and turmoil, he was by no means a provincial, backwater figure. He knew something about the kind of uncertainties that gripped much of Europe. In a life conspicuous for its unstable features—familial, financial, theological, geographical, and "racial"—Francisco Maldonado de Silva found stability, as did many others, in a "transparent" biblical text that provided comfort, certainty of belief, and inspiration for a new self-conception.

A HEBREW SCHOLAR AT THE
UNIVERSITY OF SALAMANCA

6

In 1644, a hidalgo named Lope de Vera y Alarcón was burned alive in Valladolid for judaizing, and quickly joined the ranks of the celebrated martyrs. There is no evidence or reason to believe that he had any Jewish ancestry.[1] He was denounced and arrested in 1639, at the age of nineteen, while he was at the University of Salamanca, where he had competed (by one hostile account, without success) for a chair in Hebrew.[2] His intimate acquaintance with the Hebrew Bible and his recognition of the inadequacy of the Vulgate (as a result of his reading forbidden works by Erasmus), along with his contacts with heterodox Portuguese conversos studying at Salamanca, seem to have been critical factors in raising doubts in his mind about the teachings of the Church.

Unfortunately the original trial documents have not been preserved, and we must rely primarily on the summaries of his case sent by the Valladolid tribunal to the Suprema periodically during the course of the trial.[3] However, we can glean some information about his family background from another source (which must, however, be treated with great caution). It is a dossier containing the testimony of residents of Lope de Vera's hometown, San Clemente, located in La Mancha in the heart of New Castile. The testimony concerned Lope de Vera as well as his brother Diego and their father (confusingly also named Lope de Vera). There was no tribunal in San Clemente, but a commissioner of the Inquisition stationed there was authorized to interrogate witnesses who were summoned or who came forward on their own initiative. The gathering of the testimony began a few months after Lope de Vera's arrest and continued, due to questions that began emerging about the orthodoxy of his father, well after young Lope's death at the stake.[4]

What initially triggered the interrogation of residents of San Clemente was testimony the Valladolid tribunal had gathered about an episode that had occurred prior to Lope de Vera's arrest in May, 1639. According to this testimony (which has not been preserved), Lope de Vera, while a student at the University of Salamanca, wrote his father asking him for permission to go to Japan to evangelize. The father, adamantly opposed to this, fetched both Lope de Vera and his younger brother Diego (also studying at the university) from Salamanca and took them to Madrid, presumably on their way back to San Clemente. In Madrid, one or more

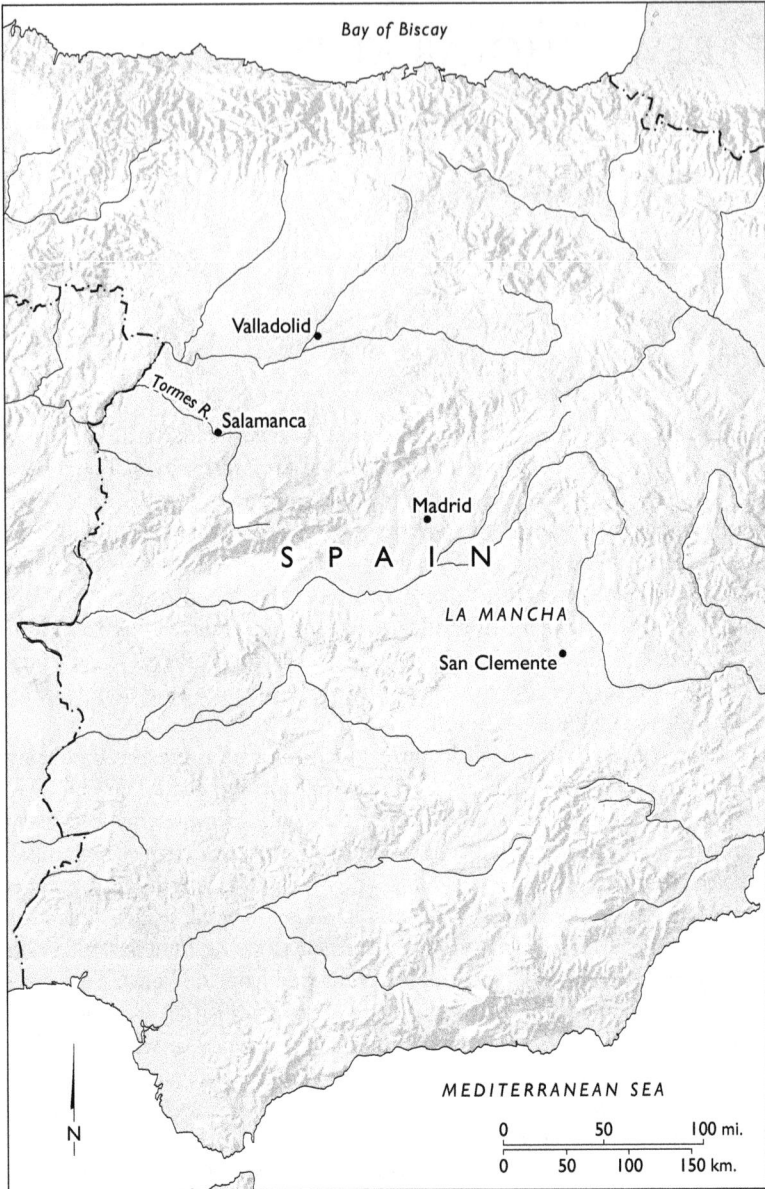

Map 4. Seventeenth-century Spain, with locations important to the career of Lope de Vera.

witnesses said, the two brothers slipped away from their father and visited the home of a "Jew from Oran." When they reached his home, they found that the Jew was not there. But his servant, also a Jew, let the brothers in, whereupon Lope de Vera began raising "certain questions and doubts" with him. The servant declined to reply, saying they should wait for his master to return—which they did not do, perhaps fearful of arousing their father's ire.

The first three witnesses who were questioned in San Clemente affirmed the main lines of this story. None of them mentioned that the Jew concerned was "from Oran" (although the presence of such a Jew in Madrid was not impossible).[5] More significant in raising questions about the information the Inquisition had received was the fact that according to the second witness, Lope de Vera had indeed asked his father for permission, but not to go to Japan to evangelize. He had wanted "to go to Algiers or Jerusalem to be converted." The witness related that after the young Lope de Vera had been arrested by the Inquisition, his widowed aunt Ana de Tévar, calling him a "wretched traitor [*perro traidor*]," revealed to her the story of his visit to the Jew in Madrid. The aunt further told her that on another occasion Diego de Vera had told her that he and his brother Lope were upset because Lope had not been able to study things at the university that he, Diego, and other students were able to study—so much so that he "had it in mind to go to Jerusalem." He did not seem to be taking any steps to do so, however: most of the time he shut himself up at home and did not go out even to go to mass.[6]

Predictably, Ana de Tévar was the next witness to be summoned to appear before the commissioner. In mid-December 1639, she testified that about fifteen months earlier Lope de Vera had written two letters to his father, which she had seen and read, in which he asked for permission to go to "those places." She said she understood that his plan was motivated by a wish to gain more merit in God's eyes—clearly implying a missionary intent. Given the previous witness's testimony, the commissioner regarded this as an evasion if not a falsification, and presented her with a detailed account of what that witness had reported her saying. Seeking to extricate herself, Ana de Tévar, without fully endorsing everything the previous witness had said, admitted that Lope de Vera himself had told her that he wanted to go to "those parts" because "in this country they did not appreciate his learning [*sus letras*], and that he would like to go to a place where he could engage in them [*donde el uviesse con ellas*], and that he wanted to save his soul more than [he wanted to own] any hacienda in this realm."

Even if we accept this testimony at face value, much is hidden from view. Had Lope de Vera selectively been denied access to works that his brother and other students were allowed to read? If so, why? Had Diego and Lope really been so indiscreet as to tell their aunt that Lope wanted to go to Jerusalem? Had the story about Lope's wish to go to Japan been concocted by the family to tell others, in order to explain the father's hasty rounding up of his sons? We don't know.

In evaluating what this testimony may or may not disclose, we must keep in mind that it was gathered at a time when Lope de Vera's arrest was well known to the residents of San Clemente. On the one hand, the witnesses would not have wanted to embroil themselves with the Inquisition by appearing to withhold information. This might have encouraged them to tell the truth. On the other hand, the tribunal presented them with detailed leading questions, which may have led them to say what they believed the Inquisition wanted to hear.

Still, as we shall see, the testimony about Lope de Vera's wish to leave Spain for a Muslim land coincides with his own direct testimony as paraphrased in the summaries to the Suprema. But before we proceed to Lope de Vera's trial, let us try to glean a bit more about his father—and indirectly about the son's upbringing—from the testimony about him gathered in San Clemente.

The senior Don Lope de Vera was a personage of some standing in that town, holding the offices of *regidor perpetuo* (councilman) and *depositario general*. In May 1640, testimony was gathered from three witnesses that raised questions about the orthodoxy of his belief. The first witness, a familiar of the Inquisition, came forward on his own to report remarks about the senior Lope de Vera that had been made by Diego de Ávalos, a first cousin of the elder Lope de Vera's wife. Ávalos had told him, in the presence of Cristóbal Ángel, that the senior Lope de Vera "was such a bad Christian" that in his home there was not a single religious image (this would certainly have been an anomaly in seventeenth-century Spain). He also reported that once on Holy Thursday, while he was visiting Don Lope's home, Lope de Vera began beating a slave at the very time when the Eucharist was passing in solemn procession outside.[7] Diego de Ávalos begged him to stop the beating, which seemed to him bad behavior on such a holy night. But Don Lope was not deterred.

The scene described by the witness is heavy with symbolic overtones. One of the principal ways of expressing hostility to the Church in early modern Spain was to express disdain for the cult of the host. It seems possible that the senior Don Lope—not, apparently, an active judaizer but quite possibly a skeptic hostile to the Church—chose to express his violent feelings about the veneration of the host by directing his anger more safely at a helpless member of his household.

In a further discussion with Diego de Ávalos (again in the presence of Cristóbal Ángel), Ávalos told the familiar that he had heard that the senior Lope de Vera once had a tutor to teach him the Bible. In post-Tridentine Spain, this piece of gossip constituted an insinuation of heterodoxy. Ávalos had also heard that when the Inquisition had initially arrested Don Lope's son and imprisoned him in a chapel of the local church in San Clemente, the young Lope had told someone (he didn't know who) that he held his father responsible for the predicament in which he found himself.[8]

Cristóbal Ángel and Diego de Ávalos were summoned to confirm this testimony, and did. Cristóbal Ángel, seventy-six years old, felt compelled to add that about twenty years earlier, his own Moorish slave had told him that one of Lope de Vera's slaves was teaching him the Bible—implying that Don Lope was "infecting" his entire household with heretical ideas. (Lope de Vera's slave, he claimed, had also tried to dissuade his Moorish slave from accepting baptism.)[9]

All of this is very questionable testimony indeed. What it tells us is that a cloud of suspicion was raised around Don Lope de Vera during the trial of his son. It could have been fueled by resentments about which we know nothing. But it may also have been stirred by a tendency in the elder Lope de Vera to exhibit bizarre and uninhibited behavior. For example, the Inquisition had heard testimony —presumably contained in the full dossier that has been lost—that it was the father's habit after eating dinner to force his children to crawl under the table and kiss his feet. His widowed sister-in-law reportedly remarked that "he could well have raised [his children] better" if he had not behaved in this way.[10] (We may be allowed to wonder how such routine humiliation affected the young Lope de Vera—assuming that the testimony is accurate.) We will see further examples of such eccentricity (and perhaps even contempt for Catholic orthodoxy) on the part of Lope de Vera senior. But eccentricity did not constitute a crime against the faith, and the Inquisition did not find sufficient basis in the testimony it gathered to pursue a case against the father.

Let us turn now to the career of the focal figure of this chapter, young Lope de Vera. Because the six summaries of the trial sent to the Inquisition—each of which traces the course of the entire trial—provide different details about the interrogation at various stages (though there is also much repetition), I have constructed a single narrative combining material from all of them.

We do not know the names of the two persons who gave eyewitness information to the Inquisition about Lope de Vera's heterodox ideas.[11] They were likely among the Portuguese students (almost certainly conversos) with whom Lope de Vera engaged in theological discussions. If so, they may well have been on trial themselves. (A letter of 1650 from Rome by a man who had apparently been a Portuguese student at Salamanca at the time of Lope de Vera's arrest suggests that a number of Portuguese intellectuals in Salamanca, shocked by the arrest, fled to Madrid.)[12] If the two witnesses were indeed on trial, they would have informed on their acquaintance under considerable pressure, possibly even torture. Whatever the case, their testimony was sufficient to justify Lope de Vera's arrest in Salamanca on May 21, 1639, at the age of nineteen. He was imprisoned in the Valladolid inquisitorial cells a few days later. The testimony of the two witnesses is of considerable interest, since it offers insight—though from two somewhat different perspectives—into Lope de Vera's thinking prior to his arrest. Although the testimony is somewhat disjointed, I will try to preserve its general flow.

The first witness was described as a "minor," meaning that he was under the age of twenty-five. Lope de Vera had told him, he said, that in the entire five years he spent in Salamanca, he had never held a rosary. He was, he said, a Jew. Once while the two of them were standing on the bank of the Tormes River (a detail that suggests they had sought out a safely remote spot), Lope de Vera had removed a small book from his pouch and told the witness it was in Hebrew. He proceeded to read it ("backwards," as the witness reported!), perhaps to demonstrate that he was conversant with Scripture in its original language. He maintained that the Law of the Jews was the law favored by God. God had prohibited the worship of images and crosses. Jesus, he said, was a fraud. He tried to persuade the witness that Jews were superior to all other peoples and were the people most favored by God.

Lope de Vera argued, the witness continued, that if Jesus were God, how could he be a man of flesh and blood? And what heavenly signs had he made to prove that he had risen from the dead? He told the witness that if he, Don Lope, only knew the "prayers of the Law of Moses," he would readily convert to that Law. The Messiah, he said, was yet to come and would restore the Jews to their original condition.[13] The supposed Messiah that the "Christian wretches" worshipped was merely a crucified man who had been put to death because he was a fraud.

Particularly intriguing is the witness's recollection that Lope de Vera expressed the wish "that someone would take a cutlass and kill these Christian wretches [perros] who were persecuting him." As we shall see from Lope de Vera's own testimony, he seems to have been regarded as suspect in his religious views by authorities at the university well before his arrest, having made public remarks that challenged orthodox thinking.

One of the details the witness provided offers evidence that his testimony is essentially reliable. Lope de Vera told him, he said, that he had discovered in a certain book that "one of the twelve tribes had a king."[14] The book in question was the so-called *Diary of David Reuveni* (of which more later), which Lope de Vera had read in a manuscript copy. For now, suffice it to say that the work is a quasi-autobiographical account of the career of David Reuveni, a remarkable imposter who appeared in Europe in the 1520s claiming to be the brother of the king of the tribe of Reuben.

The witness's account is notable for its portrayal of the young Hebraist's violent impulses. As Lope de Vera and the witness were conversing, he testified, a cleric passed by. Seeing him, Lope de Vera expressed the wish that someone would beat him up. He went on to say that if the Inquisition seized him he would kill all of his captors with a cutlass, if he had one. Even at this early stage, his anger and frustration were also reportedly expressed in disdain for his own life. He said he didn't care a song if he died. It grieved him that his blood was not Jewish—the most noble blood in the world.[15]

While this witness depicted Lope de Vera as an unmistakable judaizer, the second witness suggested a more complex type. He said that when he had been with Don Lope de Vera and a group of other students, Don Lope had said that Catholicism required belief in "many things that were difficult to believe." He found other religions, he said, "more in conformity with natural reason," possessing articles of belief that were less difficult to accept. He could profess the Law of Mohammed or that of Moses, he said, both of which seemed in conformity with natural reason. The second witness, then, depicted Lope de Vera as a rationalist and skeptic who was weighing the comparative merits of Christianity, Islam, and Judaism. Of course it would be foolhardy to accept either witness's testimony at face value. Yet the two accounts may reflect different facets of the same personality, or fluctuations in the thinking of a man who, by his own admission, had a "vacillating" nature at this point in his life.

Lope de Vera was summoned to his first audience more than a month after his arrest, on June 30, 1639. He stated that he and his ancestors were Old Christians. In response to the standard question asked at the first audience—whether he knew why he had been arrested—he confessed to having had a fight, apparently a violent one, with a cousin. As a result, he had been denied communion for some period. Under further interrogation, however, he seems to have realized that the tribunal had concrete information of a more damaging kind.

One wonders whether he had ever considered a strategy to pursue, if his heretical conversations were to become known to the Inquisition. He may have been a sufficiently rash and uncalculating person that he had not. In any case, once he got an inkling of the information the Inquisition possessed, he appears to have hoped that by making a very early confession he could minimize his punishment.

Thus in the course of his first audience he began to reveal detailed and incriminating evidence—something most defendants resisted doing. Choosing this course meant that he had little time to reflect on the most advantageous way to present his case. He stated that he had not heard mass for four months on those days when it was compulsory. This presumably included the period when he had been denied communion. During those four months, he testified, he had read prohibited books, such as the *Annotationes* of Erasmus,[16] the diary of David Reuveni ("*la Embaxada de Rabid dabid*"),[17] and some Arabic works. He had also conversed with Portuguese students about the Hebrew language. Hebrew was, he had told them, the best and most ancient tongue in the world, the language God had taught to Adam before he sinned, and the language in which he spoke to the patriarchs and prophets.

He further admitted that in conversation he had said "he was a Jew and a Moor and would very much like to abandon Catholicism and go to Algiers." But when he had said this, he hastened to say, he had had no actual intention of abandoning Catholicism. He simply had a strong desire to talk with Jews and Moors and people of other groups (*naciones*), and wanted to read the Koran (which was prohibited in Spain). If he went to Constantinople, he had said, the sultan would have to make him an *alfaquí* of the great mosque, because of his excellent knowledge of Hebrew (presumably the summary should read "Arabic": perhaps a scribal error, or a slip on Don Lope's part). He might easily be inclined, he had said, to follow the Law of the Jews or the "sect of the Moors."[18]

Lope de Vera then confessed to conversations with a certain Portuguese student. The two had discussed and condemned some articles of the Catholic faith—in particular the Trinity (because it seemed impossible for God to make himself three and one), the Incarnation, and the real presence of God in the consecrated host.[19] They had discussed their convictions that one should not worship images, that religions contrary to natural religion (*contra el precepto y bendición natural*)

Figure 11. Title page of Inquisitor-general Gaspar Quiroga's important *Index of Prohibited Books* (Madrid 1583), extending the censorship of heretical books in Spanish lands. The New York Public Library.

were pernicious, and that the miracles associated with images and human beings were fraudulent.

None of this, of course, implied intentional judaizing. But Don Lope also testified that he and the Portuguese student had discussed the possibility of killing a chicken "in the Jewish way." Given the theological thrust of their conversation, this seems puzzling. What aspect of Jewish ritual slaughter, as described in the Hebrew Bible, could have appealed to their rationalistic sensibility? Perhaps it was the prohibition of the eating of animal blood, as expressed in Leviticus 17: 10–13, which links that prohibition with expiation and the sanctity of life. But perhaps less rational impulses were at work.

Toward the end of this first audience, Lope de Vera elaborated on a defense that he had already hinted at, one that he would return to repeatedly up to a certain point in his trial. While he had uttered apparently judaizing statements, he said, he had not actually been convinced of them. Rather, he liked to propose such arguments by way of disputation. Everything to which he had confessed had thus been pronounced in a spirit of intellectual experimentation. As if to explain himself further, he stated that his nature was so unstable and delicate (*tan vario y frágil*) that, having learned Hebrew and Arabic, he might easily be inclined to follow the Law of the Jews or "the sect of the Moors." He had found himself so confused by different texts that, if he found himself among Muslims, he might well follow their law and reject Christ, were it not for the threat of excommunication.[20]

Based on what the summaries reveal, Lope de Vera appears to have expressed no remorse at this first audience. Repentance, however, was virtually the only sentiment that the inquisitors were apt to respond to favorably—and then only if they believed it was genuine. The argument of intellectual adventurism and theological confusion was only likely to deepen inquisitorial suspicions. Yet this was to be his line of defense for the next eight months. The fact that the prisoner chose this defense may have to do in part with his proud nature, which might have prevented him from expressing false remorse, even when he knew he was in mortal danger. Or he may naively have believed that the inquisitors could appreciate (or even be impressed by) the seriousness of his theological searching.

In a morning audience on July 4, Lope de Vera resumed discussion of conversations with a Portuguese student whom he named (the summary does not give the name). Given some of the contents of the conversation, it seems evident that this was the same Portuguese student mentioned in the previous audience.[21] It seems significant that the notary afterward referred to this person as the prisoner's accomplice (*cómplice*), suggesting that he had been arrested and had perhaps informed on Lope de Vera. (Lope de Vera may even have known of his arrest, which might explain why he volunteered his name.)

Don Lope testified that in a conversation, he and this student had argued over a passage in Scripture in which God revealed how the Israelites might distinguish between a true and false prophet: if someone claiming to be a prophet told the people to deviate from the Law, this was proof that he was a false prophet.[22] It appears that the student regarded this passage as proof that Jesus was a false prophet. Lope de Vera said he was aware of the passage but did not know how to interpret it. But when he saw the student on a subsequent occasion, he told him that the student's conclusion was wrong: Jesus did not call for the abandonment of the Law of Moses, and indeed explicitly proclaimed that he'd come not to abolish it but to fulfill it.[23]

Lope de Vera testified that he knew this student was a Jew (i.e., a converso crypto-Jew) and had intended to leave Spain to practice Judaism. Don Lope had given the student to understand that he shared this intention. They even discussed which destination would be the best when they left. On this and other occasions, the Old Christian Hebraist and the Portuguese converso discussed certain Catholic ceremonies and articles of faith they believed to be "impossible." Lope de Vera repeated the triad of "irrational" Catholic doctrines he had already mentioned in discussions with this Portuguese student: the Trinity, the Incarnation, and the real presence in the host. In an interesting application of Scripture to support his rejection of these doctrines, the Portuguese student had quoted a verse from Psalms, "Be not like a horse or a mule, without understanding" (Ps. 31:9)—meaning, as Don Lope told the inquisitors, "that God said we need not subjugate our reasoning, in the manner of a horse or a mule, to things that seem impossible to the mind."[24] The two students agreed, further, that God had forbidden the veneration of images, and that it was pernicious to have clerics claiming to perform miracles, which were all fraudulent.

Questioning continued that afternoon. Lope de Vera now said it was the Portuguese student who had proposed killing a chicken in the Jewish fashion and eating it, but Lope had refrained from responding to such a dangerous proposal—a less incriminating version of his previous story. However, he did cease eating meat so as not to violate the Law of Moses, he said, knowing that the butchered animal involved would not have been killed in the proper way. Moreover, he avoided going to mass or confessing—not simply because he was no longer a believing Catholic, but because he felt this would constitute a violation of the Law of Moses.[25]

Lope de Vera seems to have developed a particularly close relationship to this Portuguese student. Once on a Sabbath, Don Lope was walking with him toward a bridge over the Tormes River. As they approached, he testified, he told the student that Jews do not cross rivers on the Sabbath. They consequently turned back so as not to violate the Law of Moses.

How Lope de Vera derived this supposed precept of Jewish law offers a fascinating glimpse of crypto-Jewish ingenuity. He had learned about the legendary Sambation River by reading the Hebrew diary of David Reuveni.[26] Further, he had read in the diary of David Reuveni[27] that the Jews who lived on the other side of the Sambation River, wishing to cross it, could do so only on the Sabbath, when the river rapids miraculously became calm, but they refrained from doing so on that day in order not to violate the Law of Moses. From this, Don Lope concluded that crossing a river on the Sabbath was forbidden by the Law of Moses—even over a bridge.

Lope de Vera testified about a conversation he'd had with another person whose discretion he must have trusted, a Portuguese physician (surely also a converso). He broached the subject of Scripture being susceptible to different interpretations. When the physician said he doubted this could be true, Don Lope said it was demonstrated by the fact that different groups (*naciones*) understood it differently. Christians believed the Law of Moses was not eternal, but prefigured a new Law. The Jews, in contrast, understood Scripture literally, and believed the Law was eternal. They believed Christ was a fraud, and they continued to await the Messiah. He added that Jews were not wrong to believe as they did. Lope testified that he did not make these statements quite so explicitly, but more guardedly, yet in a way that could nevertheless be plainly understood. Once confidence had been established between them, the physician had told him, "I swear, I need to leave Spain to become an apostate or practice Judaism."[28]

Of particular interest is the work Lope de Vera mentioned as his source for the information that Jews believed Christ was a fraud. Such an idea was not uncommon among crypto-Jews. Yet Lope explained that he had learned this from "a book called *Fortalitium fidei*"—a widely disseminated anti-Jewish book by the fifteenth-century Spanish author Alonso de Espina.[29] Espina's book deals with three categories of religious "enemies"—Christian heretics, Jews, and Muslims. In order to set up his attack on the beliefs of these enemies of the faith, he cited the arguments of each of them against Christianity. Such articulations of anti-Christian claims might well have intrigued curious and educated religious malcontents of various sorts. (It is worth noting that a generation later, the ex-converso Isaac Orobio de Castro, who settled as a Jew in Amsterdam, said he had read the *Fortalitium fidei* "with great interest" while he had been in Spain.)[30] This work does, in fact, enumerate some "Jewish" arguments against the messiahship of Jesus.[31]

In a subsequent audience held some days later,[32] Lope de Vera testified that when he had been a candidate for the Hebrew chair at Salamanca, in July 1638, he had argued with a cleric about whether the Messiah had come, taking the position (astonishing as this may seem) that he had not. Don Lope based his argument on a passage from Scripture that the sixteenth-century Franciscan theologian Pietro Colonna Galatino (the notary refers to him as "Pedro Galatino") cited along with a rabbinic interpretation that apparently struck Lope de Vera as persuasive.[33] (Galatino presumably mentioned the rabbinic interpretation in order to confute it.) But, Lope de Vera told the tribunal, even though he had made this argument, he hadn't actually believed what he was saying; he simply enjoyed proposing such arguments by way of disputation. Indeed, at the university and elsewhere, when he found himself with learned friends, he debated such matters so recklessly that his friends told him he was a crazy Hebrew Jew, and that he should really escape to Turkey.

In an audience of July 8, Lope de Vera testified that in conversations with others he had praised several banned authors for their learning, including "Abraham Abencera" (Abraham ibn Ezra), the Calvinist theologian Johannes Drusio, and Erasmus. He could not deny the doubt and confusion he experienced, which had led him to speak to the Portuguese student about going to foreign countries to follow the Law of those lands—but, he added, he had never had the intention of abandoning Catholicism.[34] He had doubted the Trinity, the Incarnation, and the real presence of the host for about two months. At that time he suffered from "confusion and vacillation," as he put it, and wished that God would perform some miracle to allow him to escape this condition. It was true that he had told the Portuguese student that it was wrong to venerate images, but inwardly he had not been certain about what he was saying, and he now firmly believed the teaching of the Church that one must venerate them.

In an audience shortly thereafter,[35] he testified that he had been in a state of doubt for about a month over whether God performed miracles through the medium of the images of saints. This doubt arose because he had read Erasmus's opinion that such miracles were fabricated in order to revive and sustain the faith of Catholics. After a month, however, he was freed of his doubts, and became firm in his belief that God did perform miracles through images of the saints. He eliminated his doubts by reading Scripture—in particular the episode of the brazen serpent, which proved that God performed miracles through images. (Don Lope was quick to add that he understood that the brazen serpent, which healed men bitten by snakes, was a prefiguration of the healing Christ).[36] He had not performed any Jewish ceremonies, he emphasized, except for refraining from crossing a bridge on the Sabbath, and even this he hadn't done with the intention of observing the Law of Moses, but only because his companion observed that Law.

In contradicting his prior testimony—in which he had indicated that he had refused to cross a bridge in order to avoid desecrating the Sabbath, and had ceased eating meat because the available meat had not been slaughtered according to Jewish law—Lope de Vera was violating a cardinal rule of defense before the Inquisition. A full, consistent confession coupled with expressions of remorse might result in a milder sentence. But equivocating could only implicate the defendant more deeply. While Lope de Vera clearly had had contacts with Portuguese crypto-Jews, he seems not to have been privy to the traditions of strategy under arrest and interrogation that had developed over time in crypto-Jewish networks.

On July 15, Lope de Vera was given his second admonition, and on July 18 his third, completing the preliminary stage of the trial.[37] On July 29, he identified some books that he had had in his possession, which had presumably been sequestered at his arrest: one with an indecipherable title;[38] a Latin and Aramaic translation of Haggai; a work of Johannes Drusio; another in Greek; one that the notary recorded him as identifying as "sold in Paris by Egidio Gerum";[39] a manuscript in Hebrew that he said was the diary of David Reuveni; and another in Hebrew that contained a portion of Scripture.

A month later, he was presented with the *acusación*. Required to reply on the spot, he insisted that he had not been heretical or deviated from the Catholic faith, although for a certain period his faith had faltered, as he had confessed. He admitted to having said in anger, "I swear to God that if I had a Turkish cutlass I would chop to pieces these Christian wretches who are persecuting me." He also admitted to having said that he wished to die in the Law of Moses, and that he regretted his blood was not "of the Jewish Law." But, once again prevaricating, he said that he had not actually believed he could be saved in the Law of Moses.

When presented with the *publicación*—a litany of charges based on testimony, with names of witnesses withheld—in mid-March, 1640,[40] he confirmed the heterodox statements to which he himself had confessed, but again denied any actual intention to apostatize. He emphasized that he was an Old Christian of noble parentage, and a mere youth, and he maintained that "everything he had confessed [to having said] he had said in the manner of a dispute, as a person who was curious to know the Hebrew language." He was a good Catholic who confessed and took communion and carried a rosary. One of the witnesses who testified against him, he said (presumably inferring the identity of the witness from information in the publicación) was a poor, spineless student of little understanding.

In an audience of March 20, he ratified his confessions. He said that he had no defense to make and asked the tribunal for mercy, because he was a good and Catholic Christian, as well as an Old Christian (which was presumptive evidence of his orthodoxy), and he had confessed the entire truth. His tribunal-appointed *curador*,[41] however, told him he had to present a defense. Don Lope was given a sheet of paper on which to prepare one.

On April 18, the curador argued in Lope de Vera's defense and cross-examined him, having him name *abonos*, that is, witnesses who could give testimony proving good character and proper religious observance. Lope reiterated that he was a good Christian and an Old Christian, though in San Clemente it was believed that he had Jewish and Moorish blood.

On June 13, Don Lope requested an audience. Once again contradicting himself, he confessed that he had in fact been inclined for a while to believe that the Law of Moses was the law in which one could be saved, though he had never been convinced "decisively [*no con determinación absoluta*]." He had been in this state, he said, from Lent of 1639 until the end of May that year. Entertaining such doubts about Catholicism was blindness and weakness on his part, he conceded, but when he had gone to his parents' home (or rather, as it seems, had been dragged there from Salamanca by his father), he had thrown off his inclination toward the Law of Moses under the beneficial supervision of his parents, and came to believe firmly that the Law of Christ was the true one.

He proceeded to jeopardize his case once again by altering his testimony about the one act of "Jewish" observance that he had continued to admit to. He now claimed that he had never made a decision to refuse to cross a bridge because it was the Sabbath. It was true, he admitted, that he had been walking toward the bridge, but he was actually heading for the church of Nuestra Señora de la Vega. One can imagine the inquisitors exchanging glances.

On July 13, 1640,[42] calificadores were summoned to deliberate on the case. While Lope de Vera was by his own admission guilty of having uttered heterodox opinions, these authorities felt that further clarification was needed. Only one of the calificadores's statements is given in detail. It reflects the frustration aroused by Lope de Vera's evasions and contradictions. The calificador remarked that Lope de Vera

> is an infidel and heretic and a confused Babel (*confusa bavilonia*). He is wicked and an apostate from our holy Catholic faith, and inclines to various other sects. He seems stubbornly resistant to reason, [that is,] to the sole true law of our Lord Jesus Christ. He views [this law] as bad, as contrary to reason, and as impossible. The law the prisoner embraces is the Law of Moses, whereby he reveals his [Jewish] blood.[43] In his confessions he is a *diminuto* [withholding the full truth], and [he formulates his confessions with] cunning. He is a Jewish apostate, a Moor, and a heretic, and he is trying to avoid punishment by making frivolous excuses.[44]

In October,[45] the tribunal voted to subject Lope de Vera to torture. Inquisitorial procedure required the Suprema's consent for this, and in December the Suprema granted its approval. But in February, when the warden was called before the tribunal to report on the health of the prisoners, this minor official reported that Lope de Vera had been suffering from severe quartan fever, a form of malaria in which fever develops approximately every four days. The inquisitorial physician who had treated him reported that it had been severe but had become manageable. The illness could not have come at a more fortuitous time. Having passed the entire winter ailing, the physician declared, Lope de Vera was now so weak that he could not withstand torture.

The summaries are silent about what transpired over the next six months. It was in this period that Lope de Vera underwent a striking inner transformation. The psychic processes that were triggered as he reflected on his situation are hidden to us. What we do know is that during this time, the heretofore vacillating prisoner resolved to adopt a martyr's posture—a posture that, remarkably, he maintained unswervingly until his death more than three years later.

The members of the tribunal grasped Don Lope's volte-face only gradually. Their first inkling seems to have come at an audience he requested in the spring of 1641 (it was granted on April 16), at which the prisoner announced that he was revoking all of his prior confessions. Everything he had confessed, he said, had been false, including his denunciation of the Portuguese student. He had only made his "confessions" because he'd heard that if a person denied charges that the Inquisition believed to be founded, he was likely to receive a sentence of perpetual prison, which he hoped to avoid.

He was summoned two days later to ratify his revocation. An exhaustive catalog of his confessions was read to him, and he was asked to affirm or disavow each one. This process required a series of seven further audiences, which stretched into late May. Finally, at an audience on May 29, Don Lope refused to cooperate further with this tedious formality. He announced that he would respond to further interrogation only before the pope. (Beinart has plausibly suggested that this idea may have been suggested by his reading of the diary of David Reuveni, who was received by the pope.)[46] Then, seizing the initiative, he reclaimed the audience chamber as a platform for his own beliefs. When the minutes of the audience were read back to him, he verified their contents, then declared that he

> wanted to be a Jew and to hold and believe everything that the tribe of Judah, scattered throughout the world, held and believed, because that was the truth. He had arrived at [this truth] through the reason and truth that God had granted him. He would prefer to state this before the pope. . . . Until now he had held and believed what the Roman Church held, but from this time forward he intended to hold and believe what the tribe of Judah held and believed.[47]

It was only in the Law of the Jews, he continued, that one could be saved, and he "wanted to live and die in the Law of the Lord that Scripture calls *el pentateuco torat adonay*."[48] He denied ever having performed any Jewish ceremonies, but announced that from this time forward he would do so. To call him a Jew would not be an insult, but a commendation.

Let us pause for a moment to consider Lope de Vera's prison experience. As we have noted, his passage from a state of mind that was strongly inclined to skepticism about Christianity to unflinching certitude in the Law of Moses was not an unparalleled phenomenon in the Reformation world. His reading of Erasmus's *Annotations on the New Testament* evidently so undermined his confidence in the Church's claims for the authority of the Vulgate and so distanced him from the text of the New Testament that he found himself experiencing doubts about the reliability of a tradition that rested on such problematic foundations. His discussions with Portuguese students reflect the development of a yet more radical critique—a critique of the very core of Christian belief—as he subjected it to rational scrutiny and found it wanting. But, as was the case with many early modern religious seekers, he may well have been struggling with doubts and toying with other possible beliefs—Jewish and Muslim in particular—without having arrived at any certain conclusions. Initially, he seems to have hoped that a confession of his doubts, and feigned repentance, would offer him a way out. The failure of the inquisitors to appreciate and respect him, one senses, along with the realization that they did not believe him, provoked deeper hostility to them and the institution they symbolized. The anguish of incarceration, intensifying this hostility, seems to have precipitated an unconditional embrace of a counter-theology, namely, "what the tribe of Judah held and believed."

The tribunal, interested in getting beyond the rhetoric and extracting information about a possible network of judaizers, asked the prisoner who had taught him the Law of Moses. Lope de Vera insisted that God alone had taught it to him, and that he had relied neither on other people nor on books. Indeed, he said, God had disposed him to incline to the Law of Moses from birth. But he had had to undergo a struggle to liberate himself from the Law of Christ—a false teaching that, he implied, was forced upon him by his environment. It was God who, in his mercy, had freed him from Catholicism and led him to "the truth possessed by the tribe of Judah."

Such a declaration strikes the modern reader who has read the summaries of the trial as disingenuous, to say the least. It is quite clear that Lope de Vera drew sustenance for his heterodox views from both books and people. We must ask what he achieved by depicting himself (and perhaps actually regarding himself) as an entirely independent religious seeker. The motivation was, I believe, twofold. First, he established authority for his beliefs in a way that parallels the claims of many early modern religious dissidents (including Luis Carvajal)—men and women who were able to justify their rejection of the authority of Catholic tradition and the Church hierarchy by means of a direct revelatory relationship with God. Second, he created a heroic image of himself as a person who stood alone against the immense power of a repressive regime. These two aspects of his martyr's posture were mutually reinforcing, particularly in the circumstances of his prolonged incarceration.

But let us return to the unfolding of events. In an audience two days later, Lope de Vera ratified his new position. He had evidently developed a new rhetoric as he underwent the transition from doubt to certitude, from equivocation to heroic resistance. He reiterated his belief "in what the tribe of Judah held and believed," and his intention "to live and die in the Law of Moses." These new terms of discourse underscored and dramatized the decisiveness of inner changes that had no visible manifestation. In keeping with his new sense of self-reliance, Lope de Vera declared that he no longer wanted the services of a curador.

Three weeks later the tribunal, in an effort to help him escape his "blindness and errors," summoned the prisoner to an audience with two calificadores. The learned clerics showed him passages in Scripture that, in their view, proved that the Law of Moses had been abrogated with the coming of Christ. Some, if not all, of these passages were culled from the New Testament. By this point, however, Lope de Vera was openly rejecting the New Testament. He also denied that Jesus was the Messiah. The true Messiah, he asserted, must be embraced by both Jews and gentiles. Jesus, however, had only been embraced by gentiles.

After the prisoner left the chamber, the calificadores determined that he was "very much in his right mind" and "very pertinacious in his Judaism, defending its principles with acuity."

A further audience with the calificadores was held.[49] It seems to have covered no new ground and merely gave Lope de Vera additional opportunity to unleash his rhetoric. The calificadores concluded that because of his pertinacious malice, intelligence, and knowledge of Hebrew, it was dangerous for him to remain within the Church. But the tribunal was not satisfied that it had done enough to try to convert him. Such great efforts, it should be said, would not have been wasted on a run-of-the-mill judaizer. What prompted unusual efforts in Don Lope's case was the prospect of achieving the conversion of a learned, resolute heretic from an Old Christian, noble family (rumors of some Jewish ancestry notwithstanding). On July 5 and July 8 a new set of calificadores was summoned to try to persuade the prisoner to return to Catholicism. They were no more successful than their predecessors.

Given the turn the case had taken, the prosecutor prepared a new acusación, which was presented to Lope de Vera on July 9. At this audience, the prisoner refused to swear on a cross, an object that, he said, he did not worship. Although the purpose of the audience was to allow him to respond to the acusación, he seized the opportunity to solemnly reiterate his basic beliefs as well as his intention to die in the Law of Moses. He added that he was now observing the Sabbath. If the tribunal summoned him to an audience on the Sabbath, he said, he would refuse to descend to the audience chamber. He said he was also abstaining from eating pork. He then went on the attack. Mary, he said, had not given birth as a virgin. He rejected both the New Testament and the Vulgate, the latter of which, he said, contained more than ten thousand errors. He concluded by declaring that he would live and die in the Law of the Jews.

On July 13[50]—a Sabbath—he was summoned to an audience, perhaps in order to test his threat. He refused to leave his cell, saying he would not violate the Sabbath; if they wanted to see him in the audience chamber they would have to tie a rope around his neck and take him by force. He was left in his cell. The week passed with no follow-up to the summons. On the following Friday, perhaps anxious that the tribunal was outmanipulating him, he requested an audience, saying he wished to comply with the summons, but had not been able to do so on the Sabbath. The summaries give no further information about this audience. It is possible that the inquisitors, having fulfilled their procedural duty, gave the prisoner short shrift.

Several weeks later—almost four months after Don Lope first declared his intention to die a martyr—he took a step that had become one of the defining acts of the crypto-Jewish martyr: he performed self-circumcision. Not, however, in privacy and freedom, with reasonably suitable instruments, as Luis Carvajal and Francisco Maldonado de Silva had done, but in his Inquisition cell, with a chicken bone he had sharpened with a nail. It is possible that Lope de Vera knew of precedents in recent generations for this act (including the relatively recently publicized self-circumcision of Francisco Maldonado de Silva) through his "Portuguese" contacts.[51] But (assuming that the manuscript of the diary of David Reuveni he had read contained the relevant passage) he would certainly have been inspired by the self-circumcision of the Portuguese converso Solomon Molkho as well.[52]

The warden made the discovery of Lope de Vera's ritual surgery on the night of August 7, as he was making the rounds in the inquisitorial prison. At 8:30 that night—so he testified the next day—he sighted a light burning in Lope de Vera's cell. When he reprimanded the prisoner for this breach of discipline, a cell companion told the warden that his cellmate had circumcised himself with a bone. Lope de Vera confirmed this. The warden immediately summoned a physician.

When the physician testified before the tribunal, affirming that Lope de Vera had circumcised himself (he brought a piece of the flesh and skin Lope de Vera had removed as evidence), he reported a conversation he'd had with the prisoner. He had asked Don Lope how he could have done something so wicked. The prisoner replied that God had so commanded him through the Law of Moses, and said he considered himself a practicing Jew (*judío judaizante*). Moreover, he would regard it as a particularly good fate to be burned alive. He well knew that if he died this way he would go to heaven, and he wanted the honor of suffering martyrdom steadfastly.

A day later, Lope de Vera was summoned to an audience to explain his action. He was no doubt glad of the opportunity. He said he was an observer of the Law of Moses, and that "on the seventh day of this month" he had entered the covenant of circumcision by his own hand, cutting his foreskin. He reported that on the occasion of his circumcision he had adopted the Hebrew name "Yehudá." And, with his now standard closing flourish, he declared that he was an observer of the Law of Moses, in which he wished to live and die.[53]

While scarcely able to surpass his surgical feat, he continued to keep up the pressure on the tribunal. The tactic he devised at this point is one for which I know no precedent. When called to an audience in November,[54] he made the usual declarations about his belief in the Law of Moses and his rejection of Catholicism. When asked to read the record for ratification, he did so, but refused to sign. This may have had symbolic significance for him, indicating a rejection of the legitimacy of the proceedings. For the inquisitors, however, with their scrupulous attention to correct procedure, it had a quite practical consequence: without the prisoner's ratification, the record could not be considered in the final deliberations.

On November 21, the tribunal, seeking a way to reengage the prisoner, decided to ask him to indicate in writing the passages from Scripture on which he based his "obstinacy," in the hope that armed with this information the calificadores could better persuade him of the truth of the Church. Five days later[55] he was given a sheet of paper, which he returned to the tribunal at an audience of November 27. According to the trial summary, his statement was composed in Hebrew, Latin, and Castilian. True to character, he ignored the instructions to cite scriptural passages, and seized the opportunity to air his beliefs. The tribunal voiced its dissatisfaction and reinstructed him. Lope de Vera said he would not comply without a Bible to consult. But for the Valladolid inquisitors, this was no simple request. Lope de Vera was asking for the text that had nurtured his heresy, leaving the tribunal in a dilemma.

Displaying their usual conscientiousness, the inquisitors turned to the Suprema for an authoritative decision. The Suprema responded that not only should the prisoner be given a Bible, but he should also be given any other book he requested. Lope de Vera was soon in possession of a Bible, six pages of paper, some ink, and a quill pen. He did not, however, simply accept these materials. Demonstrating once again his talent for provocation, he refused to accept the pen, declaring that he could not write with it because to do so would be a violation of the Law of Moses (an innovative interpretation of Jewish law on his part). He was given a bronze pen.

Back in his cell, Lope de Vera covered the six pages with a written statement.

He requested an audience in order to submit his composition in January 1642.[56] It seems doubtful that he cited chapter and verse as the tribunal had requested. The summary tells us only that he wrote "many things in confirmation of the Law of Moses and concluded by saying he would defend it and be burned to death for it."

On February 5, he was presented with a second publicación of the testimony against him—presumably now including the testimony of the warden and his assistant as well as the physician, who had testified concerning his circumcision. He was expected to respond to each accusation, but, following his new course of resistance, he refused to respond in any way. As a result, he was sentenced to lashes. As he left the chamber under the supervision of the assistant warden, he turned to the latter and stated that as long as the notary was present he would not speak a word. The inquisitors, desperate to get a response from him (without which they could not proceed), ordered him to come back. The notary was told to leave, and Lope de Vera was instructed to write his response. Ever ready to vex, he took the bronze pen and wrote that he did not wish to respond to the publicación. He added that one of the persons who had testified against him, an official of the Inquisition, was his enemy.

He was nevertheless given the publicación to read. As he had done before, he took the document and read it. The trial summary notes that he responded with mirth. When he arrived at a certain passage in the testimony of the first witness ("which contained many blasphemies against our Lord Jesus Christ and the purity of the Virgin our Lady," as someone, if not the notary, recorded),

he laughed joyfully without saying a word. He [then] wrote that everything the witnesses had said was false, and that only the Law of Moses was the true one. Moreover, he regarded himself as under no obligation to obey the inquisitors, because they were not Jews as he was. Thus, he did not wish to respond to the publicación.

The farce continued. The tribunal decided to submit Don Lope's six-page defense of the Law of Moses to three different sets of calificadores so that they could respond to it and, it was still somehow hoped, convince the prisoner of his errors.[57] Lope de Vera was notified of this decision at an audience on March 16, 1642. Again he asked for a Bible (which had apparently been taken from him), saying that he would provide written proof of the literal meaning of Scripture, which he wanted to have submitted to the calificadores together with the six-page defense.

The three groups of calificadores prepared at least two separate written responses to Lope de Vera's written statements. After reading them, the prisoner dismissed them both as unpersuasive. It seems worth asking why the members of the tribunal, who surely understood that the prisoner was manipulating them, continued their efforts. They were, of course, aware that they possessed the ultimate power over Lope de Vera's fate, not vice versa; and since the proceedings were secret, the game entailed no public humiliation for the Inquisition. Apparently the distant hope of achieving this particular prisoner's conversion (or at least capitulation) kept in check the outrage his behavior must have aroused.

Thus when Lope de Vera requested an audience more than a month later, on May 2, his request was granted. When he was brought into the audience chamber, he at once indicated by signs that as long as the notary was there he would neither speak nor write. The notary was asked to leave. Lope de Vera was given a bronze pen with which to write down what he wanted to say. He wrote that he did not want the notaries of the Inquisition to be allowed to make a written record of his case, because everything they wrote was false; he would only communicate what he could write himself. The trial summary says nothing further about this audience.

The denouement of the case was a continuation of the theater of the absurd. Lope de Vera was clearly an incorrigible heretic, but the tribunal needed a ratification of his confession to bring the trial to a conclusion. On May 24, the Valladolid tribunal decided to write to the Suprema for advice on how to conclude the case. The Suprema replied with a letter of May 22 "of the same year" (clearly one of the dates is wrong), ordering that Lope de Vera be called to an audience and asked about his refusal to speak in the presence of a notary. If he responded, his case should be continued. If he refused to respond, he should be asked if some other official might serve as notary. If he still refused to speak, the tribunal should vote on his case and convey its decision to the Suprema.

On May 27, Lope de Vera was accordingly summoned, and predictably refused to speak. The tribunal was divided in its vote on how to proceed (the summary does not reveal how). The Suprema ordered that the prisoner be summoned to an audience with a notary present, and asked what complaint he had about the officials of the Holy Office. If he refused to speak, he would be given fifty lashes; and if he still refused to speak, he would again be summoned to an audience. He was summoned on June 17, refused to speak, and was given fifty lashes. This did not, however, provide the wished-for inducement, and he continued to maintain his silence (apparently with one exception: when an inquisitor made the routine weekly visit to the cells, he would cry out, "Viva la ley de Moisen!").[58]

It was decided on August 12 that a cleric with a knowledge of Hebrew should speak with the prisoner in order to persuade him (or at least to sound him out in a setting in which he would speak). Such a cleric was sent to his cell and spoke with Don Lope for two hours. It was to no avail. But perhaps the fact that he had broken his silence in his cell encouraged the tribunal to summon him again to the audience chamber. When he appeared, on September 10, he refused to speak either in the presence or absence of the notary. The tribunal came up with a new plan: they would have the prisoner's confessions read to him, and allow him to ratify them in writing. Once more they turned to the Suprema for approval. On September 20, the Suprema ordered that the case should be concluded definitively, in conformity with the regulations of the Holy Office, apparently approving this procedure.

Lope de Vera was once more summoned to an audience, and once more refused either to speak or write. As the tribunal began to read his confessions to him, he plugged his ears with his fingers. His curador intervened, saying he had no defense to offer, and requested a definitive conclusion to the case. The prosecutor

The Holy Inquisition. La Saint Inquisition.

Figure 12. Inquisition courtyard with cells, and carriage in foreground. From Isaac Martin, *The Tryal and Sufferings of Mr. Isaac Martin, who was put into the Inquisition in Spain, for the sake of the Protestant religion* (London 1723), opposite p. 8. The Jewish Theological Seminary.

requested that the prisoner be subjected to whatever punishment was needed to induce him to ratify his confessions. The inquisitors voted on this on November 4—but with mixed results, some accepting the prosecutor's proposal and some rejecting it. The Suprema was contacted, and replied with a letter of November 20 ordering that without subjecting the prisoner to torture, a vote be taken on his case and conveyed to the Suprema.

On January 25 or 27, 1643, the tribunal voted unanimously that Lope de Vera be relaxed to the secular arm, with the confiscation of his goods.[59] But the Suprema ordered that before executing the sentence, a learned cleric should be summoned to exhort and admonish him, and he should be given a copy of Luis de Granada's *Símbolo de la fe*. The tribunal dutifully complied.

By now, of course, such measures were risible. At the auto-da-fé, the Inquisition showed its more practical side: Lope de Vera was muzzled "so as not to create a scandal." That he should speak was now the last thing the Inquisition wanted.

They could not, however, prevent him from getting his wish to be burned alive at the stake. His death made an impression that reverberated widely, and took on legendary dimensions, at least in converso circles. Some years later, for example, Juan Pereira, a young man being tried by the Inquisition in Valladolid, repeatedly mentioned Lope de Vera and asserted that he had seen him after his death riding on a mule and glistening with the perspiration that had been on him when he was taken to the *quemadero*.[60] And in 1675 Benedict Spinoza reported, on the subject of Jewish martyrdom, that he knew "among others of a certain Judah called 'the faithful' who, in the midst of flames when he was already believed dead, started to sing the hymn which begins 'To thee, O God, I commit my soul,' and so singing, died."[61]

After Lope de Vera's death, the inquisitor Don Bartolemeo Marques Moscoso wrote a letter to the Marques of Monterey in which he briefly described Lope de Vera's case.[62] (It somehow reached the hands of the Sephardi apologete and poet Daniel Levi de Barrios in Amsterdam.)[63] From this account we learn that at the auto-da-fé, Lope de Vera was one of twenty-five prisoners sentenced for judaizing (two other prisoners were also sentenced, for bigamy). Of the accused judaizers, only two were burned at the stake. One was burned in effigy, and the other, Lope de Vera, was burned alive. Wrote the inquisitor of Don Lope's behavior in his final moments:

> His firmness even on the pyre was surprising. His obstinacy left everyone amazed; for throughout the reading aloud of the sentence against him, he nodded his head to show his affirmation of every point of faith [attributed to him]. From time to time, as he was able,[64] he would say "Long live the Law of Moses!" and, making signs to heaven of the confidence he felt, he displayed his pride, glorying in what was narrated of his life [in the sentence], longing to die as the most heroic martyr might do.[65]

The inquisitor's letter is particularly interesting for what it reveals about Don Lope's expressed view of the inquisitors—a view not mentioned in the trial summaries. The passage in question reads:

> Innumerable masters and calificadores spoke with him, trying by all means to bring him back, judging that at such a tender age, with God's help, it might be possible to win him back. But it was time wasted, *for he told them all that they were ignorant and did not grasp the [true] translation/interpretation (traduciones) [of Scripture], and that all [the translations/interpretations] had been composed contrary to the true [meaning of the text]*

[my emphasis]. All his trouble came to this unhappy man because of his not paying regard to the excommunication that he incurred by reading prohibited books.

If Lope de Vera had harbored the illusion, early on in his trial, that the inquisitors might understand the distress of an inquiring soul, he had been sorely deluded. Indeed, his discovery that highly trained theologians dismissed the urgent contemporary issues he raised may have been among the factors that impelled him to find certainty in a "Law of Moses" that was, to a large extent, a private religious system he created in dialogue with the Hebrew Bible.

The news of Lope de Vera's death at the stake—the exact date is in dispute, but the earliest date scholars have proposed is June 25, 1644[66]—traveled quickly to his native town of San Clemente. Naturally it became a subject of talk on the street. On July 24, some of this talk led the *caballero* Don Andres de los Herreros to appear before the San Clemente commissary on his own initiative. In a conversation in which he had participated the previous day, a notary and a young hidalgo had discussed the death of Lope de Vera in Valladolid.[67] Turning to the subject of Lope de Vera's father, they noted that the latter "showed little emotion [*poco sentimiento*] about the imprisonment of his son in the Inquisition [cells]." In the context of the conversation, this seems to have meant that the senior Lope de Vera felt little shame; for the hidalgo proceeded to say that he could not understand how the father could repeatedly contend that his son had been arrested by the Inquisition merely because he was a person of exceptional understanding.[68]

The hidalgo, Don Diego Ruíz Ángel, was immediately summoned before the Inquisition. His testimony about the senior Don Lope's reaction to his son's prosecution was even more pointed than that of the caballero. He had heard Don Lope say he was "consoled" by the fact that his son was imprisoned by the Inquisition "for being an eminent man, not for being a stupid one." He also confirmed the particulars of the conversation reported by Don Andres de los Herreros.[69]

The saga continued. In 1652, eight years after his son's death at the stake, a caballero of the Order of Calatrava came forward to denounce Don Lope. The witness had been conversing with a fellow caballero about the career and fate of Don Lope's son—evidently a topic of enduring fascination among the residents of San Clemente. In the course of the conversation, the acquaintance told the witness that he had heard from several of Don Lope's neighbors that every night between midnight and one o'clock, the *regidor* got out of bed and, stark naked, went to a high exterior corridor in his house. There, gazing at the stars, he loudly sang "the passion of Christ." (This was probably a reference to one of the devotional prayers describing the passion printed in contemporary prayer books for the laity.) Such behavior seemed to the witness indecent and irreverent and, more ominously, related to the fact that Don Lope was the father of a relaxed judaizer.

The story, however, was only very partially verified by the five witnesses who were called to affirm it. Three said they knew nothing about it. Two reported hearing Don Lope loudly singing the passion of Christ on summer evenings, but one did not see him and the other said he was dressed in a nightgown. All this had happened six, seven, or eight years earlier—that is, on the heels of the death of his son. If so, it suggests a poignant footnote to the judaizer's martyrdom career: a grieving father, evidently proud of his son, proclaiming his son's martyrdom (for being an intellectual, as he seemed to understand it) with a subversive, clamorous rendition of the passion of Christ.

There is yet another sequel to the story. In 1672, twenty-eight years after Lope de Vera's death at the stake, his brother Pedro de Vera wrote a letter to the Venetian rabbinic court.[70] It was forwarded to the rabbi Moshe Rafael d'Aguilar in Amsterdam.[71] Pedro de Vera was prompted to write the letter by reports he had heard of discussions at a certain yeshiva in Venice—discussions that, though purportedly drawing from rabbinic lore, struck him as being blasphemous and heretical. (Pedro de Vera had clearly left Spain and was apparently living in Venice.) In a message accompanying the letter, David Joshua del Soto quite explicitly identified the author as "a brother of the glorious martyr Don Lope." The letter itself reveals something more surprising about Pedro himself. He identified himself as the brother of Don Lope de Vera "who passed gloriously from the holocaust to heavenly bliss *for having defended the Law of Truth* [my emphasis]."

Don Pedro, then, had escaped Spain and now regarded himself as a Jew. There is no hard evidence that he underwent formal conversion, however. Indeed, the fact that he did not use a Hebrew name in his letter suggests otherwise.

The letter, written in Spanish, opens with a rather bombastic justification for his protest concerning statements made by some Venetian Jews:

It has come to my attention that in the meetings of this learned yeshiva, some discerning, talented men have soared up to luminous spheres, without fear of the abysses of Icarus [*Hícaros precipicios*]. But because I have inherited not only the name but also the zeal of my brother Don Lope de Vera . . . I am obliged to warn your honors that certain [of their] allegations . . . [are] mendacious, heretical, and blasphemous. Pardon my manner of speaking, to which zeal for the honor of the Lord moves me.

One assumes that Pedro, during the time he spent at the University of Salamanca, had discussed theology with his accomplished older brother. If so, he may have become oriented to a literalist, rationalistic, individualistic approach to religious belief that he felt entitled to defend, despite his inadequate knowledge, because of his kinship to the martyr and because of his loyalty to what he believed were his brother's beliefs.

He expressed dismay, in all three of the cases he raised, at propositions that were derived from midrash. The first was the proposition (as he understood it) that the examination of a single concept was more important than the entire Torah. Pedro de Vera argued that such an approach led to heresy, because the more one speculated, the further one got from the intention of Scripture.[72] Secondly, he objected to the midrashic idea that the power of peace and unity was so great among the generation of the Tower of Babel that God was not able to destroy them, an idea that he took quite literally to be a statement challenging God's omnipotence.[73] Thirdly, he objected to the midrashic idea that God had lied to Abraham for the sake of peace, repeating Sarah's words to him but omitting her statement "and my husband is old" (Gen. 18:12–13) so that Abraham would not be offended. To attribute lying to God seemed to Pedro de Vera blasphemy of the worst sort.[74] Such statements, he complained, gave ammunition to "our adversaries."

It seems obvious—and perhaps inevitable, given the fact that he had heard about the discussions he was protesting secondhand—that Pedro de Vera inhabited a mental universe that was alien, if not hostile, to rabbinic hermeneutics. He did not have the sharpness of mind of an Uriel da Costa, so he posed little threat. (Indeed, d'Aguilar wrote him a patient and compassionate reply.) Certainly he did not possess the intellectual prowess of his brother, so that he cannot throw light on how Lope de Vera might have viewed rabbinic Judaism, had he actually gone to Algiers or Constantinople.

There is one way, however, in which Pedro de Vera's letter provides a fitting close to the discussion of Lope de Vera's career. It does underscore the theological chasm that separated the Judaism of the dogmatista martyrs from rabbinic Judaism as it had evolved in seventeenth-century Europe. Pedro's "zeal" ran against the grain of a seasoned rabbinic approach to learning in which subversive irony was accepted, ambiguity was tolerated, hyperbole that verged on the absurd was used for homiletic effect, and the "simple meaning" was only one of many ways in which a biblical passage might legitimately be understood. It was true, as Pedro de Vera "warned," that midrashic traditions often provided easy targets for Christian criticism (and ridicule) of Judaism. Crypto-Judaism in general had developed in intuitive response to this. More strikingly, the elite, polemically sophisticated forms of crypto-Judaism were able to achieve a degree of invulnerability to Catholic attack by gravitating toward a straightforward, unambiguous, rationalistic interpretation of Scripture.

But this was a reaction to an unprecedented regime of repression. Outside Iberian lands, in places where internal Jewish discourse was allowed to thrive, venerable rabbinic modes of thought persisted, without regard to Christian opinion. Pedro de Vera was apparently gratified to learn that his brother had won a place of distinction within the wider Jewish world. But he failed to grasp that while his brother might be revered among members of the vibrant Jewish community of Venice, his Judaism was not a benchmark of orthodoxy there. Lope de Vera was revered because he was a great defender of Judaism under gentile attack—not because he was an authority on Judaism.

ECHOES IN THE PORTUGUESE-JEWISH DIASPORA

7

The celebrated dogmatista martyrs' resistance to the Church was shaped, in part, by an awareness of Christian religious dissent in early modern Europe. It drew strength from the insistence of Protestants that it was wrong to withhold knowledge of sacred texts in the name of ecclesiastical authority, and that indeed Scripture was the very font of religious authority. Whatever these men may have believed in principle about religious coercion (and they were not explicit), they rejected the right of the Church to enforce belief in a dogmatic "truth" whose erroneousness seemed self-evident to them. Within the clandestine circles in which they discussed their ideas, they experienced the intellectual freedom they intuitively craved. It must have seemed natural in these circumstances to associate freedom of thought with Judaism itself.

Especially after the suppression of Protestantism in academic circles in the Peninsula, crypto-Jewish polemical arguments resonated even among some Old Christians in Spain and Portugal. Some of these men incorporated "judaizing" elements into an essentially Christian perspective. Gregorio López in Mexico (whom we have met in connection with Luis Carvajal) and Bartolomé Sánchez in Castile expressed an affinity for Judaism without abandoning the foundations of Christian theology.[1] But in the cases of Diogo d'Asumpção and Lope de Vera (and perhaps Pedro de Vera as well), the persuasiveness of a "Jewish" polemical reading of Scripture led to the adoption of the Law of Moses, albeit according to a very unrabbinic interpretation.

The careers of the Old Christian judaizers hint at a phenomenon that has long remained under the radar screen of scholars. It is common knowledge by now that conversos were prominent among the figures who contributed to "Protestantish" opinion in Spain.[2] But the careers of the celebrated judaizing martyrs suggest complex interactions of another kind: namely, between educated crypto-Jews and heterodox Catholics (whether converso or Old Christian). It would seem that as inquisitorial persecution of Old Christians intensified, discontented Catholics showed greater readiness to listen to crypto-Jewish theological criticisms of Catholicism. Moreover, by the second half of the sixteenth century, clandestine judaizing possessed a certain advantage over heterodox Christian thinking: first, because it was transmitted within deeply rooted kinship networks, which made it difficult for the Inquisition to eradicate; and second, because it possessed foundations of greater antiquity, which made it less vulnerable in the face of radical scrutiny of the Gospels.

Scholars have shown just how active a conversation was taking place in innovative circles elsewhere in Europe among Jews (particularly ex-conversos) and nonconformist Christians.[3] In several notable cases outside the Peninsula, radical Christian seekers actually crossed religio-ethnic boundaries and embraced Judaism: the Italian Giovanni Laureto di Buongiorno,[4] Simon Pecs in Transylvania,[5] the Frenchman Nicolas Antoine,[6] Benedictus Sperling in Altona,[7] Johann Peter Späth from Augsburg,[8] and the Frenchman Aaron d'Antan.[9] More common was cross-pollination from behind these boundaries, which occurred in a variety of contexts.[10] But it now appears that these phenomena were not entirely absent even from the Iberian orbit.

It is interesting that the leaders of the northern European Portuguese-Jewish diaspora, who took extreme measures to guard the "purity" of their communities' Portuguese-Jewish ethnicity, seem to have been unperturbed by the fact that two of the most prominent of "their" martyrs were Old Christians. They must have known that Diogo d'Asumpção and Lope de Vera cultivated forms of belief that differed sharply from the ancestral, family-oriented Judaism practiced by many (if not most) crypto-Jews, a tradition that eased the passage of ex-conversos into a rabbinized form of Judaism. Moreover, Old Christian judaizers did not share the historical experience of forced conversion, stigma, discrimination, and inquisitorial persecution that gave the ex-converso diaspora its coherence. To put it bluntly, Old Christian judaizers were "outsiders" to Portuguese-Jewish life in a multitude of subtle and not-so-subtle ways.

Yet in so far as the Old Christian martyrs represented pure, uncompromising theological motives (as they appeared to ex-conversos to do), they became powerful symbols of a shared ideal type—one that Carsten Wilke has aptly called a "walking religious conscience."[11] For most members of the Portuguese-Jewish diaspora, this ideal was very remote indeed. Ancestral and kinship ties had played a central role in determining their own paths to normative Jewish life. They were also aware of the various self-interested motives that had led them to dissimulate, vacillate, deceive, and delay. While this seemed a normal aspect of existence, it diminished their claims to truth in the competitive polemical arena of Reformation Europe.

Thus the ex-converso diaspora became a community that, perhaps paradoxically, welcomed support from Old Christian quarters about its claims. The fact that two theologically trained Old Christians had undergone an internal struggle that led to their conversion to belief in the Law of Moses—a belief they defended despite the agonies of imprisonment and death at the stake—must have seemed to many of the émigrés incontrovertible evidence that their Law really was the true one.

At least some of the émigrés grasped the theological "logic" underlying the careers of such men as Diogo d'Assumpção and Lope de Vera. As Carsten Wilke has pointed out, elaborations of the theme of Old Christian conversion to Judaism, whether fictitious or historically-based, were a striking feature of the literature of the Portuguese-Jewish diaspora.[12] There was a common story line in such narratives. The protagonist, typically, was a pious Old Christian who underwent a crisis as a result of reading the Gospels critically. The Gospels, this person discovered, were full of contradictions. He was forced to conclude that they were nothing but a set of fables of human origin. Crisis gave way to despair. He was rescued from this condition, however, by turning to the Hebrew Bible, a revelatory experience that led him to conclude that the Law of Moses was the one eternal law of God.

Such narratives appear to have been tailored to offer reassurance to a population of ex-conversos whose members often struggled to feel at home in their new collective skin. But the stories could not have served this purpose if realities in the contemporary Christian world did not lend them some credibility. Religious experimentation, shifting loyalties, uncertain boundaries—these were hardly phenomena exclusive to the Portuguese-Jewish experience in this period. Amid such confusion, it seemed to many that only Scripture could provide a reliable compass. This, at least, was the implicit message of tales about autonomous gentile truthseekers who turned to Scripture and, as a result, chose Judaism.

Outside of this comforting scenario, however, the autonomous truthseeker was a problematic if not threatening type. Such a figure might choose any creed, not necessarily Judaism. Allowing members of the community to engage in open, independent theological investigations was antithetical to the deepest instincts of the leaders of the Portuguese-Jewish diaspora. Rabbinic and lay leaders alike understood that collective submission to rabbinic authority, the great historic backbone of Jewish existence, was a sine qua non for the survival and viability of the community. While they exalted the celebrated martyrs' defiance of Church authority, they acted vigorously within their communities to suppress vocal expressions of opposition to rabbinic authority.[13] That is, when the kind of individualistic judaizing that sustained converso resistance to the Inquisition in Iberian lands came into conflict with Jewish community building and rabbinic controls in northern Europe, it was condemned as arrogant and presumptuous. This is vividly illustrated by the cases of Uriel da Costa, Juan de Prado,[14] and Daniel Ribera (an Old Christian judaizer),[15] not to mention Benedict (Baruch) Spinoza. Da Costa, Prado, and Spinoza were excommunicated from the Jewish community of Amsterdam. Ribera would have been had he lingered.

This leads to a thorny question. Was the sort of social and theological conditioning that made possible the careers of the celebrated martyrs the same conditioning that made possible the careers of the celebrated ex-converso "heretics"? And if so, did a faint grasp of the affinity between the community's famous martyrs and its famous "heretics" affect the way the martyrs were publicly represented in the commemorative literature?

Let us first consider whether these two types did, indeed, share a common ideological orientation. A brief reexamination of the much-examined life of Uriel da

Costa will offer some insight, which unfortunately will have to suffice here, though there is much more to be said on this subject.

By his own account, Da Costa was very much a solitary seeker of truth, as a brief excerpt from his own narrative of his life will illustrate. He was raised a Catholic but found himself, he wrote, unable "to find that [spiritual] satisfaction I wanted in the Romish Church." At the same time, he was "desirous to attach myself" to an established religion. Like many another early modern religious seeker, he turned to Scripture. As he put it,

> I went through the books of Moses and the Prophets, wherein I found some things not a little contradictory to the doctrines of the New Testament, and there seemed to be the less difficulty in believing those things which were revealed by God himself.[16]

This story strikingly parallels the tales mentioned earlier of Old Christians who discovered the truth of the Law of Moses through an independent study of Scripture. However, more than four decades ago, I. S. Révah pointed out the apparent discrepancy between Uriel da Costa's account of his conversion to crypto-Judaism in Portugal and evidence about his family's crypto-judaizing.[17] Révah described the crypto-Judaism in Da Costa's family as *marranisme normale*—that is, an ancestral and unself-conscious creed with vestiges of rabbinic practice that had been transmitted orally over several generations. If so, Da Costa's autobiography conceals the contribution of family traditions to his religious development and exaggerates the degree of autonomy he exercised in determining his spiritual path.

Let us assume, as Révah conjectured, that both ancestral and individual intellectual factors were at work in the evolution of Da Costa's thought in the Peninsula. We now know what Révah only suspected, that Da Costa had had contacts with educated crypto-Jews when he studied at the University of Coimbra. Indeed, he was acquainted with António Homem, professor of canon law at Coimbra and leader of a crypto-Jewish confraternity that was, poignantly enough, named in honor of Diogo d'Asumpção.[18] Is it possible that these contacts triggered the kind of change in Da Costa that Manuel de Morales triggered in Luis Carvajal, leading him to move from a vestigial, popular form of crypto-Judaism to a more self-conscious, sophisticated, rationalistic, textually grounded one? Or perhaps he may have shifted from a rejection of a folkloristic family legacy to an enthusiastic embrace of a more intellectually satisfying conception of Judaism. And might his sense of alienation and disappointment once he encountered rabbinic Judaism, with its tangled web of traditions, its imperviousness to strict order, its structures of authority, and its essential conservatism—might his alienation not have prompted a reversion to the intellectually sophisticated crypto-Jew's posture of stubborn independence? In any event, even if Da Costa distorted his personal history to enhance such an image, it seems evident—his career would be incomprehensible otherwise—that he *had* achieved a high degree of religious autonomy by early adulthood.[19] When he arrived in Amsterdam in 1615, his theology would thus have already been somewhat detached from the visceral ethnic loyalties that provided much of the motivation for re-judaization among many of the émigrés.

Da Costa's first challenge to the communal authorities came only a few years after his arrival, with an attack on the entire post-biblical rabbinic tradition, which he characterized as a human fabrication. His point of view was bibliocentric and literalist, and probably drew from anticlerical attitudes to Rome. Even if it was not entirely consistent with a theology conceived in isolation—an unadulterated Judaism, so to speak—he sought to understand and legitimate it as such. Da Costa entered a protracted struggle with the leaders of the Amsterdam community that entailed two excommunications and two insincere recantations. He was unable to sustain an outward semblance of conformity in part because he was a demanding and aggressive person, a provocateur in spirit—traits that he shared, of course, with most of the dogmatista martyrs. He ended his tormented existence in 1640 by suicide—martyred, in his view, not by the Inquisition but by the Jewish communal authorities.[20]

Da Costa's open defiance of rabbinic authority was only one instance of the persistence, among some ex-conversos, of a crypto-Jewish sense of entitlement to religious autonomy that brought them into conflict with communal authorities. The resemblance between the careers of the famous Amsterdam "heretics" and those of the celebrated judaizing martyrs is thus not as paradoxical as it may seem. Careers of both kinds entailed the mobilization of individualistic patterns of thought and behavior—patterns that were a natural outgrowth of crypto-Jewish life—together with elements of thinking and behavior drawn from a broader Reformation orbit. However far it may have been from their minds, both the martyrs and the ex-converso "heretics" were participating in an upheaval that had repercussions far beyond the Christian-Jewish conflict—an upheaval that would eventually challenge European ecclesiastical authority everywhere and, inevitably, rabbinic authority as well. To some extent, then, the judaizing martyrs were among the harbingers of the shift in early modern Europe from the battle between well-defined orthodoxies to the battle for freedom of conscience.

This connection may be apparent with the benefit of historical hindsight. But was it apparent, even at an intuitive level, to members of the ex-converso diaspora?

I would suggest a cautious "yes." There is reason to suspect that the defiant, celebrated martyrs aroused ambivalence among at least some of those whose task it was to guide the community. To be sure, contemporary Portuguese Jews did not articulate an awareness of the fact that the evident "heroism" of Lope de Vera and the evident "arrogance" of Juan de Prado were manifestations of the same behavior, distinguished primarily by the fact that the former was defending what he believed to be the Law of Moses before *Church* authorities while the latter was defending what he believed to be the Law of Moses before *rabbinic* authorities. But if we look closely at how communal leaders chose to incorporate (or not to incorporate) the celebrated martyrs into the life of the community, we will see that they exercised a degree of circumspection.

Particularly interesting in this respect is the discussion of martyrdom in a sermon composed by the Amsterdam *hakham* Saul Levi Mortera (who was not himself an ex-converso), probably in about 1630, and certainly before 1645.[21] In this sermon, Mortera made a pointed distinction between Jewish and Christian expressions of martyrdom. Christians, he wrote, were taught that a person ought actively to seek out martyrdom. But this, he stressed, was a foolish teaching and a misunderstanding of God's will.

Mortera's generalization was, of course, a gross simplification of Christian teaching on martyrdom. Yet the Christian world's emphasis on the suffering Christ as an example for all humanity—as the ultimate expression of *imitatio Dei*—did render the martyr's death a particularly attractive goal for a Christian. It may be, too, that Mortera was aware of rash and provocative actions by Catholics and Protestants in the Reformation world, and their idealization by both sides.[22] In any case, what is important from our perspective is that Mortera portrayed the pursuit of martyrdom as something that was alien to Judaism. According to him, when God commanded, "You shall love the Lord your God with all your heart and with all your soul" (Deut. 6:5), which the rabbis understood to mean, "even if one must sacrifice one's soul," God did not mean thereby that a person should *seek* such sacrifice. Mortera continued,

> In fact, this [verse] means that [only] when one is enjoined to perform a heretical act, either by transgressing one of God's commandments or by doing something that gives the appearance of renouncing God—[only] under these terrible circumstances should one allow himself to be killed rather than transgress. This model [for allowing oneself to be killed under extreme circumstances] was provided by our father Abraham, when Nimrod had him thrown into the fiery furnace [after] ordering him to worship his [idolatrous] god. And likewise Hananiah, Mishael and Azariah in the fiery furnace, and Daniel in the lion's den.
>
> However, for a person to go and place himself in a place of danger and seek out death on his own initiative, claiming that in this way he fulfills God's will and achieves salvation—this is wrong, and such a person is actually guilty of a capital offense.

What follows is a somewhat contorted effort to minimize as far as possible the risks a person should take to adhere to God's law. It seems obvious that the "danger" Mortera refers to is the one with which his audience was so familiar, that is, the danger of arrest by the Inquisition. It was true, he said (almost as a concession), that "we are obligated to learn God's commandments and to guide others in the right path even if this entails danger." But this obligation applied only to two situations:

> First, when one can save his people from death and destruction by an act that involves danger. . . . And second, when the danger to one's life is not immediate and certain, but distant and improbable. . . . If the danger is clear and present, God does not want us to endanger our lives except in order to save the lives of many.

The unmistakable thread running through this passage is that God wants the Jew to act in a way that benefits the Jewish people, not in a way that might bring individual glory (and immediate personal salvation) but is of no value to the community. Mortera even offered a prooftext to demonstrate that in a situation of danger, God preferred that a person—even when embarking on a divine mission— choose dissimulation rather than take the risk of death. The prooftext was a biblical narrative that many in his audience would have known. When God sent Samuel to anoint the son of Jesse, an act that was to result in removing Saul as king, Samuel recognized the danger. "How can I go?" he responded. "If Saul hears it, he will kill me" (1 Sam. 16:2). Samuel thus hesitated to follow God's instruction, and yet, Mortera pointed out, God did not rebuke him. In fact, He "taught him a subterfuge, . . . [saying]: 'Take a heifer with you and say, "I have come to sacrifice to the Lord"'" (1 Sam. 16:2)." And God did this, Mortera wrote, "in order to teach us that Samuel's response [i.e., hesitating to place himself in danger] was legitimate."

Mortera had recourse to another biblical example to buttress his contention that God wanted those who served him to *avoid* martyrdom. Why did God not allow Jeremiah, pursued by his enemies, to die a martyr's death (Jer. 1:19)? Because, Mortera argued, "human beings are able to do so many more good things in the service of God while they are alive than they can by seeking an opportunity for an unnecessary and untimely death." Zealots who brought attention to themselves "by speaking insults to kings and to others, which they know will provoke a death sentence" were engaging in "foolish, ignorant behavior."

Even if Mortera was not familiar with particular cases of crypto-Jewish martyrdom we have discussed, he would have been familiar with ex-converso lore that glorified such men. It seems telling that he did not even allude to judaizing martyrs. If Mortera were not trying to alter the attitudes of members of his congregation on this subject, it would be hard to understand why he would expound on martyrdom while neglecting to mention the very men and women whose deaths would instantly have come to mind in his audience.[23] Without being explicit, he disparaged the kind of dramatic individual confrontation with authority that made these men famous, and branded it as "Christian." Implicit in this was an endorsement of the path of prudent dissimulation that most members of his audience had adopted in the Peninsula. With an eye to the realities of life in Amsterdam, Mortera may also have sought to focus the attention of his listeners on the less than glorious tasks of community life.

Mortera's discussion of martyrdom, interesting as it may be, stands out for its severity, and does not reflect the overall attitudes of Portuguese-Jewish communal leaders. Concerning the remembrance of judaizing martyrs, as in so many other matters, these leaders sought to balance the conflicting needs of a community undergoing a process of radical adaptation. On the one hand, they understood the importance of recalling crypto-Jewish martyrdom; the emotional need to do so was obvious. Moreover, invoking the men who died defiantly "in the Law of

Moses" had polemical value with reference to the Christian world. It also had internal benefit as a means both of reinforcing identification with the practice of Judaism and of gaining legitimation in the wider Jewish world. On the other hand, there was a need to control and channel expressions of reverence for the martyrs among a population that *was* more conversant with Catholic than with Jewish modes of remembrance, and that did not necessarily honor rabbinic strictures.

The polemical value of crypto-Jewish martyrdom was articulated succinctly by the ex-converso physician and apologete Isaac Orobio de Castro. Orobio noted that among those who had demonstrated the ultimate love of God were "many Papists in China, Japan, and the West Indies" and "many Protestants (*Reformados*) in France, Germany, and Italy." But the readiness for sacrifice among Christians was matched in the Jewish world by those "many Jews [i.e., conversos] over the years of [the activity of] the Inquisition of Portugal and Spain, who offered their lives and sacrificed great well-being to convert themselves to their religion, despising all things human in order to sanctify the name of God in the flames, dying while acknowledging the Divine Law."[24] Orobio, like many (but not all) Portuguese Jews and like others caught in the confessional struggles of the age, saw in acts of martyrdom support for the truth claims of his belief. In such a context, it also made perfect sense for Orobio de Castro to be indiscriminate about who was judged a martyr; he cited ambiguously the "many" persons who had died in the flames "while acknowledging the Divine Law." His phrasing suggested that *everyone* who was burned at the stake for judaizing was a martyr.

But polemics were one thing, internal communal policy another. And there were good internal reasons to curb indiscriminate communal memorialization of conversos who had died at the stake. First of all, given the not fully Jewish status of conversos in Iberian lands, there was a need to restrict the application of the term *martyr* to conform to a halakhic standard of some kind. Second, there was a need to channel the emotions around crypto-Jewish martyrdom and merge them into a more mainstream tradition of Jewish martyrology. This was part of a much broader enterprise that might be called the rabbinization of Portuguese-Jewish life.[25]

The arena of public life in which rabbinization was given its strictest expression was the synagogue, and it is there (at least in Amsterdam) that we find the most restrictive approach to the memorialization of crypto-Jewish martyrs. The problem of liturgical remembrance of such martyrs was only one aspect of the more general issue of where Peninsular conversos belonged in the realm of the sacred. This issue was almost certainly at the heart of a controversy that arose in the 1630s, when a group of Amsterdam Jews insisted that any Jew, regardless of his or her sins, whether living in a Jewish community or "in idolatry," would be saved. It required the intervention of authorities in Venice to establish firmly the orthodox teaching that only righteous Jews would be rewarded in the world to come.[26]

The issue surfaced again in 1645. Members of the community had taken to bestowing Hebrew names on relatives who had died in Iberian lands, and reciting *hashkavah* (memorial) prayers for them. The rabbinic authorities did not consider such relatives, who had lived as Catholics their entire lives (at least outwardly) and had not sought to flee "lands of idolatry," to be entitled to such formal memorialization, and prohibited the practice.[27]

The memorialization of crypto-Jews who died in the Peninsula as *martyrs* was a more complex matter. A person who died at the stake loyal to the Law of Moses could hardly be considered a person who had died with the taint of idolatry. But some criterion was needed to distinguish "true" martyrs from other converso victims of Iberian judicial violence—for example, conversos who made false confessions under torture, or *negativos,* who may or may not have been judaizers.[28] In this case, crypto-Jewish conventions and rabbinic needs coincided, and the criterion chosen was the same one that distinguished great martyrs in the crypto-Jewish world: a person who was burned *alive* at the stake for judaizing might be honored by name even in the synagogue.

There were venerable rabbinic grounds supporting such a criterion. Those who were burned alive could be regarded as having "sanctified the name" because of the principle that under pressure to perform an act of idolatry (in the case at hand, kissing a cross at the stake), a Jew must refuse to do so, regardless of the consequences.[29] Because of this final act, judaizers burned alive at the stake, despite their otherwise anomalous relationship to Judaism in general and rabbinic Judaism in particular, could be remembered as martyrs in the liturgy.

The evidence for this ruling is a prayer book in Hebrew and Spanish printed in 1687 that includes a special *hashkavah* prayer for persons burned alive at the stake, celebrated or not. It opens, "May the great, mighty, and terrible God avenge his holy servant [so-and-so] who was burned alive for the sanctity of His name [*al kiddush ha-shem*]."[30] The prayer was formulated in entirely conventional rabbinic language. The specificity of converso martyrdom was alluded to only by the use of the term "burned alive" (*ha-nisraf ḥai* [or *nisrefet ḥaya*] *al yichud kedushat shemo*), and in the Spanish translation in the prayerbook, *el quemado vivo* (or *la quemada viva*) *por la unidad de santidad de su nombre.*[31] Those who were thus honored were accorded the full status of Jewish martyrs. In this way, the Portuguese-Jewish authorities gave rabbinic recognition to the crypto-Jewish struggle as an integral part of the historical struggle of the Jewish people to honor the Covenant.

A passage from an apologetic work written in Spanish by the London rabbi David Nieto offers another case of how spiritual leaders in Portuguese-Jewish communities incorporated crypto-Jewish martyrdom into the fabric of rabbinic discourse. "Take note of the reward of the martyr who delivers himself to death to sanctify God," he wrote, alluding to the Hebrew term *kiddush ha-shem* (a term not known in crypto-Jewish circles). He continued, "because such a person, despising life in this world in order to serve God with his entire soul [cf. Deut. 6:5], even as his soul is departing, and even though he suffers terrible torments in his death, suffers [these torments] with joy and with a ready heart, as did R. Akiva and R. Ḥananiah ben Teradion, and our forefathers, and as our brethren and kin in Spain and Portugal are doing today."[32]

In this passage, Nieto seized on the parallel between the physical torments

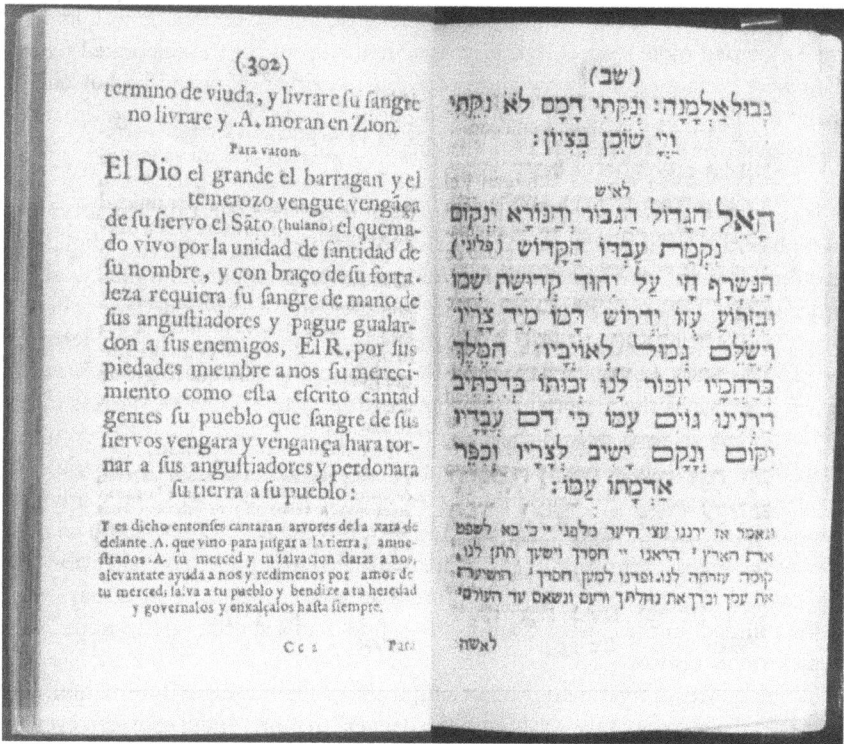

Figure 13. The *hashkavah* prayer for martyrs, in Spanish and Hebrew, from *Seder Berakhot* (Amsterdam 1687). The Jewish Theological Seminary.

suffered, according to tradition, by the rabbinic scholars R. Akiva and R. Ḥana-niah ben Teradion at the hour of their martyrdom, on the one hand, and the physical agony suffered by crypto-Jews burned alive at the stake, on the other. (He does not explicitly mention the rabbinic litmus test of being burned *alive,* but it is implicit in his reference to "terrible torments in his death.") By weaving the careers of the crypto-Jewish martyrs into the tissue of traditional rabbinic martyrdom lore, Nieto—and other authors who framed judaizing martyrdom rabbinically—divested these figures of their distinctive (and distinctively unrabbinic) way of being Jewish.[33]

As far as I know, there is no document that might throw light on an interesting issue that would naturally have arisen in this context. Did rabbinic authorities permit the recitation of the *hashkavah* prayer for persons who were not, within the bounds of halakha, Jews at all? It is certainly possible that not only Diogo d'Asumpção and Lope de Vera, but also Francisco Maldonado de Silva (whose mother was an Old Christian), were excluded. It may be, then, that conversos of matrilineal Jewish descent who were burned alive, but never became well known, were accorded more respect in the synagogue than some of the celebrated figures who were acclaimed in poetry and prose. Such a situation would be but one of many examples of a carefully monitored public sphere (and self-image) that reflected popular Portuguese-Jewish thinking only partially.

It is striking that Portuguese Jews produced no *acta*—no collection of martyrdom narratives of the kind that were widely disseminated in early modern Catholic and Protestant lands,[34] and this in spite of their astonishing output of original works of other kinds. The only efforts to gather together information on the celebrated martyrs are the two sets of brief narratives we have mentioned, one in Menasseh ben Israel's work *Esperança de Israel*,[35] the other in Isaac Cardoso's *Excelencias de los Hebreos*;[36] and the annotated list composed by Daniel Levi de Barrios in his *Triumpho del govierno popular*.[37] These thumbnail sketches (sometimes even less than that), which together scarcely cover a dozen pages, bear no comparison to the lengthy martyrologies produced by early modern Protestants and Catholics. Moreover, the narratives of Menasseh and Cardoso are not meant to stand on their own as models of exemplary lives, but are marshaled to support a certain claim—in the case of Menasseh, that biblical prophecies concerning the end of days were being fulfilled; in the case of Cardoso, that Jews had a special calling to be "witnesses to the unity of God."[38]

The brevity of treatment was not simply the result of meager information. It is true that the secrecy of the trials, and the dangers that prevented converso eyewitnesses from sending reports of the autos-da-fé to ex-conversos abroad, limited what was known in the diaspora. Yet with their ramified commercial and kinship network operating throughout Iberian lands, Portuguese Jews were unusually well positioned to obtain news. Word of autos-da-fé, in particular, traveled quickly. The auto-da-fé at which Isaac de Castro Tartas was condemned to death in Lisbon was held on December 15, 1647; news of it arrived in Amsterdam no later than January 27, 1648.[39] Portuguese Jews also obtained copies of some of the *relaciones*, or accounts of the autos printed in Iberian lands. These contained summaries of the sentencias, providing accounts of the life and trial of each condemned person. Where a "pertinacious heretic" was concerned, the account would usually be especially detailed. Isaac Cardoso relied, as he himself noted, on "the [account of the] auto which was printed in Madrid in 1640" for details about Francisco Maldonado de Silva's career. Sometimes other documentation from inquisitorial sources was obtained. Menasseh ben Israel possessed Inquisition records about Diogo d'Asumpção that the Inquisition had rather imprudently released.[40] Jews in Amsterdam also possessed a letter written by an Inquisition official describing the prison career of the martyr Lope de Vera.[41] Surely other information of this sort was available. Yet no one made the effort to compile what was known and present it in a single work.

It is not that the Portuguese-Jewish leadership failed to recognize the propaganda value of these stories. Nor could they have been oblivious to the powerful role of Protestant martyrologies (the most widely disseminated were those of John Foxe, Jean Crespin, Ludwig Rabus, and Adriaen Cornelis van Haemstede) in supporting Protestant loyalties and morale.[42] Why, then, are these narratives, such as they are, tucked away in works with broader aims? Why is there nothing more?

The leaders of the Portuguese-Jewish communities may have been hesitant to encourage a form of literature that evoked Catholic traditions of saint veneration—a concern of Protestants as well, but not one that inhibited them from producing a voluminous martyrological literature.[43] Perhaps more importantly, in the new conditions of the diaspora, "Portuguese" narratives of death at the stake could not provide, as such narratives did for so many Protestants and sectarians, examples of ideal behavior to be emulated in real life. To be sure, the persecutions of the Iberian inquisitions remained an integral part of the history, consciousness, and ongoing concerns of the "Portuguese" communities. But active resistance to a regime seeking to suppress Judaism was not a part of life in Venice, Livorno, Amsterdam, or Hamburg. The traits of the martyr—self-sufficient, defiant of authority, and eager for confrontation—were unhelpful and indeed a liability for the tasks at hand, that is, establishing internal stability and achieving conformity with the norms of the wider Jewish world. In these new circumstances, the Portuguese-Jewish elite needed to encourage a rather different set of traits: adaptability, cooperation, and respect for traditional authority. If zeal for the Law of Moses had a place, it was best expressed by learning the liturgy, making an effort to observe the precepts according to rabbinic tradition, and spending time in the service of the community.

The relatively humdrum demands of Jewish life in the diaspora could not, however, suppress the natural inclination to elaborate on the romance of life-and-death struggles in Iberian lands. It is true that Portuguese-Jewish authors refrained from sensationalizing episodes of martyrdom in the visual ways that were routine in Christian Europe. In the entire literature of this diaspora, there is not a single image that resembles the lurid illustrations of the final suffering moments of the martyr that were typical of both Catholic and Protestant martyrology—illustrations which inevitably evoked the Passion (and were meant to).[44]

Yet startlingly enough, several stories circulated of apparitions of celebrated crypto-Jewish martyrs, or other miraculous events, after or at the time of their death—a hallmark of the Catholic martyr.[45] We have already seen how a young converso being tried by the Valladolid tribunal asserted that he had seen Lope de Vera after his death, riding on a mule and glistening with the perspiration that had been on him when he was taken to the quemadero. The young man may have taken this as an omen of his own destiny. But whatever it meant, such a vision was not out of place in the framework of a way of life that drew regularly and unwittingly from Catholic sources.

What seems more surprising is that the sophisticated ex-converso apologete Isaac Cardoso introduced miracle stories into the sober, otherwise factually grounded accounts he gave of the careers of three celebrated martyrs (two of whom we have discussed). The earliest, chronologically, was that of was Diogo Lopes

The burning of William Hunter, Martyr.

Figure 14. Woodcut of the burning at the stake of the Protestant martyr William Hunter in 1554, from John Foxe, *Actes and Monuments* . . . (London 1684), vol. 3, p. 159. According to Foxe's account, a priest approached Hunter at the stake "with a popish book," hoping he would recant. William, who was sentenced after defiantly defending his reading of a Bible in English, is depicted rejecting the priest with the words, "Away thou false prophet." The New York Public Library.

Pinhanços—who as it turns out was apparently not a defiant judaizer at all, but a defiant skeptic. But Cardoso, who grew up in the region of Portugal where Pinhanços lived, drew his account of Pinhanços's martyrdom not from Inquisition documents but from the accounts of elderly Old Christians who had witnessed Pinhanços's death at the stake in 1571, more than a generation before Cardoso's birth. Cardoso related the following denouement of the story. After Pinhanços was sentenced, he was taken to the stake, tied with iron chains, and raised onto the pyre. At the moment the flames began to touch him, Cardoso wrote,

> a great portent took place, for the chains fell into the fire, and he disappeared and was never seen again. All of which caused great wonder among the multitudes of people who were present. They said that the demons had such a craving and desire for him,

that they snatched him away body and soul, and in this way they eased their suspense and astonishment.[46]

The interpretation of "multitudes of people" that this occurrence was the work of demons would have been familiar enough to ex-conversos. This was the stock explanation used by ecclesiastics to distinguish defiant heretics from steadfast saints. But those with a conflicting view (including Cardoso's readers) would automatically have inverted this interpretation, cued by his final explanatory phrase and making the martyr's miraculous rescue from the flames an act of divine intervention. Cardoso included the tale, one assumes, either because he believed the miraculous event had occurred or because the story conveyed the awe in which even Old Christians viewed judaizing martyrs.

In connection with Francisco Maldonado de Silva, too, Cardoso repeated a sensational and inspiring (though not necessarily miraculous) story about events that took place at the plaza where the ceremony of the auto-da-fé was held. Cardoso's account was drawn from an eyewitness account of the 1639 auto in Lima where Maldonado de Silva was sentenced, written by the Spanish priest Fernando Montesinos—a printed work that was given the imprimatur of the Inquisition.[47] We have already mentioned this event in connection with Maldonado de Silva's career; but let us look here at Cardoso's account, which follows Montesinos's almost word for word:

> They burned him alive at the end of thirteen years, and the [account of the] auto which was printed in Madrid in 1640 . . . states that after the announcement of the crimes of the relaxed was completed, there arose so fierce a wind that the residents of Lima affirmed they had not seen one so strong in many years. It violently rent apart the canopy over that part of the platform where [Maldonado de Silva] stood, and seeing the sky, he said, "This has been done by the God of Israel, so that he may see me face to face from heaven."[48]

Montesinos presumably included this sensational detail as testimony to the stubbornness of the judaizer. For Cardoso and his readers, though, it had the effect of draping Maldonado de Silva in an aura of sanctity, and dramatized his victory as he upstaged an event that was intended to publicize the power of the Church. The martyr's apt final remarks—a standard element of martyrologies in many cultures—served to enhance his image by giving him, as it were, the last word in the long series of his disputations with inquisitors.[49]

Finally, Cardoso reported some supernatural martyrological lore that had its origins not in Iberian lands, but in the Portuguese-Jewish community of Amsterdam. It concerned the celebrated martyr Isaac de Castro Tartas, who was raised in that community. (We have not discussed him here because, unlike the others, he had received a rabbinic education.)[50] After settling in Dutch Brazil, Isaac de Castro made a rather mysterious trip to Portuguese Brazil, where he was captured and turned over to ecclesiastical authorities. Deported to Lisbon for trial, he was burned alive at the stake as a defiant dogmatizing judaizer in 1647.

One story circulating after his death was that the young man had written to his parents before he left Dutch Brazil for Portuguese Brazil, announcing "that he was going to Rio de Janeiro to see if there he could lead some of his relatives to the fear of God, and that they should not expect a letter from him for four years." A letter did arrive four years later, as the youth had promised. But it was not from Isaac de Castro. It was written to inform his parents that he had been burned alive in the city of Lisbon.[51] Was this fulfillment of his promise not a sign from the grave?

Cardoso did not elaborate. But he did go on to report an even greater "marvel" (*maravilla*) concerning this martyr. In the Amsterdam community, he explained, it was the custom to place the names of adult male members of the community in two urns, from which names were drawn for the synagogue honors of removing the Torah scroll from the ark and being called to the Torah. When a member of the community left Amsterdam, his name was removed from the urns, and this procedure had been duly followed when Isaac de Castro left Amsterdam for Dutch Brazil at least five years earlier. Nevertheless, Cardoso reported, after news of Isaac de Castro's death reached Amsterdam,

> on the first Sabbath of his funerary honors, the hakham R. Saul Levi Mortera, peace be unto him, devoted his sermon to the blessed martyr. When they went to draw the lots, the first which emerged for the opening of the doors of the ark was that of the glorious Isaac de Castro Tartas.[52]

Stories of such events are not, to put it mildly, common features of Jewish martyrology. That they appear in a work by so enthusiastic and disciplined a supporter of rabbinic Judaism as Isaac Cardoso suggests the powerful sway of popular undercurrents about which we know very little.

Just as rabbinic culture did not share the Iberian enthusiasm for postmortem miracles, so it did not delight in flamboyant displays of manliness. Yet the defense of male honor was clearly a driving impulse in the careers of most of the celebrated martyrs. As they baited, scorned, and otherwise confronted the inquisitors, they were participating in the Reformation revival of the ancient "athletic" type of martyr.[53] But they were also behaving in a way that was triggered by Iberian patterns of male honor. To be sure, this was not inconsistent with the particular Jewish models of martyrdom they (rather infrequently) had recourse to. Francisco Maldonado de Silva did not explicitly say so, but he apparently identified with Samson—an extravagant defender of male honor (who was not regarded very highly in rabbinic literature).[54] Luis Carvajal, it may be recalled, urged his mother to follow the example of the Maccabee martyrs. It is true that one of the Maccabee martyrs was a woman. But because she took the path of Perpetua, so to speak, the author of the second book of Maccabees praised her for having "a man's courage."[55]

For communal leaders, rabbis, and apologetes of the Portuguese-Jewish diaspora, the concept of honor was no less ingrained than it was among the rank and file.[56] However, at least in public discourse they showed themselves rather adept at translating the martyrs' defense of personal male honor—that is, the display of fearlessness in the face of danger, contempt for the Inquisition, and readiness to die rather than suffer humiliation—into a conception of honor that was more useful to their aim of community building.

A fine example of this is the following excerpt from a eulogy composed by Jacob Abendana, an ex-converso rabbi in Amsterdam, for the martyrs Abraham Núñez Bernal and Isaac d'Almeida, who were burned at the stake in Cordova in 1655:

> These men demonstrated that in their hearts there reigned the perfect love of God, [which they expressed by] paying him the greatest tribute of respect of which men are capable, offering their own lives for the *honor of his holy name.* By such an act, they have brought *glory to God and luster to their stock,* and have increased the treasury of merit of *the chosen people* [my emphases].[57]

Abendana's remarks are couched in language that appealed subliminally to Iberian notions of individual honor and to converso notions of ethnic pride. But it rather neatly transferred the strong feelings associated with these to other objects: it was the honor of *God* that was being defended, and the luster of the *Jewish people* that was being enhanced.

The poets and rhymesters of the Portuguese-Jewish diaspora were quite a bit less inhibited in their treatment than members of the communal establishment, rabbinic or otherwise. Their images of the martyrs tended to emphasize individual heroism, physical courage, and intellectual brilliance. Moreover, by stressing the violence and cruelty of the Inquisition and drawing frequently on the imagery of fire, they threw into relief the crushing power of the "enemy," thus indirectly augmenting the stature of the martyr.

Let us look at two stanzas written by Daniel Levi de Barrios, memorializing Abraham Athias, a judaizer who was burned alive at the stake in Cordova in 1665. The author has Athias declare the following:

> I am a Hebrew, enemies,
> My bride is the Holy Law,
> My God, only that of Israel,
> My honor, to die for His cause.
>
> Seize me, fling me into the fire
> Just as its flame will be
> My triumphal chariot, so is
> Elijah my expectation.[58]

These stanzas are from a work by Barrios titled *There Is No Force That Can Withstand the Truth* (c. 1667). It borrows from an earlier and in many ways more interesting work, Antonio Enríquez Gómez's tribute to Judah Creyente, composed in France in the late 1640s.[59] Although the latter work circulated in the Portuguese-Jewish diaspora, Enríquez Gómez never lived in a Jewish community

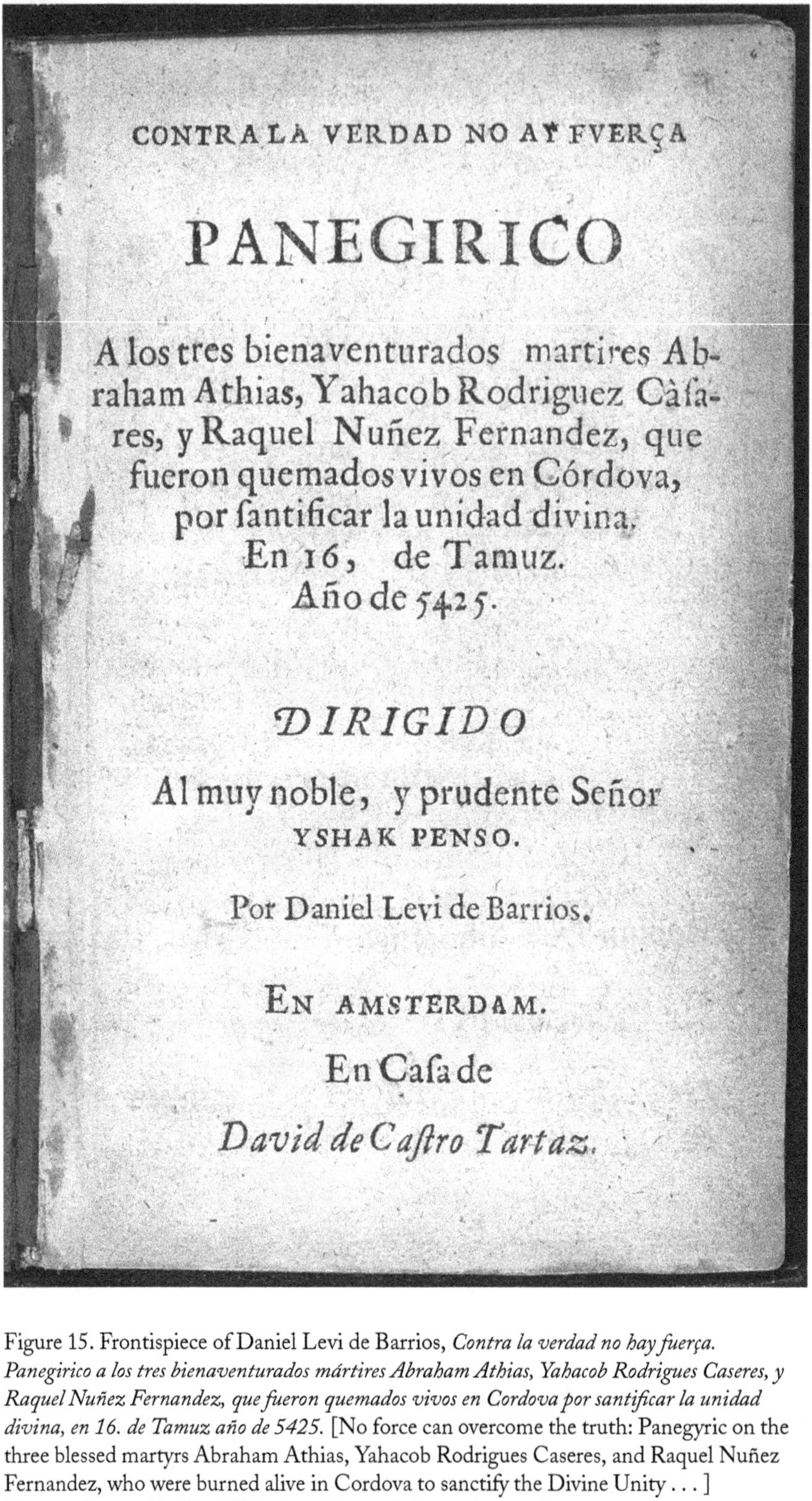

CONTRA LA VERDAD NO AY FVERÇA

PANEGIRICO

A los tres bienaventurados martires Abraham Athias, Yahacob Rodriguez Càsa-
res, y Raquel Nuñez Fernandez, que
fueron quemados vivos en Córdova,
por santificar la unidad divina.
En 16, de Tamuz.
Año de 5425.

DIRIGIDO

Al muy noble, y prudente Señor
YSHAK PENSO.

Por Daniel Levi de Barrios.

EN AMSTERDAM.

En Casa de

David de Castro Tartaz.

Figure 15. Frontispiece of Daniel Levi de Barrios, *Contra la verdad no hay fuerça.*
Panegirico a los tres bienaventurados mártires Abraham Athias, Yahacob Rodrigues Caseres, y
Raquel Nuñez Fernandez, que fueron quemados vivos en Cordova por santificar la unidad
divina, en 16. de Tamuz año de 5425. [No force can overcome the truth: Panegyric on the
three blessed martyrs Abraham Athias, Yahacob Rodrigues Caseres, and Raquel Nuñez
Fernandez, who were burned alive in Cordova to sanctify the Divine Unity . . .]
(Amsterdam, n.d.). The Bibliotheca Rosenthaliana, Amsterdam.

—which makes his lengthy "reconstruction" of Lope de Vera's theological argumentation especially worthy of analysis. Perhaps most striking, however, from the point of view of this discussion, is the poet's willingness to describe his protagonist's ardent—indeed erotic—attraction to martyrdom:

> I am a lover of your Law,
> and so much do I adore her
> that I die for love of her –
> look, O Lord, how much I love her!

> This martyrdom I undergo,
> these tortures I am suffering,
> as a lover I accept them,
> as a husband I adore them.[60]

Let us recall that this was a poet who harbored a fascination with the story of Samson, who did not hesitate to compare Lope de Vera to Samson, and who wrote an epic poem titled *Sansón Nazareno*. It is true that Samson was a popular figure generally among early modern authors. But Enríquez Gómez's interest in the biblical hero may have had special features.

Like Samson, Enríquez Gómez lived between clashing cultures. He was the child of a New Christian father and an Old Christian mother. His grandfather died in an Inquisition prison; his father was arrested by the Inquisition but later gravitated to France. Yet the poet married an Old Christian woman. When he found himself threatened by the Inquisition in 1634, he too took refuge in France. In 1647, he published a veiled attack on the Inquisition, *Política angelica*, at a time when his security was threatened there; he also wrote an only recently discovered satirical attack on the same institution.[61] Yet he returned to Spain in 1649 (under an assumed name). Discovered and arrested in 1661, he died in an inquisitorial prison. We do not know what his beliefs were in the course of his life. He clearly did not want to live in a Jewish community, but his criticism of Christianity in his *Romance al divín martír* is extended and bitter. It may be that his aversion for the Inquisition was stronger than any well-defined set of religious beliefs.

Enríquez Gómez, then, may well have nurtured a sense of profound frustration at the denial of intellectual autonomy that he yearned for—one that he would have shared with both the celebrated martyrs and the notorious ex-converso "heretics." It is interesting that his *Romance al divín martír* exists in a number of seventeenth-century copies but was never published in Amsterdam or elsewhere in the Jewish world. Was this because the author returned to Spain? Was it because he refrained from joining a Jewish community? Or was Lope de Vera represented in too strident and radical a vein? We don't know, of course. But one senses that Enríquez Gómez would not have been amenable to kindly rabbinic guidance.

The late sixteenth and the seventeenth centuries witnessed the emergence of a dizzying variety of lonely truth-seekers in Europe. Some of them produced works that would eventually contribute to the elimination of religious coercion on European soil. Some of them left no trace. It is perhaps surprising to discover a rich body of literature that records (however imperfectly) some voices of vigorous religious nonconformity in one of the least expected corners of Europe in this period—the Iberian Peninsula (and its colonial outposts). Some of the speakers whose heterodox thoughts were put in writing were sentenced as judaizers, others as *luteranos* or *alumbrados*. But the Inquisition's labels conceal the complex ties between one type and another—ties that have been overlooked for too long. Moreover, through pathways that are still dim—involving the clandestine circulation of books, maritime and commercial travel, and migration to and fro—connections were made with the Reformation world beyond Iberian frontiers, and some kind of picture of that world crystallized. We know something about the impact of Reformation (and New Christian) sensibilities on Iberian Catholicism. But we need to understand better the impact of Protestant and Iberian Catholic innovations on crypto-Judaism.

Studying the dossiers of celebrated judaizing martyrs has served to shed some light—admittedly narrowly focused—on the subject. But anyone familiar with Inquisition studies knows how much remains to be explored. Unfortunately, it is a lot easier to read *about* Inquisition dossiers than it is to read the dossiers themselves. Perhaps, nevertheless, this book will serve to stimulate interest in a question that has scarcely been asked: that is, how the wider population of Iberian judaizers—men *and women*, let me finally say—apprehended and absorbed the upheaval in religious outlook that was transforming Christian Europe.

Appendix A: Commemoration of Individual Martyrs in the Literature of the Portuguese-Jewish Diaspora, to 1683*

Asumpção, Diogo d': Poem in Portuguese by David Jesurun, published by Barrios in "En los caminos de la salvación," in *TGP,* followed by poem by Barrios; Barrios, in "Memoria de los martires" in *TGP;*[1] Barrios in "Casa de Jacob," in *TGP,* 18;[2] Menasseh ben Israel, *Esperança,*[3] 97–98.

Atias, Abraham (Jorge Mendes de Castro): Barrios, "Memoria de los martires";[1] Barrios, *Contra la verdad.*[4]

Barrocas, Tamar: Barrios, "Memoria de los martires";[1] Barrios, *Contra la verdad,*[4] 148.

Bernal, Abraham Nuñez (Manuel): Barrios, "Memoria de los martires";[1] *Elogios que zelosos dedicaron.*[5]

Bernal, Isaac de Almeida (Marcos de Almeida): Barrios, "Memoria de los martires";[1] Barrios, *Contra la verdad,*[4] 149; *Elogios que zelosos dedicaron;*[5] poem by Ruy Lopez (Ezechiel) Rosa published by Barrios in *TGP,* "Casa de Jacob."[6]

---

*For the place and date of death of the men and women listed below, see page 219n73.

1. Daniel Levi de Barrios, "Memoria de los martires que fueron quemados vivos en diferentes tiempos y ciudades de España por santificar la indivisa unidad del eterno Leguislador," in *TGP* (Amsterdam 1683–1684), "Casa de Jacob," 42–46. The copies of this work vary somewhat in their contents and arrangement; I have used the copy of the Jewish Theological Seminary of America.

2. "[Y] en el Año de 1604 passo a la Ciudad de Amsterdam con las nuevas de que Fray Diego de la Assencion siendo preso de la Lisboana Inquisicion en el año de 1601 fu[e] quemado vivo en el de 1603 por publicar que solamente la Ley de Moseh, obligava y dava gracia para la salvacion de las Almas." This passage is followed by a poem in honor of Diogo d'Asumpção.

3. Menasseh ben Israel, *Esperança de Israel* (Amsterdam 1650).

4. Daniel Levi de Barrios, *Contra la verdad no hay fuerza. Panegirico a los tres bienadenturados martires Abraham Athias, Yahacob Rodriguez Casares, y Raquel Nuñez Fernandez, que fueron quemados vivos en Córdova, por santificar la unidad divina* (Amsterdam 1665).

5. *Elogios que zelosos dedicaron a la felice memoria de Abraham Nuñez Bernal, que fue quemado vivo santificando el Nombre de su criador en Cordova a 3 de Mayo 5415* (Amsterdam 1655).

6. The poem is followed by the following remark: "Exclama *la casa de Jacob* al Dios de las Venganças como suele hasta oy dentro de Amsterdam en el Sabado de la Semana en que tiene noticia que la fiera Inquisicion entrega el ardiente suplicio a la constante Inocencia, que muere martir por sanctificar al divino nombre." Barrios refers to the martyr in the singular, and seems to allude to the young age of the martyr (Isaac de Almeida was seventeen years old when arrested and twenty-two years old when he was burned alive in March 1655). But see Cecil Roth, "Abraham Nuñez Bernal et autres martyrs contemporains de l'Inquisition," *REJ* 10 (1936), 45.

Castro de Tartas, Isaac (Joseph de Lis): Barrios, "Memoria de los martires";[1] Menasseh ben Israel, *Esperança*, 99–100; Cardoso, *Excelencias;*[7] Barrios, *Contra la verdad*, 148; Solomon de Oliveira, poem in *Sharshot gavlut* (Amsterdam 1665), 52v–54; Jonah Abarbanel, Abraham Cardoso, João Pinto Delgado.[8]

Faya, Aaron Coen (António de Aguiar):[9] Barrios, "Memoria de los martires."[1]

Ferro, Manuel: Barrios, "Memoria de los martires."[1]

Fonseca, Isaac Henriques da:[10] Barrios, "Memoria de los martires."[1]

Gomez Salsedo, Raphael: Barrios, poem in "En los caminos de la salvación," in *TGP*.

Lopez, Francisco:[11] Barrios, "Memoria de los martires."[1]

Lopez Redonda, Phelipa: Barrios, "Memoria de los martires."[1]

Lopez Redondo, Baltasar: Barrios, "Memoria de los martires."[1]

Maldonado de Silva, Francisco: Menasseh ben Israel, *Esperança de Israel*, 100; Cardoso, *Excelencias*, 323–324.

Morales, Simon de: Barrios, "Memoria de los martires."[1]

Nuñez, Clara: Barrios, "Memoria de los martires."[1]

Nuñez Fernandez, Raquel: Barrios, "Memoria de los martires";[1] Barrios, *Contra la verdad*,[4] title.

Pereyra, Abraham Lopez ("alias Gaspar Lopez Pereyra"): Barrios, "Memoria de los martires."[1]

Pereyra, Leonor: Barrios, "Memoria de los martires."[1]

Pinhanços, Diogo Lopes: Cardoso, *Excelencias*.[7]

Robles Cardoso, Gaspar de: Barrios, "Memoria de los martires."[1]

Rodriguez (Casares), Jacob: Barrios, "Memoria de los martires";[1] Barrios, *Contra la verdad*,[4] title.

Saraiva, Luis: Barrios, "Memoria de los martires."[1]

Treviño de Sobremonte, Tomás (Elias Israel): Barrios, "Corona de ley," in *TGP;* "Memoria de los martires";[1] Menasseh ben Israel, *Esperança de Israel*, 100; Cardoso, *Excelencias;*[7] Barrios, sonnet in "Luzes de la ley divina," in *TGP*.

Vera y Alarcón, Lope de (Judah Creyente): Barrios, "Memoria de los martires";[1] Antonio Enríquez Gomez, "Romance al divin Martir Juda Creyente, martirizado em Valladolid por la inquisición"; Menasseh ben Israel, *Esperança de Israel*, 98–99; Barrios, *Contra la verdad*,[4] 147, 150.

Visente, Pedro: Barrios, "Memoria de los martires."[1]

---

7. Isaac Cardoso, *Excelencias de los hebreos* (Amsterdam 1679), 323–325.

8. See Cecil Roth, "An Elegy of João Pinto Delgado on Isaac de Castro Tartas," *REJ* 121 (1962), 355–366.

9. The text of Barrios's work mistakenly reads "Aaron Coen Faya alias Don Gaspar Lopes Pereyra."

10. According to Azevedo, this judaizer was a lawyer who, during his trial, gave the inquisitors a written declaration that he signed "Misael Hisneque de Fungoca," and demanded that the inquisitors refer to him by this Hebrew name—presumably Michael. See J. Lucio d'Azevedo, *História dos Christãos Novos portugueses* (Lisbon 1921), 323.

11. Barrios identifies Francisco Lopez as "hijo del martir Joseph Lopez," although the latter is not included in the count of martyrs.

1) God gave the Law to the Jews. Even Christians accepted the Ten Commandments of this Law.

2) Scripture taught that [in Luis's words] "if at some time a prophet or dreamer rises up among you, and says he has had visions, and testifies to them with miracles, and tells you to deviate from my Law to the right or left, do not believe him, but persevere in my Law, because this is a test that I bring to make manifest whether or not you love me, and this prophet or dreamer you shall punish with death for having told you to deviate from my Law and commandments, in which you shall persevere."[1] Luis's allusion was, of course, to Jesus.

3) The condition of the Jews in exile proved that the curses in Deuteronomy 28 had been fulfilled because the Jews had failed to keep God's commandments (including a prophecy which spoke with particular power to crypto-Jews [Deut. 28:36]: "The Lord will bring you . . . to a nation that neither you nor your fathers have known; there you shall serve other gods, of wood and stone").

4) The prophecy of the Jews' exile had also been made in a song of Moses.[2] This song predicts Israel's betrayal of God and God's punishment of them (including the prophecy that God will "scatter them into corners"), but ends with the consoling message that he will avenge Israel's enemies.

5) "Everything David wrote, especially the psalm *celi etnarrant gloriam Dei,* which states that the Law of the Lord our God is a sun which lights the soul."[3]

6) Psalm 118[4]—a long psalm in which "there was no [verse] that did not praise the Law of the Lord our God," in which Law Carvajal wanted to live and die. He mentioned in particular the verse that states that "all things come to an end, but your commandment has no end."[5]

1. This is an approximation of Deut. 13: 2–6.

2. Carvajal refers to "the song of Moses that begins *Audite celi que loquor* and ends *Videte que ego sim solus et nom sitalius Deus preterme.*" This is a reference to Deut. 32: 1–43, which begins "Give ear, O heavens, and I will speak." Luis's quotations from the Vulgate, Deut. 32:1 and 39, reflect some errors of the notary.

3. In the Vulgate, Psalm 18, *caeli enarrant gloriam Dei;* Psalm 19 in the Hebrew Bible. The imagery of the sun is indeed used in this psalm, and the Law associated with enlightenment.

4. In the Vulgate; Psalm 119 in the Hebrew Bible.

5. Possibly a reference to verse 96?

7) "The psalm of Asaph that begins, *ud qui Deus repulisti imperpetuam.*"[6] This psalm petitions God to deliver Israel from the long oppression they have endured under oppressors who are clearly identified as God's enemies.

8) The prophecies of Ezekiel, which confirmed the Law of God and the coming of the Messiah and the ingathering of the people of Israel. And since this ingathering had not occurred, it was clear, Carvajal asserted, that the prophecy concerning the Messiah had not been fulfilled.

9) Various prophetic passages that elucidated the following divine promises: a) the ultimate reward granted to the Jewish people, and punishment of those who worship idols (Isaiah 76); b) God's reassurance that he has not abandoned, and would not abandon, His people (Isaiah 49);[7] c) the promise that only if the sun would cease to shine, etc., would God abandon Israel his people (Jeremiah 31 and 32); d) the salvation of Israel and the coming of the Messiah (4 Ezra); e) the fall of Christendom, identified with the fourth beast envisioned by Daniel; f) the final conversion of the gentiles (the last chapter of Tobias); g) the promise that the Temple and Jerusalem would be rebuilt (Haggai); and h) the promise that at the Final Judgment, sinners would be punished and the "servants of the Law" would be rewarded (last chapter of Malachi). He believed, he concluded, that Jesus was the Antichrist.[8]

6. In the Vulgate, Psalm 73, *ut quid Deus reppulisti in finem;* Psalm 74 in the Hebrew Bible.

7. Luis proceeded to quote Isaiah 49: 15–16, 22–23, almost verbatim, in Spanish.

8. *Antichrist* is not, of course, a concept in rabbinic Judaism. It is worth noting, however, that a prevalent view in sixteenth-century Protestant circles was that the "little horn" of Daniel 7:8 was the Antichrist, more often than not identified with the pope. See Richard Muller, "Calvin's Exegesis of Old Testament Prophecies," in David Steinmetz, ed., *The Bible in the Sixteenth Century* (Durham, N.C., 1990), 71.

Glossary

Note: All terms are Spanish unless noted otherwise.

abonos—Accumulation of evidence from witnesses called before the Inquisition on the initiative of the defendant, to prove good character and exemplary religious practice.

acusación—A text with a list of accusations derived from evidence gathered by the tribunal, presented to the accused, who was required to respond on the spot to each accusation.

alumbrados (*alumbradismo*)—Literally, "illuminists" ("illuminism"). Mystically inclined religious figures in early modern Spain who sought to perfect their souls, and who deemphasized external ceremony.

brasero—Place in a town where public burnings of heretics took place.

calificador (Portuguese: *qualificador*)—Theologian who examined inquisitorial testimony to analyze evidence of heresy.

comisario—Local representative of the Inquisition, who took testimony and collected denunciations in remote parts of a tribunal's district.

consulta de fe—Assembly of inquisitors and outside ecclesiastics who deliberated and voted to determine a prisoner's sentence.

curador—Guardian provided to an accused under the age of twenty-five, whose authority was required to ratify the defendant's confessions.

corozo—Conical mitre worn by condemned prisoners at an auto-da-fé.

diminuto—Prisoner whom the Inquisition determined had given an incomplete confession.

encomendero—A wealthy settler who possessed a grant that enabled him to become a principal miner or commercial agriculturalist in Spanish America.

familiar—Lay official of the Inquisition.

fidalgo (Portuguese)—Nobleman.

ḥakham (Hebrew)—Term (and title) for rabbinic scholar in the post-Expulsion Sephardi diaspora.

halakha (adj., *halakhic*) (Hebrew)—Rabbinic law.

libelo (Portuguese)—Equivalent of Spanish *acusación* (see above).

luterano—Any person regarded by the Inquisitions as having Protestant leanings.

mordaza—Gag applied to an impenitent heretic, particularly when he or she appeared in public.

negativo—Prisoner who persistently denied guilt, despite testimony or evidence against him or her.

oidor—A colonial judge on whom, along with others of his office, the crown relied heavily.

procurador—Inquisitorial official who served as an "adviser" to the accused.

publicación—Detailed list of assertions based on the testimony of individual witnesses, whose names and identity were concealed, to which the accused was required to respond on the spot.

quemadero—Place in a town where public burnings took place (same as *brasero*).

reconciliación—The Inquisition's formal reception back into the Church of a penitent heretic, usually in conjunction with punishment.

relajación—Transfer ("relaxation") of a prisoner from ecclesiastical to secular authorities, in order to carry out his or her execution.

relapso—Person condemned of backsliding after reconciliation, usually resulting in relaxation.

sambenito—Penitential garment of the Inquisition worn by condemned heretics.

sentencia (Portuguese, *sentença*)—Document detailing a prisoner's sentence, read publicly; it often included details of the prisoner's crimes and trial.

Shema (Hebrew)—Jewish declaration of God's unity, opening with the verse "Hear, O Israel, the Lord our God is one Lord" (Deut. 6:4).

Suprema—Supreme council of the Spanish Inquisition, with authority over all tribunals in Spanish territory.

Notes

Preface

1. This term is the English equivalent of the Castilian and Portuguese *judaizantes,* the term used by the Inquisition.

2. I refer to them as martyrs because that is how they conceived of themselves and that is how they were regarded by fellow judaizers in Iberian lands, as well as by Spanish and Portuguese Jews living as émigrés outside the Iberian Peninsula.

3. The only one that has not been examined heretofore is the fragmentary and badly damaged dossier of Diogo Lopes Pinhanços.

4. Cecil Roth's classic work *A History of the Marranos* (1932), for example, includes a chapter titled "Saints, Heroes, and Martyrs" that is essentially a set of narratives pieced together from information culled, with an eye for the sensational, from the sources. And see Yitzhak Baer, *Galut,* trans. from Hebrew by Robert Warshaw (New York 1947), 93–97.

5. The literature on converso martyrdom goes back at least a century. In 1896, George Alexandher Kohut published an eighty-six-page article on "Jewish Martyrs of the Inquisition in South America," *Publications of the American Jewish Historical Society* 4 (1896), 166–171. Most of the literature published subsequently is cited in the body of this book.

6. A striking expression of the rabbinic attitude was the initial refusal of R. Yom Tov Lippman Heller, after the Chmielnitski massacres in 1648, to compose new elegies for the martyrs, asserting that these events were merely a repetition of old ones—this, according to the publisher of the *seliḥoth* (penitential prayers) that he eventually consented to write. See Jacob Katz, *Exclusiveness and Tolerance* (London 1961), 153.

7. A notable case in point, from the work of Haim Beinart: "To a greater or lesser degree every Converso [in fifteenth-century Ciudad Real] did his best to fulfil Mosaic precepts, and one should regard as sincere the aim they all set themselves: to live as Jews and to achieve as great a degree of perfection as possible in their Judaism. The measures they took in order to keep Jewish laws, irrespective of whether they were simple folk or among the distinguished Conversos of the town, must be considered as acts of supreme self-sacrifice, and as an expression of their readiness to face martyrdom at any moment" (Haim Beinart, *Conversos on Trial: The Inquisition in Ciudad Real* [Jerusalem 1981], 242).

8. For the very rich literature on the emergence of concepts of martyrdom in Greco-Roman, Jewish, and Christian circles in antiquity, see the extensive bibliography (unfortunately lacking studies in Hebrew) in J. W. van Henten, *The Maccabean Martyrs as Saviours of the Jewish People: A Study of 2 and 4 Maccabees* (Leiden 1997). This literature includes, inter alia, W. H. C. Frend, *Martyrdom and Persecution in the Early Church: A Study of Conflict from the Maccabees to Donatus* (Oxford 1965; New York 1967); Moshe David Herr, "Persecutions and Martyrdom in Hadrian's Days," *Scripta Hierosolymitana* 23 (1972), 85–125; Saul

Lieberman, "On Persecution of the Jewish Religion" (Hebrew), *Salo Wittmayer Baron Jubilee Volume: Hebrew Section* (Jerusalem 1974), 213–245; S. Safrai, *"Kiddush ha-Shem* in the Teachings of the Tannaim" (Hebrew), *Zion* 44 (1979), 28–42; Gerald Blidstein, "Rabbis, Romans, and Martyrdom—Three Views," *Tradition* 1 (1984), 1–58; Robin Lane Fox, *Pagans and Christians* (New York 1986), ch. 9 ("Persecution and Martyrdom"); J. W. van Henten, ed., *Die Entstehung der jüdischen Martyrologie* (Leiden 1989); Arthur Droge and James Tabor, *A Noble Death: Suicide and Martyrdom among Christians and Jews in Antiquity* (San Francisco 1992); G. W. Bowersock, *Martyrdom and Rome* (Cambridge 1995); David Goodblatt, "Suicide in the Sanctuary: Traditions on Priestly Martyrdom," *Journal of Jewish Studies* 46 (1995), 10–29; Tessa Rajak, "Dying for the Law: The Martyr's Portrait in Jewish-Greek Literature," in M. J. Edwards and Simon Swain, eds., *Portraits: Biographical Representation in the Greek and Latin Literature of the Roman Empire* (Oxford 1997), 39–67; Daniel Boyarin, *Dying for God: Martyrdom and the Making of Christianity and Judaism* (Stanford 1999).

9. For an impression of issues raised in recent scholarship on martyrdom in post-antique Christendom, see the collection edited by Diana Wood, *Martyrs and Martyrologies: Papers Read at the 1992 Summer Meeting of the Ecclesiastical History Society* (Oxford 1993); and Brad S. Gregory, *Salvation at Stake: Christian Martyrdom in Early Modern Europe* (Cambridge, Mass., 1999). In the realm of Jewish history, the classic analyses are Jacob Katz, *Exclusiveness and Tolerance* (Oxford 1961), ch. 7 ("The Martyrs"); idem, "Between 1096 and 1648–9" (Hebrew), in *Sefer Yovel le-Yitzhak Baer* (Jerusalem 1961), 318–337 (and see the subsequent debate in *Zion* 61 [1996], 159–182 and 62 [1997], 23–46); Gerson Cohen, "Messianic Postures of Ashkenazim and Sephardim," *Studies of the Leo Baeck Institute*, ed. Max Kreutzberger (New York 1967), 117–156. More recently, see inter alia Haym Soloveitchik, "Halakhah, Hermeneutics, and Martyrdom in Medieval Ashkenaz," *Jewish Quarterly Review* 94 (2004), 77–108, 278–299; I. Gafni and A. Ravitzky, eds., *Sanctity of Life and Martyrdom: Studies in Memory of Amir Yekutiel* (Hebrew) (Jerusalem 1992); Jeremy Cohen, *Sanctifying the Name of God: Jewish Martyrs and Jewish Memories of the First Crusade* (Philadelphia 2004); Susan Einbinder, *Beautiful Death: Jewish Poetry and Martyrdom in Medieval France* (Princeton 2002); Simha Goldin, *The Ways of Jewish Martyrdom* (Hebrew) (Lod 2002). One can hardly ignore Israel Yuval's controversial article, "Vengeance and Damnation, Blood and Defamation: From Jewish Martyrdom to Blood Libel Accusations" (Hebrew), *Zion* 58 (1993), 33–90, which provoked strong and sometimes passionate responses (see *Zion* 59 [1994]), and Yuval's subsequent book, *"Two Nations in Your Womb": Perceptions of Jews and Christians* (Hebrew) (Tel Aviv 2000). Among analyses with a focus on the more recent past, see Alan Mintz, *Hurban: Responses to Catastrophe in Hebrew Literature* (New York 1984); and Yael Zerubavel, *Recovered Roots: Collective Memory and the Making of Israeli National Tradition* (Chicago 1995).

10. Literally, *dogmatizing*. Let me note that the term *dogmatista*, as used by the Inquisition, did not necessarily suggest that the accused was educated. It was used to designate a heresiarch—a leader and teacher of heretics. Women as well as men, unlearned persons as well as learned ones, were accused of being dogmatistas.

i. The Historical Setting

1. It is difficult to generalize the perceived "gain" from such a death, but it usually involved some combination of preserving honor, benefiting one's people, preserving freedom, gaining salvation, and propagating one's convictions.

2. Their Hebrew names are given in later sources as Hananiah, Azariah, and Mishael.

3. Maccabees is a Greek non-canonical Jewish work. The woman and her seven children appear in many subsequent versions in Jewish literature. See Gerson Cohen, "The Story of Hannah and Her Seven Sons in Hebrew Literature" (Hebrew), in *Sefer ha-yovel le-kh'vod Mordekhai Menahem Kaplan* (New York 1953), 109–122.

4. The old question of the origins of the practice of martyrdom is still debated. Its emphasis, however, has shifted. An earlier generation of scholars sought to determine whether the deepest roots of Western martyrological traditions were Jewish, Christian, or pagan, regarding each of those orbits as distinct and well defined. W. H. C. Frend, reflecting the view of one camp, regarded the story of the Jewish Maccabee martyrs as "the obvious beginning" because, in his view, this story introduces an idea of expiatory sacrifice that the Hellenic world did not possess (Frend, *Martyrdom and Persecution in the Early Church*). G. W. Bowersock, adopting a contrasting position, viewed martyrdom as a distinctive creation of the early Christian world, arguing that it "was alien to both the Greeks and the Jews" because of its core element of a trial narrative (Bowersock, *Martyrdom and Rome*). Recently, scholars have emphasized the strong intermingling of currents in Late Antiquity, so that martyrdom (among other pheonomena) has been viewed as a culturally complex construction, echoing Greco-Roman, Jewish, and Christian themes alike. For a compelling explication of this view, see J. W. van Henten, "The Martyrs as Heroes of the Christian People: Some Remarks on the Continuity between Jewish and Christian Martyrology, with Pagan Analogies," in M. Lamberights and P. van Deun, eds., *Martyrium in Multidisciplinary Perspective: Memorial Louis Reekmans* (Leuven 1995), 303–322; and see the introduction to J. W. van Henten and Friedrich Avemarie, *Martyrdom and Noble Death: Selected Texts from Graeco-Roman, Jewish, and Christian Antiquity* (London 2002), 1–8. See as well Droge and Tabor, *A Noble Death;* Carole Straw, "'A Very Special Death': Christian Death in its Classical Context," in Margaret Cormack, ed., *Sacrificing the Self: Perspectives on Martyrdom and Religion* (Oxford 2002), 39–57; and Steve Weitzman, "Josephus on How to Survive Martyrdom," *Journal of Jewish Studies* 55 (2004), 230–245. Daniel Boyarin, in his *Dying for God*, programmatically rejects the notion of distinctly "Jewish" or "Christian" modes of martyrdom in the first few centuries, drawing from recent theoretical models of culture.

5. In Judaism, the act of martyrdom was described with the variants of *masar atsmo* or *natan nafsho* ("delivered himself [to death]" or "gave up his soul") prior to the adoption of the term *kiddush ha-shem* ("sanctifying the name of God") to signify martyrdom. *Kiddush ha-shem* retained its older meaning of any act that glorified God. But a Jew gave it its ultimate expression when he or she chose death when faced with the alternative of violating the Torah. Rabbinic legal texts delineated the situations in which martyrdom was an obligation incumbent upon an adult Jew. In life, needless to say, there was always a discrepancy between prescribed and actual behavior. On the complexities of the Hebrew term *kiddush ha-shem*, see I. Gruenwald, "*Kiddush ha-Shem:* Clarification of a Term" (Hebrew), *Molad* 24 (1968), 476–484; S. Safrai, "*Kiddush ha-Shem* in the Teachings of the Tanna'im."

6. Literally, "witness." On the etymology see Hermann Strathmann, "μάρτυς etc.," *Theological Dictionary of the New Testament* 4 (1967), 475–514.

7. See André Vauchez, *Sainthood in the Later Middle Ages* (Cambridge 1997). Yet the classical tradition of choosing to die for one's faith did not disappear in western Christendom: it was carried on by members of the various heretical Christian sects who were burned at the stake. Cathars, Waldensians, and Hussites, among others, provided models of "classical" martyrdom that may have caught the attention of Jews and crypto-Jews.

8. Vauchez, *Sainthood in the Later Middle Ages*, 417.

9. See Yosef Hacker, "'If We Have Forgotten the Name of Our God' (Psalm 44:21): Interpretation in Light of the Realities in Medieval Spain" (Hebrew), *Zion* 57 (1992), 249–259. Hacker argues that it was only in the late fifteenth century that Sephardi commentators began to reevaluate the verse's meaning in light of the mass conversions in Spain.

10. The Inquisition applied the term *luterano* to any heretic who exhibited Protestant inclinations.

11. For our period, see Jean Delumeau, *Catholicism between Luther and Voltaire: A New View of the Counter-Reformation* (London 1977), esp. 161–174.

12. See literature cited by Jeremy Cohen, "The Hebrew Crusade Chronicles in Their Christian Cultural Context," in Alfred Haverkamp, ed., *Juden und Christen zur Zeit der Kreuzzüge* (Sigmaringen 1999), 17n2.

13. Jeremy Cohen has described how the sacrificial excitement of "holy war" that infused the Crusaders in 1096 stirred a counter-response in the Rhineland Jews. (See Cohen, "Hebrew Crusade Chronicles," 24–25.) In contrast, the rioters who attacked the Spanish Jews in 1391 had no such posture of self-sacrifice, and offered the Jews no similar challenge to "outdo" them.

14. Scholars have "generalized away" the phenomenon of martyrdom among the Sephardi Jews in different ways. The influential scholar Yitzhak Baer regarded the Ashkenazim as cultivating a sustained readiness for martyrdom among all classes. In contrast, much of the Spanish-Jewish elite, in his view, was drained of its religious will by "external" skeptical philosophical ideas ("Averroism"), inclining it to conversion. Baer, who identified intellectually and viscerally with the Zionist solution to the "problem of Jewish exile," was predisposed to accept such a view, since he identified the cultural autonomy and asceticism of the Ashkenazim with Jewish national strength, and the Sephardi tendency to acculturation with assimilation and weakness. For Baer's characterization of Ashkenazi society, see Baer, "The Religious-Social Tendency of *Sefer Hassidim*" (Hebrew), *Zion* 3 (1937), 1–50; and idem, "Gezerat TaTN"U" (Hebrew), in M. D. Cassuto et al., eds., *Sefer Asaf* (Jerusalem 1953), 126–140. For his view of the Spanish-Jewish elite, see his *A History of the Jews in Christian Spain*, 2 vols. (Philadelphia 1978) vol. 2, passim. Subsequently Haim Hillel Ben Sasson challenged Baer's idea that philosophy was the "culprit," but he, too, drew a picture of a Spanish Jewish society drawn to conversion, in his view through a combination of courtier assimilation and Jewish mystical currents that created a common theological ground with Christianity. See Ben Sasson's "The Generation of the Exiles on Itself" (Hebrew), *Zion* 26 (1961), 59–64. In a strikingly different vein—according to which the behavior of the Ashkenazim, however ardent their beliefs, was ultimately self-destructive—Gerson Cohen argued that Ashkenazi martyrdom was an expression of the Franco-German Jews' inclination to "passivity"; the Sephardim, being of a more "aggressive" bent, tended to messianic action. See Cohen, "Messianic Postures."

15. See the cautionary words of Elisheva Carlebach, *Between History and Hope: Jewish Messianism in Ashkenaz and Sepharad: Third Annual Lecture of the Victor J. Selmanowitz Chair of Jewish History* (New York 1998), 1–4.

16. See Cohen, "Hebrew Crusade Chronicles," esp. 21–23, 28–30; Einbinder, *Beautiful Death*, 18, 20–21; Joseph Shatzmiller, "Jewish Converts to Christianity in Medieval Europe: 1200–1500," in Michael Goodich, Sophia Menache, and Sylvia Schein, eds., *Cross-Cultural Convergences in the Crusader Period: Essays Presented to Aryeh Grabois on his Sixty-Fifth Birthday* (New York 1995), 297–318; Robert Stacey, "The Conversion of Jews to Christianity in Thirteenth-Century England," *Speculum* 67 (1992), 263–283.

17. See Abraham Gross, "On the Ashkenazi Syndrome of Jewish Martyrdom in

Portugal in 1497" (Hebrew), *Tarbiz* 64 (1995), 83–99; Ram Ben Shalom, *"Kiddush ha-Shem* and Jewish Martyrology in Aragon and Castile in 1391: A Comparison of Spain and Ashkenaz" (Hebrew), *Tarbiz* 70 (2001), 227–282; and the exchange between these two authors in *Tarbiz* 71 (2001–2002), 269–300. Gross has drawn attention to acts of martyrdom among the Portuguese Jews in 1497, which he believes were inspired by Ashkenazi culture. Ben Shalom, however, has argued for a more continuous ethos of martyrdom among Sephardim in Christian Iberia, with deep roots in the Spanish Jewish experience.

18. Einbinder, *Beautiful Death,* 25–26.

19. Many of them (or their descendants) did revert. On this episode, see Menahem ben Sasson, "On the Jewish Identity of Forced Converts: A Study of Forced Conversion in the Almohad Period" (Hebrew), *Pe'amim* 42 (1990), 16–37.

20. See Ben Shalom, *"Kiddush ha-Shem* and Jewish Martyrology," 251n111; Ben Sasson, "On the Jewish Identity of Forced Converts," 22–23.

21. This has been argued most recently and extensively in Ben Shalom, *"Kiddush ha-Shem* and Jewish Martyrology," 227–282. It is worth noting here that documents from Catalonian archives dating from half a century before the riots of 1391, examined by Paola Tartakoff, raise the possibility of a religious sensibility among Catalonian Jews that favored martyrdom as an expiatory and salvific act for Jews who had voluntarily converted to Christianity. My thanks to Paola Tartakoff for providing me with a copy of her paper, "Jews, Converts and Inquisitors in the Fourteenth-Century Crown of Aragon: A Curious Case," delivered at the annual conference of the Association for Jewish Studies in December 2005.

22. A list of elegies on the massacre of 1391 can be found in Dan Pagis, "Elegies on the Massacres of 1391 in Spain" (Hebrew), *Tarbiz* 37 (1968), 370–371.

23. See Marc Saperstein, *"Your Voice Like a Ram's Horn": Themes and Texts in Traditional Jewish Preaching* (Cincinnati 1996), 258–260.

24. See the elegy published by Pagis, "Elegies on the Massacres of 1391," 368.

25. See ibid., 364–365. For examples of this motif from the Ashkenazi literature, see Shalom Spiegel, *The Last Trial: On the Legends and Lore of the Command to Abraham to Offer Isaac as a Sacrifice: The Akedah* (Woodstock, Vt., 1993), 21–24. For further examples of specific Ashkenazi influence on Sephardi martyrological rhetoric see Gross, "On the Ashkenazi Syndrome," 100–101.

26. Scholars have long been aware that Ashkenazi attitudes to martyrdom also developed in the context of dialogue with the Christian world. See the summary in Cohen, *Sanctifying the Name,* 27–30.

27. Yet another argument has been made: namely, that the "spiritualization" of *kiddush ha-Shem* in kabbalistic circles in Spain created an ethos that encouraged acts of martyrdom when circumstances of *shemad* (anti-Jewish violence aimed at achieving conversion) arose. However, it has also been argued that this "spiritualization" had the *opposite* effect. For a discussion of this see Azriel Shochet, *"Kiddush ha-Shem* in the Thinking of the Spanish Exiles and the Kabbalists of Safed" (Hebrew), in *Milḥemet kodesh u-martyrologyah be-toldot Yisra'el uve-toldot ha-amim* (Jerusalem 1967), 143–145. For a summary of the scholarly opinions concerning the factors that brought about a changed posture to martyrdom, see Ram Ben Shalom, *"Kiddush ha-Shem* and Jewish Martyrdom," 252–255.

28. There is evidence that well before 1391, conversion was becoming more common among Spanish Jews. See Eleazar Gutwirth, "Conversions to Christianity amongst Fifteenth-Century Spanish Jews: An Alternative Explanation," in Daniel Carpi, Moshe Gil, Yosef Gorni, et al., *Shlomo Simonsohn Jubilee Volume: Studies on the History of the Jews in the Middle Ages and Renaissance Period* (Jerusalem 1993), 99.

29. On this disputation, see Robert Chazan, *Barcelona and Beyond: The Disputation of 1263 and Its Aftermath* (Berkeley, Los Angeles, Oxford 1992).

30. Disputations between Jews and apostates include the debate held in Paris in 1240, between the apostate Nicholas Donin and the French rabbi Yechiel ben Joseph; the debate between Pablo Christiani and Nachmanides in Barcelona in 1263; a debate in Paris in 1273 between the same Pablo Christiani and the Rouen Jew Abraham ben Samuel; and the debate held in Tortosa in 1413–1414 between Jerónimo de Santa Fe (previously Joshua Halorki) and a number of Spanish rabbis (to be discussed further on).

31. Solomon Halevi, who converted around 1390 and took the name Pablo de Santa Maria, became bishop of Cartagena in 1403 and of Burgos in 1415.

32. On the riots of 1391 see Baer, *History of the Jews*, 2: 95–134; Philippe Wolff, "The 1391 Pogrom in Spain: Social Crisis or Not?" *PaP* no. 50 (February 1971), 4–18.

33. This is indicated in a letter of Solomon de Piera, in which the martyrs (*chalalei ha-shem*) are set apart from the mass of those killed (*chalalei cherev ve-hereg ve-ovdan*) (Yitzhak Baer, *Toldot ha-Yehudim bi-Sefarad ha-Notsrit* [Tel Aviv 1959], 307).

34. It was published by Cecil Roth, "A Hebrew Elegy on the Martyrs of Toledo, 1391," *JQR* 39 (1948–1949), 135–150.

35. Roth analyzes the identities of these men in ibid., 127–129.

36. See the discussion of this in Jeremy Cohen, *Living Letters of the Law: Ideas of the Jew in Medieval Christianity* (Berkeley and Los Angeles 1999), 398–399.

37. My translation of the Hebrew text published in Wiener, ed., *Sefer Shevet Yehuda* (Hanover 1855), 128–130.

38. On the literature focusing on this image see Spiegel, *The Last Trial.*

39. The classic depiction of this self-image is Ben Sasson, "The Generation of the Exiles on Itself."

40. The elegy was published by J. Schirmann in the original Hebrew in *Kovets al yad* 3 (Jerusalem 1940), 64–69. The elegist employs similar imagery for Barcelona: "For Barcelona, moan! . . . She who was once a pure maid / Has raised her skirts and exposed herself" (ibid., 68).

41. "If we had forgotten the name of our God, or spread forth our hands to a strange god, would not God discover this? For he knows the secrets of the heart. Nay, for thy sake we are slain all the day long, and accounted as sheep for the slaughter" (Psalms 44: 21–23).

42. Hacker, " 'If We Have Forgotten the Name of Our God,' " 247–274.

43. Such interpretations, it should be stressed, did not entail a blanket acquittal of the converts, either at this juncture or later. Distinctions were made in both halakhic and nonhalakhic rabbinic literature—for example, between the scholarly elite and the rank and file, between the first generation of converts and their offspring who were baptized in infancy, between those who took risks to judaize and those for whom conversion was a stepping stone to wealth and social power.

44. On Profayt's conversion see Richard Emery, "New Light on Profayt Duran 'The Efodi,' " *JQR* 58 (1968), 328–337.

45. The letter has been published in Profayt Duran, *Sefer ma'aseh Efod* (Vienna 1865), 191–197. For the quotations above, see ibid., 194–195. I have used the translations in Baer, *History of the Jews* 2:156–158. The "inclusive" view of conversos continued to develop among the Spanish exiles after 1492. The rabbinic scholar Yosef Yavetz—one of the exiles from Spain in 1492—offers a case in point. Understandably, he regarded the sin of prominent rabbis who converted as inexcusable, "in that they failed to martyr themselves." But he wrote of the children of unlearned converts (*amei ha-arets*) who converted because of the

difficulties of fleeing in 1492—children who were born into Christianity without a choice—that they would be gathered into the Jewish people at the end of days. Yosef Yavetz, *Sefer ḥasdei ha-Shem* (New York 1998–1999), 59. Cf. Azriel Shochat, *"Kiddush ha-Shem* in the Thinking of the Spanish Exiles," 131. An even more embracing attitude was adopted by Sa'adyah ibn Danan, a rabbi of Granada who also left Spain in 1492. See B. Netanyahu, *The Marranos of Spain: From the Late 14th to the Early 16th Century, According to Contemporary Hebrew Sources* (Ithaca, N.Y., 1999), 61–65. For a similar later view of Solomon Alkabetz, see Hacker, " 'If We Have Forgotten the Name of Our God,' " 272–272.

46. On the use of the forced sermon in Christian missionizing of Jews, see Robert Chazan, *Daggers of Faith: Thirteenth-Century Christian Missionizing and Jewish Response* (Berkeley and Los Angeles 1989), 38–48.

47. Archival documents mention at least four and possibly ten delegates sent as Jews who returned to their communities as Christians. See Yom Tov Assis's introduction to *The Tortosa Disputation: Regesta of Documents from the Archivo de la Corona de Aragón, Fernando I, 1412–1416* (Jerusalem 1998), xxv. On the Latin and Hebrew sources for the Disputation of Tortosa, see Baer, *History of the Jews,* 2: 478–479n4.

48. For a study of how these events stirred the polemical activity of a Jewish scholar of Provence, see Ram Ben Shalom, "The Disputation of Tortosa, Vicente Ferrer and the Problem of the Conversos according to the Testimony of Isaac Nathan" (Hebrew), *Zion* 57 (1991), 21–45.

49. See David Berger, *The Jewish-Christian Debate in the High Middle Ages* (Philadelphia 1979); Chazan, *Daggers of Faith.*

50. See Daniel Lasker, *Jewish Philosophical Polemics against Christianity in the Middle Ages* (New York 1977).

51. Hasdai Crescas, *Sefer bitul ikare ha-notsrim,* ed. Daniel Lasker (Jerusalem 2002), 73–74. I have used Lasker's translation, *Hasdai Crescas, The Refutation of the Christian Principles* (Albany 1992), 61.

52. The letter is known, after its refrain, as *Al tehi ke-avotekha* ("Be Not Like Unto Thy Fathers"). According to Yitzhak Akrish, the sixteenth-century Sephardi scholar who published it in Constantinople in the 1570s, the letter was known among Christians, who referred to it as "Alteca boteca." It has been published with notes by Ephraim [Frank] Talmage, *The Polemical Writings of Profayt Duran: The Reproach of the Gentiles and "Be Not Like Unto Thy Fathers"* (Hebrew) (Jerusalem 1981), 71–83.

53. Ibid., 74.

54. See Lasker, *Jewish Philosophical Polemics,* 3–6.

55. Jeremy Cohen, "Profiat Duran's *The Reproach of the Gentiles* and the Development of Jewish Anti-Christian Polemic," in *Shlomo Simonsohn Jubilee Volume: Studies on the History of the Jews in the Middle Ages and Renaissance Period* (Jerusalem 1993), 71–84.

56. Eleazar Gutwirth, "History and Apologetics in XVth Century Hispano-Jewish Thought," *Helmantica* 35 (1984), 231–242; Frank Talmage, "The Polemical Writings of Profiat Duran," *Immanuel* 13 (1981), 69–85; Baer, *History of the Jews,* 2: 474–475n41.

57. Alonso de Espina, *Fortalitium Fidei* (c. 1464), Book II.6.ii: "Secunda heresis est eorum qui dicunt Evangelium esse falsum."

58. According to Frank Talmage, the Institute of Microfilmed Hebrew Manuscripts in Jerusalem lists more than thirty manuscripts of *Kelimat ha-goyim.* See Talmage, *Polemical Writings of Profayt Duran,* xxvi.

59. Lasker, *Jewish Philosophical Polemics,* 41–2, 186n65.

60. Baer, *History of the Jews,* 2: 222.

61. The latter has survived only in the Hebrew translation from 1451, but the translator mentions that the original was composed in *lashon artso* (the language of his land)—probably Catalan. See the translator's preface in *Sefer bitul ikare ha-notsrim*, trans. to Hebrew by Joseph ben Shem Tov, 33.

62. See ibid., editor's introduction, 18–19.

63. On the Spanish Jews' increasing resort to "romance" Bibles see Eleazar Gutwirth, "Religión, historia y las *Biblias Romanceadas*," *Revista Catalana de Teología* 13 (1988), 115–134.

64. Eleazar Gutwirth, "Towards Expulsion: 1391–1492," in Elie Kedourie, ed., *Spain and the Jews: The Sephardi Experience, 1492 and After* (London 1992), 56.

65. "Proceso contra Jaime Ferrer, relapso, judaizante relaxado," published by Bernardino Llorca in *Analecta Sacra Tarraconensia* 12 (1936), 410–414. Cf. Baer, *History of the Jews* 2: 361.

66. See Miriam Bodian, "'Men of the Nation': The Shaping of Converso Identity in Early Modern Europe," *PaP* no. 143 (1994), 51–54.

67. The riots and their aftermath have been studied by Eloy Benito Ruano, *Toledo en el siglo XV: vida política* (Madrid 1961), 33–81; idem, "La 'Sentencia-Estatuto' de Pedro Sarmiento contra los conversos toledanos," *Revista de la Universidad de Madrid*, 6 (1957), 277–306. See also Nicholas Round, "La rebelión toledana de 1449: aspectos ideológicos," *Archivum* 16 (1966), 385–446; Baer, *History of the Jews*, 2: 277–283.

68. On this trial and "auto-da-fé" by the rebels, see Eloy Benito Ruano, "El memorial contra los conversos del Bachiller Marcos García de Mora (Marquillos de Mazarambroz)," *Sefarad* 17 (1957), 330–337, 348. According to the account published in this article, the "heretics," when they were being put to death at the stake, "did not repent and said nothing but 'ay Adonai el biejo.'" The Hebrew expression *"chaye Adonai"* was apparently used by conversos in this corrupted form (see David Gitlitz, *Secrecy and Deceit: The Religion of the Crypto-Jews* [Philadelphia 1996], 477).

69. For the sources on this activity, see William Monter, *Frontiers of Heresy: The Spanish Inquisition from the Basque Lands to Sicily* (Cambridge 1990), 4n3.

70. Such was the reaction of Alonso de Hojeda, a Dominican in Seville, after the apprehension and immediate burning in Llerena in September 1467 of two conversos accused of crypto-judaizing. See Henry Kamen, *The Spanish Inquisition: A Historical Revision* (New Haven and London 1997), 43.

71. On this episode see Yitzhak Baer, *Die Juden im christlichen Spanien*, 2 vols. (Berlin 1929, 1936), #399, 2: 472. And cf. idem, *History of the Jews*, 2: 299; idem, "The Messianic Movement in Spain at the Time of the Expulsion" (Hebrew), *Measef Zion* 5 (1933), 64.

72. We should note, however, that the Inquisition did try unbaptized Jews who abetted judaizing. In 1489, three Jews were burned at the stake (two of them alive) for having participated in the circumcision of a converso in Huesca in the 1460s. See Baer, *Die Juden*, #410, 2: 484–509; idem, *History of the Jews*, 2: 297–299, 384–389; Encarnación Marin Padilla, "Relación judeoconversa durante la segunda mitad del siglo XV en Aragón," *Sefarad* 42 (1982), 59–76. The martyrdom of those burned alive at the stake was memorialized by a grandson of one of them, R. Moses Almosnino of Salonica.

73. Baer, *History of the Jews*, 2: 405.

74. In contrast to Protestant martyrologies, which granted the status of martyrdom to persons who died in prison before their trials had been completed. See Gregory, *Salvation at Stake*, 191.

75. Encarnación Marin Padilla, *Relación judeoconvera durante la segunda mitad del siglo XV en Aragón: La Ley* (Madrid 1988), 16.

76. Haim Beinart, "The Judaizing Movement in the Order of San Jeronimo in Castile," *Scripta Hierosolymitana* 7 (1961), 179. The friar was also reported to have "praised greatly the Maccabee martyrs, saying that they were very fine and glorious because they died for the Law of Moses" (Baer, *Die Juden*, #403, 2: 473–476).

77. A similar sentiment was echoed by another converso at the same time, though he did not expressly used the term *martyr*. See the statement attributed to Pedro Serrano of Montalvan in Baer, *Die Juden*, # 404, 2: 476. Cf. Baer, *History of the Jews*, 2: 349–350, with whose interpretation of this statement I do not necessarily agree.

78. Haim Beinart, "The Conversos of Almagro and Daimiel" (Hebrew), *Zion* 35 (1970), 85.

79. Haim Beinart, "The Prophetess Inés and her Messianic Movement in Herrera del Duque" (Hebrew), in Y. Dan and Y. Kaplan, eds., *Studies in Kabbalah, Jewish Philosophy and Ethical Literature in Honor of Isaiah Tishby on his Seventy-fifth Birthday* (Jerusalem 1986), 502n3, 503n4.

80. *Records of the Trials of the Spanish Inquisition in Ciudad Real*, 4 vols. (Jerusalem 1974–1985), 2: 193.

81. The accounts of Inés's vision, of which she herself gave more than one and which were spread by word of mouth, not surprisingly vary in content and detail. But the mostly consistent testimony leaves little doubt of the episode's essential authenticity. It has been studied by several scholars. It was first studied by Baer, "The Messianic Movement in Spain," 66–70; idem, *Die Juden*, 2, #423; idem, *History of the Jews*, 2: 356–358. See also Beinart, "The Prophetess Inés and Her Movement"; Haim Beinart, "Conversos of Chillón and the Prophecies of Mari Gómez and Inés, the Daughter of Juan Esteban" (Hebrew), *Zion* 48 (1983), 241–272; Renee Melammed Levine, *Heretics or Daughters of Israel? The Crypto-Jewish Women of Castile* (New York and Oxford 1999), 45–72.

82. Hopes of imminent redemption were widespread among Spanish Jews and conversos from as early as the fall of Constantinople in 1453, but appear to have reached a crescendo in the wake of the Expulsion. See, in addition to the bibliography above, Baer, "The Messianic Movement in Spain," 61–74; Rivka Shatz, "An Outline of the Image of the Political-Messianic Arousal after the Spanish Expulsion" (Hebrew), *Da'at* 11 (1982–1983), 53–66; Isaiah Tishby, *Messianism in the Time of the Expulsion from Spain and Portugal* (Hebrew) (Jerusalem 1985); Beinart, "The Prophetess Inés and Her Movement," 459–506; Carlos Carrete Parrondo, "Nostalgia for the Past (and for the Future?) among Castilian *Judeoconversos*," *Mediterranean Historical Review* 6 (1991), 36. For the pre-Inquisition period see Alisa Meyuhas Ginio, "Las aspiraciones mesianicas de los conversos en la Castilla de mediados del siglo XV," *El Olivo* 13 (1989), 217–233. These expectations drew from Jewish sources but were also stirred by Catholic speculations. As one scholar has shown, contemporary European apocalyptic thinking reveals fascinating interactions between Jews and Christians; figures from both groups competed, appropriated from each other, and envisioned a variety of messianic scenarios on the basis of some of the same "evidence." See David Ruderman, "Hope Against Hope: Jewish and Christian Messianic Expectations in the Late Middle Ages," in Aharon Mirsky, Avraham Grossman, and Yosef Kaplan, eds., *Exile and Diaspora* (Jerusalem 1991), 185–202. The Christians mentioned by Ruderman are almost all from Italy, and he notes the need for further study of the Spanish context, 197n56. It is hardly surprising to find, among the conversos in an Extremaduran village, a striking freedom in their weaving together of Christian and Jewish lore.

83. William Christian, Jr., *Apparitions in Late Medieval and Renaissance Spain* (Princeton 1981), 80. Visions of ascent to heaven—not infrequently by young girls—were part of the popular culture of rural Castilian villages like Herrera and Chillón, as William Christian has vividly shown in this book. See also Agne Beijer, "Visions célestes et infernales dans le théâtre du moyen-âge et de la Renaissance," 413 in *Journées Internationales d'Études, Les Fêtes de la Renaissance,* vol. 1 (Paris 1956), 405–417. On the antique sources of this motif, see Martha Himmelfarb, *Ascent to Heaven in Jewish and Christian Apocalypses* (New York and Oxford 1983). For an example of a thirteenth-century Beguine who saw both heaven and purgatory in her ascent to heaven see Jacques Le Goff, *The Birth of Purgatory* (Chicago 1984), 331–332. It was rumored that Inés had brought back evidence testifying to her ascent—"a corn ear, an olive, and a letter" (see Haim Beinart, "Inés of Herrera del Duque, The Prophetess of Extremadura," in Mary Giles, ed., *Women in the Inquisition: Spain and the New World* [Baltimore 1999], 46, 307n15; and see ibid., 47, 308n25), as was commonly reported in such cases. On converso visions, see also Baer, "The Messianic Movement in Spain," 68–69; Beinart, "Conversos of Chillón," 247; Carlos Carrete Parrondo, ed., *Fontes Iudaeorum Regni Castellae,* vol. 2, *El Tribunal de la Inquisicón en el Obispado de Soria [1486–1502]* (Salamanca 1985); Haim Beinart, "A Prophesying Movement in Cordova in 1499–1502," *Zion* 44 (1979), 190–200.

84. Baer, *Die Juden,* # 423, 2: 528–29.

85. The Christian source for the vision of martyrs on thrones is the Book of Revelation: "Then I saw thrones, and seated on them were those to whom judgment was committed, and I saw the souls of those who had been beheaded for their testimony to Jesus and for the word of God . . ." (Rev. 20: 4).

86. Inés's theatrical account drew considerable attention to her, and before long the story of her vision had been disseminated among a relatively wide circle of conversos in the region. In the wake of Inés's vision, Mari Gómez of Chillón, a converso who knew Inés, also reported seeing in heaven "the burnt ones on thrones of gold." Beinart, "Conversos of Chillón," 245.

87. See Francisco Bethencourt, "The 'Auto da Fé': Ritual and Imagery," *Journal of the Warburg and Courtauld Institute* 55 (1992), 155–168; Maureen Flynn, "Mimesis of the Last Judgment: The Spanish *Auto de Fe,*" *The Sixteenth Century Journal* 22, no. 2 (1991), 281–297.

88. For a description of such inversion, see Bodian, "'Men of the Nation,'" 61–62.

89. On the efficacy of suffering during one's life for the purging of sin, see Carlos Eire, *From Madrid to Purgatory: The Art and Craft of Dying in Sixteenth-Century Spain* (Cambridge and New York 1995); Le Goff, *The Birth of Purgatory,* passim, and see p. 260 with regard to the special efficacy of the martyr's death.

90. For an illuminating glimpse of that path, see Linda Martz, *A Network of Converso Families in Early Modern Toledo: Assimilating a Minority* (Ann Arbor, Mich., 2003).

91. The great pioneering work in this area is Marcel Bataillon, *Erasmo y España: estudios sobre la historia spiritual del siglo XVI* (Mexico City 1982). See the summary of José-Carlos Gómez-Menor, "Linaje judío de escritores religiosos y místicos españoles del siglo XVI," in Angel Alcalá, ed., *Judíos, Sefarditas, Conversos: La expulsion de 1492 y sus consecuencias* (Valladolid 1995), 587–600. On antitrinitarian currents, see Richard Popkin, "Marranos, New Christians and the Beginnings of Modern Anti-Trinitarianism," in Yom Tov Assis and Yosef Kaplan, eds., *Jews and Conversos at the Time of the Expulsion* (Jerusalem 1999), 143–160.

92. See Gross, "On the Ashkenazi Syndrome," 83–95.

93. For a more detailed narrative of these events, see Yosef Hayim Yerushalmi, "A Jewish Classic in the Portuguese Language," introduction to Samuel Usque, *Consolação às Tribulações de Israel*, 2 vols. (Lisbon, 1989), 1: 19–28. Royal decrees of April 20 and 22, 1499, were the first to forbid any New Christian from leaving the realm.

94. Manuel's edict of May 1497 is published in M. Kayserling, *Geschichte der Juden in Portugal* (Leipzig 1867), 347–349.

95. The difference between the two converso populations has long been recognized. See See I. S. Révah, "Les Marranes," *REJ*, 108 (1959–1960), 36–39; Yosef Hayim Yerushalmi, *From Spanish Court to Italian Ghetto: Isaac Cardoso, A Study in Seventeenth-Century Marranism and Jewish Apologetics* (Seattle 1971), 4–5.

96. The intricate machinations by all parties that preceded the establishment of the Portuguese Inquisition are described in detail in Alexandre Herculano's classic work *História da origem e estabelecimento da Inquisição portuguesa*, originally published in 1854–1859. The most recent edition (Lisbon 1975–1976) includes a long introduction by Jorge Borges de Macedo. The work is available in English translation as *History of the Origin and Establishment of the Inquisition in Portugal* (New York 1972).

2. The Dogmatista Crypto-Jewish Martyrs

1. This is not to say that accident did not sometimes play a role in determining who was commemorated and who was forgotten. A case in point is that of Manuel López, a judaizer who debated with numerous theologians and was burned alive at the stake, defiant, in Cordova in 1625. Knowledge of his career simply did not reach the ex-converso communities of northern Europe. See the documentation on his career in Rafael Gracia Boix, *Autos de fe y causas de la Inquisición de Córdoba* (Cordova 1983), 391–394.

2. See Henry Charles Lea, *A History of the Inquisition of Spain*, 4 vols. (New York 1906–1907), 2: 458, 3: 185; Beinart, *Conversos on Trial*, 188; Herculano, *Origin and Establishment*, 430. For concrete examples in Spain, see the many trials in Ciudad Real that were held from beginning to end between 14 November 1483 and the autos-da-fé of 23 and 24 February 1484 (Beinart, *Records*, 1: 1–314).

3. We unfortunately do not have the kind of data for the Portuguese Inquisition that we have for the Spanish. But see the statistics in Carlos Moreira Azevedo, ed., *História religiosa de Portugal*, 3 vols. (Lisbon 2000–2002), 2: 129.

4. Imprisonment conditions were considerably more relaxed after sentencing than during the trial.

5. See Kamen, *The Spanish Inquisition*, 118.

6. José Ignacio Tellechea Idígoras, "Biblias publicadas fuera de España secuestradas por la Inquisición de Sevilla en 1552," *Bulletin Hispanique* 64 (1962), 236. The impressive production of these volumes outside the Peninsula is treated in Enrique Fernandez y Fernandez, *Las biblias castellanas del exilio: Historia de las biblias castellanas del siglo XVI* (Miami 1976).

7. Henry Kamen cites as an example of this view a passage from R. O. Jones, *The Golden Age: Prose and Poetry* (London 1971) that opens: "By 1560 the traditionalists had won: the Spain of Philip II remained closed to the new current of ideas beyond its frontiers . . ." (Henry Kamen, *The Phoenix and the Flame: Catalonia and the Counter Reformation* [New Haven 1993], 486n9). Virtually none of the treatments of Erasmian, illuminist, and Protestant thinking in Spain goes beyond 1560. Marcel Bataillon, in his magisterial work on the impact of Erasmus in Spain, concluded that the Spanish humanist impulse "lost its

vitality and power to irradiate" with the advent of the Counterreformation under Philip II; he dealt only fleetingly with the residue. (Bataillon, *Erasmo y España*, 804.)

8. For a rare (if brief) treatment of the topic in English, see José Pedro Paiva, "Spain and Portugal," in R. Po-chia Hsia, ed., *A Companion to the Reformation World* (Malden, Mass., Oxford, and Melbourne 2004), 294–295, and see bibliography there, 305–310. It is telling that in the recent multivolume *História religiosa de Portugal*, the volume which deals with the period of humanism and reform devotes only a few pages to Protestantism (2: 68–75).

9. Most of these later cases were cases of casual anticlericalism that were mislabeled in an atmosphere of intense anxiety about Protestantism. See Miguel Jiménez Monteserín, "Los luteranos ante el tribunal de la Inquisición de Cuenca, 1525–1600" in Joaquín Pérez Villanueva, ed., *La Inquisición española: Nueva vision, nuevos horizontes* (Madrid 1980), 689–736.

10. António Baião, *Inquisição em Portugal e no Brazil: Subsidos para a sua historia* (Lisbon 1906), 110.

11. Ibid., 112.

12. See Thomas Freeman and Marcelo Borges, "'A grave and heinous incident against our holy Catholic Faith': Two Accounts of William Gardiner's Desecration of the Portuguese Royal Chapel in 1552," in *Historical Research* 69 (1996), 1–17.

13. Baião, *Inquisição em Portugal e no Brazil*, 163; see also José Sebastião da Silva Dias, *Correntes de sentimento religioso em Portugal (séculos XVI a XVIII)*, 2 vols. (Coimbra 1960), 1: 217n. 1.

14. See Lea, *History of the Inquisition*, 3: 193. On Spanish "Protestant" martyrs of the Inquisition, see C. Wagner, "Los luteranos ante la Inquisición de Toledo en el siglo XVI," *Hispania Sacra* 46/94 (1994), 474–505; Gordon Kinder, "Spanish Protestants and Foxe's Book: Sources," in *BHR* 60 (1998), 107–116.

15. Nieto's remarks were picked up when they were repeated by an Old Christian cellmate. The Calvinist heretic to whom Nieto referred was a "Simón de Santiago" from a town near Bremen. See Eva Alexandra Uchmany, *La vida entre el judaísmo y el cristianismo en la Nueva España, 1580–1606* (Mexico City 1992), 329.

16. The various prohibitions barring conversos or some subset of them (Portuguese conversos, conversos reconciled by the Inquisition, etc.) from settling in the overseas territories were enforced with great unevenness, and frequently evaded. See Eva Alexandra Uchmany, "The Participation of New Christians and Crypto-Jews in the Conquest, Colonization, and Trade of Spanish America, 1521–1660," in Paulo Bernardini and Norman Fiering, eds., *The Jews and the Expansion of Europe to the West, 1450 to 1800* (New York 2001), 187–195; Günter Böhm, "Crypto-Jews and New Christians in Colonial Peru and Chile," in ibid., 205–210.

17. See Miriam Bodian, *Hebrews of the Portuguese Nation: Conversos and Community in Early Modern Amsterdam* (Bloomington 1997), 132–146.

18. For a detailed history and description of the auto, see Consuelo Maqueda Abreu, *El Auto de Fe* (Madrid 1992). See also Francisco Bethencourt, *La Inquisición en la Época Moderna: España, Portugal e Italia, siglos XV–XIX* (Madrid 1997), 281–366; Miguel Jiménez Montserín, "El auto de fe de la Inquisición Española," in *Inquisición y Conversos: Conferencias pronunciadas en el III Curso de Cultura Hispano-Judía y Sefardí de la Universidad de Castilla-La Mancha* (Toledo 1994), 203–223; Miguel Avilés, "The Auto de Fe and the Social Model of Counter-Reformation Spain," in Alcalá, ed., *The Spanish Inquisition and the Inquisitorial Mind*, 249–264. On the symbolic power and dramatic impact of the auto,

see Flynn, "Mimesis of the Last Judgment." Flynn evokes the impact of the auto on a public susceptible to suggestion; the perception of the proceedings by a defiant, provocative, and contemptuous heretic would have been quite different.

19. It is true that technically, even in the early period of the Spanish Inquisition's activity a distinction was supposed to be made between last-minute penitents (who were to be garroted before being burned) and defiant heretics (who were to be burned alive). But evidence indicates that in the early period this did not happen. See Herculano, *Origin and Establishment*, 431, for a report of an auto-da-fé by an inquisitor describing the burning alive of nineteen *negativos*. Even in a later period, application of the rule was not always consistent. In 1691, three pertinacious female judaizers were granted the mercy of being garroted before being burnt. However, such evidence is impressionistic. Unfortunately, as late as the eighteenth century the documents do not always specify whether a victim who was "relaxed" was strangled or burned alive. See Lea, *A History of the Inquisition*, 3: 192–195, 197. Scholars have confused the issue because they have often translated *quemado en persona* (a term used to distinguish live victims from fugitives burned in effigy or previously deceased persons who were disinterred and burned) as "burned alive," making it appear that there were many more such cases than there really were.

20. On the Black Legend, see Benjamin Keen, "The Black Legend Revisited: Assumptions and Realities," *The Hispanic American Historical Review* 49 (1969), 703–719; Gordon Kinder, "The Creation of the Black Legend: Literary Contributions of Spanish Protestant Exiles," *Mediterranean Studies* 6 (1996), 67–78.

21. There is an enormous literature on the "decline of Spain." See R. A. Stradling, *Europe and the Decline of Spain: A Study of the Spanish System, 1580–1720* (London 1981), bibliographical prologue, 1–23.

22. On the special efforts to convert the pertinacious, see Lea, *History of the Inquisition*, 3: 196.

23. Apparently an act of seeking forgiveness. For a similar scene, see Pieter Spierenburg, *The Spectacle of Suffering: Executions and the Evolution of Repression* (Cambridge 1984), 43.

24. Gracia Boix, *Autos de Fe*, 506, 601, 629–636.

25. There is some ambiguity about what actually happened. See the account of Luis Carvajal's last-minute "conversion" in 1596 by the friar who accompanied him ("Ultimos momentos y conversion de Luis de Carvajal," *Anales del Museo Nacional de Arqueología, Historia y Etnografía* 3 [1925], 64–78), and the analysis of Martin Cohen, *The Martyr: The Story of a Secret Jew and the Mexican Inquisition in the Sixteenth Century* (Philadelphia 1973), 257–259.

26. Whether the events occurred as they are related in the Franciscans' letter is, for us, not important. For the letter and analysis of the circumstances, see Jesús-Antonio Cid, "Jacob Bueno, martír: Cuatro judíos portugueses ante la razon del estado," *Sefarad* 47 (1987), 283–299.

27. Isaac Cardoso, *Las Excelencias de los Hebreos* (Amsterdam 1679), 323–324.

28. *Auto de la fe celebrado en Lima a 23. De Enero de 1639* (Madrid 1640), fo. 21v.

29. J. H. Elliott, "Self-perception and Decline in Early Seventeenth-Century Spain," *PaP*, no. 74 (May 1977), 60.

30. "[S]ino por confundirlos y convertirlos, y por decir con verdad lo que dice el salmo ciento y veinte y ocho, y luego dijo ciento y diez y ocho, que dice [Ps. 119:46]: *loquebar de testimonys tuis inconspectu regum et no confundebar* [I will also speak of thy testimonies before kings, and shall not be put to shame], por quanto los Sres. Inquisidores son reyes y príncipes,

pues tienen el poder del Papa y del Rey." L. González Obregón, ed., *Procesos de Luis de Carvajal (el Mozo)* [hereafter *PLC*] (Mexico City 1935), 294. And cf. ibid., 417, 453. It is interesting that during the Disputation of Tortosa in the early fourteenth century this same verse had been invoked to demonstrate that Jews had a religious duty to engage in religious disputation. See Baer, *History of the Jews*, 2: 187; see also 202–204.

31. Arquivo Nacional da Torre do Tombo, Lisbon (henceforth ANTT), Inquisição de Lisboa (henceforth IL), Processo no. 104, fo. 212v.

32. See Perez Zagorin's study of this debate and its context, *Ways of Lying: Dissimulation, Persecution, and Conformity in Early Modern Europe* (Cambridge, Mass., and London 1990).

33. The term is derived from John Calvin's term "Nicodemites" used in reference to crypto-Protestants in Catholic lands. Calvin was alluding to the story of Nicodemus who out of fear visited Jesus only secretly at night (see John 3:1–2).

34. On this revival of interest in the Christian martyrs of late antiquity see Gregory, *Salvation at Stake*, 251. On the prevalence of anti-Nicodemite arguments among Catholics and well as Protestants see ibid., 252.

35. Accounts of the martyrdom of Catholics during the persecutions in England provided sixteenth-century Spaniards with anti-Protestant propaganda in a period when Protestantism had largely been suppressed in Spain. Important works included an account by Pedro de Rivadeneira, *Historia eclesiastica del schisma del reyno de Inglaterra* (1588); a compendium compiled by Diego de Yepes, bishop of Tarrasma, with help from the English Jesuit Joseph Creswell, *Historia particular de la persecución de Inglaterra* (1599); and an account of the martyrdom of a Spanish Jesuit by Joseph Creswell, *Historia de la vida y martirio que padeció este año de 1595 el P. Henrico Valpolo* (1595). See Gregory, *Salvation at Stake*, 290; Elizabeth Rhodes, "Luisa de Carvajal's Counter-Reformation Journey to Selfhood (1566–1614)," *Renaissance Quarterly* 51 (1998), 896n17.

36. On the Spiera episode see M.A. Overell, "The Exploitation of Francesco Spiera," *Sixteenth Century Journal* 26 (1995), 619–637; Michael MacDonald, "'The Fearful Estate of Francis Spiera': Narrative, Identity and Emotion in Early Modern England," *Journal of British Studies* 31 (1992), 32–61. A similar but unverifiable story is told of the French humanist Jacques Lefèvre d'Etaples, who before his death in 1536 was reported to have experienced remorse and fear of damnation because he had not openly professed his Protestant faith. See Zagorin, *Ways of Lying*, 36–37.

37. See also Lev. 18:5.

38. See Yerushalmi, *Spanish Court*, 38n56.

39. "When you see a multitude before you and behind you bowing down, say in your hearts, thou only art to be adored, O Lord" (Baruch 6:5). See Yerushalmi, *Spanish Court*, 38–39n56.

40. See Bodian, *Hebrews of the Portuguese Nation*, 100–101.

41. Isaac Orobio de Castro, *Epístola Invectiva*, Ms. EH 48A23. Cf. Kaplan, *From Christianity*, 330.

42. Nathan Wachtel, *La Foi du souvenir: Labyrinthes marranes* (Paris 2001), 77–101, esp. 97–98.

43. Herculano, *Origin and Establishment*, 161.

44. Martin Cohen, *The Canonization of a Myth: Portugal's "Jewish Problem" and the Assembly of Tomar 1629* (Cincinnati 2002), 38.

45. Ibid., 45.

46. Ibid., 45. The report routinely generalizes outrageously about all New Christians.

47. See Victor Turner, *Dramas, Fields, and Metaphors: Symbolic Action in Human Society* (Ithaca 1974), 71.

48. Ibid., 64.

49. Ibid., 69. My emphasis.

50. On the *ars moriendi* literature, see Roger Chartier, "Les arts de mourir, 1450–1600," *Annales E.S.C.* 31 (1976), 51–75; Marianne Carbonnier-Burkard, "Les manuels reformes de preparation a la mort," *RHR* 217 (2000), 363–380. See also Philippe Ariès, *The Hour of Our Death* (New York 1991), 99–110; Eire, *From Madrid to Purgatory*, 24–29 and *passim*.

51. As penitent Catholics, of course. Note the language used by an eyewitness to the auto-da-fé at which the judaizing martyr Luis Carvajal was burned at the stake: a cleric was at his side "exhorting him to die well" [*que le exhortase á bien morir*]. See Medina, *Inquisición en México* 93, and cf. ibid. 97.

52. See Solange Alberro, *Inquisición y sociedad en México, 1571–1700* (Mexico City 1988), 261. During his second trial, Treviño de Sobremonte was examined by four surgeons who declared him to have been cut on two sides of his member, and considered him circumcized. See the entry for December 15, 1644 (AGN Inq. vol. 1495; I have used the transcription by A. J. Baker in the G. R. G. Conway Archives at the Library of Congress).

53. It is significant that the ex-converso Isaac Cardoso, despite his rabbinic education after he arrived in Italy, referred to circumcision in such terms, writing that God ordained it "as a mysterious sacrifice, to mortify the flesh and lessen the sensual impulses." Cardoso, *Las excelencias de los Hebreos*, 90. Cf. Yerushalmi, *Spanish Court*, 380.

54. *PLC*, 470–471, and cf. ibid., 224. It is striking that although Luis was on hand, Baltasar performed the circumcision on himself. It may be that Luis and his brother understood it to be especially praiseworthy to perform the command ("And you shall circumcise the flesh of your foreskin," Gen. 17:11) as Abraham did.

55. On Solomon Molkho see Zvi Werblowsky, "R. Joseph Caro, Solomon Molcho, Don Joseph Nasi," in Haim Beinart, ed., *The Sephardi Legacy*, 2 vols. (Jerusalem 1992), 2: 179–191.

56. Carl Gebhardt was influential in disseminating this idea. He wrote, in reference to Uriel da Costa, that this Jewish "heretic" in Amsterdam had "a fixed picture of Judaism solely from the Law and the Prophets. The post-biblical religious sources were inaccessible to him because of his unfamiliarity with the Hebrew language" (Carl Gebhardt, *Die Schriften des Uriel da Costa* [Amsterdam 1922], xix. Cf. Yerushalmi, *Spanish Court*, 297.)

57. Baer, *Die Juden*, #429, 2: 544. On New Christians who visited the Jewish community of Fez, see José Alberto Rodrigues da Silva Tavim, *Os judeus na expansão portuguesa em Marrocos durante o século XVI: origens e actividades duma comunidade* (Braga 1997), 103–104. A number of New Christians in Portugal were denounced to the Inquisition for having lived in Jewish communities—particularly in Ferrara, but also in Avignon, Lyons, Ancona, Pisa, Venice, and Salonica. See Baião, *Inquisição em Portugal e no Brasil*, 176, 204, 205, 207, 210, 211, 280.

58. On Jewish visitors to the Peninsula, see João Lúcio d'Azevedo, *História dos Christãos-Novos portugueses* (Lisbon 1921), 374n. 3; Yosef Kaplan, "The Travels of Portuguese Jews from Amsterdam to the 'Lands of Idolatry' (1644–1724)," in Kaplan, ed., *Jews and Conversos: Studies in Society and the Inquisition* (Jerusalem 1985), 197–224; Maximiano Lemos, *Zacuto Lusitano* (Porto 1909), 30, #6; Tavim, *Os judeus na expansão*, 494–509; Yosef Hayim Yerushalmi, "Professing Jews in Post-Expulsion Spain and Portugal," in Saul Lieberman, ed., *Salo Wittmayer Baron Jubilee Volume*, 3 vols. (Jerusalem 1974), 2: 1023–

1058; Haim Beinart, "A Jew of Salonica in Spain in the Seventeenth Century" (Hebrew), *Sefunot* 12 (1971–1978), 189–197; idem, "Ties between Jews and Conversos of Italy and Spain," in idem, ed., *Jews in Italy: Studies Dedicated to the Memory of U. Cassuto* (Hebrew) (Jerusalem 1988), 275–288; Salo Wittmayer Baron, *A Social and Religious History of the Jews*, 2nd ed., 18 vols. (New York 1952–1983), 15: 162, 481n. 71; Julio Caro Baroja, *Los judíos en la España moderna y contemporánea*, 3 vols. (Madrid 1986), 3: 361 (Appendix 29).

59. On these contacts, see Maria José Ferro Tavares, "The Portuguese Jews after the Expulsion," in Katz and Serels, eds., *Studies on the History of Portuguese Jews from Their Expulsion in 1497 through Their Dispersion* (New York 2000), 7–28; Claude Stuczynski, "Apóstatas marroquíes de origen judío en Portugal en los siglos XVI–XVII: Entre la misión y la Inquisición," in Mercedes García-Arenal, ed., *Los judíos magrebíes en la Edad Moderna* (Madrid 2003), 125–152.

60. On Jews from Fez who lived in Madrid, see Mercedes García-Arenal and Gerard Wiegers, *A Man of Three Worlds: Samuel Pallache, A Moroccan Jew in Catholic and Protestant Europe* (Baltimore and London 1999), 14–20.

61. Yerushalmi, *Spanish Court*, 271–301.

62. These works were a collection of usages and prayers for the minor fast days; a prayer book for the pilgrim festivals; a prayer book for the High Holidays; a comprehensive prayer book for weekdays, Sabbaths, and holidays; and a copy of Menasseh ben Israel's *Thesouro dos dinim que o povo de Israel e obrigado saber e observar*—a compendium of rabbinic practice. The Inquisition inventory of these books has been published by Lucía García de Proodian, *Los judíos en América: Sus actividades en los Virreinatos de Nueva Castilla y Nueva Granada S. XVII* (Madrid 1966), 478–479.

63. Elvira Cunha de Azevedo, "Orações judaicas na Inquisição portuguesa—século XVI," in Yosef Kaplan, ed., *Jews and Conversos*, 162. On the persistence of certain Jewish prayers in general, see Gitlitz, *Secrecy and Deceit*, 459–468.

64. David Gitlitz reports finding no references after 1480 of conversos possessing a Talmud, either in Spanish or Portuguese lands (Gitlitz, *Secrecy and Deceit*, 426). It is not clear how significant this is. A Talmud, printed or in manuscript, is not an easy thing to conceal. It would also soon have become inaccessible to conversos because of its language and inherent difficulty. The lack of *reference* in Inquisition documents to the Talmud or Mishnah seems more significant.

65. See Baer, *History of the Jews*, 2: 184–185.

66. This general strategy is stated quite explicitly by Haym ibn Musa in his *Magen ve-Romaḥ*, in the context of philosophical polemics. See Gutwirth, "Religión, historia y las biblias romanceadas," 118. It is perhaps worth noting the increased emphasis Profayt Duran placed on biblical, rather than talmudic, education. See Duran's introduction to his *Sefer ma'aseh Efod* (Vienna 1865), 1–25, and discussion in Eleazar Gutwirth, "Religion and Social Criticism in Late Medieval Rousillon: An Aspect of Profayt Duran's Activities," *Michael* 12 (1991), 150–156.

67. It seems significant that when Isaac Orobio de Castro, a newcomer to the Amsterdam Portuguese-Jewish community, was challenged by Christian theologians on the issue of the Talmud, he turned to the experienced rabbinic scholar Moses d'Aguilar for guidance. See Yosef Kaplan, *From Christianity to Judaism: The Story of Isaac Orobio de Castro* (Oxford 1989), 116.

68. Carlos Carrete Parrondo and Yolanda Moreno Koch, "Movimiento mesiánico hispano-portugués: Badajoz 1525," *Sefarad* 52 (1992), 65–68. Cf. Herculano, *Origin and Establishment*, 161.

69. On the sermons, see Edward Glaser, "Invitation to Intolerance: A Study of the Portuguese Sermons Preached at Autos-da-fé," *Hebrew Union College Annual* 27 (1956), 327–385.

70. See the example cited by Maureen Flynn, "Mimesis of the Last Judgment," 289–290.

71. Maureen Flynn, "Mimesis of the Last Judgment," 295–296.

72. It is now apparent that Antonio Llorente's figures for the total number of persons accused and the number burned at the stake in Spain between 1547 and 1699 are hopelessly exaggerated—84,400 accused, of whom 12, 536 were burned at the stake. (Juan Antonio Llorente, *Histoire critique de l'Inquisition d'Espagne*, 4 vols. [Paris 1817–1818], 4:259–265). The best effort to obtain accurate numbers thus far has been a project initiated by Gustav Henningsen to analyze the summaries of cases sent to the Suprema by the various tribunals. On the findings of this project see Gustav Henningsen, "El 'Banco de datos' del Santo Officio," *Boletin de la Real Academia de la Historia* 174 (1977), 542–570; Jaime Contreras and Gustav Henningsen, "Forty-four Thousand Cases of the Spanish Inquisition (1540–1700): Analysis of a Historical Data Bank," in Henningsen and Tedeschi, eds., *The Inquisition in Early Modern Europe* (Dekalb, Illinois 1986), 100–129; "The Database of the Spanish Inquisition: The *'relaciones de causas'* project revisited," in H. Mohnhaupt and D. Simon, eds., *Vorträge zur Justizforschung: Geschichte und Theorie*, 2: 43–85. This survey yielded the following data for 44,674 of the estimated 82,573 cases reported to the Suprema between 1540 and 1700. A total of 4,397 persons were accused of judaizing. Although the study does not indicate how many of the "judaizers" were burned at the stake, it indicates that a total of 826 persons out of the 44,674 were burned at the stake for crimes of any kind. Even these painstakingly gathered data are flawed, however. See Kamen, *Spanish Inquisition*, 198 and 341nn11,12; Bethencourt, *La Inquisición en la época moderna*, 13–14.

73. They are, in chronological order, Diogo d'Asumpção (burned alive in Lisbon 1603); Francisco Maldonado da Silva (Lima 1639); Lope de Vera (Valladolid 1644); Isaac de Castro Tartas (Lisbon 1647); Tomás Treviño de Sobremonte (Mexico City 1649); Balthazar Lopez [Redondo??] (Cuenca 1654??); Abraham Núñez Bernal (Cordova 1655); Isaac de Almeida Bernal (Compostela de Galicia, March 1655); Abraham Athias, Jacob Rodriguez Caseres, and Raquel Núñez Fernandez (Cordova 1665); Felipa Lopez Redonda, Leonor Pereyra, Luis Saraiva, Gaspar de Robles Cardoso, Balthasar Lopez Redondo, Simon de Morales, Pedro Visente (Madrid, June 1680); Aaron Coen Faya = António de Aguiar, Abraham Lopez Pereyra = Don Gaspar Lopez Pereyra (Lisbon, May 1682); Antonio Cabicho (according to Cecil Roth, Lisbon 1684); and "los tres martires de Sevilla" Francisco Lopez, Manuel Ferro, and Clara Núñez (no date). Some scholars have created the impression that more than a few persons were burned alive at the stake when they have translated "relajado en persona" (meaning burned in person rather than in effigy or after being exhumed) as "burned alive." Thus, for example, Seymour Liebman's translation of the account of the great auto in Mexico City in 1649—where in fact only one person was burned alive at the stake—suggests quite a few more (Seymour Liebman, *The Great Auto de fe of 1649* [Lawrence, Kans., 1974], 77, 97, 98, 101, 104).

74. Notably missing from his list is Francisco Maldonado de Silva.

75. John Edwards has pointed out that in accusations brought before the Inquisition in Soria between 1486 and 1502, there was some gender imbalance in terms of the "crimes" allegedly committed. Men were more likely to commit blasphemy. They were more likely to adopt general skepticism about Christianity. And they were more likely to have materialist or skeptical notions concerning the afterlife. See John Edwards, "Male and Female Re-

ligious Experience among Spanish New Christians, 1450–1500," in Raymond Waddington and Arthur Williamson, eds., *The Expulsion of the Jews: 1492 and After* (New York and London 1994), 41–51.

76. Martin A. Cohen, *Canonization of a Myth*, 34.

77. The outstanding example of this is Francisco Maldonado de Silva, who reported that his examination of Pablo de Santa Maria's anti-Jewish polemical work *Scrutinium Scripturarum* played a key role in his conversion to Judaism.

78. ANTT, Inquisição de Coimbra, processo 634. About twenty-three folio pages of the original dossier remain, of which some are mere fragments. I am grateful to Pedro Cardim for locating this dossier and having it microfilmed for me.

79. Cardoso hispanizes his name as "Diego Lópes de Piñancos."

80. He also mentions a fourth martyr, Tomás Treviño de Sobremonte, but only with the greatest brevity, as "un Trebiño" who was burned at the stake "en Mexico." Cardoso, *Excelencias*, 323.

81. Cardoso, *Excelencias*, 324. I have relied on Yerushalmi's translation, *From Spanish Court*, 396–397, with modifications. I have not been able to establish whether such a painting was hung in the Mosteiro de Santa Cruz in Coimbra or whether, if so, it has survived.

82. The record of this audience appears in the entry before that of January 25; the opening lines that would have included the date have not survived.

83. There is some ambiguity about what actually happened. See the account of Luis Carvajal's last minute "conversion" in 1596 by the friar who accompanied him ("Ultimos momentos," 64–78), and the analysis of Cohen, *The Martyr*, 257–259.

84. A typewritten transcription of his dossier can be found in the G. R. C. Conway Collection at the Library of Congress. It has been published, with changes to conform to modern usage, as "Causa criminal contra Tomas Treviño de Sobremonte, por judaizante" in *Boletín del Archivo General de la Nación*, seriatum, 6 (1935), 7 (1936), 8 (1937).

85. ANTT, IL, processo no. 11.550.

86. On the three Cordova martyrs—two members of the Bernal family and Abraham Athias = Jorge Méndez de Castro—see Cecil Roth, "Abraham Nuñez Bernal et autres martyrs contemporains de l'Inquisition,"*REJ* 100 [1936], 38–51; Gracia Boix, *Autos de fe*, 435–437, 444–464, 493.

3. A Conquistador's Nephew in New Spain

1. Anyone knowledgeable about crypto-Jewish history in New Spain will be familiar with Luis Carvajal. Martin Cohen has written a detailed biography of him based on archival documents, *The Martyr: The Story of a Secret Jew and the Mexican Inquisition in the Sixteenth Century*. His "autobiography" and letters have been published in English translation by Seymour Liebman, *The Enlightened: The Writings of Luis de Carvajal, el Mozo* (Coral Gables 1967), 55–84. Yet there is reason to revisit his life if we are to try to understand his prison career, which has not been sufficiently analyzed or contextualized.

2. *PLC*, 222, and cf. ibid., 463. Such an initiation on Yom Kippur may have been a custom in the family. Luis's younger sister Mariana testified in 1590 that about ten years earlier (she would have been only nine in 1580), her mother had taken her aside and said to her that she should no longer believe what the Church taught, and that when she went to mass she should not believe that God was there (in the host), rather that He was in heaven, and that she must believe in the Law of Moses "which is the law of God Almighty which he

gave to Moses on Mount Sinai." Her mother told her this on the day they called "*dia grande*"—Yom Kippur. Dossier of Manuel Morales, Archivo General de la Nación (henceforth AGN), Mexico City, Ramo de la Inquisición (henceforth Inq.), vol. 127, 381r.

3. Martin Cohen states rather categorically that Luis Carvajal did not even know that his family were New Christians (*The Martyr*, 25, 28–30), but I do not know on what basis he arrived at this conclusion.

4. This, according to his own account given to the Inquisition. See the document in Alfonso Toro, ed., *Los judíos en la Nueva España* (Mexico City 1982), 281.

5. While the crown was in general trying to discontinue the practice of granting *conquistadores* the title of *governador*, which gave them the right to dispose of Indians and land, this practice was continued in remote and "unpacified" areas in order to encourage the recipients to conduct further campaigns of conquest. See Leslie Bethell, ed., *The Cambridge History of Latin America*, 11 vols. (Cambridge 1984–), 1: 292.

6. Such investigations were aimed at preventing the emigration of New Christians, in accordance with a policy introduced in 1501 that was never enforced very effectively. See Boleslao Lewin, *Los judíos bajo la Inquisición en Hispano America* (Buenos Aires 1960), 25–26.

7. Cohen, *The Martyr*, 58. Evidence about conditions in Mexico supports such a supposition. In the frontier conditions of New Spain, with vast territories supposedly supervised by a single tribunal, the detection of judaizers was far more difficult than in Spain. Moreover, there existed a certain social solidarity between the inquisitors and the wealthy entrepreneurs, who belonged to the same privileged colonial elite. Since the Mexican Inquisition was also notoriously corrupt, complicity between inquisitors and wealthy judaizers was possible in a way that could hardly have been imagined in Spain. See Solange Alberro, *Inquisición y sociedad*, 23–28, 41, 45.

8. Cohen, *The Martyr*, 35.

9. Ibid., 61.

10. See ibid., 71. Cohen implies elsewhere that Morales was known to the family prior to the voyage. Discussing crypto-judaizing in Medina del Campo, he calls Morales "a dear friend of the [Carvajal] family's" and states that "Luis's parents regularly sought him out for religious counsel and instruction and transmitted his teachings to their children." Ibid., 36. However, there is no evidence of this in Morales's Inquisition dossier, AGN, Inq., vol. 127.

11. AGN, Inq., vol. 127, 343r-343v. Luis Carvajal seems to have believed that Morales settled in Salonica (*PLC*, 240).

12. See José Toribio Medina, *Historia del Tribunal del Santo Oficio de la Inquisición en México* (Santiago de Chile 1905), 88. And cf. Cohen, *The Martyr*, 78.

13. *PLC*, 427.

14. *PLC*, 40–68; on Morales, see esp. ibid., 53. By the time of Luis's second trial, Morales, by this time in Italy, had been tried *in absentia* and burned in effigy, and the Inquisition was not interested in him.

15. The aspects of Judaism that Francisca claimed to have learned from Morales were the usual crypto-Jewish ritual practices (Sabbath and holiday observances, and the dietary laws) and some essential theological dicta concerning the unity of God and the messianic expectations of the Jews. Her observance had no doubt become more ramified under his tutelage, but she was determined to hold Morales (who was safely abroad) responsible for *all* of her judaizing. An inquisitor chastised her for just that, remarking that she had better reconsider her testimony and "remember" what she had been taught by "a person very close to her," presumably Luis. AGN, Inq., vol. 127, 358r-372v; for the castigation, see 370v–371r.

16. As was the rule in all Inquisition trials, she was read a set of charges against her and asked to respond to them on the spot. The charges discussed here were clearly based on the testimony of others.

17. Diego Díaz Nieto, another accused judaizer in New Spain, reported that Carvajal's sister Mariana had told him "que tenían todos un libro guardado enque estaba escrita la ley de Moysén, el cual les había dejado un doctor que se fue de esta tierra, que cree que se llamaba el doctor Morales" (Uchmany, *La vida,* 77). Another witness who testified about Morales, a young New Christian from Portugal named Hernando Rodríguez de Serrera, also drew attention to this book, stating that "a Licenciado Morales, from Portugal, came to this land from Spain (to which he has returned), and he extracted from the Bible everything one needs [to know] to observe the Law of Moses, and made a book of it." (AGN, Inq., vol. 127, 387r.)

18. For Catalina's testimony, see AGN, Inq., vol. 127, 374r–379r.

19. AGN, Inq., vol. 127, 381v–382r.

20. AGN, Inq., vol. 127, 382v.

21. See Bodian, *Hebrews of the Portuguese Nation,* 36–43, 99–103.

22. In 1552, 450 copies of Bibles published abroad were seized by the Inquisition in Guadalquivir and taken to Seville for examination. See Tellechea Idígoras, "Biblias publicadas fuera de España," 236–247. See also Eugénie Droz, "Notes sur les impressions genevoises transportées par Hernández," *BHR* 22 (1960), 119–132; Georges Bonnant, "Notes sur quelques ouvrages en langue espanole imprimés a Genève par Jean Crespin (1557–1560)," *BHR* 24 (1962), 50–57.

23. The first edict concerning Bibles was issued in 1554. (See José Ignacio Tellechea Idígoras, "La censura inquisitorial de Biblias de 1554," *Anthologia Annua* 10 [1962], 89–142.) The Spanish Inquisition's Index of 1559 prohibited some vernacular Bibles; the 1583 Index prohibited *all* vernacular Bibles. (See Virgilio Pinto Crespo, *Inquisición y control ideológico en la España del siglo XVI* [Madrid 1983], 68–81.) The Inquisition also discovered that the book of hours—an enormously popular type of collection that contained, in addition to prayers and instructions, vernacular translations of certain psalms and other passages of Scripture—could lead to or lend support to nonorthodox ideas. Vernacular books of hours were thus banned in 1573. Pinto Crespo, *Inquisición y control,* 280–283.

24. For Portugal, see I.-S. Révah, *La censure inquisitoriale portugaise au XVIe siècle,* vol. 1 (Lisbon 1960) (vol. 2 never appeared).

25. See Joaquín Pérez Villanueva and Bartolomé Escandell Bonet, eds., *Historia de la Inquisición en España y América,* 3 vols. (Madrid 1984–2000), 3: 918.

26. *PLC,* 464.

27. Cohen, *The Martyr,* 69–71.

28. Ibid., 73–76. On the Chichimeca wars, see Philip Wayne Powell, *Soldiers, Indians, and Silver: The Northward Advance of New Spain, 1550–1600* (Berkeley and Los Angeles 1952).

29. The memoirs are published in *PLC,* 463–534.

30. On the religious strife in the family, see Cohen, *The Martyr,* 79–92.

31. See *PLC,* 17. May 12, 1589.

32. *PLC,* 46. Royal policy prohibited the enslavement of Indians, but during the Chichimeca wars that policy was modified, and traffic in Chichimeca slaves became widespread by the 1580s. See Powell, *Soldiers, Indians and Silver,* 105–111.

33. On the activity of itinerant merchants in New Spain, see P. J. Bakewell, *Silver Mining and Society in Colonial Mexico, Zacatecas 1546–1700* (Cambridge 1971), 58–80.

34. The obtaining of any new text was an event worthy of mention. On one occasion, Carvajal and his elder brother visited an elderly and ailing crypto-Jew in Mexico City, with whom Morales had left a copy of his translation of Deuteronomy into Spanish. The Carvajal brothers borrowed it and were especially impressed by "the chapter that contains the curses of the Holy Law. We saw that those truths had been fulfilled 'to the letter' (*a la letra*)" (*PLC*, 470). No doubt he was referring in particular to Deut. 28: 64–67, "The Lord will scatter you among all peoples . . . , and there you shall serve other gods, of wood and stone," a *locus classicus* among crypto-Jews. On another occasion the Carvajal brothers obtained a manuscript book with some Hebrew prayers translated into Spanish and Portuguese, from a New Christian merchant who had escaped from the Peninsula to Italy. (*PLC*, 471–472).

35. Such use of the third person was a characteristic of spiritual memoirs written in early modern Spain by mystics and *alumbrados*. See Melquíades Andrés, "Alumbrados, Erasmians, 'Lutherans,' and Mystics: The Risk of a More 'Intimate' Spirituality," in Angel Alcalá, ed., *The Spanish Inquisition and the Inquisitorial Mind* (New York 1987), 457.

36. This is an interesting rendering of Gen. 17:14. The Vulgate reads: "non fuerit delebitur anima illa de populo suo quia pactum meum irritum fecit." At the second audience of his second trial, Luis quoted the verse in question from memory and the notary recorded it thus: "amina enim quem circuncisa fuerit delebitur de libro viventium" (*PLC*, 222).

37. There are two accounts of Luis's self-circumcision, the first, in his memoirs (*PLC*, 464–465), the second, from his testimony at his second trial (*PLC*, 222).

38. 2 Chronicles 6: 7–9. *PLC*, 465.

39. On this crypto-Jewish belief see Bodian, *Hebrews of the Portuguese Nation*, 100–101.

40. The memoirs have been published twice in the original Spanish: *PLC*, 461–496; Alfonso Toro, *La Familia Carvajal: Studio histórico sobre los judíos y la Inquisición de la Nueva España*, 2 vols. (Mexico City 1944), 2: 315–339. For an English translation, see Liebman, *The Enlightened*, 55–84.

41. Carvajal noted, for example, that on a trip with his uncles to some recently discovered mines, he carried with him a notebook into which had been copied the Fourth Book of Esdras (or Ezra), a late first-century Jewish apocalypse that appears in an appendix to the Vulgate, to which Luis ascribed an important role in his earlier conversion. "Not having the sacred Bible with him," he wrote (referring to himself in the third person), "he spent his time reading Esdras in that land of savage Chichimecas" (*PLC*, 465–466). Luis's brother Baltasar, while hiding from the Inquisition, spent his time "holed up with the Holy Bible and other holy books the Lord provided him; their assiduous reading was his sole occupation" (ibid., 475).

42. This booklet, lined with green velvet, merited mention in the memoirs because on one occasion it had been lost in a public place, sending the family into a panic (*PLC*, 487 and cf. ibid., 245).

43. According to his memoirs, *PLC*, 465.

44. See *PLC*, 465–467, 468–469.

45. This engagement touched off a melodrama even by soap-opera standards; suffice it to say that Mariana never married her fiancé or anyone else. See Cohen, *The Martyr*, 115, 120–123; Uchmany, *La vida*, 93–94.

46. *PLC*, 469.

47. Five of the seventeen witnesses who testified about Luis Carvajal's judaizing were itinerant merchants of Portuguese origin imprisoned by the Inquisition for judaizing: Man-

uel de Lucena, Sebastian Rodríguez, Sebastian de la Peña Cardoso, Diego López, and Duarte Rodríguez.

48. *PLC,* 229. Judaizers sometimes also escaped to Indian villages to hide from the Inquisition, when they knew they were being sought. For a striking example in New Spain, see Wachtel, *La Foi du souvenir,* 120.

49. See Amos Megged, *Exporting the Catholic Reformation: Local Religion in Early-Colonial Mexico* (Leiden 1996), 53, 56–57.

50. *PLC,* 240–241.

51. *PLC,* 470.

52. For Luis's recitation of these Hebrew lines, see *PLC,* 225.

53. *PLC,* 224, 471.

54. *PLC,* 195–199.

55. Particularly striking are the apparent allusions in one poem to the family's experience in New Spain: "confieso que por ser inobedientes / fuimos de nuestra patria desechados / vivimos entre incircuncisas gentes / con hambres y con guerras afrentados, / todos con crueldades diferentes / fuimos de nuestra patria deshechados" (*PLC,* 195).

56. *PLC,* 200–202. The Inquisition recorded verbatim the thirty-seven-line introduction and twelve five-line stanzas, before summarizing the rest in the interest of time. To give an example of the many signs that the author's native language was Portuguese, the fourth stanza has "meu nome" for *mi nombre,* "muyta" for *muy,* and "ficieres" for *hicieres.*

57. When confessing under torture, Luis Carvajal recalled that these two men had also lived in the Jewish communities of Rome and Florence (*PLC* 347). On Carvajal's contact with Ruy and Diego Díaz Nieto, see Uchmany, *La vida.*

58. See Uchmany, *La vida,* 250.

59. *PLC,* 357.

60. *PLC,* 354.

61. This is Martin Cohen's explanation. See *The Martyr,* 95–96.

62. *PLC,* 471.

63. For Luis's testimony, see *PLC* 221, 316–317. For the chapter on the Talmud, see Luis de Granada, *Obras completas,* Alvaro Huerga ed., (Madrid 1994–), 12: 203–210. It is clear from Luis's testimony that he and members of his crypto-Jewish circle mined this verbose work (which was intended to "convert" judaizers back to Catholicism) for its abundant quotations of Old Testament passages in Spanish. One wonders how Luis responded to the chapter on the Talmud, which relied entirely on the anti-Jewish work of apostate Jerónimo de Santa Fe, *De Judaeis Erroribus ex Talmuth.* (Luis de Granada appears to have used a recent Portuguese translation. See ibid., 12: 204.)

64. On Díaz Nieto's knowledge of rabbinic Judaism, see the relevant passages of his testimony at his second trial, published in Uchmany, *La vida,* 226–233, 255–271; discussion of the Fast of Esther on p. 265.

65. This, according to his only contemporary biographer, Bishop Francisco Losa, who was initially recruited to investigate him. See Fernando Ocaranza, *Gregorio López, el hombre celestial* (Mexico City 1944), based on Losa's work, 63–70. On Losa and López, see Jodi Binkoff, "Francisco Losa and Gregorio López: Spiritual Friendship and Identity Formation on the New Spain Frontier," in Allen Greer and Jodi Bilinkoff, eds., *Colonial Saints: Discovery of the Holy in the Americas, 1500–1800* (New York and London 2003), 115–128.

66. This work has recently been published with an introductory essay by Álvaro Huerga: Gregorio López, *Declaración del apocalipsis* (Madrid 1999).

67. The testimony of Bishop Francisco Losa, who knew him intimately, includes the

statement "que una vez le havia preguntado nueve lugares de los mas oscuros y dificiles que havia visto en la Biblia y que el [Gregorio López] los avia declarado todos en sentido literal con tanta propriedad que parecia un San Geronimo," and mentions another person who had heard Gregorio López discuss on many occasions biblical stories from the creation of the world to the time of Jesus, recounting all the wars and other events (*Información sumaria de las virtudes y milagros de Gregorio López, año de 1620*, Ms. 7819, Biblioteca Nacional, Madrid, 39v–40r).

68. *PLC*, 151–152.

69. *PLC*, 20–22.

70. See Cohen, *The Martyr*, 138–139.

71. Baltasar surely did not actually use this derogatory Jewish epithet to refer to Jesus. Luis employed it in his memoirs for polemical effect.

72. A paraphrase of Matthew 5: 17–18.

73. *PLC*, 472–473.

74. For a discussion of shifting early modern attitudes concerning access to knowledge about momentous matters, see Carlo Ginzburg, "The High and the Low: The Theme of Forbidden Knowledge in the 16th and 17th Centuries," in idem, *Clues, Myths, and the Historical Method* (Baltimore 1989), 60–76.

75. Cohen, *The Martyr*, 143–144.

76. *PLC*, 31–34. The first accusation was that Luis had abandoned Catholicism for the Law of Moses; the second, that his father had asked him to wash his corpse after his death according to Jewish custom; the fourth, that certain persons suspected him in respect to his belief in the Trinity and Ascension; fifth, that in a discussion with a certain person [Gaspar], he had confirmed his false belief; sixth, that he rejected the christological reading of a psalm; seventh, that he had fled to Veracruz with his brother Baltasar after hearing of his sister Isabel's arrest, and deceived the Inquisition about Baltasar's whereabouts; and eighth, that he had committed other crimes which would be enumerated in the course of the trial.

77. *PLC*, 35.

78. *PLC*, 40, 44.

79. *PLC*, 47–48.

80. *PLC*, 53.

81. *PLC*, 477.

82. *PLC*, 476.

83. *PLC*, 445–446.

84. *PLC*, 234.

85. See Alberro, *Inquisición y sociedad*, 223.

86. Luis's sensitivity to light deprivation is reflected in a letter he wrote during his second imprisonment to Leonor and Isabel, in which he reported having been confined to a dark cell for three weeks, during which the only light he saw was some candlelight when his meals were brought. But "my blessed God" had taken him out of there and brought him to a prison with a window "through which I watch the sky day and night." *PLC*, 501. On the Inquisition's punitive use of dark, closed cells see Alberro, *Inquisición y sociedad*, 224.

87. Francisca Núñez de Carvajal was tortured on November 10, 1589. Cohen, *The Martyr*, 171, 172.

88. *PLC*, 477–478.

89. See Medina, *Inquisición en México*, 83–84. Luis Carvajal alluded to the friar's lack of Jewish ancestry in his memoirs, in which he referred to the friar as an "hombre de estraña nacion" (*PLC*, 486).

90. The dogmatizing martyrs' sense of engagement with the Christian world parallels that of the major polemicists in western Sephardi communities, who were strongly prepared, and often eager, to spar with Christians in theological debate. For an impression of the richness and diversity of such contacts, see Yosef Kaplan, Henry Méchoulan, and Richard Popkin, eds., *Menasseh ben Israel and His World* (Leiden 1989). And cf. Yerushalmi, *Spanish Court*, 350–412; Kaplan, *From Christianity*, 235–307.

91. See Medina, *Inquisición en México*, 83–84.

92. See Alberro, *Inquisición y sociedad*, 225.

93. *PLC*, 478.

94. On this notion among believing Christians, see Alastair Hamilton, *Heresy and Mysticism in Sixteenth-Century Spain: The Alumbrados* (Cambridge 1992), 36.

95. See Medina, *Inquisición en México*, 83–84.

96. *PLC*, 478–479.

97. Medina, *Inquisición en México*, 83–84.

98. Medina, *Inquisición en México*, 84–85.

99. This news was reported in a letter of Jorge de Almeida from Spain. Baltasar also wrote to Luis prior to his departure, on November 15, 1590, noting that "in France there are great wars and the whole country is becoming Lutheran, and two popes have died in one month" (*PLC*, 256). And see Cohen, *The Martyr*, 196–197.

100. *PLC*, 480.

101. Two inventories of the library of the Colegio de Santa Cruz, dating from 1572 and 1584, respectively, have been published in *Códice Mendieta: documentos franciscanos, siglos XVI y XVII*, 2 vols. (Mexico City 1892), 2: 255–261. According to these lists, the library possessed a volume of letters by Erasmus, and "six books by [Juan] Luis Vives," which might have attracted Carvajal's attention, as well as a copy of Josephus's *Antiquities*, which he took from the library and must have read, since we know he lent it to a fellow converso (see Uchmany, *La vida*, 69).

102. This work is not mentioned in the existing late sixteenth-century inventories (see previous footnote).

103. *PLC*, 481–482.

104. *PLC*, 486–487.

105. Medina, *Inquisición en México*, 86.

106. *PLC*, 495–496.

107. *PLC*, 125–134. For details of the arrests, see Cohen, *The Martyr*, 235.

108. The transfer is noted in an entry in the dossier, *PLC*, 124. On Gaspar de los Reyes Plata, see Eva Alexandra Uchmany, "La vida en las cárceles del Santo Oficio en la Ciudad de México entre 1589 a 1660," in Henri Méchoulan and Gerard Nahon, eds., *Mémorial I.-S. Révah: Études sur le marranisme, l'hétérodoxie juive et Spinoza* (Paris and Louvain 2001), 475–476.

109. Luis Díaz reported in a morning audience of February 11, 1595, that Luis had discovered "who he was" the day before (*PLC*, 156).

110. *PLC*, 225.

111. This detail appears in an account by a Dominican who was familiar with at least one of the tribunal's inquisitors. See [Contreras], "Ultimos momentos," 67.

112. In the notary's rendition, "El primero dice: oye, Israel, y en ebrero [*sic*] *Semha Israel, Adonay Alhieno Varocsem que voz malcuto leolamvaet*, que quiere decir: oye Israel Adonay, tu Dios uno solo es, uno bendito nombre de honra de su Reino para consigo y siempre. . . ." *PLC*, 225. The butchered rendition of the Hebrew is no doubt partly the

notary's fault, but Luis did not actually know Hebrew. Aside from these phrases, he knew a few other Hebrew words—*Quippur* (a term he used to refer to Yom Kippur), *Sequina* (for *shekhina*), and *nesse* (Hebrew *nes*, meaning "miracle").

113. *PLC*, 227-229, 235.

114. *PLC*, 154-155.

115. He identified as judaizers only his brother Baltasar, at this point in Italy; Antonio Machado, deceased; and two men in New Spain—Manuel de Lucena and Manuel Gómez Navarro—who were under arrest and, as he must have assumed, had revealed their own as well as Luis's judaizing.

116. *PLC*, 167.

117. *PLC*, 222, 234-235.

118. *PLC*, 235-238. For a summary of Luis Carvajal's statement, see Appendix B.

119. *PLC*, 238.

120. *PLC*, 221. I have not been able to identify one of them, titled *Diálogos del Amor de Dios*.

121. Sara Nalle, *God in La Mancha: Religious Reform and the People of Cuenca, 1500–1659* (Baltimore 1992), 148. And see Baião, *Inquisição em Portugal e no Brasil*, 232, for a confession by a Portuguese judaizer in 1587, in which this work was mentioned as a source of "cousas da ley velha." I have examined only the third part of this work, *Espejo de consolación de tristes: en la qual se veran muchas y grandes hystorias de la sagrada escriptura para consolación de los que en esta vida padecen tribulación. Tercera parte* (Barcelona 1580), at the Houghton Library at Harvard University.

122. *Guía de Pecadores* was actually listed in the notorious 1559 Index of Valdés, but this was of little interest to Luis's interrogators. See Antonio Márquez, *Literatura e inquisición en España (1478–1834)* (Madrid 1980), 152.

123. *PLC*, 316.

124. See the condemnation of two of the works mentioned by Carvajal in a letter to Mexican inquisitors sent to the Suprema in March 1595 (Alvaro Huerga, "Judíos de Ferrara en las Inquisición de México," *Annuario dell'Istituto storico italiano per l'età moderna e contemporanea* 35–36 [1983–1984], 125–126).

125. The problem of giving a single descriptive title to a collection of innovative Spanish religious personalities that included saints as well as "heretics" burned at the stake, rationalist anticlerical figures as well as ecstatic mystics, has long troubled scholars. The great seminal work on this subject is Marcel Bataillon's *Erasmo y España*—which deals primarily with the period to 1560 and is noted for having first revealed the startling predominance of conversos among these innovative and/or radical thinkers. By Luis Carvajal's time, inquisitorial repression and the Index had made caution necessary. Figures of his generation who supported a rejection of scholasticism, a greater emphasis on interior religious experience, and a focus on lay education in the vernacular—Luis de Granada was one—existed in an uneasy alliance with the Church hierarchy.

126. The dream of the sweet potato in association with his mother's torture is a case in point. Whatever its Freudian meanings might be, the imagery is also strongly reminiscent of Catholic hagiography, in which great saints, having endured much suffering and violence to the body, exude a sweet odor after death. Among sixteenth-century Spanish mystics, moreover, a sweet taste was often associated with the presence of God.

127. For some of the many examples, see *PLC*, 146–152.

128. See Uchmany, *La vida*, 72 (Manuel de Lucena), 77 (Diego Díaz Nieto).

129. *PLC*, 413.

130. *PLC,* 294.

131. *PLC,* 415.

132. From an anonymous pamphlet printed in the Netherlands. See Benjamin Kaplan, *Calvinists and Libertines: Confession and Community in Utrecht, 1578–1620* (Oxford 1995), 49.

133. On the early *alumbrados'* approach to Scripture and authority, see José C. Nieto, "The Nonmystical Nature of the Sixteenth-Century Alumbrados of Toledo," in A. Alcalá, ed., *The Spanish Inquisition,* 431–456; idem, *Juan de Valdés and the Origins of the Spanish and Italian Reformation* (Geneva 1970), esp. 239–255.

134. Alastair Hamilton, *Heresy and Mysticism in Sixteenth-Century Spain: The Alumbrados* (Cambridge1992), 35.

135. Antonio Márquez, *Los Alumbrados: Orígenes y filosofía (1525–1559),* (Madrid 1980), 175.

136. Nieto, *Juan de Valdés,* 68.

137. It is worth noting that the idea of possessing an inner light of the spirit is ubiquitous in Luis de Granada's writing.

138. The sense of being specially granted this "light" or "love" differs from that of Protestants who believed Scripture provided all people with the necessary light for its understanding. The Christian Hebraist Johann Jacob Schudt, for example, regarded Scripture as "in itself a light that explains its own terms and words, and builds in us useful and necessary teachings about the natural things that God wishes to reveal." (See Allison Coudert, "Judaizing in the Seventeenth Century: Francis Mercury van Helmont and Johann Peter Späth [Moses Germanus]," in Martin Mulsow and Richard Popkin, eds., *Secret Conversions to Judaism in Early Modern Europe* [Leiden and Boston 2004], 82n28.) What is common to both conceptions is a conviction of the existence of a human capacity to understand Scripture that derives not through institutions but directly from God.

139. According to Carvajal, the verse meant he was required to debate the inquisitors, "whose power came from the pope and king" (*PLC,* 294, and cf. 417, 453).

140. *PLC,* 261.

141. On the messages, see *PLC,* 171–184. Martin Cohen implies (*The Martyr,* 235, 240) that none of the messages reached their addressees, but this is clearly not the case.

142. The surviving letters are published in *PLC,* 499–534. Two letters to Leonor predate May 22, 1595; a letter to Leonor and two to Isabel were written between May 22 and May 26; to his mother, Catalina, Anica and Leonor, before May 28; to Catalina and Leonor, before May 30; to Leonor, before June 1, and to Anica, before June 3. Several other letters, including one to Mariana, cannot be dated.

143. Luis did acknowledge receiving a letter from Leonor, and a brief letter from one of them; in another letter he asked Leonor to write him. But mainly he asked them to send him food items or paper on which he could write, or objects (like an olive pit) that would have some significance.

144. On the rather routine exchange of messages and foodstuffs between prisoners in the secret cells in Mexico City see Alberro, *Inquisición y sociedad,* 229–251.

145. The twentieth charge deals with his proselytizing, and notes that he was responsible for "reconverting" his mother and sisters to the Law of Moses after they returned to Catholic practice in the wake of their first trial. *PLC,* 271.

146. See, in particular, charges #3, 5, 6, and 7, *PLC,* 264–266.

147. Charge #9, PLC, 267; see his response, *PLC,* 274.

148. These are charges #17, 18, 19, *PLC,* 269–271; for Luis's responses, see ibid., 284.

149. *PLC,* 285.

150. These meetings took place on October 30 and October 31, 1595. See *PLC,* 290–292.

151. *PLC,* 293–294.

152. *PLC,* 299–365. Torture was applied on February 8 and February 12. For details of these sessions in English, see Cohen, *The Martyr,* 244–246.

153. *PLC,* 366–367.

154. See the entry for March 4, 1596, in *PLC,* 377.

155. *PLC,* 368–369. The following day, Lobo Guerrero returned to his cell, where Luis was still in great pain and bedridden, to ask him specifically about his testimony that Gregorio López was a judaizer. Luis said this piece of testimony was *not* true. *PLC,* 370–371.

156. See Medina, *Inquisición en México,* 96, and Toro, *La familia Carvajal,* 233n. 15. To be sure, the Inquisition's conclusions should be regarded with some skepticism. Unfortunately, other scholars have not taken note of this episode and I have not had an opportunity to examine Benítez's dossier (according to Alfonso Toro, AGN, Inq., vol. 151), which might throw some light on his "conversion."

157. In an audience of July 13, 1596. *PLC,* 395.

158. *PLC,* 405.

159. This may have been why he requested paper and ink in an audience of August 14, though he gave a different reason; but given the frequency with which messages were smuggled in the Mexican Inquisition prison, he may have had little difficulty obtaining these items. (One of the prisoners sentenced at the auto-da-fé where Luis was finally sentenced was an African slave accused of passing messages between prisoners, and providing them with writing materials [Medina, *Inquisición de México,* 94]). For the Testament, see *PLC,* 411–418. For an English translation, see Liebman, *The Enlightened,* 125–133.

160. He appears to have intended to make a list of ten "truths," but inadvertently skipped the fifth and ninth. This may suggest that, at least after the first three were composed, he worked hastily. Or it may reflect a state of exhaustion that produced inattention to the neatness of his presentation.

161. He cited Psalm 110: 7–9 (of the Vulgate, Psalm 111 of the Hebrew Bible: "... all his precepts are trustworthy, they are established for ever and ever ... he has commanded his covenant for ever."); Malachi 3:6 ("For I the Lord do not change"); all of Psalm 118 (119 of the Hebrew Bible); Eccles. 3:14 (" I know that whatever God does endures for ever: nothing can be added to it, nor anything taken from it"); and Deut. 4:2 ("You shall not add to the word which I command you, nor take from it").

162. Matt. 5: 17–18. It may be recalled that in his memoirs, Luis mentioned Baltasar's quoting both of these verses in an attempt to convert his brother Gaspar. See *PLC* 473. These verses were naturally of interest to radical Protestant Bible readers as well. An English millenarian of the seventeenth century saw them, like Luis Carvajal, as prooftexts justifying the continuation of contemporary Jewish observance—although he hoped it would occur *along with* an acceptance of Christ. See Richard Popkin, "Can One Be a True Christian and a Faithful Follower of the Law of Moses? The Answer of John Dury," in Martin Mulsow and Richard Popkin, eds., *Secret Conversions to Judaism in Early Modern Europe* (Leiden and Boston 2004), 47.

163. "[E]l ánimo, y el hombre que no fuere circuncidado será borrado de la lista de los vivientes: Gens. 17." *PLC,* 414.

164. Among the condemned were forty-five judaizers. Eight other judaizers were

sentenced (and burned) in effigy, including Luis's brother Miguel and a nephew of Manuel de Morales.

165. Luis's sister Mariana was burned at the stake, and his sister Ana was reconciled, at a later auto, in 1601.

166. Some of the many persons Luis had denounced were also at the auto. Four of them were also headed for the quemadero: Manuel Díaz, Beatriz Enríquez de Payba, Diego Enríquez, and Manuel de Lucena. (See Medina, *Inquisición en México*, 97.) At least a dozen other persons against whom Luis had testified were given lesser sentences. Compare the list of persons against whom Luis testified (*PLC*, 375) with the (incomplete) list of other judaizers sentenced at this auto (Medina, *Inquisición en México*, 95–96).

167. *PLC*, 457.

168. [Contreras], "Ultimos momentos."

169. The account includes long, perfectly worded conversations and speeches, and attempts to refute a variety of claims by eyewitnesses (who surely did not report to Contreras immediately after the event) that Luis had not undergone a sincere conversion.

170. According to Martin Cohen, this account was appended to the Inquisition dossier, indicating the Inquisition's interest in claiming "victory" (Cohen, *The Martyr*, 258). It was not published in *PLC*.

4. A MONK OF CASTANHEIRA

1. The dossier of his trial is ANTT, Inquisição de Lisboa, no. 104. Extracts have been published in A. J. Teixera, *Antonio Homem e a Inquisição* (Coimbra 1895–1902), 217–247, edited to conform to modern usage and in some places paraphrased. Menasseh ben Israel possessed a copy of the Inquisition's *sentença* (summary of trial and sentence), very likely the copy found by L. D. Barnett in the British Museum and published in his "Two Documents of the Inquisition," *Jewish Quarterly Review* 15 (1924–1925), 221–229; it differs somewhat from the *sentença* found in the dossier, which Teixeira published with the aforementioned extracts.

2. In his dossier, the town is referred to as "Viana de Caminha."

3. "Determinou de fugir pera frandes ou frança ou pera qualquer outra parte q podesse for a deste reino pera la viver a sua vontade e em sua liberdade" (ANTT, IL, no. 104, fo. 103v). According to the testimony of a fidalgo he approached after his escape, he mentioned the Netherlands and England, not France.

4. See José Mattoso, ed., *História de Portugal—Edição Académica*, vol. 3, *No alvorecer da modernidad (1480–1620)*, (Lisbon 1997), 197–198.

5. ANTT, IL, no. 104, 10v. Frei Diogo testified that he did not know this man, who was living outside Lisbon due to the plague epidemic in the region, but he believed that being "of the *nação*" he would show him favor. Ibid., 103v–104r.

6. Diogo de Sousa identified himself as the son of Jorge de Sousa and Dona Francisca, thirty-seven years old, and was a member of the military Order of Christ.

7. The fidalgo testified that he had never seen Frei Diogo and did not know him. ANTT, IL, no. 104, 9r. August 27, 1599.

8. In his testimony, the nobleman said he had at some point asked Frei Diogo whether he had told Gaspar Boccarro the things he had told him. The friar said no, he hadn't, because there were other people present. In any case, the dossier contains no testimony given by Gaspar Boccarro.

9. Diogo de Sousa recorded it in great detail, and it is corroborated by the friar's own

testimony days later. For the fidalgo's testimony, see ANTT, IL, no 104, fos. 3r–6r. For Frei Diogo's corroborating testimony, ibid., fos. 101r–114r.

10. Frei Diogo's notebooks and papers were seized by the Inquisition (ibid., 19v), but have not been preserved. An inventory of the monastery library's holdings from 1834 lists a number of books that Frei Diogo might have consulted to find support for his thinking. See ANTT, Arquivo Histórico do Ministério das Finanças, Conventos Extintos (CX.2204, Capilha 3)—Convento de Santo António da Ordem de S. Francisco de Castanheira, Auttos de Inventário do Convento de Santo António dos Capuchos, fo. 14v. My thanks to Luisa França Luzio for providing me with a transcript of this inventory. Of particular interest is a volume listed as "João Esqui contra Lutero."

11. Isaiah 7: 14.

12. "[Que] Deos mandava no Deuteronomio q as suas palavras se não trocessem nem lhe desem outro sentido mais q o literal" (ANTT, IL, no. 104, 12r, and cf. 117v). The depiction of Jesus and his followers as ignorant was common in medieval Jewish polemics, and may have passed into Portuguese crypto-Jewish circles. We have no concrete evidence, however, that Frei Diogo had contact with such circles. On this medieval polemical theme see David Berger, "On the Uses of History in Medieval Jewish Polemic against Christianity: The Quest for the Historical Jesus," in E. Carlebach, J. Efron, and D. Myers, eds., *Jewish History and Jewish Memory: Essays in Honor of Yosef Hayim Yerushalmi* (Hanover, N.H., 1998), 32.

13. This was a common image in the Reformation period, used in reference to allegorical or philosophical interpretations of Scripture. It is a borrowing from the medieval dictum "authority has a nose of wax." The image was used by Erasmus, Luther, and Calvin, among others.

14. It may be an error on Frei Diogo's part—or on the notary's part—to classify Domingo de Soto, a Dominican, in this way.

15. The problem of the status of a consecrated host eaten by a mouse or other animal was a subject of controversy as early as the thirteenth century, not long after the doctrine of transubstantiation became official Church doctrine. And, indeed, the thirteenth-century Dominican Peter de La Palu contended that if a mouse consumed a consecrated host, it should be caught and burned, and its ashes washed down a sacrarium. See Miri Rubin, *Corpus Christi: The Eucharist in Late Medieval Culture* (Cambridge 1991), 67–68.

16. The social denigration of Jesus and his followers has a venerable history that can be traced back to pagan critics of the early Christians. See Wayne Meeks, *The First Urban Christians: The Social World of the Apostle Paul* (New Haven 1983), 51. It was not, however, a prominent feature of anti-Christian Jewish polemics. It is thus striking that Frei Diogo echoes a theme touched on by Luis Carvajal, who testified to having said that Jesus "was born among shepherds and had disciples who were lowly and vile, not kings and princes, and was crucified between thieves."

17. Acts 16: 1–3.

18. On familiarity with Martin Luther in Spain, see John Longhurst, *Luther's Ghost in Spain, 1517–1546* (Lawrence, Kansas 1969); Augustin Redondo, "Luther et l'Espagne de 1520 à 1536," *Mélanges de la Casa de Velázquez* 1 (1965), 109–165.

19. Presumably he preferred to embark from Setúbal, a port city south of Lisbon, because he had spent time in the Capuchin monastery in Lisbon, and was known in that city.

20. This is a reference to the great pilgrim shrine in Santiago de Compostela, the supposed burial place of St. James.

21. ANTT, IL, no. 104, 110r.

22. For the record of this session, see ANTT, IL, no. 104, 101r–106r.

23. "[E] não ter raça nenhuma de christão novo."

24. In testimony two days later, returning to the subject of his reading, he recalled that the title contained the phrase *Notationes in sacram scripturam*—quite possibly a work by the Jesuit Emmanuel Sa. See ANTT, IL, no. 104, 109r.

25. ANTT, Arquivo Histórico do Ministério das Finanças, Conventos Extintos (CX.2204, Capilha 3) Auttos de Inventário, do Convento de Santo António dos Capuchos, fo. 14v.

26. ANTT, IL, no. 104, 106r–114r.

27. ANTT, IL, no. 104, 24r (Sept. 30, 1599), 115v (October 25, 1599).

28. ANTT, IL, no. 104, 9r–21v. In my account of events, I have combined information from the two texts, Diego de Sousa's letter and the transcript of his testimony.

29. ANTT, IL, no. 104, 115v–117v.

30. The books he mentioned were a *Summa de sacramenti* by Francisco de Vitoria, a work recorded as "*Flosculus sacramentora*," the *Summa silvestrina*, and the *Manual de confessores* by the Coimbra professor Martim de Azpilcueta Navarro.

31. His father was from Cantanhede; his mother's family was mainly from Aveiro. The Coimbra tribunal reported its findings on January 11, 1600. ANTT, IL, no. 104, 26r–v.

32. For the genealogical investigation, see ANTT, IL, no. 104, fos. 26r–40v.

33. "[Que] ele declarasse as razões q elle neste seu processo appontava."

34. ANTT, IL, no. 104, 118r–119v.

35. "Ego sum deus Abraham, deus Isac, deus Jacob, et hoc est nomen meum in sempiternum, et in generatione et generationem." Cf. Exod. 3: 14–15.

36. "Respondome, muito milhor porq estou alumiado de N. S. na verdadeira Ley q he a dos Judeos em q de presente estou." ANTT, IL, no. 104, 41r.

37. "[Que] todo aquelle tempo andara frio . . . assi (uso da sua palabra) a qual eu entendi q andara como vacillando." ANTT, IL, no. 104, 41r.

38. The Inquisition expected prisoners to provide their own cell furnishings, though it did routinely provide necessities for the indigent. Having taken the Capuchin vows, Frei Diogo would not have owned such furnishings.

39. For the inquisitor's record of this session, see ANTT, IL, no. 104, 41r–41v; further details were reported when the inquisitor himself was questioned, ibid., 44r–45v.

40. ANTT, IL, no. 104, 41v–43r.

41. The Catholic recitation of a psalm was followed by this formula, a brief affirmation of the Trinity. Its omission was a hallmark of crypto-Jewish prayer.

42. He most likely studied at the seminary founded there by the Frei Bartolomeu dos Mártires, one of the leading figures of the Catholic Reformation in Portugal. Azevedo, ed., *História religiosa de Portugal,* 2: 215.

43. "Respondeome, Enfadado eu do meu ministro q me tratava mal lhe pus apreta hum escrito q dizia assi, qui suggerit mel de petra, oleumq de saxo duressimo e as[sinei em] baixo, Christus Dominus." ANTT, IL, no. 104, 42r.

44. In the Vulgate, Ps. 83:11: *elegi abiectus esse in domo Dei mei magis quam habitare in tabernaculis impietatis.*

45. He is referring to his incarceration in the monastery in Castanheira, in the monastery in Lisbon, and in the Inquisition cells.

46. On this figure, see Columba Stewart, *Cassian the Monk* (New York and Oxford 1998).

47. ANTT, IL, no. 104, 43r.

48. John Cassian, *The Conferences*, trans. and annotated by Boniface Ramsey (New York 1997), Book 2, chapter 8, 89–90.

49. ANTT, IL, no. 104, 43v–45r.

50. ANTT, IL, no. 104, 120r–122r.

51. At his first audience on November 4, 1599. The record for two subsequent audiences, on April 6 and April 7, 1600, is silent on this matter.

52. "[N]otus in Judea deus, et in Israel magna nomen eius" (cf. Ps. 76: 1; in the Vulgate, Ps. 75:2).

53. "[E]go servus tuus e filias ancilae tuae" (cf. Ps. 116: 16, in the Vulgate Ps. 115: 16).

54. "[Q]ui anunciat verba seum Jacob et . . . juditia sua Israel" (cf. Ps. 147: 19).

55. Cf. Exod. 20: 3, 7–8.

56. See the testimony of Miguel Siguet (ANTT, IL, no. 104, 54r) and Antonio Gomes Gorião (Ibid., 67v). On days other than Friday and Saturday, Frei Diogo ate only the midday meal.

57. See especially David S. Katz, *Sabbath and Sectarianism in Seventeenth-Century England* (Leiden 1988).

58. In a treatise of 1523, Luther wrote, "If I had been a Jew and seen such oafs and numbskulls governing and teaching the Christian faith, I would rather have become a sow than a Christian." See *Martin Luthers Werke: Kritische Gesamtausgabe, Abteilung Werke* (Weimar 1883–1993), 11: 314–315.

59. ANTT, IL, no. 104, 46r–49r.

60. See Elias Lipiner, *Santa Inquisição: Terror e linguagem* (Rio de Janeiro 1977), 176–177.

61. ANTT, IL, no. 104, 50r–55r.

62. Cf. Psalm 119: 176 (in the Vulgate, Ps. 118. 176).

63. ANTT, IL, no. 104, 56r–v. Frei Diogo's prison companion Pero Domingues gave a slightly different account of the friar's refusal to bare his head, in his testimony of Dec. 10, 1600. Ibid., 61r–v.

64. ANTT, IL, no. 104, 57r–62r.

65. ANTT, IL, no. 104, 62v–66v.

66. ANTT, IL, no. 104, 67r–68v. The testimony was given on July 24, 1601.

67. ANTT, IL, no. 104, 122v–126v.

68. Ps. 78: 1 (Vulgate, Ps. 77:1).

69. Deut. 32: 1. My emphasis.

70. Ps. 23: 3 (Vulgate, Ps. 22:3).

71. Ps. 119: 105 (Vulgate 118: 105).

72. ANTT, IL, no. 104, 126v–129v.

73. In the Vulgate, Ps. 126:1.

74. In the Vulgate, Ps. 145:2–3.

75. "[Q]ue o ditto Frei Diogo em todo o ditto tempo esteve muito sesudo e callado ouvindo e respondendo com muito siso e como homen de muito bem entendimento." ANTT, IL, no. 104, 129r–v.

76. On the *libelo*, see Lipiner, *Terror e linguagem*, 159–160.

77. The *libelo* is recorded in ANTT, IL, no. 104, 132r–139r.

78. On the role of the procurador, see Lipiner, *Terror e linguagem*, 199–200.

79. ANTT, IL, no. 104, 139r–140r.

80. ANTT, IL, no. 104, 174v–179r.

81. Cf. Ps. 26:10 (Ps. 27:10 in the Vulgate).

82. The Inquisitors seem never to have considered the possibility of applying torture. Frei Diogo was not exempt by virtue of being a cleric, so there must have been other considerations. On the application of torture to clerics, see Lea, *History of the Inquisition*, 3: 13.

83. On this custom, see Gitlitz, *Secrecy and Deceit*, 321–322.

84. It is consistent with our picture of Frei Diogo's development that the friar seems not to have actively sought out information about judaizing practices before his arrest. A prior indifference to Jewish practices may help explain his ignorance of the fact that the Sabbath began at sundown on Friday. Although a standard edict of faith read aloud in Portuguese parishes explicitly mentions, among many other practices, the lighting of Sabbath lamps on "Friday afternoon" (*nas ditas sestas ferias á tarde*), an uninterested listener might well fail to take note of this detail. See Charles Amiel, "Crypto-judaisme et Inquisition: La matière juive dans les edits de la foi des Inquisitions ibériques," *RHR* 210 (1993), 167.

85. ANTT, IL, no. 104, 179r–181r.

86. Cf. Wisdom 6: 12–13.

87. He used the accepted abbreviation, which can be approximately reproduced as "Xp's dn's."

88. ANTT, IL, no. 104, 79r-81r. Statement of December 11, 1602.

89. See Azevedo, ed., *História religiosa de Portugal*, 2: 221.

90. These were the first two of the three "sacred orders," the third being *missa*, which he did not receive (see further on). See Azevedo, ed., *História religiosa de Portugal*, 2: 220.

91. See the testimony of Frei Jeronimo of March 6, 1603, ANTT, IL, no. 104, 88v.

92. ANTT, IL, no. 104, 82r–83v. The entry is undated.

93. The identity of the two is suggested by the many biographical details that tally, but it is established by the fact that Jeronimo de Jesus gave his mother's name as Maria Fagundez (recorded by the notary as "Fagandes"). ANTT, IL, no. 104, 88v.

94. ANTT, IL, no. 104, 85r–v. The letter is dated January 1, 1603. Frei Jeronimo's name is missing from the document, but the handwriting matches that of his letter of April 15, and the contents confirm his identity.

95. I have not seen this quite rare book, titled *Questionarium conciliationis simul et expositionis locorum difficilium Sacrae Scripturae. . . .*

96. ANTT, IL, no. 104, 90v.

97. ANTT, IL, no. 104, 70r–v.

98. ANTT, IL, no. 104, 73r–74r.

99. On Sebastianism, see Jacqueline Hermann, *No reino do desejado: a construção do sebastianismo em Portugal, séculos XVI e XVII* (São Paulo 1998).

100. "[Q]uando claramente se via convencido."

101. ANTT, IL, no. 104, 182r–v.

102. Cf. Ps. 119:4 (in the Vulgate, Ps. 118: 4).

103. ANTT, IL, no. 104, 183r-192r. This phase of the trial was called the *publicação da prova da justiça*. See Lipiner, *Terror e linguagem*, 202–203.

104. ANTT, IL, no. 104, 202r–v.

105. ANTT, IL, no 104, 203r.

106. ANTT, IL, no. 104, 204r.

107. João Manuel Andrade, *Confraria de S. Diogo: judeus secretos na Coimbra do séc. XVII* (Lisbon 1999), 47.

108. ANTT, IL, no. 104, 211v–212v.

109. My emphasis.

110. "[M]orrio quemado vivo." ANTT, IL, no. 104, 213v.

111. Baião, *Inquisição em Portugal e no Brasil*, 231.

112. Ibid., 260.

113. Two of them were doing military service in the Indies.

114. There is no evidence that any of the founders of this confraternity, which was uncovered by the Inquisition, had known Diogo personally. See J. M. de Almeida Saraiva de Carvalho, "The Fellowship of St. Diogo: New Christian Judaisers in Coimbra in the Early Seventeenth Century" (Ph.D. dissertation, University of Leeds, 1990), 43–79; Teixera, *Antonio Homem*, 155–159, 161–164, 184–187, 206; Andrade, *Confraria de S. Diogo*.

115. See Elvira Cunha Azevedo Mea, "Frei Diogo d'Assunção, o martir marano," *Proceedings of the Eleventh World Congress of Jewish Studies*, Division B, vol. 1 (Jerusalem 1994), 114.

116. See Paul Hauben, "Reform and Counter-Reform: The Case of the Spanish Heretics," in Theodore Rabb and Jerrold Siegel, eds., *Action and Conviction in Early Modern Europe: Essays in Memory of E. H. Harbison* (Princeton 1969), 164. See also the interesting cases of two Spaniards who left the Peninsula and found social and ideological support in Spanish Protestant conventicles abroad, before returning to Spain, where they were burned alive as defiant Protestants: John E. Longhurst, "Julián Hernández, Protestant Martyr," *BHR* 20 (1960), 90–118; and José I. Tellechea Idígoras, "Francisco de San Román, un mártir protestante burgalés (1542)," *Cuadernos de Investigación Histórica* 7 (1984), 223–260.

117. "[E] asim mais disse elle confitente q nas religiões não avia a sanctidade q de for a parecia, e q algũs frades das religiões terião tambem pera si estas mesmas cousas q elle confitente pera si tinha, mas q porq nas religiões comião e bebião e porq não inquietarem o não manifestarião asi como elle confitente manifestava ali a elle ditto Diogo de Sousa." ANTT, IL, no. 104, 107r–v.

118. "[Que] muitos avia q conhecião todas estas cousas mas q por comerem, e viverem, sofrião" (ANTT, IL, no. 104, 5a); "muitas pessoas avia q conhecião e sabião estas verdades cousas q elle denunciado dizia, mas q por comerem e viverem sofrião" (ibid., 14b).

119. Martinho do Amor de Deos, *Escola de penitencia, caminho de perfeição, Estrada secura para a vida eternal, chronica da santa provincial de S. Antonio da regular e estreita observancia da Ordem do Serafico Patriarca S. Francisco, no Instituto Capucho neste reyno de Portugal* (Lisbon 1740), Libro I, 120–153. I have studied a copy of this work at Houghton Library. My thanks to Luisa França Luzio for bringing the work to my attention.

120. The most detailed description of the Capuchins in the context of Portuguese religious life in the sixteenth century is Silva Dias, *Correntes de sentimento religioso*, esp. chs. 2, 5, 8, 9.

121. Silva Dias, *Correntes de sentimento religioso*, 514. Cf. Baião, *Inquisição em Portugal e no Brasil*, 145, 150, 151; António Baião, *Episódios dramaticos da Inquisição Portuguesa*, 3 vols. (Lisbon 1992), 1:17–19.

122. On the theme of Jesus as a fraud, see Morton Smith, *Jesus the Magician* (New York 1977). By the sixteenth century, skeptics were embroidering on the idea that Moses, Jesus, and Mohammed were all imposters. See Silvia Berti, "Unmasking the Truth: The Theme of Imposture in Early Modern European Culture, 1660–1730," in James E. Force and David S. Katz, eds., *Everything Connects: In Conference with Richard H. Popkin* (Leiden 1999), 21–36.

123. See, in particular, Richard Popkin, "The Third Force in Seventeenth-Century

Thought: Scepticism, Science and Millenarianism," in idem, *The Third Force in Seventeenth-Century Thought* (Leiden 1992), 90–119.

124. Ibid., 95.

5. A CONVERSO SURGEON IN THE VICEROYALTY OF PERU

1. Fittingly, the most important document pertaining to his case has been published not once but twice. The full dossier compiled by the Lima tribunal is not extant. The summary (*relación*) sent to the Suprema was published, along with three letters by the prisoner, in García de Proodian, *Los Judíos en America*, 340–387; they were published subsequently, along with some additional records pertaining to the case, in Günter Böhm, *Historia de los judíos en Chile*, vol. 1, *El Bachiller Francisco Maldonado de Silva, 1592–1639* (Santiago de Chile 1984) [henceforth *FMS*], 219–325. Well before this, lengthy passages from the trial summary were published by José Toribio Medina in his *El Tribunal del Santo Oficio de la Inquisición en las provincias del Plata* (Buenos Aires 1945), 175–202, and again in his *Historia del Santo Oficio de la Inquisición en Chile* (Santiago de Chile 1952), 341–356, 370. The original set of summaries can be examined at the AHN, Inq., Libro 1031.

2. Although his reading habits indicate he was highly educated, Diego Núñes de Silva apparently did not complete university training for a degree, since his name is always mentioned in documents without a title. (The Inquisition—and Spanish officialdom in general—invariably mentioned the titles of persons who had received degrees—an important marker of status.)

3. It was relatively easy for Portuguese in useful occupations to enter Spanish America, either legally or illegally. See Harry E. Cross, "Commerce and Orthodoxy: A Spanish Response to Portuguese Commercial Penetration in the Viceroyalty of Peru, 1580–1640," *The Americas* 35 (1978), 152–153. The Inquisition was soon concerned about such émigrés. A letter of the Lima tribunal of 1611 complained of the entry of "mucha gente portuguesa de la nación hebrea y otras personas extranjeras sospechosas en nuestra sancta fee" through Buenos Aires and the province of Río de la Plata, and sought to block their entry. See Günter Böhm, *Los judíos en Chile durante la Colonia* (Santiago de Chile 1948), 123–124. For a more detailed discussion of the flow of Portuguese into Río de la Plata, and efforts to prevent it, see Medina, *Inquisición en las provincias del Plata*, 158–165.

4. His original name was presumably Diogo Nunes da Silva.

5. See Paulino Castañeda Delgado and Pilar Hernández Aparicio, *La Inquisición de Lima*, 3 vols. (Madrid 1989–1998), 1: 419.

6. The present-day city of San Miguel de Tucumán is not at the original site. The town was relocated in 1685, to gain access to a purer source of water.

7. See Medina, *Inquisición en las provincias del Plata*, 141–142. It is worth noting that one such settler, Diego López, apparently escaped to Tucumán after his father and uncle were burned at the stake in Lisbon. See ibid., 172. He was denounced to the Inquisition for judaizing, and may have been the same person as the Diego López de Fonseca who was burned at the stake on the same occasion as Maldonado de Silva. (See Montesinos, *Auto de la fe celebrado en Lima*, 21.)

8. See the chapter on "Buenos Aires, Tucumán and the River Plate Route" in Jonathan Israel, *Diasporas within a Diaspora: Jews, Crypto-Jews and the World Maritime Empires (1540–1740)* (Leiden 2002), 125–150. See also Cross, "Commerce and Orthodoxy."

9. Prior to the installation of Antonio Ordoñez y Flores as inquisitor in February, 1594,

the Lima tribunal's activity was focused on errant clerics and the occasional—usually foreign —Protestant. See José Toribio Medina, *Historia del Tribunal del Santo Oficio de la Inquisición de Lima (1569–1820)*, 2 vols. (Santiago de Chile 1956), 1: 1–301.

10. Summaries of their trials are extant: AHN, Inq., Libro 1029, fos. 52v–53v, and AHN, Inq., Libro 1029, fos. 55v–57r, respectively. These men are also named as witnesses against Núñez de Silva in a document about the latter's trial recorded after the latter was sentenced by the Inquisition. See Böhm, *FMS*, 219.

11. The name that appears in the trial summary is the Spanish form of the name, "Dionisio Cartujano."

12. For two discussions of crypto-Jewish reading of Christian sources, see Gitlitz, *Secrecy and Deceit*, 429–432; Yerushalmi, *Spanish Court*, 271–301.

13. Böhm, *FMS*, 219.

14. A lack of development in the young Diego might conceivably suggest why it was the younger son, Francisco, who inherited his father's library and who became responsible for the support of his two unmarried sisters after his father's death in 1616. On the other hand, Francisco's older brother disappears from the record after 1605, and he may have moved to other parts or died.

15. Böhm must be in error in stating that he was born around 1584. See Böhm, *FMS*, 8, 21, and compare it to the Inquisition document, ibid., 219.

16. In fact, a papal brief pardoning Portuguese New Christians was issued on August 23, 1604. (The Portuguese New Christians paid a huge sum for this dispensation.) It empowered religious authorities to reconcile all Portuguese New Christians, wherever they lived (including those in the hands of Spanish tribunals), with sentences of spiritual penances alone. It included all persons who were on trial, or who had been found guilty but whose sentences had not yet been published. Although the brief was not formally issued until January 16, 1605, a royal cédula was issued in October of 1604 prohibiting the sentencing of Portuguese New Christians until the brief took effect. On this *perdon general*, see Lea, *Spanish Inquisition* 3: 267–268.

17. See Castañeda Delgado and Hernández Aparicio, *Inquisición de Lima*, 1: 425.

18. Böhm, *FMS*, 11.

19. The rather brief Inquisition records on the trials of Diego Núñez de Silva and his son Diego have been published in Böhm, *FMS*, 217–224. Except where otherwise noted, the account I have given is drawn from this material.

20. See Böhm, *FMS*, 7–8 n. 14; Medina, *Inquisicón de Lima*, 1: 337.

21. AHN, Inq., Libro 1029, fos. 322r–324r. The case is mentioned in Castañeda Delgado and Hernández Aparicio, *Inquisición de Lima* 1: 434–435; Böhm, *FMS*, 219; Medina, *Inquisición de Lima*, 1: 338.

22. This was one of the works that the converso physicians Isaac Cardoso and Isaac Orobio de Castro would examine in Spain a generation later, as part of their own Jewish self-education (Yerushalmi, *From Spanish Court*, 288; Kaplan, *From Christianity*, 114). Interestingly, it was also studied by the antitrinitarian heretic Michael Servetus. (See Jerome Friedman, *Michael Servetus: A Case Study in Total Heresy* [Geneva 1978], 129.)

23. There is no doubt about his access to it. A copy of the *Scrutinium* was listed in the Inquisition's inventory of the books Francisco Maldonado de Silva possessed, confiscated after his arrest in 1627 (Böhm, *FMS*, 231).

24. On Francisco's "conversion" in Callao see the testimony from his first audience, Böhm, *FMS*, 285–286.

25. Although he was invariably titled *bachiller,* he had not necessarily completed his university studies. On the fluid use of degree titles in colonial Peru, see James Lockhart, *Spanish Peru, 1532–1560: A Social History* (2nd ed., Madison 1994), 69.

26. See Böhm, *FMS,* 29–30.

27. He later testified that he and his siblings had inherited this collection of over a hundred books, but that it remained in his possession—one would assume, because of his practice of medicine and his intellectual interests. See the record of Maldonado's account of his property on July 23, 1627, in Böhm, *FMS,* 227.

28. See Böhm, *FMS,* 30.

29. See Böhm, *FMS,* 31–32.

30. See the marriage contract signed by Francisco Maldonado de Silva on September 3, 1622, in Böhm, *FMS,* 243.

31. On the sisters see Böhm, *FMS,* 53–54nn61,62. Felipa, who was fifteen years old when her father was reconciled, certainly could not have expected a dowry, which would have allowed her to join a convent or marry. Isabel, four years Felipa's senior, conceivably married before her father's arrest.

32. On Iberian beatas, see Mary Elizabeth Perry, "Beatas and the Inquisition in Early Modern Seville," in Stephen Haliczer, ed., *Inquisition and Society in Early Modern Europe* (Totowa, NJ 1987), 147–168.

33. The first item in the inventory of Francisco Maldonado de Silva's sequestered property is listed as "estas casas con lo edificado en ellas y solar." It is followed by a brief description of four slaves. Böhm, *FMS,* 231.

34. Böhm, *FMS,* 287.

35. Castañeda Delgado and Hernández Aparicio, *Inquisición de Lima* 1: 436, 436nn89,90.

36. Böhm, *FMS,* 281–282.

37. "[Q]ue en ella estaba su vida o su muerte."

38. This is presumably a reference to Jesus's presence and activity at the wedding at Cana. See John 2: 1–11. It may also allude to the accusation that Jesus was "a glutton and a drunkard" in Mt. 11:19.

39. It is not clear on this last point whether she was reporting what he said to her at the baths or during a conversation after they returned to Santiago.

40. For the notary's account of his sister's testimony, see Böhm, *FMS,* 281–282.

41. See Böhm's inferences, Böhm, *FMS,* 57–58.

42. Böhm, *FMS,* 234.

43. Böhm's date of March 2 (*FMS,* 282) is not correct.

44. Böhm, *FMS,* 282–283.

45. Böhm, *FMS,* 283–284.

46. Böhm, *FMS,* 285. When interrogated by the *receptor general* about his possessions, separately but on the same day, he also refused to take an oath on a crucifix (Böhm, *FMS,* 227).

47. Böhm, *FMS,* 285–286.

48. For the account of the second audience, see Böhm, *FMS,* 285–286.

49. Presumably Exod. 20: 8–11.

50. That is, "el salmo que comiença *Ut quid Deus repulisti infinem*"—Psalm 73 of the Vulgate. Böhm, *FMS,* 287.

51. The trial summary cites the passage as "el cantico que dixo dios a Moises en el

Deuteronomio capitulo 30 que comiença *Audite celi quae locor,*" in fact a reference to Deuteronomy 32.

52. It may be remembered that Luis Carvajal memorized the "prophecies of Esdras."

53. José Toribio Medina published an extract from this witness's trial. See Medina, *Tribunal del Santo Oficio en las Provincias del Plata, 182–184n1.*

54. For the mulatta's testimony, see Böhm, *FMS,* 284. It seems curious that Maldonado would have asked a strange woman about this person. However, Montesinos makes a point of noting that in Lima the Portuguese-born Cuaresma treated not only "all those of the Hebrew nation" but also "los negros y negras boçales," so that he may have been well-known among Limeños of African descent. Perhaps for this reason Maldonado ventured to find out from her whether he had been arrested. It is likely that Cuaresma, who was seventy years old when he was burned at the stake as a negativo after the auto of 1639, belonged to the judaizing network to which his father had belonged prior to his arrest. See Böhm, *FMS,* 423. (Since this is the age given in the "Publicación del auto de la fe" of the Inquisition, it is presumably correct. He is listed as being forty-seven years old in 1635, by Alfonso Quiroz, "La expropriación inquisitorial de cristianos nuevos portugueses en Los Reyes, Cartagena y México, 1635–1649," *Historica* [Peru] 10 [1986], 283–284.)

55. And that had also drawn the attention of Diogo d'Assumpção.

56. The date is given correctly in the entry for October 5 (Böhm, *FMS,* 288).

57. He is presumably wrong in citing Deuteronomy. He is probably alluding to Lev. 23:27, "adfligetisque animas vestras"—"you shall afflict your souls."

58. "[U]n silicio para ceñir el cuerpo, de cerdas" (Böhm, *FMS,* 231).

59. Böhm, *FMS,* 287. It is interesting that the ex-converso apologist Isaac Cardoso, who underwent adult circumcision, termed that rite "a mysterious sacrifice, to mortify the flesh and lessen the sensual impulses." See Yerushalmi, *Spanish Court,* 380.

60. See Böhm, *FMS,* 284.

61. Böhm, *FMS,* 287–288. The inquisitors indeed found among Maldonado's papers a notebook enclosed in vellum "with some Jewish prayers" and with a calendar of the festivals of the Law of Moses, presumably copied from Génebrard's book. Böhm, *FMS,* 284.

62. Gilbert Génebrard, *Psalmi Davidis, calendario Hebraeo, Syro, Graeco, Latino . . .* (Lyon 1592), 1v.

63. Böhm, *FMS,* 288.

64. For details on these figures see Böhm, *FMS,* 91; Medina, *Inquisición en Chile,* 87–88.

65. Böhm, *FMS,* 288.

66. They were held on Jan. 13, Feb. 29, Nov. 9, and Nov. 16.

67. Böhm, *FMS,* 289.

68. Böhm, *FMS,* 289.

69. Alonso de Maldonado, *Chronica universal de todas las naciones y tiempos . . .* (Madrid 1624). See the chapter on the hebdomad, folios 25r–38r.

70. In the summary, "*haternum.*"

71. Like the dossier itself, they have not been preserved.

72. Böhm, *FMS,* 290.

73. So we are informed by Montesinos's account of the auto, Montesino, *El auto da la fè,* 21v.

74. The text has the ambiguous expression "como los Nazarenos," which may be why this term—which may also mean *Nazarene*—was picked up by Portuguese Jews in the

diaspora. See Miriam Bodian, "Death at the Stake as Seen in the Northern Sephardi Diaspora" (Hebrew), *Pe'amim* 75 (Spring 1998), 49 n. 6.

75. Montesinos, *El auto de la fe*, 21v.

76. The biblical source is Num. 6: 1–21.

77. Böhm, *FMS*, 291.

78. See Böhm, *FMS*, 129–132; Medina, *Inquisición de Lima*, 2: 93–97.

79. One was accused of bigamy, the other was a priest who was accused of concubinage.

80. Both copies of the letter, neither complete to the end, have been preserved. They differ only slightly. They are published with a Spanish translation in Böhm, *FMS*, 305–325.

81. Böhm, *FMS*, 291.

82. For a description of the psychic factors involved, see Bodian, "'Men of the Nation,'" 60–63.

83. Böhm, *FMS*, 305 (Spanish translation, 311–312).

84. In the Vulgate; Psalm 110 in the Hebrew Bible.

85. The full Hebrew phrase is "*ne'um adonai le-adoni.*" See Lasker, *Jewish Philosophical Polemics*, 4, 173n. 14.

86. That is, the copy of the letter that does not break off earlier. For the three arguments, see Böhm, *FMS*, 313–316.

87. See Jean-Pierre Tardieu, *L'inquisition de Lima et les hérétiques étrangers (XVIe–XVIIe siècles)* (Paris 1995).

88. See Medina, *Inquisición de Lima*, 2: 93.

89. The sentencia has been published in Medina, *Inquisición de Lima*, 2: 127–154. On the Complicidad Grande sentencing and its wider context see also Cross, "Commerce and Orthodoxy," 151–167. Inquisitorial documents on the episode are published in Böhm, *FMS*, 327–374.

90. For one thing, the confessions, as summarized in the sentencias, are for the most part suspiciously general and superficial. Irene Silverblatt, "New Christians and New World Fears in Seventeenth-Century Peru," *Comparative Studies of Society and History* 42 (2000), 524–546, has emphasized the psycho-social anxieties that lay behind the mass arrests. Vividly reflecting the atmosphere of hostility to Portuguese New Christians is the Lima tribunal's letter to the Suprema of May 18, 1636. It opens by noting that "For about six to eight years in these parts, a great many Portuguese have entered this kingdom of Peru. . . . In this city there is much grumbling about them. . . . They have made themselves the masters over trade; the street they call 'the Merchants' Street' became almost all theirs . . . They owned all the dry-goods stores, all the stalls where they sold their goods. . . . They took over the retail trade, so that from gold brocade to sackcloth, from diamonds to cumin seed, and from the lowest black slave from Guinea to the most precious pearl, [everything] passes through their hands. . . ." and so on. (The letter is published in Böhm, *FMS*, 345–367.) But most scholars have stressed the self-serving financial motives of the Inquisition. Only two of the sixty-three persons sentenced were women (a fact that scholars have not noted). Forty-seven of them were engaged in commercial activity of some kind, and some of them were extremely wealthy. José Toribio Medina notes the violence with which the inquisitors, "ávidos del dinero de sus víctimas," extorted confessions from the accused. See Medina, *Tribunal del Santo Oficio en las Provincias del Plata*, 197. The goods confiscated from the wealthiest of the victims alone, Manuel Bautista Pérez, yielded the tribunal the huge sum of 212,869 pesos. Overall, the confiscations made the Lima tribunal among the wealthiest of the Spanish Inquisition. See René Millar Corbacho, "Las confiscaciones de la Inquisición de Lima a los comerciantes de origen judeo-portugués de 'La Gran Complicidad' de 1635,"

Revista de Indias 43 (1983), 27–58; Quiroz, "La expropriación inquisitorial," 237–303. It should also be noted, however, that political factors played into the hands of the Inquisition in this episode: Spanish anger at the successful revolt of Portugal against Spanish domination in 1640; the fall of Count-Duke Olivares, a supporter of Portuguese New Christians, in 1643; and fears of a Dutch attack aided and abetted by the "Portuguese."

91. The passage refers to the "auto de 23 de Henero de 639," and was thus entered after Maldonado's death. See Böhm, *FMS*, 291. Maldonado's temporary deafness is also mentioned in the account of the auto, Montesinos, *El auto de la fe*, 31v.

92. See Lea, *Spanish Inquisition*, 2: 497–498. On the particular issue of dowries, see Lea, *Spanish Inquisition*, index, "Dowry of Catholic wife."

93. Böhm, *FMS*, 241–242.

94. She asked that her request be granted "por ser como es grande la necesidad que padezco y estar enferma no poder trabajar para mi sustento y el de mis hijos que tengo de mi marido."

95. Böhm, *FMS*, 247.

96. Böhm, *FMS*, 248.

97. See Böhm, *FMS*, 252, 262, 264.

98. Böhm, *FMS*, 257, 269.

99. Böhm, *FMS*, 292.

100. It may be recalled that this widely disseminated book had been used by Luis Carvajal.

101. Böhm, *FMS*, 418.

102. Montesinos, *El auto de la fe*, 21v. Isaac Cardoso includes it in his brief narrative of the career of Maldonado de Silva which is quoted in chapter 2 above; it is found in his *Excelencias de los Hebreos*, 323–324.

103. For the account of the public notification, see Fernando de Montesinos, *Auto de la fe*, 2r–3v.

104. Böhm, *FMS*, 292.

105. See Böhm, *FMS*, 292, 301.

106. He would have been relying on such passages as Hosea 3:5, Ezekiel 34: 23–24, and Amos 9:12.

107. The term I have translated "contradiction" is transcribed "opinión" by Böhm; Nathan Wachtel corrects to "oposición": See Wachtel, *La foi du souvenir*, 393.

108. Sirach 4:30 in the Vulgate; Sirach 5:13–14 in the Vulgate.

109. Actually the verse is Amos 3:7.

110. The letter is published in Böhm, *FMS*, 295–301.

111. Montesinos, *Auto de la fe*, 3v–5r.

112. Ibid., 7r.

113. Ibid., 23r–24r.

114. Ibid., 21v–22r.

115. Böhm, *FMS*, 292.

116. Medina, *Inquisición de Lima*, 1: 337.

117. Ibid., 1: 52–55.

118. Ibid., 1: 150–156.

119. Wachtel, *La foi du souvenir.*

120. The inventory is published in Böhm, *FMS*, 231–232.

121. The work was published in several editions, the first in Strasburg in 1469, the last in Burgos in 1591.

122. As he wrote, "Per scrutinium scripturarum contra iudaeos non est quaerendus sensus mysticus, sed solum literalis." Cited in Nicolás López Martínez, "Teología de controversia sobre judíos y judaizantes españoles del siglo XV: Ambientación y principales escritos," *Anuario de historia de la iglesia* 1 (1992), 61. Incidentally, Santa María also made use in this work of talmudic texts, which he cited in support of Christian doctrines. One wonders how Maldonado de Silva read these passages.

123. To be sure, with the exception of Pablo de Santa María's *Scrutinium Scripturarum*, there is no way of knowing which of the books sequestered at the time of Francisco Maldonado's arrest were originally his father's and which he acquired himself after his practice began to flourish. But this makes little difference in terms of trying to determine what was available to him.

124. Gitlitz, *Secrecy and Deceit*, 436.

125. Perhaps he got rid of it at some point after his failed approach to his sister Isabel, or it may simply be missing from the inventory.

126. Ambrosio Calepino's dictionary was first printed in Reggio in 1502, but was printed in numerous subsequent and expanded editions, some of them including Hebrew terms.

127. Francisco's older brother Diego was born in 1579. If his father "revealed" himself to this older son when the latter was seventeen or eighteen, and afterwards had Álvaro Núñez reveal himself to him, this would place the visit of Diego Núñez de Silva's fellow crypto-judaizer in 1596 or thereafter.

128. See Castañeda Delgado and Hernández Aparicio, *Inquisición de Lima*, 1: 433.

129. Ibid., 1: 433–434.

130. See Samuel Morell, "The Samson Nazirite Vow in the Sixteenth Century," *AJS Review*, 14 (1989), especially 230–232.

131. Joseph Wittreich, *Interpreting "Samson Agonistes"* (Princeton 1986), xv. On this theme, see also Watson Kirkconnell, *That Invincible Samson: The Theme of Samson Agonistes in World Literature with Translations of the Major Analogues* (Toronto 1964); and F. Michael Krouse, *Milton's Samson and the Christian Tradition* (Princeton 1949).

132. Antonio Enríquez Gómez, *Sánson Nazareno* (Rouen 1656). The work was published only after Enríquez Gómez had returned to Spain under an assumed name. A critical edition of the work has recently been published by María del Carmen Artigas (Madrid 1999).

133. Juan Pérez de Montalbán's *El valiente Nazareno Sanson*, published in Madrid in 1638, and the play *Sanson*, written by Francisco de Rojas y Zorilla and performed in Madrid in 1641, but probably never printed.

134. Antonio Enríquez Gómez, *Romance al divín mártyr, Judá Creyente [don Lope de Vera y Alarcon] martirizado en Valladolid por la Inquisición*, Timothy Oelman, ed. (London and Toronto 1986), 142, lines 10–14. Not surprisingly, the Maccabees were frequently invoked in converso martyrology. See, inter alia, ibid., 164, line 18; Daniel Levi de Barrios, *Contra la verdad no hay fuerza* (Amsterdam n.d.), 147.

135. Enríquez Gómez, *Romance*, 148, lines 275–278.

6. A Hebrew Scholar at the University of Salamanca

1. There was evidently some testimony indicating that Lope de Vera had a minor degree of Jewish ancestry, but this appears to have been mere rumor.

2. An explicit report of Lope de Vera's lack of success comes from a hostile account

summarized by Cecil Roth, "Le chant du cygne de Don Lope de Vera," *REJ* 97 (1934), 112–113. According to the author, the candidate was rejected because he defended Hebrew as being superior to all other languages. It is worth noting that Salamanca was at the time the only university in Spain where Hebrew was taught. Humanist learning, including the study of Hebrew, had a distinguished history at Salamanca; but the scholastic backlash against humanist learning there resulted in a series of inquisitorial trials in the 1570s. Among the theologians tried was Fray Luis de León. On these trials see Lea, *History of the Inquisition of Spain*, 4: 149–168; Miguel de la Pinta Llorente, *Procesos inquisitoriales contra los catedráticos hebraístas de Salamanca: Gaspar de Grajal, Martínez de Cantalapiedra, y Fr. Luis de León* (Madrid 1925); idem, *Proceso criminal contra el hebraísta salmantino Martín Martínez de Cantalapiedra* (Madrid 1946).

3. Archivo Histórico Nacional [henceforth AHN], Inquisición, Legajo 2135, No. 15, fos. 49r–51r (1639); No. 16, fols. 15r–19r (1641); No. 17, fos. 24v–31r (1643); No. 18, in two parts, 4v–6r, 12v–22r (1643); No. 19, 5v–7r (1644). Each summary offers an account of the trial from the time of arrest, repeating contents of earlier summaries, but sometimes, at unpredictable junctures, offering greater detail. The summaries were studied by Lea, *History of the Inquisition*, 3: 294–295.

4. Archivo Diocesana de Cuenca [henceforth ADC], Inquisición 458/6317. I am grateful to Kenneth Brown for supplying me with a photocopy of this forty-page document and his transcription. The text is unpaginated so I will refer to the manuscript pages in order, starting from page one. Some of the testimony has been presented uncritically in Juan Blazquez Miguel, *San Clemente y la Inquisición de Cuenca* (Madrid 1988).

5. On the rather free movement of North African Jews in Spain, see García-Arenal and Wiegers, *Man of Three Worlds*, esp. 4–10, 14–20.

6. ADC, Inq. 458/6317, 7.

7. Holy Thursday, commemorating the day of the Last Supper and thus also the institution of the Eucharist, was one of the annual processions in which the host was regularly carried in procession, encased in an ornately decorated vessel and accompanied by dignitaries and other townspeople. Don Lope could not have been ignorant of what was happening in the street outside his home.

8. ADC, Inq. 458/6317, 12–13. If the prisoner indeed said this, he may of course have been referring to the tongue wagging set off by his father's fetching him home.

9. ADC, Inq. 458/6317, 14–15 (Cristóbal Angel); 16–17 (Diego de Ávalos).

10. ADC, Inq. 458/6317, 8.

11. Hearsay evidence was gathered from five other witnesses.

12. See the letter published in A. S. Halkin, "A *Contra Christianos* by a Marrano," in Moshe Davis, ed., *Mordecai M. Kaplan: Jubilee Volume on the Occasion of His Seventieth Birthday* (New York 1953), 405.

13. "El mesías abrá de venir y volver por el estado Judaico" (AHN Inq., Legajo 2135, No. 17, 24r). The statement is ambiguous, but I concur with Beinart's suggestion as to its meaning. See Haim Beinart, "The Convert Lope de Vera y Alarcón and His Martyrdom as Judah Creyente" (Hebrew), in Z. Malachi, ed., *Sefer yovel li-khevod Aharon Mirski* [Lod 1989], 32n5.

14. This and the previous statement appear only in the last of the summaries, AHN Inq., Legajo 2135, No. 19, 6r. It is not entirely clear whether this statement was made by the first or second witness, since the testimony of the two is conflated in this final summary.

15. The theme of the nobility of Jewish blood was not uncommon in crypto-Jewish and Portuguese-Jewish thinking. See Bodian, *Hebrews of the Portuguese Nation*, 86–89. Since it

is evident that Lope de Vera had contact with Portuguese converso students, he may have heard this claim from one or more of them.

16. The reference is to the *Annotationes in Novum Testamentum,* first printed in 1516, which Erasmus successively expanded in four subsequent editions. Among other things, this work pointed out errors in the Latin translation of the Greek text, compared New Testament quotations from the Old Testament to the original Hebrew passages, and argued for the need to arrive at a proper understanding of the literal sense of Scripture. See Jerry Bentley, "Erasmus' *Annotationes in Novum Testamentum* and the Textual Criticism of the Gospels," *Archiv für Reformationsgeschichte* 67 (1976), 33–53.

17. While the summaries refer to this work only as the *"Embajada de Rabid Dabid"* or the *"Itinerario de Rabid David,"* Beinart's identification of the work as the diary of David Reuveni seems justified by Lope de Vera's knowledge of certain contents of this work, particularly the story of the Sambation River (of which more later). See Haim Beinart, "The Convert Lope de Vera y Alarcón," 37.

18. AHN Inq., Legajo 2135, No. 16, 16v–17r.

19. If Lope de Vera had read Espina's *Fortalitium fidei,* as he later testified, he would have been acquainted with the sixth section of the third book, cataloguing Jewish arguments for the "impossibility" of a number of Christian doctrines.

20. "[Y] que tenía un natural tan vario y frágil que aviendo savido las lenguas hebrea y aráviga fácilmente se inclinara a seguir la ley de los judíos o la secta de los moros y se hallava tan confuso con las varias lecturas que si se viera entre moros no savía si siguiera su ley y se apartara de la de cristo por el de verse excomulgado." This statement appears in only two summaries, AHN Inq., Legajo 2135, No. 17, 25v and, with minor orthographic variations, No. 18a, 13r.

21. Beinart, however, believes the two were different persons, though it is unclear why. See Beinart, "The Convert Lope de Vera y Alarcón," 35.

22. See Deut. 13: 1–5. This passage was the second of nine reasons Luis Carvajal gave for adhering to the Law of Moses. See appendix B.

23. AHN Inq., Legajo 2135, No. 17, 25v; No. 18a, 13r–14r.

24. " . . . el dho complice trajo un lugar de un salmo que dice nolite fieri sicut equus et mulus quibus non est intelectu [*sic*], el qual declaro diciendo que dios decia que no abiamos de subjetar el entendimiento sicut equs, et mulus, a las cosas que parecen inpusibles al entendimiento" (AHN Inq., Legajo 2135, No. 17, 25v, and cf. No. 18, 13r). It is worth noting that Antonio Vaez Castelblanco (= Antonio Vaez Tirado), a brother of one of the key judaizers in New Spain in the 1630s, who was himself burned at the stake as a dogmatizer, said that Christians died as if they were beasts, citing the same psalm, "*Sicut equus et mulus quibus non est intellectus* [like a horse and mule lacking in intelligence]," and that Jews, in contrast, "as a rational people . . . would go to enjoy eternal rest with the God of Israel." ("Dezia que los Christianos morian y acabavan como vestias, alegando . . . las palabras de David: *Sicut equus, et mulus, quibus non est intellectus,* y que los judios como gente [segun el dezia] racional, y de discurso iban a gozar de descansos eternos con el Dios de Israel.") Matías de Bocanegra, *Auto general de la fee: celebrado . . . en la . . . ciudad de Mexico . . . Dominica in albis 11 de abril de 1649 . . .* (Mexico 1649), unpaginated.

25. Beinart understands the passage concerning avoidance of meat and confession as referring to the student, but this seems to me a problematic reading. See Beinart, "The Convert Lope de Vera y Alarcón," 36. For the passage in question, see AHN Inq., Legajo 2135, No. 17, 26r.

26. "[E]l licionario de David Rabid tahuien" (AHN Inq., Legajo 2135, No. 17, 26r;

and see No. 18a, 14v). I accept Beinart's identification of this work, despite the notary's garbled rendering of its author's name, since the Sambation River legend does indeed figure in this work. Apparently the University of Salamanca library possessed a manuscript copy of the diary.

27. "[E]l Itenerario de Raví David Sarraceabat" (AHN Inq., Legajo 2135, No. 17, 26r; and see No. 18a, 14v). Beinart understands "Sarraceabat" as the notary's effort to render "*sar tseva'ot.*"

28. "[P]or dios que me tengo de yr fuera de españa a rrenegar o Judayçar" (AHN Inq., Legajo 2135, No. 18, 15r).

29. On Espina's *Fortalitium fidei*, see Alisa Meyuhas Ginio, "The Fortress of Faith—At the End of the West: Alonso de Espina and his *Fortalitium Fidei*," in Ora Limor and Guy Stroumsa, eds., *Contra Iudaeos: Ancient and Medieval Polemics Between Christians and Jews* (Tübingen 1996), 215–237.

30. Kaplan, *From Christianity*, 235–236.

31. These appear in the third of the five books that comprise this work, a section that is devoted to responding to Jewish arguments. Alonso de Espina, *Fortalitium fidei* (Nuremberg [1485]), esp. 47r–54v.

32. AHN Inq., Legajo 2135, No. 17, 26v places it on July 5; No. 18, 15r, on July 9.

33. Galatino's work *De Arcanis Catholicae Veritatis* (1516) was popular and had been printed in several editions.

34. "[Q]ue no puede negar la dubda y confusión en que se hallava" (AHN Inq., Legajo 2135, No. 17, 26v).

35. AHN Inq., Legajo 2135, No. 17, 26v, has July 12; No. 18, 15v, has July 11.

36. See Num. 21:8 and John 3:14.

37. On the three *moniciones,* see Lea, *Spanish Inquisition,* 3: 38–39.

38. The book is identified as *hipachivi tini in arati eterodoxi* (AHN Inq., Legajo 2135, No. 17, 26v); and in the following summary as *hepachibi = tine ynbati = exetudos =* (No. 18, 16r). Beinart contends that this is a rhymed work on astronomy by an ancient Greek poet named Artos. See Beinart, "The Convert Lope de Vera y Alarcón," 37 n. 25.

39. "*[V]enundatur parisis apud*" (AHN Inq., Legajo 2135, No. 17, 26v); "*benundatur payses apud exidio gerum* que al pricipio esta traducido en latín" (No. 18a, 16r).

40. AHN Inq., Legajo 2135, No. 16, 18r gives the date as March 15; No. 17, 26v gives it as March 19. The former is evidently correct, because according to No. 17 the session continued on March 16.

41. The assent of a curador was required to validate the legal acts of a minor, that is, a defendant under the age of twenty-five.

42. AHN Inq., Legajo 2135, No. 17, 27v and No. 18, 17v give the date as June 13 but it was almost certainly July.

43. The belief that a noble Old Christian could not have become a judaizer without some physical link to the Jews reveals the intensity of racial paranoia in seventeenth-century Spain. Particularly interesting is the rationalization for Lope de Vera's judaizing offered by the virulently anti-Jewish author Francisco Torrejoncillo in a work written in 1673 and first printed in 1691. He claimed that it was at some point discovered that Lope de Vera had had a wet-nurse with "infected blood." See Torrejoncillo, *Centinela contra Judíos* (Barcelona 1731), 214.

44. AHN Inq., Legajo 2135, No. 17, 28r.

45. AHN Inq., Legajo 2135, No. 16, 19r gives the date as Oct 26; No. 17, 17v and No. 18a, 17v as October 28; No. 18b, 7v as October 18; No. 19, 6r as October 6.

46. Beinart, "The Convert Lope de Vera y Alarcón," 40. For the relevant passage in the manuscript that has been published, see David Reuveni, *The Story of David Hareuveni, Copied from the Oxford Manuscript* (Hebrew), A. Z. Aescoly, ed. (Jerusalem 1993), 34–47.

47. AHN Inq., Legajo 2135, No. 17, 28v–29r.

48. AHN Inq., Legajo 2135, No. 17, 28v–29r.

49. AHN Inq., Legajo 2135, No. 17, 29v gives the date as June 15; No. 18, 18v, gives it as June 29, which is presumably correct.

50. AHN Inq., Legajo 2135, No. 19, 6v mistakenly gives the date as July 19.

51. Maldonado de Silva was burned at the stake on January 23, 1639; Lope de Vera was arrested in June of that year. Given the notoriety of Francisco Maldonado de Silva even before his death, it is possible Lope de Vera had learned details of his career before his own arrest.

52. See *Story of David Hareuveni*, 93–94.

53. The trial summaries do not mention the full name the prisoner apparently adopted at this time, and by which he became known in the Portuguese-Jewish diaspora, namely, "Judah Creyente." This name may have become known through the reading of his sentencia at the auto-da-fé at which he was condemned.

54. November 15 (AHN Inq., Legajo 2135, No. 17, 31r), or November 19 (No. 18a, 19v).

55. AHN Inq., Legajo 2135, No. 19, 6v apparently errs in giving the date as November 29.

56. AHN Inq., Legajo 2135, No. 18a, 20r gives date as Jan 24; No. 19, 6v, as January 6.

57. The final summary (AHN Inq., Legajo 2135, No. 19, 6v–7r) notes that the statement Lope de Vera wrote was submitted to "los calificadores del Santo offiçio y a los de la conpañía de Jesus y a los de la Trinidad calçada que cada uno dio su Respuesta."

58. See the letter of a Jesuit dated January 16, 1644, in *Cartas de algunos PP. de la Compañia de Jesus entre los años de 1634 y 1648*, vol. 17 of *Memorial Histórico Español* 17 (Madrid 1863), 418–419. Cited in Barnett, "Two Documents," 230.

59. AHN Inq., Legajo 2135, No 18a, 22r gives date as January 27; No. 19, 7r, as January 25.

60. Barnett, "Two Documents," 231.

61. Benedict Spinoza, *The Letters* (Indianapolis and Cambridge 1995), #76, 343.

62. It has been published, with an English translation, by L. D. Barnett, "Two Documents," 235–239.

63. It was found in the British Museum and published in the 1920s. See Barnett, "Two Documents," 214, 234–235.

64. This seems odd, given that he was gagged. But Moscoso's letter reports that he cried out when the gag was removed—perhaps before his burning at the stake: "tuvo siempre puesta una mordasa por que no Blasfemase contra nuestra fe catolica y enxalsase la de Mosseh como dizia el tiempo que se la quitavan" (Barnett, "Two Documents," 237).

65. Barnett, "Two Documents," 236, English translation (which I have modified), 238.

66. Both Haim Beinart and Cecil Roth have given the date of his death as July 25, 1644 (Roth, "Chant du cygne," 101; Beinart, "The Convert Lope de Vera y Alárcon," 49). But this date is clearly not correct, since news of Lope de Vera's death had reached San Clemente by July 23, 1644. The reason some scholars have relied on the July 25 date is because "Don Lope de Vera, natural de San Clemente" is mentioned in an Inquisition document as having been relaxed at an auto-da-fé in Cordova on that date. See Blazquez Miguel, *San Clemente*, 63n. 27. For details of the record involved, see Pedro Rubio Merino, "Autos de fe de la

Inquisición de Cordoba durante el siglo XVII a traves de la documentación del Archivo de la Santa Iglesia Catedral de Sevilla," in Joaquim Pérez Villanueva, ed., *La Inquisición Española, Nueva Vision, Nuevas Horizontes* (Madrid 1980), 347. However, there is no evidence that Lope de Vera had been transferred to Cordova, and it is very clear from the many references in the set of testimonies from San Clemente that the auto was held in Valladolid, not in Cordova. Other dates scholars have given are June 25 or July 15. Lea saw documentation that persuaded him of the date June 25. See Lea, *History of the Inquisition,* 3: 293.

67. This is only one of the many statements placing of the auto-da-fé in Valladolid, significant because of scholarly speculation that Lope de Vera was burned at an auto in Cordova (see above note).

68. ADC, Inq. 458/6317, 19.

69. ADC, Inq. 458/6317, 20–21. Perhaps not surprisingly under the circumstances, shortly after this testimony a maidservant of Don Lope threatened, in the presence of another person, to reveal "aquello de los sábados." However, the testimony was less than persuasive, especially in view of the fact that it was common knowledge that the maidservant had been a lover of the senior Don Lope. ADC, Inq. 458/6317, 23–26.

70. I have consulted Ets Haim ms. 48A11, 48r–54v. I wish to thank Kenneth Brown for kindly sending me his transcription of this document.

71. Yosef Kaplan has discussed the letter of Pedro de Vera. See Kaplan, "The Role of Rabbi Moshe d'Aguilar in his Contacts with the Refugees from Spain and Portugal in the Seventeenth Century" (Hebrew), *Proceedings of the Sixth World Congress of Jewish Studies,* vol. 2 (Jerusalem 1975), 103–105.

72. Moshe Rafael d'Aguilar guided him to the passage in Tractate Kidushin 40b where the Sages defend R. Akiva's assertion that study (*talmud*) is more important than action (*ma'aseh*).

73. Moshe Rafael d'Aguilar explicates the passage in Bereshit Raba 38, which states that God is not able, "as it were," to overcome even idol worshippers, when there is peace and unity between them.

74. Moshe Rafael d'Aguilar again directed Pedro de Vera to the actual source, Tractate Yebamot 65b, and explicated it.

7. Echoes in the Portuguese-Jewish Diaspora

This chapter incorporates material that I have previously published in "Death at the Stake," *Pe'amim* 75 (1998), 66–104, and "In the Cross-Currents of the Reformation: Crypto-Jewish Martyrs of the Inquisition, 1570–1670," *PaP,* No. 176 (2002), 99–104.

1. See Martin Cohen, "Don Gregorio López: Friend of the Secret Jew," *Hebrew Union College Annual* 38 (1967), 259–284; Nalle, *Mad for God.*

2. The list of such conversos would include Juan Luis Vives, the brothers Juan and Francisco de Vergara, Isabel de la Cruz, Pedro Ruiz de Alcaraz, Alonso Gudiel, Alfonso de Zamora, Luis de León, and quite possibly Juan and Alfonso de Valdés.

3. See, inter alia, Jerome Friedman, "The Reformation and Jewish Antichristian Polemics," *BHR* 41 (1979), 83–97; and idem, "New Religious Alternatives," in Raymond Waddington and Arthur Williamson, eds., *The Expulsion of the Jews: 1492 and After* (New York and London 1994), 19–40. See also essays in J. van den Berg and E. G. E. van der Wall, eds., *Jewish-Christian Relations in the Seventeenth Century* (Dordrecht 1988); and Richard Popkin and Gordon Weiner, eds., *Jewish Christians and Christian Jews* (Dordrecht 1994). At least one major Jewish scholar outside the converso sphere, Leon de Modena, also

absorbed something of radical converso ideas. See Talya Fishman, *Shaking the Pillars of Exile* (Stanford 1997), index, "conversos," "Uriel da Costa."

4. Laureto, who joined antitrinitarian Anabaptist circles in Italy, fled at one point to Salonica, where he joined a community of Sephardi Jews and was circumcised. (He was soon disillusioned by rabbinic Judaism, however, and eventually recanted before the Venetian Inquisition in 1553.) See George Williams, "The Two Social Strands in Italian Anabaptism, ca. 1526–1565" in Lawrence Buck and Jonathan Zophy, eds., *The Social History of the Reformation* (Columbus, Ohio, 1972), 179–84.

5. According to one author, Simon Pecs (Péchi) and his group of anti-Trinitarians in Hungary turned to Judaism around 1600. See Esther Seidel, "Out of the Ghetto and into the Open Society: Conversion from the Renaissance to the Twentieth Century," in Walter Homulka, Walter Jacob and Esther Seidel, eds., *Not by Birth Alone: Conversion to Judaism* (London and Washington 1997), 41–42.

6. Antoine was born a Catholic in France but converted to Calvinism in his youth. His Hebrew and Old Testament studies (which included discussions with rabbis in Metz) led him to adopt Judaism of a sort, but he was rejected by cautious communal leaders when he sought to join a Jewish community in Italy. He died at the stake in Geneva in 1632. See S. Balitzer, "Nicolas Antoine," *REJ* 36 (1898), 161–196; Julien Weill, "Nicolas Antoine," *REJ* 37 (1898), 161–180; Bernard Lescaze, "La confession de foi de Nicolas Antoine (1632)," *Bulletin de la Societé d'Histoire et d'Archéologie de Genève* 14 (1970), 277–323; Elisabeth Labrousse, "Vie et mort de Nicolas Antoine," *Etudes Théologiques et Religieuses* 52 (1977), 421–433.

7. See Gerald Strauss, "A Seventeenth Century Conversion to Judaism: Two Letters from Benedictus Sperling to His Mother," *Jewish Social Studies* 36 (1974), 166–174. It should be said that the two letters, which constitute our only source of information about Sperling, reveal an eclectic and idiosyncratic set of ideas, many of which would not have been regarded as compatible with Judaism at all.

8. See Coudert, "Judaizing in the Seventeenth Century," 71–121. Writes Coudert, "[Späth] repeatedly argues that Christians have misunderstood and misinterpreted Old Testament prophecies. By showing that Old Testament prophecies are not fulfilled in the New Testament, Späth . . . effectively separated the Old and New Testaments, thus removing the historical and theological rationale for Christianity. Once this was done, it was possible for other questions to be asked" (ibid., 83).

9. See Martin Mulsow, "Cartesianism, Skepticism and Conversion to Judaism: The Case of Aaron d'Antan," in *SCJ*, 123–181.

10. See, inter alia, Robert Dán, "Isaac Troky and his 'Antitrinitarian' Sources" in idem, ed., *Occident and Orient: A Tribute to the Memory of A. Scheiber* (Budapest 1988), 69–82; Frank Manuel, *The Broken Staff: Judaism through Christian Eyes* (Cambridge, Mass. 1992), 51–107.

11. Carsten Wilke, "Conversion ou retour? La métamorphose du nouveau chrétien en juif portugais dans l'imaginaire sépharade du XVIIe siècle," in Esther Benbassa, ed., *Memoires juives d'Espagne et du Portugal* (Paris 1996), 57.

12. Wilke, "Conversion ou retour?" 53–67. Wilke emphasizes the imaginative origins of this type in a way that obscures the real historical manifestations of Old Christian conversion.

13. Bodian, *Hebrews of the Portuguese Nation*, 96–125. On the various cases of conflict, see Kaplan, *From Christianity*, 122–159; Miriam Bodian, "Amsterdam, Venice and the

Marrano Diaspora in the Seventeenth Century," *Dutch Jewish History* 2 (1989), 51–58; and on Spinoza, inter alia, Steven Nadler, *Spinoza: A Life* (Cambridge 1999), 116–154.

14. It is significant that Juan de Prado seems to have made a shift from crypto-Jewish beliefs to a deistic form of skepticism while still in the Peninsula. According to inquisitorial testimony given by Baltasar Orobio de Castro in Seville, Prado had by 1643 adopted a skeptical view toward all revealed religions, including Judaism; he was safely beyond the reach of the Inquisition at the time of the testimony. See I. S. Révah, "Aux origines de la rupture spinozienne: nouvel examen des origines, du déroulement et des consequences de l'affaire Spinoza-Prado-Ribera," *Annuaire du Collège de France* 72 (1972), 650–651.

15. Originally José Carreras, a Catholic priest with no apparent Jewish ancestry, Daniel Ribera converted to Judaism in Amsterdam in 1655, preached his radical ideas there, and apparently left that city before he could be excommunicated. He went to England where he became a Protestant. I. S. Révah, "Aux origines de la rupture spinozienne: nouvel examen des origines, du déroulement et des consequences de l'affaire Spinoza-Prado-Ribera," *Annuaire du Collège de France* 70 (1970), 563.

16. Uriel da Costa, *Exemplar humanae vitae*, trans. John Whiston (London 1740), appendix in Salomon and Sasson, *Examination*, 556–564. The authenticity of this work is problematic. But while the text may have been tampered with, the *Exemplar* offers details of Da Costa's life in the Peninsula that are corroborated by Inquisition documents, confirming its fundamental authenticity.

17. See I. S. Révah, "La religion d'Uriel da Costa, Marrane de Porto," *RHR* 161 (1962), 50–76. An aunt and half-sister of Da Costa's mother was burned at the stake in Coimbra in 1568 for judaizing, a fact that must have been alive in family memory. Other family members were also tried by the Inquisition.

18. Saraiva de Carvalho, "The Fellowship of St. Diogo," 33, 199n50. Homem was burned at the stake in 1624.

19. Cf. Yerushalmi, *Spanish Court*, 298–299; Yirmiyahu Yovel, *Spinoza and Other Heretics: The Marrano of Reason* (Princeton 1989), 47–48. I. S. Révah depicts Da Costa somewhat differently. While Révah was the first scholar to grasp Da Costa's need to exaggerate his independence from outside factors in his theological development, he attributed the heretical direction taken by Da Costa and other ex-conversos in Amsterdam not primarily to mental habits developed in the Peninsula, but to a loss of status in the transition to life in Amsterdam that interfered with normal adaptive processes. See I. S. Révah, *Uriel da Costa et les Marranes de Porto: Cours au Collège de France, 1966–1972* (Paris 2004), 76–79, 64–65.

20. For a brief account of Da Costa's life, see H. P. Salomon's introduction to Da Costa, *Examination*, 1–24.

21. The text appears in Saul Levi Mortera, *Giv'at Sha'ul* (Amsterdam 1645), 70v–71r. I have used, with a few modifications, the translation by Marc Saperstein, *Exile in Amsterdam: Saul Levi Morteira's Sermons to a Congregation of "New Jews"* (Cincinnati 2005), 423–425. Saperstein arrived at the approximate date for the composition of the sermon as being during the week when the Torah portion *Va-etchanan* was read in the year 1630 a) because the sermon is listed in *Giv'at Sha'ul* as belonging to the tenth cycle of sermons, and Mortera had begun preaching in 1619; and b) because the theme verse for the sermon, Deut. 4: 2, is the ninth verse of the Torah portion, through which Mortera moved fairly systematically year by year. (My thanks to Marc Saperstein for his e-mail communication.)

22. On the active courting of martyrdom by early modern Christians, see Gregory, *Salvation at Stake*, 104, 276–280. On efforts to curb this impulse see ibid., 105, 285–286.

23. To be sure, he may have mentioned them in the sermon he actually delivered.

24. Isaac Orobio de Castro, "Respuesta a un escrito que presentò un Predicante frances a el Author contra la observancia de la divina ley de Moseh," EH 48C 12 (in the version published by M. B. Amzalak, *La observancia de la Divina Ley de Mosseh* [Coimbra 1925], 20–21).

25. I have examined this process elsewhere in some detail for the community of Amsterdam. See Bodian, *Hebrews of the Portuguese Nation.*

26. See Bodian, *Hebrews of the Portuguese Nation,* 121–122.

27. Gemeentelijke Archief, Amsterdam, Particuliere Archieven 334, No. 19, 195 (21 Av 5405).

28. In the early modern period a similar boundary issue arose concerning the status of Protestants who were victims of mass violence at the hands of Catholics, and who thus had not clearly chosen to die for their faith. See Gregory, *Salvation at Stake,* 191–192.

29. Tractate Sanhedrin 74a.

30. *Seder Berakhot, Orden de Bendiciones y las ocaziones en que se deven dezir, con muchas adiciones a las precedentes impreciones, y por major methodo dispuestas* (Amsterdam 1687), 300–303. Cecil Roth maintains that this prayer could be found "in the prayer books of the time" (Roth, *History of the Marranos,* 141), but I have found it only in one.

31. *Seder Berakhot,* 300–303 (Hebrew and Spanish on facing pages). In the Hebrew version the prayer is titled *Hashkavat ha-serufim al kiddush ha-shem.*

32. David Nieto, *Matteh Dan* (London 1714), 149–150.

33. For another example of martyrdom framed rabbinically, see Cardoso, *Excelencias,* 323, where, before launching into his long passage on celebrated crypto-Jewish martyrs, Cardoso mentions the Jewish martyrs Hananiah, Mishael, and Azariah, Daniel, the Maccabee mother and her seven sons, and (leaping across many centuries) the victims of the 1391 pogroms in Spain.

34. The Protestant works are well known; on the Catholic works, see Gregory, *Salvation at Stake,* 289–290.

35. Menasseh ben Israel, *Esperança de Israel* (Amsterdam 1650), 97–100. Also published that year in English and Latin editions, and later in the seventeenth century in Dutch, Yiddish, and Hebrew. For a list of the editions, see Menasseh ben Israel, *The Hope of Israel,* ed. Henry Méchoulan and Gérard Nahon (Oxford 1987), ix–xi.

36. Cardoso, *Excelencias,* 323–325.

37. Daniel Levi de Barrios, "Memoria de los martires que fueron quemados vivos en diferentes tiempos y ciudades de España por santificar la indivisa unidad del eterno Leguislador," in his *Triumpho del govierno popular* (Amsterdam 1683–1684), in the opuscule titled "Casa de Jacob," 42–46.

38. It is interesting that even Spinoza believed the Jews were superior to any gentile people in their record of martyrdom. An acquaintance of his who had converted to Catholicism, and who wrote to the philosopher in the rather absurd hope of convincing him to do the same, mentioned by way of persuasion the Church's many martyrs. In his reply, Spinoza rejected this argument and, remarkably, asserted that Judaism was superior to any other faith in its tradition of martyrdom, mentioning the case of Judah Creyente (Lope de Vera). See Y. H. Yerushalmi, "Spinoza on the Survival of the Jewish People" (Hebrew), *Proceedings of the Israel National Academy of Sciences* 3 (1984), 187–188.

39. Arnold Wiznitzer, *Jews in Colonial Brazil* (New York 1960), 109.

40. He wrote that the inquisitors were "grieved that they had published the reasons which he [Diogo d'Asumpção] had alleged" and "would have recalled their sentence; but it

was then too late, for it was divulged through the world, which I myself have by me." Menasseh, *Hope of Israel,* 149. In the 1920s the scholar L. D. Barnett recognized a copy of the documents mentioned by Menasseh in the British Museum and published them. See Barnett, "Two Documents," 213–239.

41. The letter is mentioned by Daniel Levi de Barrios in his "Memorial de los Mártires," in *Triumpho del govierno popular* (Amsterdam 1683), in the opuscule titled "Govierno popular judaico," 43–44: "Su maravillosa firmeza celebran los versos de Antonio Henriques Gomez, de Manuel de Pina, y a un carta que escrivió entonces el Inquisidor Moscoso a la Condesa de Monterey." A copy of the letter was located in the British Museum and was published in Barnett, "Two Documents," 213–239. A further document that may have been available to Portuguese Jews is a *relacion* dealing with Lope de Vera, a copy of which is housed in the British Museum, Ms. Egerton 2058, fos. 201v–204r. A summary of it, in French, was published by Roth, "Chant du cygne," 112–113.

42. John Foxe, *Acts and Monuments* (London 1563, and many subsequent editions); Jean Crespin, *Recueil de plusieurs personnes . . .* (Geneva 1554); Ludwig Rabus, *Historien der Heyligen Ausserwölten Gottes Zeügen . . .* (Strasbourg 1552–1558); Adriaen Cornelis van Haemstede, *De Geschiedenisse ende den doodt der vromer Martelaren . . .* (Emden 1559). On Reformation period martyrologies, see Gregory, *Salvation at Stake.*

43. For a discussion of underlying features of Judaism that militated against the creation of anything resembling a cult of saints, see Robert Cohn, "Sainthood on the Periphery: The Case of Judaism," in John Stratton Hawley, ed., *Saints and Virtues* (Berkeley 1987), 87–108. On the Protestant attitude, see Gregory, *Salvation at Stake,* 140, 146–147.

44. Protestants, in marked contrast to the Portuguese Jews, demonstrated no inhibitions about drawing from traditional Church images of martyrs, despite their associations with saint veneration. See the analysis of Margaret Aston and Elizabeth Ingram, in David Loades, ed., *John Foxe and the English Reformation* (Aldershot, England, 1997), 66–142.

45. Protestant and Anabaptist martyrs were also associated with miracles. On miracles associated with martyrs in early modern Christian narratives see Gregory, *Salvation at Stake,* 307–310. In contrast to miracles associated with Christian martyrs after their death, we should note, crypto-Jewish martyrs were not depicted as performing intercessory miracles on behalf of others.

46. Cardoso, *Excelencias,* 324. I have relied partially on the translation in Yerushalmi, *Spanish Court,* 396.

47. Montesinos's account was discussed in chapter 5. It has been published by Böhm, *FMS,* 418–419.

48. Cardoso, *Excelencias,* 324. I have relied for the most part on the translation in Yerushalmi, *Spanish Court,* 396. It is worth noting that the last words of Maldonado de Silva, as related by Montesinos and repeated by Cardoso, resemble the final words of St. Stephen at the time of his martyrdom: "Behold, I see the heavens opened, and the Son of man standing at the right hand of God" (Acts 7:56). While the stories differ in significant ways, in both cases the ordinarily impenetrable barriers between heaven and earth are mysteriously removed for the martyr at the hour of death.

49. This phenomenon in a Christian context was the topic of a study by J. A. Sharpe, "'Last Dying Speeches': Religion, Ideology and Public Execution in Seventeenth-Century England," *PaP* 107 (May 1985), 144–167.

50. For a detailed description of his career see Elias Lipiner, *Izaque de Castro.*

51. Cardoso, *Excelencias,* 325. I have relied on the translation in Yerushalmi, *Spanish Court,* 398.

52. Cardoso, *Excelencias*, 325.

53. For an example of the explicit use of the imagery of the athlete in the Reformation discourse of martyrdom, see Gregory, *Salvation at Stake*, 287 and 487n178.

54. The sages of the Talmud and the medieval exegetes showed due respect to Samson as a liberator of his people from Philistine oppression, but they were not afraid to raise some rather pointed questions about his violent rampages and his relations with Philistine women. For example, Samson was identified in the Talmud with Bedan (1 Sam. 12:11), who was regarded as one of the most unworthy of Israelite leaders (Rosh Hashanah, 25a–b). Abarbanel simply asked, "How could Samson have been so foolish as to tell a prostitute how he could be bound and how his strength could be removed?" (Abarbanel on Judges 14).

55. Maccabees 7:21.

56. For a general discussion of Iberian notions of honor in ex-converso thinking see Bodian, *Hebrews of the Portuguese Nation*, 85–92.

57. *Elogios que zelosos dedicaron a la felice memoria de Abraham Nuñez Bernal, que fue quemado vivo santificando el Nombre de su criador en Cordova a 3 de Mayo 5415* (Amsterdam 1655), 169.

58. "Hebreo soy, enemigos, / mi esposa es la Ley sagrada, / mi Dios, solo el de Israel, / mi honor, morir por su causa. / Prendedme, echadme al incendio, / que por que sea su flama / mi carro triumphal, ya es / de Elias mi vigilancia." Barrios, *Contra la verdad no hay fuerça*, 128.

59. Enríquez Gómez, *Romance al divín martír*. Compare Barrios's stanzas above with lines 275–279 and 295–299 of this work.

60. "Amante soy de tu Ley / y de tal suerte la celo, / que muero por adorarla: / ¡mira, Señor, si la quiero!/ Estos martirios que paso, / estas penas que padezco, / como amante las admito, / como esposo las venero." Enríquez Gómez, *Romance al divín martír*, lines 340–349. Translation by Timothy Oelman.

61. *La inquisición de Lucifer y visita de todos los diablos*, ed. Constance Hubbard Rose (Amsterdam 1992).

Bibliography

Manuscripts and Archival Sources

Mexico

Mexico City. Archivo General de la Nación. Proceso of Manuel Morales. Inq. vol. 127.
Mexico City. Archivo General de la Nación. Procesos of Tomás Treviño de Sobremonte. Inq. vol. 1495.

The Netherlands

Amsterdam. Ets Haim Collection. Ms. 48A23. Isaac Orobio de Castro, "Epístola Invectiva."
Amsterdam. Ets Haim Collection. Ms. H48D6. Isaac Orobio de Castro. "Respuesta a un escrito que presentó un Predicante Francés a el Author contra la observancia de la Divina Ley de Mosseh."
Amsterdam. Gemeentelijke Archief. Particuliere Archieven 334, No. 19.

Portugal

Lisbon. Arquivo Nacional da Torre do Tombo. Inquisição de Lisboa, Processo no. 104.
Lisbon. Arquivo Nacional da Torre do Tombo. Inquisição de Lisboa, Processo no. 11.550.
Lisbon. Arquivo Nacional da Torre do Tombo. Arquivo Histórico do Ministério das Finanças, Conventos Extintos (CX.2204, Capilha 3)—Convento de Santo António da Ordem de S. Francisco de Castanheira, Auttos de Inventário do Convento de Santo António dos Capuchos.

Spain

Cuenca. Archivo Diocesana de Cuenca. Inquisición 458/6317.
Madrid. Archivo Histórico Nacional. Inquisición. Legajo 2135, No. 15 (1639); No. 16 (1641); No. 17 (1643); No. 18, (1643); No. 19 (1644).
——. Inquisición, Libro 1029, fos. 322r–324r.
Madrid. Biblioteca Nacional. Ms. 7819. Información sumaria de las virtudes y milagros de Gregorio López, año de 1620.

Primary Sources

Barrios, Daniel Levi de. *Contra la verdad no hay fuerza: Panegirico a los tres bienaventurados martires Abraham Athias, Yahacob Rodriguez Càseres, y Raquel Nuñez Fernandez, que fueron quemados vivos en Córdova, por santificar la unidad divina.* Amsterdam [1667?].
——. *Triumpho del govierno popular.* Amsterdam 1683.

Bocanegra, Matías de. *Auto general de la fee: Celebrado . . . en la . . . ciudad de Mexico . . . Dominica in albis 11 de abril de 1649 . . .* Mexico 1649.

Cardoso, Isaac. *Las Excelencias de los Hebreos.* Amsterdam 1679.

Cartas de algunos PP. de la Compañia de Jesus entre los años de 1634 y 1648. (= *Memorial Histórico Español,* vol. 17). Madrid 1863.

Cassian, John. *The Conferences.* Trans. and annotated by Boniface Ramsey. New York 1997.

"Causa criminal contra Tomas Treviño de Sobremonte, por judaizante," in *Boletín del Archivo General de la Nación,* seriatum, 6 (1935), 7 (1936), 8 (1937).

[Contreras, Alonso]. "Ultimos momentos y conversión de Luis de Carvajal," *Anales del Museo Nacional de Arqueología, Historia y Etnografía* 3 (1925), 64–78.

Costa, Uriel da. *Examination of Pharasaic Traditions.* Amsterdam 1624. Facsimile edition, ed. and trans. by H. P. Salomon and I. S. D. Sassoon. Leiden 1993.

——. *Exemplar humanae vitae.* Trans. by John Whiston (London 1740), republished as appendix in Da Costa, *Examination of Pharasaic Traditions,* 556–564.

Crescas, Hasdai. Letter to the Jews of Avignon, in Wiener (ed.), *Sefer Shevet Yehudah* (Hanover 1855), 128–130.

——. *The Refutation of the Christian Principles.* Trans. by Daniel Lasker. Albany 1992.

——. *Sefer bitul ikare ha-Notsrim.* Ed. by Daniel Lasker. Jerusalem 2002.

Delgado, João Pinto. *Poema de la Reyna Ester. Lamentaciones del Propheta Ieremias. Historia de Rut, y varias Poesías.* Facsimile edition of original Rouen edition of 1627. Lisbon 1954.

Dueñas, Juan de. *Espejo de consolación de tristes: En la qual se veran muchas y grandes hystorias de la sagrada escriptura para consolación de los que en esta vida padecen tribulación. Tercera parte.* Barcelona 1580.

Duran, Profiat. *Sefer ma'aseh Efod.* Vienna 1865.

——. *The Polemical Writings of Profiat Duran: The Reproach of the Gentiles and "Be Not Like Unto Thy Fathers"* (Hebrew). Ed. by Ephraim Talmage. Jerusalem 1981.

Elogios que zelosos dedicaron a la felice memoria de Abraham Nuñez Bernal, que fue quemado vivo santificando el Nombre de su criador en Cordova a 3 de Mayo 5415. Amsterdam 1655.

Enríquez Gómez, Antonio. *La Inquisición de Lucifer y visita de todos los diablos.* Ed. by Constance Hubbard Rose and Maxim Kerkhof. Amsterdam 1992.

——. *Romance al divin mártyr, Judá Creyente [don Lope de Vera y Alarcon] martirizado en Valladolid por la Inquisición.* Ed. by Timothy Oelman. London and Toronto 1986.

——. *Sánson Nazareno.* [Rouen 1656]. Ed. by María del Carmen Artigas. Madrid 1999.

Espina, Alonso de. *Fortalitium Fidei.* Nuremberg 1485.

Fontes Iudaeorum Regni Castellae, vol. 2, *El tribunal de la Inquisición en el Obispado de Soria [1486–1502].* Ed. by Carlos Carrete Parrondo. Salamanca 1985.

Genebrard, Gilbert. *Psalmi Davidis, calendario Hebraeo, Syro, Graeco, Latino . . .* Lyon, 1592.

Granada, Luis de. *Obras completas.* Ed. by Alvaro Huerga. Madrid 1994.

López, Gregorio. *Declaración del apocalipsis.* Madrid 1999.

Luther, Martin. *Martin Luthers Werke: Kritische Gesamtausgabe, Abteilung Werke.* Weimar 1883–1993.

Maldonado, Alonso de. *Chronica universal de todas las naciones y tiempos . . .* Madrid 1624.

Martinho do Amor de Deos. *Escola de penitencia, caminho de perfeição, Estrada secura para a vida eternal, chronica da santa provincial de S. Antonio da regular e estreita observancia da Ordem do Serafico Patriarca S. Francisco, no Instituto Capucho neste reyno de Portugal.* Lisbon 1740.

Menasseh ben Israel. *Esperança de Israel.* Amsterdam 1650.

——. *The Hope of Israel: The English Translation by Moses Wall, 1652.* Henry Méchoulan and Gérard Nahon (eds.). Oxford 1987.

Montesinos, Fernando. *Auto de la fe celebrado en Lima a 23. de enero de 1639.* Madrid 1640.

Mortera, Saul Levi. *Giv'at Sha'ul.* Amsterdam 1645.

Nieto, David. *Matteh Dan, y segunda parte de Cuzari.* London 1714.

Nueva colección de documentos para la historia de México. Ed. by J. García Icazbalceta. 3 vols. Mexico City 1941.

Orobio de Castro, Isaac. *Epístola Invectiva.* Ets Haim Collection, Amsterdam, Ms. 48A23.

——. "Respuesta a un escrito que presentò un Predicante frances a el Author contra la observancia de la divina ley de Moseh," Ets Haim Collection, Ms. 48C 12, fos. 340v–381v.

"Proceso contra Jaime Ferrer, relapso, judaizante relaxado," published by Bernardino Llorca in *Analecta Sacra Tarraconensia* 12 (1936), 410–414.

Procesos de Luis de Carvajal (el Mozo). Ed. by L. González Obregón. Mexico City, 1935.

Records of the Trials of the Spanish Inquisition in Ciudad Real. Ed. by Haim Beinart. 4 vols. Jerusalem 1974–1985.

Reuveni, David. *The Story of David Hareuveni, Copied from the Oxford Manuscript* (Hebrew). Ed. by Aaron Zeev Aescoly. Jerusalem 1993.

Schirmann, J. (ed.), anonymous elegy, *Kovets al yad* 3 (Jerusalem 1940), 64–69.

Seder Berakhot, Orden de Bendiciones y las ocaziones en que se deven dezir, con muchas adiciones a las precedentes impreciones, y por major methodo dispuestas. Amsterdam 1687.

Simancas, Diego de. *Defensio statuti Toletani.* Antwerp 1575.

Spinoza, Benedict. *The Letters.* Trans. by Samuel Shirley. Indianapolis and Cambridge 1995.

Torrejoncillo, Francisco. *Centinela contra Judíos.* Barcelona 1731.

Yavetz, Yosef. *Sefer ḥasdei ha-shem.* New York 1998–1999.

SECONDARY SOURCES

Alberro, Solange. *Inquisición y sociedad en México, 1571–1700.* Mexico City 1988.

Amiel, Charles. "Crypto-judaïsme et Inquisition: La matière juive dans les édits de la foi des Inquisitions ibériques," *RHR* 210 (1993), 145–168.

Andrade, João Manuel. *Confraria de S. Diogo: Judeus secretos na Coimbra do séc. XVII.* Lisbon 1999.

Andrés, Melquíades. "Alumbrados, Erasmians, 'Lutherans,' and Mystics: The Risk of a More 'Intimate' Spirituality," in Angel Alcalá (ed.), *The Spanish Inquisition and the Inquisitorial Mind* (New York 1987), 457–494.

Ariès, Philippe. *The Hour of Our Death.* New York 1991.

Aston, Margaret and Betty Ingram. "The Iconography of *Acts and Monuments,*" in David Loades (ed.), *John Foxe and the English Reformation* (Aldershot, England 1997), 66–142.

Avilés, Miguel. "The Auto de Fe and the Social Model of Counter-Reformation Spain," in Angel Alcalá (ed.), *The Spanish Inquisition and the Inquisitorial Mind,* 249–264.

Azevedo, Carlos Moreira (ed.). *História religiosa de Portugal,* vol. 2, *Humanismos e Reformas.* Rio de Mouro 2000.

Azevedo, João Lúcio d'. *História dos Christãos-Novos portugueses.* Lisbon 1921.

Baer, Yitzhak. *Galut.* Trans. from Hebrew by Robert Warshaw. New York 1947.

——. "Gezerat TaTN"U" (Hebrew), in M. D. Cassuto et al (eds.), *Sefer Asaf* (Jerusalem 1953), 126–140.

——. *A History of the Jews in Christian Spain.* 2 vols. Philadelphia 1978.

——. *Die Juden im christlichen Spanien,* 2 vols. Berlin 1929, 1936.

——. "The Messianic Movement in Spain at the Time of the Expulsion" (Hebrew), *Measef Zion* 5 (1933), 61–78.

——. "The Religious-Social Tendency of *Sefer Hassidim*" (Hebrew), *Zion* 3 (1937), 1–50.

——. *Toldot ha-Yehudim bi-Sefarad ha-Notsrit.* Tel Aviv 1959.

Baião, António. *Episódios dramáticos da Inquisição Portuguesa,* 3 vols. Lisbon 1992.

——. *Inquisição em Portugal e no Brazil: Subsidos para a sua historia.* Lisbon 1906.

Bakewell, P. J. *Silver Mining and Society in Colonial Mexico, Zacatecas 1546–1700.* Cambridge 1971.

Balitzer, S. "Nicolas Antoine," *REJ* 36 (1898), 161–196.

Barnett, L. D. "Two Documents of the Inquisition," *JQR* 15 (1924–1925), 213–239.

Baron, Salo Wittmayer. *A Social and Religious History of the Jews,* 2nd ed., 18 vols. New York 1952–1983.

Bataillon, Marcel. *Erasmo y España: Estudios sobre la historia spiritual del siglo XVI.* 2nd ed., trans. by Antonio Alatorre. Mexico City 1982.

Beijer, Agne. "Visions célestes et infernales dans le théâtre du moyen-âge et de la Renaissance," in *Journées Internationales d'Études, Les Fêtes de la Renaissance,* vol. 1 (Paris 1956), 405–417.

Beinart, Haim. "The Conversos of Almagro and Daimiel" (Hebrew), *Zion* 35 (1970), 80–95.

——. "Conversos of Chillón and the Prophecies of Mari Gómez and Inés, the Daughter of Juan Esteban" (Hebrew), *Zion* 48 (1983), 241–272.

——. *Conversos on Trial: The Inquisition in Ciudad Real.* Jerusalem 1981.

——. "The Convert Lope de Vera y Alarcón and His Martyrdom as Judah Creyente" (Hebrew), in Z. Malachi (ed.), *Sefer yovel li-khevod Aharon Mirski* (Lod 1989), 31–55.

——. "Inés of Herrera del Duque, The Prophetess of Extremadura," in Mary Giles (ed.), *Women in the Inquisition: Spain and the New World* (Baltimore 1999), 42–52, 304–310.

——. "A Jew of Salonica in Spain in the Seventeenth Century" (Hebrew), *Sefunot* 12 (1971–1978), 189–197.

——. "The Judaizing Movement in the Order of San Jeronimo in Castile," *Scripta Hierosolymitana* 7 (1961), 167–192.

——. "A Prophesying Movement in Cordova in 1499–1502," *Zion* 44 (1979), 190–200.

——. "The Prophetess Inés and Her Messianic Movement in Herrera del Duque" (Hebrew), in Y. Dan and Y. Kaplan (eds.), *Studies in Kabbalah, Jewish Philosophy and Ethical Literature in Honor of Isaiah Tishby on his Seventy-fifth Birthday* (Jerusalem 1986), 459–506.

——. "Ties between Jews and Conversos of Italy and Spain," in idem (ed.), *Jews in Italy: Studies Dedicated to the Memory of U. Cassuto* (Hebrew) (Jerusalem 1988), 275–288.

Ben Sasson, Haim Hillel. "The Generation of the Exiles on Itself" (Hebrew), *Zion* 26 (1961), 59–64.

Ben Sasson, Menahem. "On the Jewish Identity of Forced Converts: A Study of Forced Conversion in the Almohad Period" (Hebrew), *Pe'amim* 42 (1990), 16–37.

Ben Shalom, Ram. "The Disputation of Tortosa, Vicente Ferrer and the Problem of the Conversos according to the Testimony of Isaac Nathan" (Hebrew), *Zion* 57 (1991), 21–45.

——. "Jewish Martyrdom and Conversion in Sepharad and Ashkenaz in the Middle Ages: An Assessment of the Reassessment" (Hebrew), *Tarbiz* 71 (2001–2002), 279–300.

——. "*Kiddush ha-Shem* and Jewish Martyrology in Aragon and Castile in 1391: A Comparison of Spain and Ashkenaz" (Hebrew), *Tarbiz* 70 (2001), 227–282.

Benito Ruano, Eloy. "El memorial contra los conversos del Bachiller Marcos García de Mora (Marquillos de Mazarambroz)," *Sefarad* 17 (1957), 330–337, 348.

——. "La 'Sentencia-Estatuto' de Pedro Sarmiento contra los conversos toledanos," *Revista de la Universidad de Madrid*, 6 (1957), 277–306.

——. *Toledo en el siglo XV: Vida política.* Madrid 1961.

Bennassar, Bartolomé. *L'Inquisition espagnole XVe–XIXe siècle.* Paris 1979.

Bentley, Jerry. "Erasmus' *Annotationes in Novum Testamentum* and the Textual Criticism of the Gospels," *Archiv für Reformationsgeschichte* 67 (1976), 33–53.

Berg, J. van den and E. G. E. van der Wall (eds.). *Jewish-Christian Relations in the Seventeenth Century.* Dordrecht 1988.

Berger, David. "On the Uses of History in Medieval Jewish Polemic against Christianity: The Quest for the Historical Jesus," in E. Carlebach, J. Efron, and D. Myers (eds.), *Jewish History and Jewish Memory: Essays in Honor of Yosef Hayim Yerushalmi* (Hanover, N.H. 1998), 25–39.

——. *The Jewish-Christian Debate in the High Middle Ages.* Philadelphia 1979.

Berti, Silvia. "Unmasking the Truth: The Theme of Imposture in Early Modern European Culture, 1660–1730," in James E. Force and David S. Katz (eds.), *Everything Connects: In Conference with Richard H. Popkin* (Leiden 1999), 19–36.

Bethencourt, Francisco. "The 'auto da fé': ritual and imagery," *Journal of the Warburg and Courtauld Institute* 55 (1992), 155–168.

——. *La Inquisición en la época moderna: España, Portugal, Italia, siglos XV–XIX.* Madrid 1997.

Bilinkoff, Jodi. "Francisco Losa and Gregorio López: Spiritual Friendship and Identity Formation on the New Spain Frontier," in Allen Greer and Jodi Bilinkoff (eds.), *Colonial Saints: Discovery of the Holy in the Americas, 1500–1800* (New York and London 2003), 115–128.

Blazquez Miguel, Juan. *San Clemente y la Inquisición de Cuenca.* Madrid 1988.

Blidstein, Gerald. "Rabbis, Romans, and Martyrdom—Three Views," *Tradition* 1 (1984), 1–58.

Bodian, Miriam. "Amsterdam, Venice and the Marrano Diaspora in the Seventeenth Century," *Dutch Jewish History* 2 (1989), 47–65.

——. "Death at the Stake as Seen in the Northern Sephardi Diaspora" (Hebrew), *Pe'amim* 75 (1998), 47–62.

——. *Hebrews of the Portuguese Nation: Conversos and Community in Early Modern Amsterdam.* Bloomington 1997.

——. "In the Cross-Currents of the Reformation: Crypto-Jewish Martyrs of the Inquisition, 1570–1670," *PaP*, No. 176 (2002), 66–104.

——. "Les juifs portugais d'Amsterdam et la question identitaire," in *La Diaspora des "Nouveaux-Chrétiens"* (= *Arquivos do Centro Cultural Calouste Gulbenkian*, vol. 48) (Lisbon 2004), 103–116.

——. "'Men of the Nation': The Shaping of Converso Identity in Early Modern Europe," *PaP*, no. 143 (1994), 48–76.

Böhm, Günter. "Crypto-Jews and New Christians in Colonial Peru and Chile," in *JEEW*, 203–212.

——. *Historia de los judíos en Chile*. Vol. 1, *El Bachiller Francisco Maldonado de Silva, 1592–1639*. Santiago de Chile 1984.

——. *Los judíos en Chile durante la Colonia*. Santiago de Chile 1948.

Bonnant, Georges. "Notes sur quelques ouvrages en langue espagnole imprimés a Genève par Jean Crespin (1557–1560)," *BHR* 24 (1962), 50–57.

Bowersock, G. W. *Martyrdom and Rome*. Cambridge 1995.

Boyarin, Daniel. *Dying for God*. Stanford 1999.

Carbonnier-Burkard, Marianne. "Les manuels reformes de preparation à la mort," *RHR* 217 (2000), 363–380.

Carlebach, Elisheva. *Between History and Hope: Jewish Messianism in Ashkenaz and Sepharad: Third Annual Lecture of the Victor J. Selmanowitz Chair of Jewish History* (New York 1998).

Caro Baroja, Julio. *Los judíos en la España moderna y contemporánea*. 3 vols. Madrid 1986.

Carrete Parrondo, Carlos. "Nostalgia for the Past (and for the Future?) among Castilian *Judeoconversos*," *Mediterranean Historical Review* 6 (1991), 25–43.

Carrete Parrondo, Carlos and Yolanda Moreno Koch, "Movimiento mesiánico hispano-portugués: Badajoz 1525," *Sefarad* 52 (1992), 65–68.

Castañeda Delgado, Paulino and Pilar Hernández Aparicio, *La Inquisición de Lima (1570–1635)*, 3 vols. Madrid 1989–1998, 1995.

Chartier, Roger. "Les arts de mourir, 1450–1600," *Annales E.S.C.* 31 (1976), 51–75.

Chazan, Robert. *Barcelona and Beyond: The Disputation of 1263 and Its Aftermath*. Berkeley, Los Angeles, Oxford 1992.

——. *Daggers of Faith: Thirteenth-Century Christian Missionizing and Jewish Response*. Berkeley and Los Angeles 1989.

Christian, William Jr. *Apparitions in Late Medieval and Renaissance Spain*. Princeton 1981.

Cid, Jesús-Antonio. "Jacob Bueno, mártir: Cuatro judíos portugueses ante la razon del estado," *Sefarad* 47 (1987), 283–299.

Cohen, Gerson. "Messianic Postures of Ashkenazim and Sephardim," *Studies of the Leo Baeck Institute*, ed. by Max Kreutzberger (New York 1967), 117–156.

——. "The Story of Hannah and her Seven Sons in Hebrew Literature" (Hebrew), in *Sefer ha-yovel le-kh'vod Mordekhai Menahem Kaplan* (New York 1953), 109–122.

Cohen, Jeremy. "The Hebrew Crusade Chronicles in Their Christian Cultural Context," in Alfred Haverkamp (ed.), *Juden und Christen zur Zeit der Kreuzzüge*. Sigmaringen 1999, 17–34.

——. *Living Letters of the Law: Ideas of the Jew in Medieval Christianity*. Berkeley and Los Angeles 1999.

——. "Profiat Duran's *The Reproach of the Gentiles* and the Development of Jewish Anti-Christian Polemic," in *Shlomo Simonsohn Jubilee Volume: Studies on the History of the Jews in the Middle Ages and Renaissance Period* (Jerusalem 1993), 71–84.

——. *Sanctifying the Name of God: Jewish Martyrs and Jewish Memories of the First Crusade*. Philadelphia 2004.

Cohen, Martin. *The Canonization of a Myth: Portugal's "Jewish Problem" and the Assembly of Tomar 1629*. Cincinnati 2002.

——. "Don Gregorio López: Friend of the Secret Jew," *Hebrew Union College Annual* 38 (1967), 259–284.

——. *The Martyr: The Story of a Secret Jew and the Mexican Inquisition in the Sixteenth Century*. Philadelphia 1973.

Cohn, Robert. "Sainthood on the Periphery: The Case of Judaism," in John Stratton Hawley (ed.), *Saints and Virtues* (Berkeley 1987), 87–108.

Contreras, Jaime and Gustav Henningsen, "Forty-four Thousand Cases of the Spanish Inquisition (1540–1700): Analysis of a Historical Data Bank," in Henningsen and Tedeschi (eds.), *The Inquisition in Early Modern Europe* (De Kalb, Illinois 1986), 100–129.

Coudert, Allison. "Judaizing in the Seventeenth Century: Francis Mercury van Helmont and Johann Peter Späth (Moses Germanus)," in *SCJ*, 71–121.

Cross, Harry E. "Commerce and Orthodoxy: A Spanish Response to Portuguese Commercial Penetration in the Viceroyalty of Peru, 1580–1640," *The Americas* 35 (1978), 151–167.

Cunha de Azevedo, Elvira. "Orações judaicas na Inquisição portuguesa—século XVI," in Yosef Kaplan (ed.), *Jews and Conversos: Studies in Society and the Inquisition* (Jerusalem 1981), 149–178.

Dán, Robert. "Isaac Troky and his 'Antitrinitarian' Sources" in Robert Dán (ed.), *Occident and Orient: A Tribute to the Memory of A. Scheiber* (Budapest 1988), 69–82.

Delumeau, Jean. *Catholicism between Luther and Voltaire: A New View of the Counter-Reformation*. Eng. trans. London 1977.

Droge, Arthur and James Tabor. *A Noble Death: Suicide and Martyrdom among Christians and Jews in Antiquity*. San Francisco 1992.

Droz, Eugénie. "Notes sur les impressions genevoises transportées par Hernández," *BHR* 22 (1960), 119–132.

Edwards, John. "Male and Female Religious Experience among Spanish New Christians, 1450–1500," in Raymond Waddington and Arthur Williamson (eds.), *The Expulsion of the Jews: 1492 and After* (New York and London 1994), 41–51.

Einbinder, Susan. *Beautiful Death: Jewish Poetry and Martyrdom in Medieval France*. Princeton 2002.

Eire, Carlos. *From Madrid to Purgatory: The Art and Craft of Dying in Sixteenth-Century Spain*. Cambridge and New York 1995.

Elliott, J. H. "Self-perception and Decline in Early Seventeenth-Century Spain," *PaP*, no. 74 (May 1977), 41–61.

Emery, Richard. "New Light on Profayt Duran 'The Efodi,' " *JQR* 58 (1968), 328–337.

Fernandez y Fernandez, Enrique. *Las biblias castellanas del exilio: Historia de las biblias castellanas del siglo XVI*. Miami 1976.

Ferro Tavares, Maria José. "The Portuguese Jews After the Expulsion," in Katz and Serels (eds.), *Studies on the History of Portuguese Jews from Their Expulsion in 1497 through Their Dispersion* (New York 2000), 7–28.

Fishman, Talya. *Shaking the Pillars of Exile*. Stanford 1997.

Flynn, Maureen. "Mimesis of the Last Judgment: The Spanish Auto de Fe," *The Sixteenth Century Journal* 22 (1991), 281–297.

Freeman, Thomas and Marcelo Borges. " 'A grave and heinous incident against our holy Catholic Faith': Two Accounts of William Gardiner's Desecration of the Portuguese Royal Chapel in 1552," in *Historical Research* 69 (1996), 1–17.

Frend, W. H. C. *Martyrdom and Persecution in the Early Church: A Study of Conflict from the Maccabees to Donatus*. New York 1967.

Friedman, Jerome. *Michael Servetus: A Case Study in Total Heresy*. Geneva 1978.

———. "New Religious Alternatives," in Raymond Waddington and Arthur Williamson (eds.), *The Expulsion of the Jews: 1492 and After* (New York and London 1994), 19–40.

——. "The Reformation and Jewish Antichristian Polemics," *BHR* 41 (1979), 83–97.

Gafni, I. and A. Ravitzky (eds.). *Sanctity of Life and Martyrdom: Studies in Memory of Amir Yekutiel* (Hebrew). Jerusalem 1992.

García de Proodian, Lucía. *Los judíos en América: Sus actividades en los Virreinatos de Nueva Castilla y Nueva Granada S. XVII.* Madrid 1966.

García-Arenal, Mercedes and Gerard Wiegers. *A Man of Three Worlds: Samuel Pallache, A Moroccan Jew in Catholic and Protestant Europe.* Baltimore and London 1999.

Gebhardt, Carl. *Die Schriften des Uriel da Costa.* Amsterdam 1922.

Ginzburg, Carlo. "The High and the Low: The Theme of Forbidden Knowledge in the 16th and 17th Centuries," in Carlo Ginzburg, *Clues, Myths, and the Historical Method,* trans. by John and Anne Tedeschi (Baltimore 1989), 60–76.

Gitlitz, David. *Secrecy and Deceit: The Religion of the Crypto-Jews.* Philadelphia 1996.

Glaser, Edward. "Invitation to Intolerance: A Study of the Portuguese Sermons Preached at Autos-da-fé," *Hebrew Union College Annual* 27 (1956), 327–385.

Goldin, Simha. *Alamot ahevukha, al-mot ahevukha* [The ways of Jewish martyrdom]. Lod 2002.

Gómez-Menor Fuentes, José-Carlos. "Linaje judío de escritores religiosos y místicos españoles del siglo XVI," in Angel Alcalá (ed.), *Judíos, Sefarditas, Conversos: La expulsión de 1492 y sus consecuencias* (Valladolid 1995), 587–600.

Goodblatt, David. "Suicide in the Sanctuary: Traditions on Priestly Martyrdom," *Journal of Jewish Studies* 46 (1995), 10–29.

Gracia Boix, Rafael. *Autos de fe y Causas de la Inquisición de Córdoba.* Cordova 1983.

Gregory, Brad. *Salvation at Stake: Christian Martyrdom in Early Modern Europe.* Cambridge Mass., 1999.

Griffiths, Nicholas. "Popular Religious Scepticism and Idiosyncrasy in post-Tridentine Cuenca" in L. Twomey (ed.), *Faith and Fanaticism: Religious Fervour in Early Modern Spain* (Aldershot 1997), 95–126.

Gross, Abraham. "Conversions and Martyrdom in Spain in 1391: A Reassessment of Ram Ben-Shalom (*Tarbiz,* 70 [2001] pp. 227–282)" (Hebrew), *Tarbiz* 17 (2001–2002), 269–277.

——. "On the Ashkenazi Syndrome of Jewish Martyrdom in Portugal in 1497" (Hebrew), *Tarbiz* 64 (1995), 83–99.

Gruenwald, I. "*Kiddush ha-Shem:* Clarification of a Term" (Hebrew), *Molad* 24 (1968), 476–484.

Gutwirth, Eleazar. "Conversions to Christianity amongst Fifteenth-Century Spanish Jews: An Alternative Explanation," in Daniel Carpi, Moshe Gil, Yosef Gorni et al. (eds.), *Shlomo Simonsohn Jubilee Volume: Studies on the History of the Jews in the Middle Ages and Renaissance Period* (Jerusalem 1993), 97–121.

——. "History and Apologetics in XVth Century Hispano-Jewish Thought," *Helmantica* 35 (1984), 231–242.

——. "Religion and Social Criticism in Late Medieval Roussillon: An Aspect of Profayt Duran's Activities," *Michael* 12 (1991), 135–156.

——. "Religion, historia y las *Biblias Romanceadas,*" *Revista Catalana de Teología* 13 (1988), 115–134.

——. "Towards Expulsion: 1391–1492," in Elie Kedourie (ed.), *Spain and the Jews: The Sephardi Experience, 1492 and After* (London 1992), 51–73.

Hacker, Yosef. "'If We Have Forgotten the Name of Our God' (Psalm 44:21): Interpretation in Light of the Realities in Medieval Spain" (Hebrew), *Zion* 57 (1992), 247–274.

Halkin, A. S. "A *Contra Christianos* by a Marrano," in Moshe Davis (ed.), *Mordecai M. Kaplan: Jubilee Volume on the Occasion of His Seventieth Birthday* (New York 1953), 399–416.

Hamilton, Alastair. *Heresy and Mysticism in Sixteenth-Century Spain: The Alumbrados.* Cambridge 1992.

Hauben, Paul. "Reform and Counter-Reform: The Case of the Spanish Heretics," in Theodore Rabb and Jerrold Siegel (eds.), *Action and Conviction in Early Modern Europe: Essays in Memory of E. H. Harbison* (Princeton 1969), 154–168.

Henningsen, Gustav. "El 'Banco de datos' del Santo Officio," *Boletín de la Real Academia de la Historia* 174 (1977), 542–570.

———. "The Database of the Spanish Inquisition: The '*relaciones de causas*' project revisited," in H. Mohnhaupt and D. Simon (eds.), *Vorträge zur Justizforschung: Geschichte und Theorie,* 2 vols. (Frankfurt am Main 1992–1993), 2: 43–85.

Henten, J. W. van (ed.). *Die Entstehung der jüdischen Martyrologie.* Leiden 1989.

———. *The Maccabean Martyrs as Saviours of the Jewish People: A Study of 2 and 4 Maccabees.* Leiden 1997.

———. "The Martyrs as Heroes of the Christian People: Some Remarks on the Continuity between Jewish and Christian Martyrology, with Pagan Analogies," in M. Lamberights and P. van Deun (eds.), *Martyrium in Multidisciplinary Perspective: Memorial Louis Reekmans* (Leuven 1995), 303–322.

Henten, J. W. van and Friedrich Avemarie. *Martyrdom and Noble Death: Selected Texts from Graeco-Roman, Jewish, and Christian Antiquity.* London 2002.

Herculano, Alexandre. *History of the Origin and Establishment of the Inquisition in Portugal.* Trans. by John Branner. New York 1972.

Hermann, Jacqueline. *No reino do desejado: a construção do sebastianismo em Portugal, séculos XVI e XVII.* São Paulo 1998.

Herr, Moshe David. "Persecutions and Martyrdom in Hadrian's Days," *Scripta Hierosolymitana* 23 (1972), 85–125.

Himmelfarb, Martha. *Ascent to Heaven in Jewish and Christian Apocalypses.* New York and Oxford 1983.

Huerga, Alvaro. "Judíos de Ferrara en la Inquisición de México," *Annuario dell'Istituto storico italiano per l'età moderna e contemporanea* 35–36 (1983–1984), 117–157.

Israel, Jonathan. *Diasporas within a Diaspora: Jews, Crypto-Jews and the World Maritime Empires (1540–1740).* Leiden 2002.

Jiménez Monteserín, Miguel. "El auto de fe de la Inquisición española," in *Inquisición y Conversos: Conferencias pronunciadas en el III Curso de Cultura Hispano-Judía y Sefardí de la Universidad de Castilla–La Mancha* (Toledo 1994), 203–223.

———. "Los luteranos ante el tribunal de la Inquisición de Cuenca, 1525–1600" in Joaquín Pérez Villanueva (ed.), *La Inquisición española: Nueva vision, nuevos horizontes* (Madrid, 1980), 689–736.

Kamen, Henry. *The Phoenix and the Flame: Catalonia and the Counter Reformation.* New Haven, 1993.

———. *The Spanish Inquisition: A Historical Revision.* New Haven and London 1997.

Kaplan, Benjamin. *Calvinists and Libertines: Confession and Community in Utrecht, 1578–1620.* Oxford 1995.

Kaplan, Yosef. *From Christianity to Judaism: The Story of Isaac Orobio de Castro.* Oxford 1989.

——. "The Role of Rabbi Moshe d'Aguilar in his Contacts with the Refugees from Spain and Portugal in the Seventeenth Century" (Hebrew), *Proceedings of the Sixth World Congress of Jewish Studies*, vol. 2 (Jerusalem 1975), 95–106.

——. "The Travels of Portuguese Jews from Amsterdam to the 'Lands of Idolatry' (1644–1724)," in idem (ed.), *Jews and Conversos: Studies in Society and the Inquisition* (Jerusalem 1985), 197–224.

Kaplan, Yosef, Henry Méchoulan, and Richard Popkin (eds.). *Menasseh ben Israel and His World.* Leiden 1989.

Katz, David S. *Sabbath and Sectarianism in Seventeenth-Century England.* Leiden 1988.

Katz, Jacob. "Between 1096 and 1648–1649" (Hebrew), in *Sefer yovel le-Yitzhak Baer* (Jerusalem 1961), 318–337.

——. *Exclusiveness and Tolerance.* London 1961.

Kayserling, M. *Geschichte der Juden in Portugal.* Leipzig 1867.

Keen, Benjamin. "The Black Legend Revisited: Assumptions and Realities," *The Hispanic American Historical Review* 49 (1969), 703–719.

Kerkhof, Maxim. "La 'Ynquisiçion de Luzifer y visita de todos los diablos,' texto desconocido de Antonio Enríquez Gómez, edición de unos fragmentos," *Sefarad* 38 (1978), 319–331.

Kinder, Gordon. "The Creation of the Black Legend: Literary Contributions of Spanish Protestant Exiles," *Mediterranean Studies* 6 (1996), 67–78.

——. "Spanish Protestants and Foxe's Book: Sources," in *BHR* 60 (1998), 107–116.

Kirkconnell, Watson. *That Invincible Samson: The Theme of Samson Agonistes in World Literature with Translations of the Major Analogues.* Toronto 1964.

Kleinberg, Aviad. *Prophets in Their Own Country: Living Saints and the Making of Sainthood in the Later Middle Ages.* Chicago 1992.

Kohut, George Alexander. "Jewish Martyrs of the Inquisition in South America," *Publications of the American Jewish Historical Society* 4 (1896), 166–171.

——. "The Trial of Francisco Maldonado de Silva," in Martin Cohen (ed.), *The Jewish Experience in Latin America*, 2 vols. (New York 1971), 2: 39–55.

Krouse, F. Michael. *Milton's Samson and the Christian Tradition.* Princeton 1949.

Labrousse, Elisabeth. "Vie et mort de Nicolas Antoine," *Etudes Théologiques et Religieuses* 52 (1977), 421–433.

Lane Fox, Robin. *Pagans and Christians.* New York 1986.

Lasker, Daniel. *Jewish Philosophical Polemics against Christianity in the Middle Ages.* New York 1977.

Lea, Henry Charles. *A History of the Inquisition of Spain.* 4 vols. New York 1906–1907.

Le Goff, Jacques. *The Birth of Purgatory.* Trans. by Arthur Goldhammer. Chicago 1984.

Lemos, Maximiano. *Zacuto Lusitano.* Porto 1909.

Lescaze, Bernard. "La confession de foi de Nicolas Antoine (1632)," *Bulletin de la Societé d'Histoire et d'Archéologie de Genève* 14 (1970), 277–323.

Levine, Renee Melammed. *Heretics or Daughters of Israel? The Crypto-Jewish Women of Castile.* New York and Oxford 1999.

Lewin, Boleslao. *Los judíos bajo la Inquisición en Hispano America.* Buenos Aires 1960.

Lieberman, Saul. "On Persecution of the Jewish Religion" (Hebrew), *Salo Wittmayer Baron Jubilee Volume: Hebrew Section* (Jerusalem 1974), 213–245.

Liebman, Seymour. *The Enlightened: The Writings of Luis de Carvajal, el Mozo.* Coral Gables 1967.

Liebman, Seymour (trans. and ed.). *Jews and the Inquisition of Mexico: The Great Auto de fe of 1649 as Related by Mathias de Bocanegra.* Lawrence, Kans., 1974.

Lipiner, Elias. *Izaque de Castro: O mancebo que veio preso do Brasil.* Recife 1992.

———. *Santa Inquisição: Terror e linguagem, um dicionário da Santa Inquisição.* Rio de Janeiro 1977.

Llorente, Juan Antonio. *Histoire critique de l'Inquisition d'Espagne.* 4 vols. Paris 1817–1818.

Llorente, M. de la Pinta. *Procesos inquisitoriales contra los catedráticos hebraístas de Salamanca.* Madrid 1925.

Lockhart, James. *Spanish Peru, 1532–1560: A Social History.* 2nd ed. Madison 1994.

Longhurst, John E. "Julián Hernández, Protestant Martyr," *BHR* 20 (1960), 90–118.

———. *Luther's Ghost in Spain, 1517–1546.* Lawrence, Kans., 1969.

López Martínez, Nicolás. "Teología de controversia sobre judíos y judaizantes españoles del siglo XV: Ambientación y principales escritos," *Anuario de Historia de la Iglesia* 1 (1992), 39–70.

MacDonald, Michael. "'The Fearful Estate of Francis Spiera': Narrative, Identity and Emotion in Early Modern England," *Journal of British Studies* 31 (1992), 32–61.

Manuel, Frank. *The Broken Staff: Judaism through Christian Eyes.* Cambridge, Mass., 1992.

Maqueda Abreu, Consuelo. *El Auto de Fe.* Madrid 1992.

Marin Padilla, Encarnación. "Relación judeoconversa durante la segunda mitad del siglo XV en Aragón," *Sefarad* 42 (1982), 59–76.

———. *Relación judeoconversa durante la segunda mitad del siglo XV en Aragón: La Ley.* Madrid 1988.

Márquez, Antonio. *Los Alumbrados: Orígenes y filosofía (1525–1559).* Madrid 1980.

———. *Literatura e inquisición en España (1478–1834).* Madrid 1980.

Martz, Linda. *A Network of Converso Families in Early Modern Toledo: Assimilating a Minority.* Ann Arbor 2003.

Mattoso, José (ed.). *História de Portugal—Edição Académica.* Vol. 3. *No alvorecer da modernidad (1480–1620).* Lisbon 1997.

Mea, Elvira Cunha Azevedo. "Frei Diogo d'Assunção, o martir marano," *Proceedings of the Eleventh World Congress of Jewish Studies,* Division B, vol. 1 (Jerusalem 1994), 107–114.

Medina, José Toribio. *Historia del Tribunal del Santo Oficio de la Inquisición de Lima (1569–1820),* 2 vols. Santiago de Chile 1956.

———. *Historia delTribunal del Santo Oficio de la Inquisición en Chile.* Santiago de Chile 1952.

———. *Historia del Tribunal del Santo Oficio de la Inquisición en México.* Santiago de Chile 1905.

———. *El Tribunal del Santo Oficio de la Inquisición en las provincias del Plata.* Buenos Aires 1945.

Meeks, Wayne. *The First Urban Christians: The Social World of the Apostle Paul.* New Haven 1983.

Megged, Amos. *Exporting the Catholic Reformation: Local Religion in Early-Colonial Mexico.* Leiden 1996.

Meyuhas Ginio, Alisa. "Las aspiraciones mesianicas de los conversos en la Castilla de mediados del siglo XV," *El Olivo* 13 (1989), 217–233.

———. "The Fortress of Faith—At the End of the West: Alonso de Espina and his *Fortalitium Fidei,*" in Ora Limor and Guy Stroumsa (eds.), *Contra Iudaeos: Ancient and Medieval Polemics Between Christians and Jews* (Tübingen 1996), 215–237.

Millar Corbacho, René. "Las confiscaciones de la Inquisición de Lima a los comerciantes de orígen judeo-portugués de 'La Gran Complicidad' de 1635," *Revista de Indias* 43 (1983), 27–58.

Mintz, Alan. *Hurban: Responses to Catastrophe in Hebrew Literature.* New York 1984.

Monter, William. *Frontiers of Heresy: The Spanish Inquisition from the Basque Lands to Sicily.* Cambridge 1990.

Morell, Sanmuel. "The Samson Nazirite Vow in the Sixteenth Century," *AJS Review* 14 (1989), 223–262.

Muller, Richard. "Calvin's Exegesis of Old Testament Prophecies," in David Steinmetz (ed.), *The Bible in the Sixteenth Century* (Durham, N.C., 1990), 68–82.

Mulsow, Martin. "Cartesianism, Skepticism and Conversion to Judaism: The Case of Aaron d'Antan," in *SCJ,* 123–181.

Nadler, Steven. *Spinoza: A Life.* Cambridge 1999.

Nalle, Sara. *God in La Mancha: Religious Reform and the People of Cuenca, 1500–1659.* Baltimore 1992.

——. *Mad for God: Bartolomé Sánchez, The Secret Messiah of Cardenete.* Charlottesville 2001.

Netanyahu, B. *The Marranos of Spain: From the Late 14th to the Early 16th Century, According to Contemporary Hebrew Sources.* Ithaca, N.Y., 1999.

Nieto, José C. *Juan de Valdés and the Origins of the Spanish and Italian Reformation.* Geneva 1970.

——. "The Nonmystical Nature of the Sixteenth-Century Alumbrados of Toledo," in Angel Alcalá (ed.), *The Spanish Inquisition and the Inquisitorial Mind* (New York 1987), 431–456.

Ocaranza, Fernando. *Gregorio López, el hombre celestial.* Mexico City 1944.

Overell, M.A. "The Exploitation of Francesco Spiera," *Sixteenth Century Journal* 26 (1995), 619–637.

Pagis, Dan. "Elegies on the Massacres of 1391 in Spain" (Hebrew), *Tarbiz* 37 (1968), 370–371.

Paiva, José Pedro. "Spain and Portugal," in R. Po-chia Hsia (ed.), *A Companion to the Reformation World* (Malden, Mass., Oxford, and Melbourne 2004), 291–310.

Pérez Villanueva, Joaquín and Bartolomé Escandell Bonet (eds.). *Historia de la Inquisición en España y América,* 3 vols. Madrid 1984–2000.

Perry, Mary Elizabeth. "Beatas and the Inquisition in Early Modern Seville," in Stephen Haliczer (ed.), *Inquisition and Society in Early Modern Europe* (Totowa, NJ 1987), 147–168.

Peters, Edward. *The Inquisition.* Berkeley and Los Angeles 1989.

Pinta Llorente, Miguel de la. *Proceso criminal contra el hebraísta salmantino Martín Martínez de Cantalapiedra.* Madrid 1946.

——. *Procesos inquisitoriales contra los catedráticos hebraístas de Salamanca: Gaspar de Grajal, Martínez de Cantalapiedra, y Fr. Luis de León.* Madrid 1925.

Pinto Crespo, Virgilio. *Inquisición y control ideológico en la España del siglo XVI.* Madrid 1983.

Popkin, Richard. "Can One Be a True Christian and a Faithful Follower of the Law of Moses? The Answer of John Dury," in *SCJ,* 33–50.

——. "Marranos, New Christians and the Beginnings of Modern Anti-Trinitarianism," in Yom Tov Assis and Yosef Kaplan (eds.), *Jews and Conversos at the Time of the Expulsion* (Jerusalem 1999), 143–160.

——. "The Third Force in Seventeenth-Century Thought: Scepticism, Science and Millenarianism," in idem, *The Third Force in Seventeenth-Century Thought* (Leiden 1992), 90–119.

Popkin, Richard and Gordon Weiner (eds.). *Jewish Christians and Christian Jews*. Dordrecht 1994.

Powell, Philip Wayne. *Soldiers, Indians, and Silver: The Northward Advance of New Spain, 1550–1600*. Berkeley and Los Angeles 1952.

Quiroz, Alfonso. "La expropriación inquisitorial de cristianos nuevos portugueses en Los Reyes, Cartagena y México, 1635–1649," *Histórica* (Peru) 10 (1986), 237–303.

Rajak, Tessa. "Dying for the Law: The Martyr's Portrait in Jewish-Greek Literature," in M. J. Edwards and Simon Swain (eds.), *Portraits: Biographical Representation in the Greek and Latin Literature of the Roman Empire* (Oxford 1997), 39–67.

Redondo, Augustin. "Luther et l'Espagne de 1520 à 1536," *Mélanges de la Casa de Velázquez*, 1 (1965), 109–165.

Révah, I. S. "Aux origines de la rupture spinozienne: Nouvel examen des origines, du déroulement et des conséquences de l'affaire Spinoza-Prado-Ribera," *Annuaire du Collège de France* 70 (1970), 562–568.

——. "Aux origines de la rupture spinozienne: Nouvel examen des origines, du déroulement et des conséquences de l'affaire Spinoza-Prado-Ribera," *Annuaire du Collège de France* 72 (1972), 641–653.

——. *La censure inquisitoriale portugaise au XVIe siècle*. Lisbon 1960.

——. "Les Marranes," *REJ* 108 (1959–1960), 29–77.

——. "La religion d'Uriel da Costa, Marrane de Porto," *RHR* 161 (1962), 45–76.

——. *Uriel da Costa et les Marranes de Porto: Cours au Collège de France, 1966–1972*. Ed. by Carsten Wilke. Paris 2004.

Rhodes, Elizabeth. "Luisa de Carvajal's Counter-Reformation Journey to Selfhood (1566–1614)," *Renaissance Quarterly* 51 (1998), 887–911.

Roth, Cecil. "Abraham Nuñez Bernal et autres martyrs contemporains de l'Inquisition," *REJ* 100 (1936), 38–51.

——. "Le Chant du cygne de Don Lope de Vera," *REJ* 97 (1934), 97–113.

——. "A Hebrew Elegy on the Martyrs of Toledo, 1391," *JQR* 39 (1948–1949), 135–150.

——. *A History of the Marranos*. New York 1974.

Round, Nicholas. "La rebelión toledana de 1449: Aspectos ideológicos," *Archivum* 16 (1966), 385–446.

Rubin, Miri. *Corpus Christi: The Eucharist in Late Medieval Culture*. Cambridge 1991.

Rubio Merino, Pedro. "Autos de fe de la Inquisición de Córdoba durante el siglo XVII a traves de la documentación del Archivo de la Santa Iglesia Catedral de Sevilla," in Joaquim Pérez Villanueva (ed.), *La Inquisición Española: Nueva Vision, Nuevas Horizontes* (Madrid 1980), 329–349.

Ruderman, David. "Hope Against Hope: Jewish and Christian Messianic Expectations in the Late Middle Ages," in Aharon Mirsky, Avraham Grossman, and Yosef Kaplan (eds.), *Exile and Diaspora* (Jerusalem 1991), 185–202.

Safrai, S. "*Kiddush ha-Shem* in the Teachings of the Tannaim" (Hebrew), *Zion* 44 (1979), 28–42.

Saperstein, Marc. *Exile in Amsterdam: Saul Levi Morteira's Sermons to a Congregation of "New Jews."* Cincinnati 2005.

——. "*Your Voice Like a Ram's Horn*": *Themes and Texts in Traditional Jewish Preaching*. Cincinnati 1996.

Saraiva de Carvalho, J. M. de Almeida. "The Fellowship of St. Diogo: New Christian

Judaisers in Coimbra in the Early Seventeenth Century." Ph.D. dissertation, University of Leeds, 1990.

Seidel, Esther, "Out of the Ghetto and into the Open Society: Conversion from the Renaissance to the Twentieth Century," in Walter Homulka, Walter Jacob and Esther Seidel (eds.), *Not by Birth Alone: Conversion to Judaism* (London and Washington 1997), 36–52.

Sharpe, J. A. "'Last Dying Speeches': Religion, Ideology and Public Execution in Seventeenth-Century England," *PaP* no. 107 (May 1985), 144–167.

Shatz, Rivka. "An Outline of the Image of the Political-Messianic Arousal after the Spanish Expulsion" (Hebrew), *Da'at* 11 (1982–1983), 53–66.

Shatzmiller, Joseph. "Jewish Converts to Christianity in Medieval Europe: 1200–1500," in Michael Goodich, Sophia Menache, and Sylvia Schein (eds.), *Cross-Cultural Convergences in the Crusader Period: Essays Presented to Aryeh Grabois on his Sixty-Fifth Birthday* (New York 1995), 297–318.

Shochet, Azriel. "*Kiddush ha-Shem* in the Thinking of the Spanish Exiles and the Kabbalists of Safed" (Hebrew), in *Milḥemet kodesh u-martyrologyah be-toldot Yisra'el uve-toldot ha-amim* (Jerusalem 1967), 143–145.

Silva Dias, José Sebastião da. *Correntes de sentimento religioso em Portugal (séculos XVI a XVIII)*, 2 vols. Coimbra 1960.

Silverblatt, Irene. "New Christians and New World Fears in Seventeenth-Century Peru," *Comparative Studies of Society and History* 42 (2000), 524–546.

Smith, Morton. *Jesus the Magician*. New York 1977.

Soloveitchik, Haym. "Halakhah, Hermeneutics, and Martyrdom in Medieval Ashkenaz," *JQR* 94 (2004), 77–108, 278–299.

Spiegel, Shalom. *The Last Trial: On the Legends and Lore of the Command to Abraham to Offer Isaac as a Sacrifice: The Akedah*. Trans. by Judah Goldin. Woodstock, Vt., 1993.

Spierenburg, Pieter. *The Spectacle of Suffering: Executions and the Evolution of Repression*. Cambridge 1984.

Stacey, Robert. "The Conversion of Jews to Christianity in Thirteenth-Century England," *Speculum* 67 (1992), 263–283.

Stewart, Columba. *Cassian the Monk*. New York and Oxford 1998.

Stradling, R. A. *Europe and the Decline of Spain: A Study of the Spanish System, 1580–1720*. London 1981.

Strathmann, Hermann. "μάρτυς etc.," *Theological Dictionary of the New Testament* 4 (1967), 475–514.

Strauss, Gerald. "A Seventeenth Century Conversion to Judaism: Two Letters from Benedictus Sperling to His Mother," *Jewish Social Studies* 36 (1974), 166–174.

Straw, Carole. "'A Very Special Death': Christian Death in its Classical Context," in Margaret Cormack (ed.), *Sacrificing the Self: Perspectives on Martyrdom and Religion* (Oxford 2002), 39–57.

Stuczynski, Claude. "Apóstatas marroquíes de origen judío en Portugal en los siglos XVI–XVII: Entre la misión y la Inquisición," in Mercedes García-Arenal (ed.), *Los judíos magrebíes en la Edad Moderna* (Madrid 2003), 125–152.

Talmage, Frank. "The Polemical Writings of Profiat Duran," *Immanuel* 13 (1981), 69–85.

Tardieu, Jean-Pierre. *L'inquisition de Lima et les hérétiques étrangers (XVIe–XVIIe siècles)*. Paris 1995.

Tavim, José Alberto Rodrigues da Silva. *Os judeus na expansão portuguesa em Marrocos durante o século XVI: Origens e actividades duma comunidade*. Braga 1997.

Teixeira, A. J. *Antonio Homem e a Inquisição.* Coimbra, 1895.

Tellechea Idígoras, José Ignacio. "Biblias publicadas fuera de España secuestradas por la Inquisición de Sevilla en 1552," *Bulletin Hispanique* 64 (1962), 236–247.

——. "La censura inquisitorial de Biblias de 1554," *Anthología Annua* 10 (1962), 89–142.

——. "Francisco de San Román, un mártir protestante burgalés (1542)," *Cuadernos de Investigación Histórica* 7 (1984), 223–260.

Tishby, Isaiah. *Messianism in the Time of the Expulsion from Spain and Portugal* (Hebrew). Jerusalem 1985.

Toro, Alfonso. *La Familia Carvajal: Estudio histórico sobre los judíos y la Inquisición de la Nueva España.* 2 vols. Mexico City 1944.

Turner, Victor. *Dramas, Fields, and Metaphors: Symbolic Action in Human Society.* Ithaca, N.Y., 1974.

Uchmany, Eva Alexandra. "The Participation of New Christians and Crypto-Jews in the Conquest, Colonization, and Trade of Spanish America, 1521–1660," in *JEEW,* 186–202.

——. "La vida en las cárceles del Santo Oficio en la Ciudad de México entre 1589 a 1660," in Henri Méchoulan and Gerard Nahon (eds.), *Mémorial I. S. Revah: Études sur le marranisme, l'hétérodoxie juive et Spinoza* (Paris and Louvain 2001), 471–489.

——. *La vida entre el judaísmo y el cristianismo en la Nueva España, 1580–1606.* Mexico City 1992.

——. Vauchez, André. *Sainthood in the Later Middle Ages.* Trans. by Jean Birrell. Cambridge 1997.

Wachtel, Nathan. *La Foi du souvenir: Labyrinthes marranes.* Paris 2001.

——. "Marrano Religiosity in Hispanic America in the Seventeenth Century," in *JEEW,* 149–171.

Wagner, C. "Los luteranos ante la Inquisición de Toledo en el siglo XVI," *Hispania Sacra* 46/94 (1994), 474–505.

Weill, Julien. "Nicolas Antoine," *REJ* 37 (1898), 161–180.

Weitzman, Steve. "Josephus on How to Survive Martyrdom," *Journal of Jewish Studies* 55 (2004), 230–245.

Werblowsky, Zvi. "R. Joseph Caro, Solomon Molcho, Don Joseph Nasi," in Haim Beinart (ed.), *The Sephardi Legacy,* 2 vols. (Jerusalem 1992), 2: 179–191.

Wilke, Carsten. "Conversion ou retour? La métamorphose du nouveau chrétien en juif portugais dans l'imaginaire sépharade du XVIIe siècle," in Esther Benbassa (ed.), *Memoires juives d'Espagne et du Portugal* (Paris 1996), 53–67.

Williams, George. "The Two Social Strands in Italian Anabaptism, ca. 1526–1565" in Lawrence Buck and Jonathan Zophy (eds.), *The Social History of the Reformation* (Columbus, Ohio, 1972), 156–207.

Wittreich, Joseph. *Interpreting "Samson Agonistes."* Princeton 1986.

Wiznitzer, Arnold. *Jews in Colonial Brazil.* New York 1960.

Wolff, Philippe. "The 1391 Pogrom in Spain: Social Crisis or Not?" *PaP* no. 50 (February 1971), 4–18.

Wood, Diana, ed. *Martyrs and Martyrologies: Papers Read at the 1992 Summer Meeting of the Ecclesiastical History Society.* Oxford 1993.

Yerushalmi, Yosef Hayim. *From Spanish Court to Italian Ghetto: Isaac Cardoso, A Study in Seventeenth-Century Marranism and Jewish Apologetics.* Seattle 1971.

——. "A Jewish Classic in the Portuguese Language," introduction to Samuel Usque, *Consolação às Tribulações de Israel,* 2 vols. (Lisbon 1989), 1: 19–123.

——. "Professing Jews in Post-Expulsion Spain and Portugal," in Saul Lieberman (ed.), *Salo Wittmayer Baron Jubilee Volume*, 3 vols. (Jerusalem 1974), 2: 1023–1058.

——. "Spinoza on the Survival of the Jewish People" (Hebrew), *Proceedings of the Israel National Academy of Sciences* 6 (1984), 171–213.

Yovel, Yirmiyahu. *Spinoza and Other Heretics: The Marrano of Reason*. Princeton 1989.

Yuval, Israel. "Vengeance and Damnation, Blood and Defamation: From Jewish Martyrdom to Blood Libel Accusations" (Hebrew), *Zion* 58 (1993), 33–90.

Zagorin, Perez. *Ways of Lying: Dissimulation, Persecution, and Conformity in Early Modern Europe*. Cambridge, Mass.,and London 1990.

Zerubavel, Yael. *Recovered Roots: Collective Memory and the Making of Israeli National Tradition*. Chicago 1995.

Index

Italicized page numbers indicate illustrations.

Abendana, Jacob, 193
Abraham ben Ophrit, 7
Abrunhosa, Frei Antonio d', 112
acusación, 70, 71, 72, 97, 122, 133, 164, 169
aggadah/aggadoth, 38
Aguilar, Moshe Rafael d', 176, 177
Akiva, Rabbi, 3, 186, 187
Alfonso de Toledo, 16
Almeida, Isaac d', 193
Almeida, Jorge de, 55, 65, 67
Almohads, 5
Alonso de Espina, 12, 163
alumbradismo, 21, 69–70, 78, 196
Amsterdam, 30, 32, 80, 82, 163, 249n19;
    crypto-Jewish martyrs memorialized in, 185;
    excommunication from Jewish community of,
    180, 182, 249n15; Jewish community of, 26,
    46, 137, 176; news of Iberian martyrdom in,
    188, 191–192; Spanish-language texts pub-
    lished in, 37
Anabaptists, 33, 248n4
Ángel, Cristóbal, 156
*Annotationes in Novum Testamentum [Annota-
    tions on the New Testament]* (Erasmus), 159,
    167, 244n16
Antan, Aaron d', 179
Antiochus, 1, 75
Antoine, Nicolas, 179, 248n6
apocalypticism, 17–18, 82
apostates, Jewish, 6–7, 148, 166, 208n30
Arabic language, 159, 161
Aragon, 5, 6, 10, 14, 15
Aramaic language, 164
Aristotle, 142
ars moriendi literature, 34
Asher ben Yechiel, 7
Ashkenazim, 4–5, 5–6, 8, 206n14
Assembly of Tomar, 42
assimilation, 9, 26, 206n14

Asumpção, Frei Diogo d', 31, 137, 178, 187;
    ambiguous Jewish ancestry of, 79, 87, 89, 95,
    113; behavior in Capuchin order, 101–104,
    106–107, 116; conversion to "Judaism," 95–
    96, 98, 111, 179; critique of Catholic Church,
    79–82, 113; crypto-judaizing practices and,
    112, 234n84; denounced by fellow prisoners,
    91–95, 99; "diagnosis" of heresy of, 107–109;
    first audience with Inquisition, 85–86; genea-
    logical inquiry into, 84–85; identification with
    Messiah, 100–101, 108; Inquisition records
    about, 188; interrogations of, 82–84, 87–91,
    96–99; martyrdom of, 93, 109, 111–112;
    "Protestantish" beliefs, 108–109, 111, 113;
    psychology of, 114–116
Athias, Abraham, 193, 194
Augustine (Church Father), 90–91, 96
Augustinian order, 150
autos-da-fé, 15, 18, 23, *28,* 40, 100; burning in
    effigy, 41, 49, 174; as grand spectacle, 27; in
    Lima, 118, 122–123, 141, 144; in Lisbon,
    109, *110,* 111–112; muzzling of condemned
    prisoners, 40, 174; news spread abroad of, 188.
    See also stake, burning at the
Auxilio de la religión [Ezer ha-da'at] (Moses ha-
    Kohen), 13
Ávalos, Diego de, 156
Avignon, anti-papacy of, 12
Azambuja, Jerónimo de (Jerónimo Oleastro), 64

Babylonia, 1, 89
baptism, 4, 5, 6, 38, 83, 156; apostasy and, 97–
    98; coerced, 32; Jesus and, 81; martyrdom
    and, 14; religious disputations and, 10; sacra-
    mental nature denied, 97–98; suicide as
    resistance to, 21
Barcelona, 7, 8
Barrios, Daniel Levi de, 41, 174, 188, 193, 194,
    195
Bataillon, Marcel, 213–214n7, 227n125

Bautista Pérez, Manuel, 32, 146, 240n90
Becket, Thomas, 34
Beinart, Haim, 166–167, 203n7
Belchior, Frei, 103
Benedict XIII, anti-pope, 10
Benítez, Daniel, 73–74, 229n156
Bernal, Abraham Nuñez, 193
Bernal, Juan, 147
Bible, 12, 29, 50, 52–53, 74, 121, 156, 175; foreign-published Bibles banned in Spain, 24; vernacular translations, 13, 51, 118. *See also* New Testament; Old Testament; Scripture
Bible, books of: Baruch, 32; Daniel, 1; Ecclesiastes, 143; Exodus, 59, 66, 130; Ezekiel, 10; Ezra, Fourth Book of (Vulgate), 54; Genesis, 52, 75, 131, 177, 223n36; Haggai, 138, 164; Jeremiah, 11, 108, 184, 200; Lamentations, 76; Leviticus, 132, 161; 2 Maccabees, 1, 64, 192; 1 Samuel, 184; Wisdom, 100. *See also* Deuteronomy, Book of; Psalms, Book of
Bitul ikare ha-notsrim [Refutation of Christian Principles] (Crescas), 11, 13
Bivach (Bibago), Abraham, 11, 12
Black Legend, 27
blood libels, 2, 6, 15
Boccarro, Gaspar, 79, 230n8
body, resurrection of, 107
Bonafed, Solomon, 12–13
Brazil, 117, 191–192
Bueno, Jacob, 30
Burgos, 7, 9, 148
"burnt ones" (*los quemados*), 18, 20, 212n86

Cáceres, Antonio Díaz de, 54
Calepino, Ambrosio, 150
calificadores/qualificadores (inquisitorial theologians), 29, 123; Carvajal (Luis) and, 74; Maldonado de Silva and, 129, 133, 134, 138, 140, 144; Vera (Lope de) and, 165–166, 168–169, 171, 174
Calvin, John, 26
Calvinists, 31, 163, 214n15, 248n6
Camara, Fray Marcos de la, 83, 106
Capuchin order, 79, 83–84, 101–104, 106–107, 113
Cardoso, Isaac: on Castro Tartas (Isaac de), 191–192; on circumcision, 217n53, 239n59; on Maldonado de Silva, 30, 188; on Pinhanços, 42–43, 45, 189–191
Carvajal, Baltasar, 35, 47, 48, 50, 52, 57; in hiding, 61, 64, 223n41; in Italy, 71; plan to escape New Spain, 58–60, 64
Carvajal, Catalina, 49, 60, 76

Carvajal, Francisca, 49, 65, 221n15
Carvajal, Gaspar, 48, 52, 58–60, 61, 63–64
Carvajal, Isabel, 52, 54, 60, 63, 76
Carvajal, Leonor, 70, 76, 228nn142–143
Carvajal, Luis, 31, 46, 97, 137, 151, 168, 178; *alumbradismo* and, 69–70, 78; early life, 47; family of, 47–50, 65, 71; Hebrew name taken by, 36, 62, 67, 72, 73; immigration to New Spain, 47–48; imprisonment and trials of, 60–68, 70–74, 225n86, 229n159; interpretation of Scripture, 68–70; Italian Jewish communities and, 55, 57; last-minute "conversion," 30, 76, 215n25; life in Mexico, 51–55; Maccabees as model and, 192; memoirs, 33, 53; Morales's influence on, 48–51, 73, 78, 181; plan to escape New Spain, 58–60; reading habits, 52–54, 67–68, 223n34, 226n101; reasons for adhering to Law of Moses, 199–200; as *relapso*, 65; self-circumcision, 35, 54, 66, 169; sentences meted out to, 63–64, 74; suicide attempt, 73–74
Carvajal, Luis (elder), 47–48, 51–52, 60
Carvajal, Mariana, 49–50, 60, 220–221n2, 230n165
Carvajal, Miguel, 64, 71
Caseres, Yahacob Rodrigues, 194
Cassian, John, 89
Castanheira, Portugal, 79, 82, 83, 102, 113
Castile, 5, 10, 14, 47; autos-da-fé in, 15; "culture of visions" in, 18; economic decline of, 48
Castro, Alfonso de, 51
Castro Tartas, Isaac de, 42–43, 46, 188, 191–192
Cathars, 205n7
Catholic Church, 3, 178; apocalyptic visions and, 18; campaign to convert Iberian Jews, 4, 6; cult of the host, 156; dogmatista defiance against, 40; erosion of authority of, 138–139; establishment of, 97; Frei Diogo's critique of, 79–82; "idolatry" of, 51; Jewish apostates in, 6–7; martyrologies of, 188, 189, 250n38; Protestant martyrs and, 26; rabbinical polemics and, 12; reconciliation with, 24; reformist attacks on, 12; sacraments of, 83; saint veneration, 189; Talmud attacked by, 38. *See also* Christianity; Jesuits; papacy/popes; theologians, Catholic
Cerda y Sotomayor, Don Cristóbal de la, 125
Chagas, Frei Francisco das, 102, 103, 104
Charles I, king of England, 151
Charles V, Emperor, 27
Chichimeca Indians (Mexico), 47, 51, 54, 57, 222n32

Chile, 122, 124–125, 130

Chmielnitski massacres (1648), 203n6

Christ, Law of, 35, 37, 67, 72, 92, 165; abandonment of, 122; Frei Diogo's critique of, 81, 83; rejection of, 167

Christian, William, 18, 212n83

Christiani, Pablo, 6, 10, 208n30

Christianity, 5, 38, 100, 158; Christendom as fourth beast, 75; early period of, 12; Hebrew Scripture and, 37; Judaism and Christian dissenters, 179; martyrdom in theology of, 2; rabbinical polemics against, 10–13, 25; skepticism about, 167. *See also* Catholic Church; Jesus Christ; Protestantism; Reformation

Chronica universal (Alonso de Maldonado), 134

circumcision, 35, 116, 210n72, 217n53; of Carvajal (Luis), 52–54, 66; in Cassian's *Conferences,* 89; as eternal "sacrament," 75; of Maldonado de Silva, 126, 131, 150, 151; Saint Paul and, 81; of Vera (Lope de), 169, 171

Cohen, Gerson, 5

Cohen, Martin, 47–48, 220n1

Coimbra, 45, 84, 101, 103, *105,* 112, 181; inquisitorial prison in, 91, 92; tribunal of, 42, 43

Complicidad Grande, 139, 146

Conceição, Frei Diogo da, 101, 103, 106

Conciliarists, 12

Conferences (Cassian), 89, 90

confession, Catholic sacrament of, 13, 127

Constantine (Roman emperor), 97

Constantinople, 71, 177

Contreras, Alonso, 76, 230n169

conversion, 8, 10, 208–209n45; campaign of 1391, 5–8, 9; of Portuguese Jews, 21–22

conversos, 8, 162; anti-Christian polemics and, 12–13; conceptions of martyrdom among, 17–18; crypto-Jews abandoned by, 20; Inquisition and, 16; Judaism practiced clandestinely, 9; messianism and, 39; penitent, 24; Portuguese, 21–22, 26, 117; "Protestantish" opinion and, 178; Sabbath observance and, 91; ties to émigré diaspora, 26–27; violence against, 14. *See also* New Christians

Cordera, Antonio, 139

Cordova, 7, 14, 29, 46, 193

coroza, wearing of, 40, 141

Correa, Manoel, 86–87, 89–90, 96

Costa, Pero da, 84

Costa, Uriel da, 177, 180–182, 217n56

Council of Trent, 22, 51, 130

Covenant, 1, 9, 10, 35, 70, 186

Crescas, Hasdai, 8, 11, 13

Crespin, Jean, 31, 189

Creyente, Judah, 36, 152, 193, 246n53. *See also* Vera, Lope de

Crusades/Crusaders, 2, 4, 5–6, 8, 16–17, 206n13

Cruz, Isabel del la, 69

crypto-Jews: anti-Christian polemics and, 12; appropriation of Catholic values, 15, 18; Catholic texts used by, 67, 68, 130, 163; conceptions of martyrdom, 20; defense strategy against Inquisition, 164; dissimulation of faith by, 32–33; fasting practices of, 99, 121; "good death" ideal and, 34–35; Inquisition and, 15–16; Jesuit education and, 58; judaizing practice among, 47; kinship networks of, 39, 179; medieval philosophy and, 142; in New Spain, 49, 51, 54–55, 68, 78; news of martyrdom and, 30; open declaration of faith and, 31, 33; in Peru, 117, 147; in Portugal, 21–22, 23–24, 114; pride of, 9; rabbinic Judaism and, 177, 180, 186; Reformation and, 24–26, 196; Scripture as anchor of belief, 120. *See also* martyrs, (crypto-)Jewish

Cuaresma, Tomé, 124, 131, 146, 239n54

Daniel (biblical), 1, 65, 75, 183

Darius, 1

De los nombres de Cristo (Luis de Léon), 148, 150

De Sacramentis (Francis de Vitoria), 83, 86

death, noble, 1, 2, 34–35

Decalogue, 124

Descartes, René, 115

Deuteronomy, Book of, 66, 69, 199, 223n34; "law of Christ" and, 80; martyrdom and, 31, 183, 186; on oneness of God, 143; on salvation, 10; song of Moses, 130, 132. *See also* Bible, books of

devotio moderna, 68

Diary of David Reuveni, 158, 162, 164, 167, 169

Dias, Bernaldo, 85

Dias, Tristão, 91

diaspora, Jewish, 4, 179, 180, 188, 189, 193

Díaz, Jorge, 55, 57

Díaz, Luis, 65–66

Díaz de Cáceres, Antonio, 54

Díaz Nieto, Diego (Isaac), 55, 57

Díaz Nieto, Ruy (Jacob), 55

Díaz of Almagro, Constanza, 16

Díaz Tavares, Gregorio, 123, 124, 126, 128, 151

dietary laws, 8, 49, 63

Dionysius Carthusianus, 120, 121

Disputation of Barcelona, 38, 208n30

Disputation of Tortosa, 38, 208n30

disputations, religious, 6–7, 10, 29

dissimulation, 125, 184
dogmatista martyrs, 23, 25, 111, 204n10; Christian dissent and, 178; defiant death of, 27; disputations with inquisitors, 36–37; masculine self-image of, 151; numbers of, 41, 219n72; open declaration of faith by, 40; proselytizing of, 63; provocative traits of, 182; rabbinic Judaism and, 177; Scripture and, 120; theological disputes and, 29, 226n90. *See also* martyrs, (crypto-)Jewish
Domingo de Soto, 80
Domingues, Pero, 91–92, 93, 94
Dominican order, 80, 83, 133, 231n15
dreams, 65, 116, 227n126
Drusio, Johannes, 163, 164
Duarte, Sebastian, 146
Dueñas, Fray Juan de, 67
Duns Scotus, 80
Duran, Profayt, 9–10, 11, 12
Dury, John, 115
"dying in Law of Moses," 3, 14, 33, 123, 151; Asumpção (Frei Diogo de), 97; Carvajal (Luis), 66, 67, 70, 74; Maldonado de Silva, 128, 129, 132, 133; Pinhanços, 45; Vera (Lope de), 165, 167, 169, 170, 171. *See also* martyrs, (crypto-)Jewish; Moses, Law of

effigy, burning in, 41, 49, 174
"Efodi, the." *See* Duran, Profayt
Egypt, Jews enslaved in, 32, 50, 75, 143
Eleazar (biblical), 64, 72
Elliott, J. H., 30
Emblemas Morales (Horozco y Covarrubias), 148
encomenderos, 117–118
England, 25, 81, 113, 216n35
Enríquez Gómez, Antonio, 151–152, 193, 195, 242n132
Erasmus, 3, 153, 163, 213n7; *Annotationes,* 159, 167, 244n16; *luteranos* and, 147
Espejo de Consolación (Juan de Dueñas), 67
Esperança de Israel (Menasseh ben Israel), 188
Esplugas, Gracia de, 16
Esther, Fast of, 50, 57, 99
Eucharist, 13, 114, 156, 243n7
Excelencias de los Hebreos, Las (Cardoso), 42, 188
excommunication: from Catholic Church, 97, 131, 161, 175; from Jewish community, 180, 249n15
exegesis, biblical, 3, 75
Ezekiel (biblical prophet), 10, 200

Fagundez, Frei Jeronimo (de Jesus), 83, 101–104, 106

Fagundez, Baltasar Vaz, 104
fasting, 50, 55, 91, 99, 121, 133, 135, 139
Fernandes, Francisco, 111–112
Fernandez de Luna, Miguel, 93, 94
Ferrara, 56, 57
Ferraz, Gaspar, 87
Ferrer, Jaime, 13
Ferrer, Vicente, 10
Flanders, 25, 27, 33
Flynn, Maureen, 40–41
Fonseca, Manuel. *See* Tavares, Manuel Álvarez
Foreiro, Frei Paulo, 107–109
Fortalitium fidei (Alonso de Espina), 12, 163
Foxe, John, 31, 189, 190
France, 25, 79, 83, 113, 151, 195
Francis, Saint, 82
Franciscan order, 80, 113, 133
friars, mendicant, 38

Galatino, Pietro Colonna, 163
García, Benito, 15
Gardiner, William, 25
garrote, execution by, 27, 30, 46, 76, 146–147, 215n19. *See also* stake, burning at the
Génebrard, Gilbert, 132, 148
Gitlitz, David, 148, 150, 218n64
God, perfection of, 143
God of Heaven, 44
Gomes, Antonio, 92, 108
Gomes, Pero, 92
Gómez Navarro, Manuel, 65, 227n115
Gómez Piñero, Pero, 118
González, Maria, 17
Gorião, Antonio Gomes, 93, 94
Gospels, 74–75, 87, 90, 142, 179; Catholic Church teachings and, 12; crisis from critical reading of, 180. *See also* New Testament
Granada, Luis de, 57, 67–68, 68, 74, 140, 150, 174
Greco-Roman culture, 1–2, 205n4
Guerrero, Lobo, 66, 73, 229n155
Guía de pecadores (Luis de Granada), 67

Hacker, Yosef, 9
Haemstede, Adriaen Cornelis van, 189
Halevi, Isaac ben Moses. *See* Duran, Profayt
Hananiah ben Teradion, Rabbi, 3, 186, 187
Hartlib, Samuel, 115
hashkavah prayer, 185, 186, 187
Hebrew language, 13, 42, 66, 133, 157; taught at University of Salamanca, 153, 243n2; Vera (Lope de) and, 159, 161, 165, 170
hell, 18, *19*

Henry II, king of England, 34
heresy/heretics, 12, 13, 45, 83; burning of heretics, 25–26; classification of, 163; contempt for the Church, 27; "diagnosis" of, 107–109; disputations with inquisitors, 29; dissimulation and, 32; ex-conversos of Amsterdam as, 180, 182; "good death" and, 35; judaizers accused of, 14, 96; martyrdom and, 16, 17; "Protestantish," 111; public humiliation and, 40; "talmudic" Jews as heretics, 39; vernacular Scripture as source of, 51
Herreros, Don Andres de los, 175
Herrezuelo, Bachiller, 25
holidays, Jewish, 8, 99
Homem, António, 181
Horozco y Covarrubias, Juan de, 148
host, real presence in, 162, 164, 231n15
humanism, 99, 138, 147, 213–214n7, 243n2
Hunter, William, *190*
Hus, Jan, 12
Hussites, 205n7

Ibn Ezra, Abraham, 133, 163
"idolatry," 5, 25, 51, 75, 97, 185–186; Christianity accused of, 126, 131; Protestant attack on, 147
Ignatius Loyola, 68
illuminists, 113, 213n7. *See also alumbradismo*
images, veneration of, 124, 162, 164
Incarnation, Catholic doctrine of, 7, 11, 12, 159, 162, 164
Index of Prohibited Books, 160
Inés de Herrara, 18, 20, 211n81, 212n86
Inquisition, 23, 36, 84; autos-da-fé as grand spectacle, 27, 40–41; books banned by, 31, 50, 159, *160*, 222n23; confession as defense before, 164, 166; cruelty of, 112, 193; crypto-Jewish kinship networks and, 179; crypto-Jewish notions of martyrdom and, 15–16; documentation/dossiers of, 4, 20, 43, 46, 101, 150, 188, 196; early stages of, 17, 215n19; establishment of, 12, 14, 15, 23; informers for, 63, 65–66, 91–95; Jews seen as heretics, 39; Judeo-Christian polemics and, 13; *luterano* martyrs and, 3, 150, 206n10; medieval, 24; in New Spain, 48, 221n7; pace of trials, 23; in Peru, 120, 126, 130–131, 139, 240n90; in Portugal, 22, 23, 24, 38, 109, 185; prison cells of, 30; procedures of, 97–98; psychological effect on inmates, 115; Reformation and, 24–25, 27, 29; in Spain, *173*, 174, 185, 195; torture used as tool of, 73, 157, 166, 173; Venetian, 31; vernacular Bibles suppressed by, 51;

witnesses and denunciations, 60, 121, 153, 155–159. *See also calificadores/qualificadores* (inquisitorial theologians)
Introducción del símbolo de la fe (Luis de Granada), 57, 67–68, 74, 140, 150, 174
Isaac ben Shushan, 7
Islam, 5, 6, 158. *See also* Moors; Muslims
Israel, people of, 9, 75, 130
Israel al-Nakawa, 7
Israelites, ancient, 86, 88, 132, 143, 161
Italy, 25, 33, 55, 57, 64, 130

Jerome (Church Father), 12, 90
Jesuits, 31, 45, 58, 64; at autos-da-fé, 111; *beatas* (lay sisters), 126, 127; Carvajal (Luis) and, 72, 74; as inquisitors, 87; Maldonado de Silva and, 133, 134, 140
Jesus Christ, 9, 44, 45, 81–82, 132, 231n16; as Antichrist, 200; apostles and, 81; authority of Catholic Church and, 36; birth of, 80, 83, 126; charge of blaspheming Christ, 13, 71, 171; Christian teaching on martyrdom and, 183; Church teachings about, 122; divinity challenged by Jewish polemics, 12, 127; as example for humanity, 183; as false prophet, 67, 114, 158, 162, 163; identification with, 2, 100–101, 108; Law of Moses and, 74–75, 81; messiahship denied, 50, 61, 80, 93, 120, 128, 142, 163, 168; Samson identified with, 151. *See also* Christianity
Jesus, Frei Jeronimo de. *See* Fagundez, Frei Jeronimo
Jews and Jewish communities: in Amsterdam, 26, 46, 137, 176; Ashkenazi, 4–5, 8; conversos and, 8–9; as "enemies" of Christianity, 163; Expulsion from Spain, 5, 12, 20, 23; forcible conversion of, 7; Iberian exiles in Europe, 26, 32; Jews as God's people, 67; Law of Moses and, 189; martyrdom and, 184; Messiah and, 88–89, 163; mob violence against, 2, 5, 7, 10; in North Africa, 37; as people favored by God, 158; as persecuted people, 2–3; Sephardi (Iberian), 4–5; twelve tribes, 158; in Venice, 49, 57, 137
Joseph ben Shem Tov, 11
Joshua del Soto, David, 176
Juan de Madrid, 14–15
Juan de Segovia, 18
Juan II of Aragon, 12
Judah, kingdom of, 1
Judah, Rabbi, 7
Judaism, 11, 30, 45, 89, 100, 158; anti-Nicodemite tradition in, 31–32; appropriation

Judaism (*continued*)
of Catholic usage, 15; converts' reversion to, 5, 8; defended against Inquisition, 168; as "deformed" faith, 90; embraced by Christian dissenters, 179, 180; "errors" of, 107; freedom of thought associated with, 178; freely practiced in exile, 32, 49, 163; Hebrew Scripture and, 37; "historicist" attacks on, 12; holidays, 8, 99; information gleaned from Catholic texts, 120; martyrdom and, 2, 183, 205n5, 250n38; in northern Europe, 113; rabbinic, 37, 57, 69, 177, 181, 186, 192; Talmud and, 38

judaizers/judaizing, 14, 24, 65, 99–100, 196; acts associated with, 43; anomalous relation to Judaism, 186; burned alive at the stake, 41, 42; Catholic texts used by, 120–121, 150; within Christian perspective, 178; disputations with inquisitors, 29; last-minute "conversion" of, 29–30; martyrdom and, 16; pardoned in Spain, 122, 237n16; in Peru, 146; Portuguese conversos in Spain, 26; reconciled to the Church, 112, 122–123, 125; in Spanish America, 26, 37, 55; taxonomy of heresy and, 96

Judith, Fast of, 50

Karaites, 39
kedoshim. See martyrs, (crypto-)Jewish
Kelimat ha-goyim [Reproach of the Gentiles] (Duran), 12
kiddush ha-shem, 2, 186
Kimchi, David, 133
Koran, 159

Last Judgment, 18, *19*, 41, 94
Last Judgment, The (Van Eyck, studio of), *19*
Latin language, 13, 23, 42, 65, 81, 90, 150; biblical verses in, 93, 95; Catholic laity and, 80; Inquisition interrogations and, 67, 85, 88, 134, 170; vernacular translations from, 118
Laureto di Buongiorno, Giovanni, 179, 248n4
Leeuwen, Denys van. *See* Dionysius Carthusianus
León, Catalina de, 52
León, Fray Luis de, 148, 150, 243n2
León, New Kingdom of, 47, 60
libelo, 97, 98, 109
Lima, 32, *119*, 122, 191; autos-da-fé in, 151; tribunal of, 117, 118, 122, 125, 126, 139
Lisbon, 25, 36, 46, 49, 79, *105;* autos-da-fé in, 109, *110*, 111–112; Capuchin monastery in, 101, 103; Inquisition in, 82

López, Gregorio, 57–58, 65, 68, 78, 178, 229n155
López, Manuel, 213n1
Lucena, Gaspar de, 118, 121
Lucena, Manuel de, 65, 227n115, 230n166
Lumbroso, Joseph. *See* Carvajal, Luis
Luna, Pedro de, 10
luteranismo, 24–26, 29, 33, 108–109
luterano(s), 3, 29, 57, 68, 73, 147, 150, 196, 206n10
Luther, Martin, 3, 81, 91, 147, 233n58
Lyra, Nicholas, 142–143

Maccabees, 33, 75, 152, 192, 205n4, 242n134
Machado, Antonio, 55, 227n115
Madrid, 7, *28*, 31, 153, *154*, 155
Maimi, R. Simon, 21
Maimonides, 64
Maldonado, Aldonza, 118
Maldonado, Fray Alsonso de, 133, 134
Maldonado de Silva, Francisco, 29, 30, 42, 151–152; arrest and first audience, 127–130; disputations with inquisitors, 131–134, 135, 140–144, 191; early life of, 117, 118, 120, 123; escape attempt, 135, 137; fasting in prison, 135; *hashkavah* prayer and, 187; Hebrew name of, 36; judaizing practices and sources, 130–131, *136*, 137; martyrdom of, 117, 144, *145*, 146–147, 191, 246n51; medical practice of, 124–125; news of career spread abroad, 188; path to martyrdom, 128, 131, 137–138; Reformation thinking and, 147–148, 150, 152; reunion with father, 123–124; self-circumcision, 126, 131, 150, 151, 169; sentencing of, 134–135, 141; sisters of, 125–127, 128, 132, 146, 238n31
Manasseh, Prayer of, 130
Manuel I, king of Portugal, 21
Marques Moscoco, Don Bartolomeo, 174
Martínez, Maria, 17, 130
martyrdom: defiance and, 27; historical origins of, 1–2, 205n4; Jewish and Christian views of, 1, 183; root paradigm of, 34
martyrologies, 31, 188, 189, 210n74, 250n38
martyrs, Christian, 1–2, 34, 205n7, 251n45; Catholic, 26, 185, 216n35; emphasis on violent death, 2, 6; Protestant, 3, 25–26, 185, *190*
martyrs, (crypto-)Jewish, 4, 7, 20, 151, 180, 250n33; Ashkenazi and Sephardi, 4–5; Chmielnitski massacres, 203n6; Crusades and, 4, 5–6, 8, 16–17; example of, 9; first, 14; gender of, 41–42, 196, 219n75; in Greco-Roman world, 1–3, 3; identification with Maccabees,

75, 192; memorialization of, 193, *194*, 195, 197–198; muzzling of, 174; Pinhanços (Diogo Lopes), 42–46; polemics and, 5, 184–185. *See also* crypto-Jews; dogmatista martyrs; "dying in Law of Moses"

Menasseh ben Israel, 188, 218n62

Méndez Chavez, Luis, 37

Mendoza, Antonio de, 64

Messiah, 10, 75, 85, 131; Church doctrine and, 86–87; identification with, 108, 114; inquisitorial interrogation and, 87–88, 138; Judeo-Christian debate over, 92–93; Law of Moses and, 158, 163. *See also* Jesus Christ

messianism, 20, 36, 39, 108, 211n82

Mexico, *56*, 147, 178

Mexico City, 26, 31, 35, 49, 54, 58, *59*; autos-da-fé in, 63, 76; Carvajal in, 52; inquisitorial prison in, 60

midrash, 177

Miguel, Frei, 103

Milton, John, 151

miracles, 162, 164, 189–190, 251n45

Mishnah, 38

Mohammed, Law of, 158

Molkho, Solomon, 36, 169

Moncada, Juan de, 141

Montesinos, Fernando, 144, 146, 191, 239n54

Moors, 159, 161

Morales, Manuel de, 61, 73, 75, 78, 181; *alumbradismo* and, 69; biblical texts and, 50–51; crypto-Jewish practices and, 50, 52, 78, 221n15; departure from New Spain, 52; influence on Carvajal family, 48–49

Mortera, Saul Levi, 183–184, 192, 249n21

Moses, Law of, 15, 25, 43, 51, 62, 109; biblical authority and, 50; Carvajal's nine reasons for adhering to, 199–200; circumcision and, 170; crypto-Jews' knowledge of Judaism and, 38; customs associated with, 127; disputations with inquisitors and, 31, 36; fasting and, 91; "good death" and, 35; "idolatry" and, 186; inquisitors' view of, 71, 72; internal struggle in conversion to, 179; Jesus and, 83, 142, 158; judaizing activity and, 49, 167; "Law of God" as alternative term, 99; natural reason and, 158; New Christian ancestry and, 118; observed *con perfección*, 49, 68; Old Christians converted to, 63; polemical value of martyrs and, 184–185; profession of faith and, 129; psychology and conversion to, 115; rabbinic tradition and, 57, 182, 189; superseded in Christian view, 36, 59, 69, 74, 92; "talmudic" and "true" Jews, 39; taught within families,

121; unrabbinic interpretation of, 178. *See also* "dying in Law of Moses"

Moses ben Asher, 7

Moses ha-Kohen of Tordesillas, 11, 13

Moura, Christoção de, 111

Muslims, 2, 101, 156, 161, 163. *See also* Islam

Nachmanides, 6, 38, 208n30

Nazareo, Heli. *See* Maldonado de Silva, Francisco

Nazirites, 135, 137, 151

Nebuchadnezzar, 1

negativos, 13, 92, 186; burned at stake, 24, 146–147, 215n19; defined, 16

Netherlands, 79, 81, 83, 113

New Christians, 9, 14, 237n16; Capuchin order and, 101; dissimulation by, 32–33; genealogy examined, 84–85, 87; Iberian Catholicism and, 196; Latin language and, 42; in New Spain, 55; in Peru, 118, 125; Portuguese, 20–21, 22, 47, 139, 146; Portuguese Inquisition and, 91–92, 99; Protestant influence on, 25–26. *See also* conversos; crypto-Jews; judaizers/judaizing

New Spain, 36, 47, 48, 56, 64, 221n7

New Testament, 12, 59, 95, 133, 181, 244n16; authenticity rejected, 95; Erasmus on, 167; John, Book of, 124; rejection of, 168, 169; Revelation, Book of, 212n85; soteriological contradiction with Old Testament, 81. *See also* Bible; Gospels

Nicodemus, 216n33

Nieto, David, 186–187

Nieto, Diego Díaz, 25–26, 55, 222n17

Nieto, José, 69

Nieto, Ruy Díaz, 55

nominalism, 142

North Africa, 37, 55, 82, 94

Núñez, Álvaro, 122, 123, 151

Núñez, Felipe, 54, 60

Núñez de Silva, Diego, 117–118, 128, 131, 147, 236n2; arrest of, 120–122; Carvajal and, 151; circle of, 147; reconciliation of, 122–123, 151

Núñez Fernandez, Raquel, 194

Ochino, Bernardino, 107

Old Christians, 15, 45, 82; anti-converso attitudes of, 14, 32–33; imprisoned by Inquisition, 63, 91, 92, 93, 108, 165; intermarriage with conversos/New Christians, 9, 14, 120, 125, 129, 195; as judaizers, 178, 179, 180; in Peru, 117

Old Testament, 58, 61, 67, 244n16; anointed kings of, 80; illumination experience and, 96, 100; prophecies about Messiah, 142; soteriological contradiction with New Testament, 81. *See also* Bible

Oleastro, Jerónimo. *See* Azambuja, Jerónimo de (Jerónimo Oleastro)

Orobio de Castro, Isaac, 32, 163, 185, 218n67

Oroz, Fray Pedro de, 64

Otáñez, Isabel de, 125, 139–140

Pánuco, 52, *53,* 61, 64

papacy/popes, 12, 14, 87; Law of Moses and, 91; New Christian criticism of, 25; obedience to, 97; Portuguese Inquisition and, 22; prayers and, 82; Protestant and humanist attacks on, 138. *See also specific popes*

Passover, 8, 35, 43, 50, 99

Pater Noster prayer, 82, 91

patriotism, 1

Paul, Apostle, 124

Paul III, Pope, 22

Pecs, Simon, 179

Peralta, Alonso de, 73

Pereira, Juan, 174

Pérez Ferro, Gonzalo, 52

Peru, Viceroyalty of, 117, *119,* 147; Portuguese New Christians in, 139, 240n90; Protestantism in, 139

Piedade, Frei Pedro de, 101

Pina, Fernão de, 114

Pinhanços, Diogo Lopes, 42–46, 189–191

Pires, Diogo, 36, 39. *See also* Molkho, Solomon

Pisa, 57, 88

polemics, Christian, 38, 39, 69

polemics, Jewish, 6, 10–13, 124, 126, 231n16; arguments for truth of Law of Moses, 138; Protestants/Christian dissenters and, 25, 26; value of crypto-Jewish martyrdom and, 184–185

Política angelica (Enríquez Gómez), 195

Portugal, 4, 18, *105,* 147; annexed by Spanish Empire, 26, 27, 82, 241n90; Capuchin order in, 113; end of public Jewish life in, 13; forced conversion of Jews, 21–22, 23; kings of, 32–33, 38–39, 75, 95, 108; *luteranos* persecuted in, 25; Spanish Jews exiled in, 10–11

Portuguese language, 37, 55, 130, 224n56

Potosí, 117, 118, *119,* 120, 123, 147

Prado, Juan de, 180, 182, 249n14

prayers: Catholic, 91, 129, 175; crypto-Jewish, 130, 132; *hashkavah* (memorial) prayers, 185, 186, 187, *187*

property, confiscation of, 17, 24, 64, 120, 122; hardship on martyrs' families, 128; Maldonado de Silva, 128, 129; recovered by kin of martyrs, 139–140; Vera (Lope de), 174

Protestantism, 107, 138, 228n138; anti-Catholic propaganda in Iberia, 24–25, 51; Catholic post-apostolic traditions and, 147; dogmatista martyrs and, 178; erosion of Iberian power and, 27; martyrologies of, 188, 189, 210n74; open declaration of faith and, 31. *See also* Reformation

Psalmi Davidis (Génebrand), 132, 148

Psalms, Book of, 3, 9; Asumpção (Frei Diogo de) and, 86, 93, 95, 97, 99; Carvajal (Luis) and, 54, 64, 69, 199; Maldonado de Silva and, 130, 133, 138. *See also* Bible, books of

purgatory, 18, 20, 34

qualificadores, 107

quemadero, 27, 29, 40

rabbis, 3–4, 70; anti-Christian polemicizing of, 6, 10–13; conversos and, 9, 17; martyrdom of rabbinic scholars, 7–8; rabbinical authority and Jewish existence, 180

Rabus, Ludwig, 189

Reconquest, 6

Reformation, 3, 24–26, 29, 82, 91, 167; crypto-Jews and, 147–148, 150, 196; *devotio moderna,* 68; erosion of Church's authority and, 138–139; individualistic thought and, 182; polemical strategy and, 69; revival of "athletic" martyrdom and, 192; Scripture and, 231n13. *See also* Protestantism

relapsos, 13, 24, 40, 65, 70

repentance, 16, 24, 161

Reuveni, David, 36, 39, 158, 162, 164, 167, 169

Révah, I. S., 181, 249n19

Reyes Plata, Gaspar de los, 65, 70

Ribera, Daniel, 180, 249n15

Rodríguez, Francisco, 55, 57

Rodríguez, Juan, 61

Rodriguez de Leon, Antonio, 147

Romance al divín martír (Enríquez Gómez), 195

Rome, 71, 137, 157

root paradigm, 34

Ruíz Ángel, Don Diego, 175

Ruiz de Alcaraz, Pedro, 69

Ruiz de Luna, Francisco, 62–63, 64–65

Sabbath, Jewish, 132, 162, 164, 169, 234n84; conversos and, 8; crypto-judaizing practices

and, 43, 56, 57, 91, 99, 162; literalist reading of Scripture and, 91
Saduccees, 107
saints, Christian, 2, 3, 18, 82; cult of, 13; images of, 164; intercessory power of, 147; veneration of, 5, 189
Salado, Mateo, 147
Salamanca, University of, 153, 163, 243n2
Salvatierra, Fray Martín de, 128
salvation, personal, 15, 23, 184, 204n1
sambenito, wearing of, 64, 65, 122, 141; flame-and-devil imagery, 40, 77; humiliation of, 27; prisoners condemned to death, 76; reconciled prisoners, 24
Samson (biblical), 151–152, 195, 252n54
Samuel ha-Katan, 7
Sánchez, Bartolomé, 178
sanity, religious heterodoxy and, 85, 114, 128, 168
Sánson Nazareno (Enríquez Gómez), 152, 195, 242n132
Santa Fe, Jerónimo de, 10, 208n30, 224n63
Santa Maria, Pablo de, 124, 143, 148, 220n77, 242n123
Santiago de Chile, 125, 126
Saul (Apostle Paul), 124
Scripture, 11, 12, 37, 53–54, 115; aggadoth and, 38; alumbradismo and, 69–70; Apocrypha included in, 52; authority of, 39, 178; Catholic Church and, 87; Christian treatment of, 80; contradictions in, 106; crypto-Jewish practices and, 99; in Hebrew, 157, 164; independent study of, 181; in Latin, 93; polemics and, 67; Protestant doctrine concerning, 74, 228n138; search of, 124; Trinity and, 128. See also Bible
Scrutinium scripturarum (Pablo de Santa Maria), 124, 125, 143, 148, 220n77, 237n23; frontispiece, 149; sequestered by Inquisition, 242n123
Sebastianism, 108
Segovia, 7
self-sacrifice, 1, 2, 8
Sephardim, 4–5, 11, 26, 30, 206n14
Serveto, Miguel (Michael Servetus), 26, 237n22
Seville, 15, 24, 31
Shem Tov ben Isaac ibn Shaprut, 11
Shema prayer, 37, 55, 66
Siguet, Miguel, 91–93, 94
skepticism, materialist, 45, 158, 249n14
slaughter, ritual, 6, 161, 162
sola fide, 51
sola scriptura, 39
Solomon, King (biblical), 62, 72

Solomon Ha-Levi, 148
soul, immortality of, 107
Sousa, Diogo de, 79, 95, 96, 107, 113; family of, 230n6; as informer for Inquisition, 82
Spain, 4, 147, 154, 195; annexation of Portugal, 26, 27, 82, 241n90; conversos in, 8; end of public Jewish life in, 13; forcible conversion of Jews in, 7–8; kings of, 75; luteranos persecuted in, 25; under Muslim rule, 5; Protestant literature in, 24
Spanish (Castilian) language, 122, 130, 170; Old Testament in, 67–68; Ten Commandments in, 50, 64
Späth, Johann Peter, 179, 248n8
Sperling, Benedictus, 179
Spiera, Francesco, 31
Spinoza, Benedict, 174, 180, 250n38
stake, burning at the, 14, 15, 36; conversionist disputations and, 29; gender of victims, 41–42; in Lisbon, 110; Maldonado de Silva (Francisco), 147; martyrdom associated with, 16, 17, 187–188; of negativos, 24; open declaration of faith and, 33; of Protestants and "Protestantish," 25, 147, 190; as public spectacle, 30; purgatory and, 20; refusal of idolatry and, 186; in Spanish America, 31, 32, 35. See also autos-da-fé; garrote, execution by
suffering, physical, 2, 3, 27, 35, 187
suicide, 5, 6, 21, 30, 73–74, 182
Summa Silvestrina, 83
synagogues, 8, 21, 185

Talmud, 10, 38, 218n64, 224n63, 252n54
Tampico, Mexico, 51, 52, 54
Tavares, Manuel Álvarez, 101, 126, 151
Taxco, 54, 58
Temple, in Jerusalem, 138
Ten Commandments, 50, 66, 91, 124, 199
Teresa of Ávila, 68
Tévar, Ana de, 155
theodicy, 2
theologians, Catholic, 43, 45, 46, 72, 133; controversies among, 80; at disputations, 33, 42; on Messiah, 163. See also calificadores/qualificadores (inquisitorial theologians)
There Is No Force That Can Withstand the Truth (Levi de Barrios), 193, 194, 195
Thirteen Articles of Faith (Maimonides), 64
Thomas Aquinas, 80, 142
Toledo, 7–8, 18
Torah, 7, 12, 55, 176, 192, 205n5, 249n21
Torres Zevallos, Antonio Gabriel de, 29–30
Tortosa, 7, 10

transubstantiation, 12, 25
Travassos, Jorge Velho, 104
Treviño de Sobremonte, Tomás, 35, 46, 220n80
Trinity, Catholic doctrine of, 87, 93, 121, 159, 162, 164; Law of Moses and, 132; polemics against, 7, 11, 12, 142–143
Triumpho del govierno popular (Levi de Barrios), 188
Tucumán, San Miguel de, 117, 118
Turner, Victor, 34

Uruña (Urvina), Diego de, 128

Valencia, 7, 14
Valladolid, 153, *154*, 157, 174
Vauchez, André, 2
Vega, Lope de, 148
Venice, 37, 189; Jewish ghetto of, 49, 57, 137; rabbinical authorities in, 176, 185
Vera, Diego de, 153, 155
Vera, Lope de, 36, 152, 176–177, 182; arrest and first audience, 153, 155, 159, 161; charges against, 164–166; desire to leave Spain, 155–156, 159; *hashkavah* prayer and, 187; Inquisition records about, 188; martyrdom of, 153, 174–176, 176, 189; path to martyrdom, 166–

170; resistance to inquisitors, 171–173; Samson compared to, 195; Scripture interpreted by, 161–164; self-circumcision, 169–170, 171; unorthodox Judaism of, 179; witnesses against, 153, 155–159. *See also* Creyente, Judah
Vera, Lope de (elder), 153, 156–157, 158, 175–176
Vera, Pedro de, 176–177, 178
vernacular, religious texts in, 13, 34, 50
Virgin Birth, Catholic doctrine of, 7, 11, 12, 80, 83, 126, 169
visions and visionaries, 18, 20, 212n83
Vitoria, Francis de, 83, 86
Vulgate, 12, 52, 130, 138, 167, 169

Wachtel, Nathan, 147
Waldensians, 205n7
Wilke, Carsten, 179–180
Wyclif, John, 12

Yáñez de Zurita, Antonio, 127
Yerushalmi, Yosef Hayim, 31–32, 37, 251n48
Yom Kippur, 43, 47, 55, 99, 132, 220–221n2

Zacatecas, 52

MIRIAM BODIAN

is Professor of Jewish History at the Graduate School of
Jewish Studies at Touro College, New York.